016232

780.9444/PAG

THE OWL AND
THE NIGHTINGALE

ma· æ libere contulit ea constantinus ecclijs.
æ adulatio prelatorũ· æ pusillanimitas illorũ
redegit ecclias in huĩmodi seruitutẽ· Si quetas
de opis minorũ puta de sc̃ptoribʒ in nundinis
qui locant opas suas æ sc̃pturas feneratoribus·
cambiatoribʒ: dico ut supra q̃d tenent̃ ad restitu

Solutio·

tionẽ om̃ium eoꝛ que a feneratoribʒ receperũt.

ſ· Similiter dicam̃ q̃d illicite sũt opere magistrorũ
organicorũ qui scurrilia æ effeminata ꝓponũt
iuuenibʒ æ rudibʒ ad effeminandos animos ipoꝛ
tamen locare possent opas suas in licitis cantibus
in quibʒ seruit ecclijs· Si autẽ prelatus lasciuus
lasciuijs talibʒ cantatoribʒ det beneficia· ut huĩ
modi scurrilia æ lasciuia audiat in ecclia sua:
credo q̃d lepram symonie incurrit. Si tamen in
aliqua sollemnitate pro consuetudine terre de
cantent aliqui in organis· dũ tñ scurriles noti

6 le tñ admisceant̃: tolerari possunt· De cyrurgi
cis dicim̃ q̃d non habent̃ locare opas suas in inci
dendis calculosis aut herniosis· nisi ubi uehemen
ter credũt se debere curare illos· Nam si alias
tracti cupiditate incidũt eos æ occidũt: homici
Solutio·
de fiunt· Ex dictis patet q̃d oñs cuiũcũqʒ conditio
nis homines siue sint religiosi· albi ut̃ nigri· si

THE OWL AND
THE NIGHTINGALE

Musical Life and Ideas
in France 1100–1300

Christopher Page

J. M. DENT & SONS LTD · LONDON

First published 1989
© Christopher Page 1989

This book is set in 10 ½ /12 pt Baskerville
by BP Datagraphics

Printed and bound in Great Britain
by The Bath Press, Avon for
J.M.Dent & Sons Ltd
91 Clapham High Street, London SW4 7TA

British Library Cataloguing in Publication Data
Page, Christopher
    The owl and the nightingale : musical life and ideas in France
1100–1300.
    1. France. Music, 1200–1500
    I. Title
    780′.944

    ISBN 0–460–04777–9

Frontispiece
*Robert of Courson, Master of Theology at the University of Paris
and Papal Legate, discusses the 'Masters of organum' in his* Summa,
*compiled 1208–1212/13. Bruges, Stedelijke Openbare Bibliotheek, MS
247, f.46r. Reproduced by permission.*

CONTENTS

ILLUSTRATIONS

Singing, playing the fiddle, dancing, exercise, acting and the recitation of epics – these are things which the statesman should regulate so that every citizen can be happy.

Albertus Magnus,
Commentary upon the *Politics* of Aristotle

PREFACE

The period 1100-1300 is an imposing one in the history of music and literature. It witnessed the rise of the troubadours and trouvères, the elaboration of Notre Dame polyphony, the emergence of Romance, and many other developments which have inspired historians to regard the twelfth century as a time of renaissance and the thirteenth as a time of consolidation. This book is an attempt to view the musical life of those centuries through the eyes of contemporary writers. The picture that emerges has a touch of strangeness. Many details of musical life are buried in sermons, in treatises on the Seven Deadly Sins and in other works which have been little used by historians of music, but the men who wrote these works rarely think as we do. The ground level of thought has changed in many places since the Middle Ages, and like ghosts who enter an old room through doors that are no longer there, these writers remind us that we too have our time and place; many have thrived independently of ideals and conditions which we have come to regard as essential to human dignity and fellowship. To capture that strangeness, and even to savour it, seems a worthwhile task; it is one way to understand the musical life of the twelfth and thirteenth centuries in contemporary terms.

It is a pleasant duty to acknowledge my debt to friends and colleagues who have given their help and advice. Stephen Haynes read the entire book in his meticulous fashion and improved both my text and the translations from Latin, Old Occitan, Old French and Catalan. I am responsible for any slips or infelicities that remain. Professor John Stevens of Magdalene College, Cambridge, read chapters 1-3 and returned them with comments so subtle, and yet so searching, that I was able to revise those chapters and give them whatever merit they may now possess. Ann Lewis of Keble College, Oxford, though busy with research of her own, found the time to discuss many parts of the book with me and to give her advice whenever it was needed. Dr Patricia Morison, of All Souls College, Oxford, has continued to be an inexhaustible fund of information about the latest and most stimulating research in medieval history. Among librarians I owe a special debt of thanks to Heather Owens of Gonville and Caius College, Cambridge, and to her staff, who put their magnificent collection of medieval theological manuscripts at my disposal time and time again. My thanks are due to Malcolm Gerratt of J. M. Dent & Sons for his unflagging interest in this book, and to Valerie Gardner who edited it. Copy-editors are the true heroes and heroines of publishing; they save authors from the consequences of their own illiteracy and laziness and yet they rarely win the thanks that they deserve. Régine, as always, did everything, and my debt to Professor Derek Pearsall, as to Professor Elizabeth Salter, knows no bounds. I owe a special debt of gratitude to the Master and Fellows of Sidney Sussex College, Cambridge.

CAMBRIDGE

ix

ABBREVIATIONS

Abbreviations have been kept to an absolute minimum, both in the text and in the notes. The following, however, have been retained:

AV   The Authorised Version of the Bible
b.   completed before
fl.   flourished
Grove 6   *The New Grove Dictionary of Music and Musicians*, ed. Stanley Sadie, 20 vols (London, 1980)
MED   Middle English Dictionary, ed. H. Kurath and S. H. Kuhn (University of Michigan Press, 1959–)
OED   Oxford English Dictionary
PL   Patrologiae Cursus Completus: Series Latina, 221 vols (Paris, 1844–64)

INTRODUCTION

Nine large volumes of parchment, compiled about 1320, lie in the municipal library at Douai. In dense and closely-written columns of Latin they present the wisdom that a Dominican friar had gathered in his studies of the psalms. His name was Pierre de Palude and his books represent a great labour. Page after page, the psalms are sifted through a mesh of commentary so fine that it retains everything of substance in the text. The great Christian themes of Grace, Charity and Redemption appear on every folio, and at first glance there seems little reason to suspect that these nine books of theology will have anything to disclose about contemporary musical life. A second glance, however, reveals that they contain numerous references to minstrels, to clerical singers and even to contemporary musical forms such as the motet. These arise in various ways, and especially through the frequent use of extended similes where an aspect of religious doctrine is illuminated by means of a comparison. Here, for example, is a passage in which Pierre de Palude glosses the words 'a new song' (*canticum novum*; for the text see below p. 201):

> *Sing a new song* . . . because a new song requires a renewed man. For
> see, a minstrel wishing to play the fiddle takes off his outer clothing,
> adjusts his inner garments, takes off the belt of his tunic, puts down
> his hood, smoothes down his hair and puts a woollen cap on top of it . . .

This is perhaps the most vivid description in existence of a medieval musician preparing himself to perform. Such sharp-eyed observation as this in a work of theology should remind us that there is virtually no limit to the variety of medieval writings which can disclose information about musical customs and practices: who performers were, how they behaved, how they were regarded, where they performed, and so on through a list of questions that will recur throughout this book.

The variety of the evidence is indeed enormous, for it includes sermons, treatises on the Seven Deadly Sins, manuals for confessors, theological encyclopedias, vernacular romances and more besides, much of it unpublished. No single person could hope to read it all, but I believe that enough has been encompassed here to frame two basic questions: what do these writings say about musical life, and what pattern does their testimony form? An attempt to answer the question of what these writings say occupies Chapters 1–7. As for the pattern which their testimony forms, we can sharpen a question which we have already posed: what do these writings *really* say? The answer offered in this book is that they make a statement which is intimately related to the emergence of the French State and to the way in which its laws and controls were elaborated by clerical bureaucrats with special interests and prejudices. The later-twelfth and thirteenth centuries saw the realm of France consolidated under a supreme monarch, saw a proliferation of the legal controls which centralised authorities exercised over individuals, and saw the Church discover the efficacy of concerted action against its enemies, chiefly Jews and heretics. It was lawyers, bureaucrats, theologians, preachers and confessors – the clerical *literati* – who provided the literate skills and the literacy-based ideas which made this centralisation possible by a process which Cheyette has described as 'the invention of the State'.[1] This was a gradual development whereby this *literati* 'slowly imposed upon the non-literate their ways of thinking about politics and law'.[2] We can map this evolution, as it affected the perception of secular musical life, by comparing two Parisian authors working a century apart: Peter the Chanter and Johannes de Grocheio.

At some time towards 1200, on the verge of a momentous period in the history of music, the celebrated theologian Peter the Chanter cast an eye over the various ways in which craftsmen contributed to the common good of the Church.[3] Peter was a canon of Notre Dame of Paris, and the French capital was a good place to attempt such a survey for it had become the largest city in northern Europe, 'swarming with boats, groaning with goods and abounding with things to be bought and sold'. Peter concludes that there is a place within the Church for tailors, and so too for the tanners and carpenters 'who make basic objects'. He also admits weavers 'who produce plain work' and painters who depict instructive narrative scenes. What of musicians? Players of musical instruments, Peter rules, are acceptable within the community of the Church because their music helps to relieve sadness and tedium.

About a century later, another Parisian scholar, Johannes de Grocheio, decided to survey the social importance of secular music in the city where he had been trained.[4] Once again, Paris was the ideal place for such a review, for since the time of Peter the Chanter it had witnessed an astonishing burst of experiment and creativity in the realm of polyphonic music, both sacred and secular. At the same time, the dense concentration of young men in the university, combined with a demographic increase which all the major cities of northern Europe had known, ensured that dance-music and other popular forms were thriving. Exhilarated by these things, Johannes de Grocheio was able to attempt a systematic survey of the uses of secular music such as Peter the Chanter could not have dreamed possible. Grocheio concludes, for example, that narrative epics help to reconcile old people, labourers and citizens of middle station to their trials and therefore contribute to the stability of the whole city, while trouvère songs in the best style help to draw kings and nobles to magnanimity, thus contributing to good government.

Peter the Chanter and Johannes de Grocheio were both scholars who knew

Paris intimately, and we recognise a relationship between the way in which they interpret the usefulness of secular music even though Peter has only a few lines on the subject while Grocheio devotes a third of a treatise to it. And yet there is a striking difference between them. Peter is concerned with the good of the Church (*Ecclesia*), but Johannes de Grocheio is preoccupied with the welfare of the State (*Civitas*). Indeed, Grocheio systematically imposes his literacy-based notions of good governance upon the secular music of the illiterate (or barely literate) laity, and in this respect his *De musica* is a microcosm of the process whereby the French State was brought into being.

In part, this shift of emphasis in social thought from the welfare of *Ecclesia* to the safety of the *Civitas* – which was by no means universally accomplished, even in France, during the thirteenth century – can be regarded as the result of a powerful secularising impulse which is manifest in many areas of cultural life between 1100 and 1300. In the realm of learning it is revealed in the transfer of intellectual leadership from the monasteries to the urban schools. In vernacular literature it is apparent in the emergence of the Old French romances soon after 1150 where the fundamental tone of life is set by love and by the leisure offered by major court festivities, not by the crusading fervour of the *chansons de geste* or by the bitter sense, ubiquitous in these epics, that only Divine Providence can free the barons from the feuds which bind them together in enmity.

The force of this secularising impulse in musical life deserves a longer look. For a sense of how it was manifested in northern France and the Anglo-Norman realm we cannot do better than turn to an anonymous poet of *c.* 1200 who observes it with a broader vision and a keener wit than any other writer of his time. His poem, entitled *The Owl and the Nightingale*,[5] tells how the two birds of the title engage in a heated and wide-ranging debate, always returning to the subject of their contrasting songs and their attitude to the usefulness of music. The owl's voice, ominous and mournful, sounds one of the deepest notes of Christian spirituality, for the sadness in her cry is man's awareness of his sinful nature and the anguish of his wretchedness before God:[6]

> Men shall discover that they must beseech for grace for the forgiveness of their sins with long weeping before they may come to heaven. [In my song] I therefore counsel men who set out to seek the king of heaven to be ready, and to weep more than they sing, for no man is without sin. Therefore, before they go hence, they must make amends with tears and weeping, so that which was formerly sweet to them becomes sour. I help them to that, God knows it, for there is no foolish snare in my singing. For all my song is of longing, and mixed somewhat with lamentation, so that man may look to himself and may groan for his misdeeds. I assail him with my song so that he may groan for his guilt.

The nightingale, in contrast, is a courtly creature. She flies towards the richest people and loves to sing where a lord and lady lie abed or where young maidens are gathered;[7] she scorns the people of the north who have not yet adopted the gentler customs and the sophisticated diet belonging to the new courtliness;[8] her beautiful song, evoked in the opening lines of many troubadour and trouvère lyrics, is an expression of ebullient joy:[9]

> One song from my mouth is better than all those which you know.
> Listen! I will tell you why this is so. Do you know for what man was
> born? For the bliss of the kingdom of heaven where there is song and
> joy forever and without change; every man who is capable of any good
> deeds sets out for that place. This is why men sing in Holy Church
> and why clerics compose chants, so that mankind may ponder, in that
> song, where he will go and stay for a long while.

The nightingale aligns herself with composers, the clerics who *ginneth songes wirche*, and as early as 1159 John of Salisbury was inveighing against singers who abandon all decorum and sing in a way that 'neither the nightingale, the parrot, nor any bird with greater range than these can rival'.[10] Even the fragmentary remains of English polyphony from the time of *The Owl and the Nightingale* are sufficient to convey a vivid impression of what John may mean. The final flourish of *Exultemus et letemur*,[11] a two-part piece in honour of St Nicholas, may show the kind of *writelinge* ('chirping') to which the owl takes such exception and which put John of Salisbury in mind of the nightingale and the parrot (Figure 1 and Music example 1):

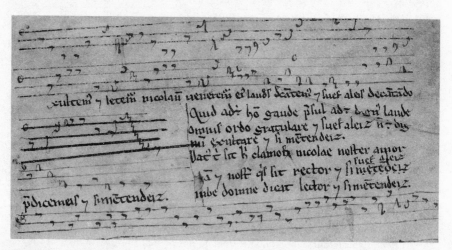

Figure 1   [E]xultemus et letemur, *A two-voice conductus in honour of St Nicholas. Cambridge, University Library, MS Ff.1.17 (1), f.4r; English, probably late twelfth century. Reproduced by permission.*

Example no. 1

[E]xultemus et letemur,
Nicolaum veneremur,
Eius laudes decantemus
   Et suef Aleis;
Decantando predicemus;   [MS predicemeis]
   Et si m'entendeiz!

It is possible to discern a form of Humanism in the nightingale – at least if we take that word to imply a liberal esteem for the works of human skill and a measure of respect (or at least a measure of tolerance) that can be extended to all human wants judged to be natural. In this sense the nightingale represents some of the most profound intellectual and spiritual changes of the twelfth century.[12] There is something of her spirit in the romances, in the writings of confessors who sought to soften the rigour of the older penitential canons,[13] in the pages of the theologians who could recognise – as Peter the Chanter recognised – the power of secular music to heal the body or to console the mind, and in the writings of the schoolmen who submitted many of the harsh doctrines of the Fathers to fresh scrutiny.

But there was another aspect to the renaissance of the twelfth century, and one which Moore has aptly called its 'dark underside'.[14] Within the lifetime of the poet who composed *The Owl and the Nightingale*, the Third Lateran Council of 1179 ruled that lepers should be deprived of legal rights and protection, and of their property. 'The leper was treated thenceforth as being effectively dead, with all the cruelty and all the ambivalence that implies'.[15] The Fourth Lateran Council of 1215 decreed that Jews should distinguish themselves from Christians in their dress, prohibited them from holding public office, and initiated the first concerted effort of the Western Church to persecute heretics.[16] Thus the foundations were laid for what Moore calls 'a persecuting society': one in which the clerical *literati* developed a neurotic fear of the subversive threat which lepers, Jews and heretics – all indiscriminately imagined as creatures of the Devil – posed to the State and the clerics' power within it. Viewed in this context the central concern of this book proves to be the investigation of a paradox. Why was it that amongst the clerical *literati* an increasingly rational and tolerant view of some secular music and secular musicians coexisted with an intensified fear of supernatural power, with a neurotic dread of subversion, and with a desire to tighten the grip of centralised authority on all human relations?

In Chapter 8 I have attempted to frame an answer to that question based upon the material assembled in Chapters 1–7. It is a consequence of the kind of source material used that these chapters should assume the character of a sequence of essays. The literary evidence presents a huge field, and searching within it is like excavating an archaeological site; there is no time to dig everywhere so one must choose a series of promising places. Some of these may yield a rich seam of connected and broadly dateable finds; others may reveal nothing, or may disclose something so isolated and devoid of a context that one can do little more than speculate as to what it might mean. Other finds are rich and self-contained. The Cistercian evidence used in Chapter 7, for example, lies in the texts which contain it like brilliant coins in a jar turned up by a plough. The significance of such material can be very wide indeed, however, and I believe that to be the case here.

Within the limitations imposed both by the evidence and by the pattern of what was discovered, Chapters 1–7 explore musical activities of both a professional and an amateur kind in courtly and popular contexts. These terms are not particularly happy ones, but they will serve for the present. The major categories of twelfth- and thirteenth-century music are also repre-sented in these first seven chapters: the unwritten tradition of the minstrels and written instrumental music (Chapters 1–3), the courtly monody of the trouvères and the *carole*, the latter both in courtly and in urban contexts (Chapters 4 and 5), composed polyphony of the Parisian tradition (Chapter 6), and finally plainchant (Chapter 7).

CHAPTER ONE

MINSTRELS AND THE CLERGY

Pupil: Do *joculatores* have any hope of salvation?
Master: None.

Honorius Augustodunensis

'And Heaven and Hell?' said the parson. The host then bid him 'not
to prophane: for those were things not to be mentioned nor thought
of but in church.' Adams asked him, 'why he went to church, if what
he learned there had no influence on his conduct in life?' 'I go to
church', answered the host, 'to say my prayers and behave godly.' 'And
dost not thou', cry'd Adams, 'believe what thou hearest at church?'
'Most part of it, master', returned the host. 'And dost not thou then
tremble', cries Adams, 'at the thought of eternal punishment?' 'As for
that, master', said he, 'I never once thought about it: but what signifies
talking about matters so far off? The mug is out, shall I draw another?'

Henry Fielding *Joseph Andrews*

When Honorius Augustodunensis decided that the Master in his colloquy
should deny minstrels *all* hope of salvation he created the most famous of
all medieval references to minstrelsy. It has often been quoted,[1] and there
is a consensus today that the ecclesiastical authorities of the Middle Ages
damned all professional entertainers save the tiny handful who sang the lives
of the saints and other stories of an improving sort. In his fundamental study
of French minstrelsy in the twelfth and thirteenth centuries, Edmond Faral
devotes a chapter to this clerical animosity, 'l'attitude ordinaire de l'Eglise
pendant tout le moyen âge à l'égard des agents de dissipation'.[2] In more
recent times Edmund Bowles has endorsed this view in an article whose
influence upon the study of medieval performance practice has been considerable. 'With the exception of those who sang or played music in praise of
Christianity or famous saints and heroes', he writes, 'the attitude of the
Church towards secular performers never varied throughout the Middle
Ages'.[3] Geremek sees things in a similar light, for he finds that the severity
of the official opinion 'never flagged'.[4]

We do not know whether the minstrels themselves paid much attention to the official opinions of the Church; perhaps they sometimes affected the airy disregard for damnation which the host uses to amaze the parson in *Joseph Andrews*. We do know, however, that medieval people did not all think in the same way. That is a trite but true observation (to quote Fielding once more), and its truth is worth dwelling upon; our sense of the texture of medieval culture owes much to the delicacy with which we separate the finer threads of belief and opinion. The more we come to admire the energy of dialectic and theology in medieval France – especially during the thirteenth century – the more difficult it becomes to accept the picture of unchallenged authority and spiritual quiescence presented by Bowles and Geremek. Urban expansion, the recovery of Aristotle's philosophy, the rise of the schools, the emergence of an urban poor, changes of approach to the sacrament of penance – what impact did these forces have upon the way in which minstrels were perceived in thirteenth-century society? There are many questions to be answered here; some will be discussed in this chapter while others will present themselves later. Nonetheless it can be plainly said here that the thirteenth century was indeed a time when the predicament of the minstrel changed.

Sermons: a test-case

For signs of a virulent clerical hostility to professional entertainers, musicians among them, we naturally turn to sermons. It was in his *sermones* that a churchman with pastoral responsibilities wielded the most powerful weapon of his ministry, his faculty of speech (*sermo*). From the sermon literature we may reasonably expect orthodox opinion and fervent expression. Orthodoxy was required, because a cleric who preached fulfilled his role as one appointed to speak the word of God and pass it to the laity; fervour was inevitable, because a sermon was a demonstration of love and ardour; by constantly taking his cue from a biblical text, only to return almost immediately to another by a route of commentary and metaphor, the preacher displayed in himself the irresistible attraction which the word of God, not severe but 'joyous and refreshing', held for a reflective mind and an alert spirit.[5]

Let us examine one of the most striking collections of sermons from the thirteenth century: the anthology of 216 sermons in MS lat.16481 of the Bibliothèque Nationale in Paris (Figure 2).[6] This collection, owned and annotated by the scholar Pierre de Limoges (d.1306), merits attention for several reasons. Firstly, the items it contains are rich in *similitudines*, one of the literary devices which are responsible for so many of the allusions to contemporary customs and attitudes that are to be found in sermons (*see* Appendix). Secondly, most of the homilies in MS lat.16481 can be localised and dated. They were all preached in Paris during the years 1272–3 in churches ranging from the Ste Chapelle to urban churches such as St Gervais. They therefore

9

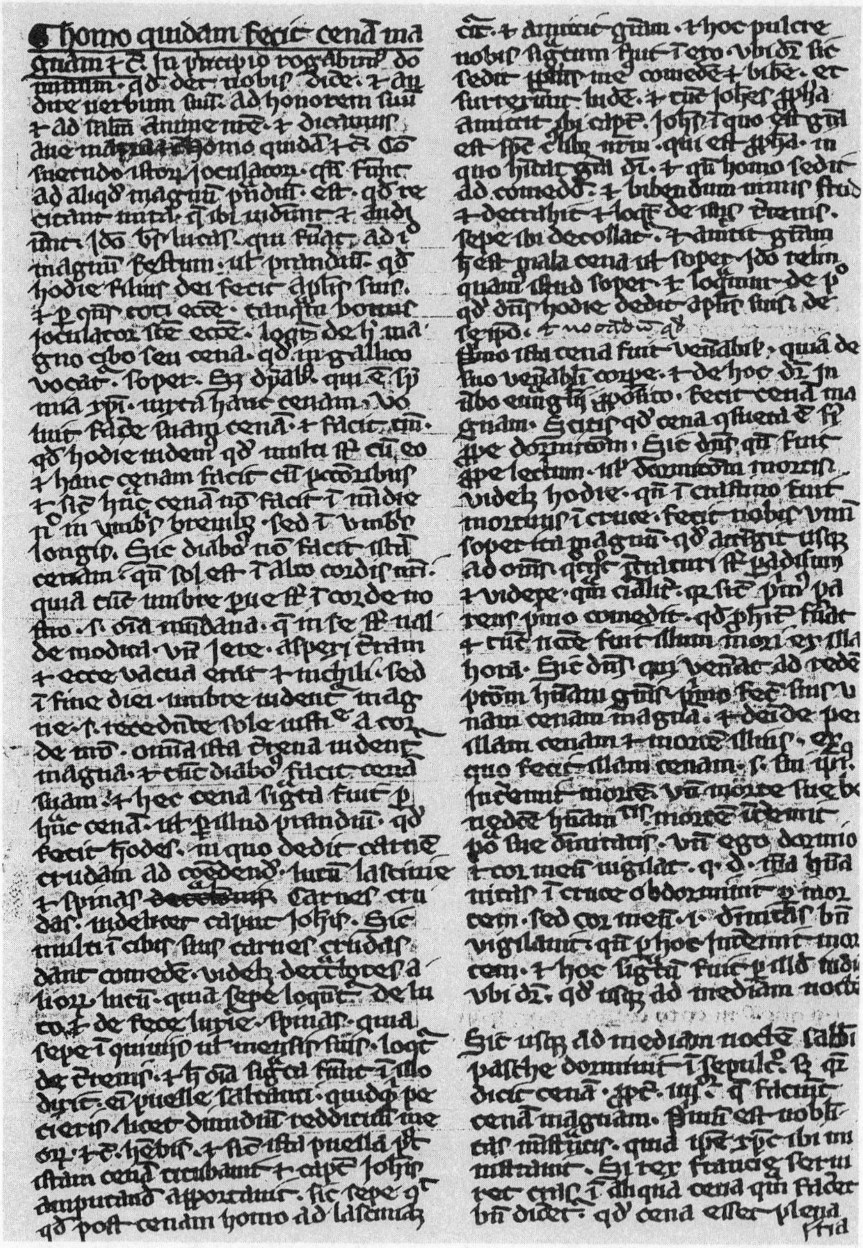

Figure 2   *A sermon by Pierre de Limoges, preached in the Ste Chapelle, Paris, in 1273. The opening lines refer to the activities of minstrels who have been present at great feasts. Paris, Bibliothèque Nationale, MS lat.16481, f.186v. Reproduced by permission.*

derive from a city which enjoyed an exceptionally rich musical life and which drew gifted theologians and preachers from all over the Christian world.[7]

In MS lat.16481 I find five references to minstrels, all brief enough to be quoted in their entirety:

I f.17v From a sermon preached by Daniel of Paris in 1272 at the church of St Leufroy, referring to St Martin who divided his cloak with a pauper, using a knife for the purpose.

> hic fuit pulcher ictus . . . Satis cantatur de Rolando et Olivero et dicitur quod Rolandus percussit unum per caput ita quod scidit ipsum usque ad dentes, Oliverus scidit alium per medium ventrem totum ultra. Sed hoc nichil est totum quia nec de Rolando, Olivero, Karolo maiore nec de Hogero le Danois invenitur quod fecerit ita pulchrum ictum quia numquam erit usque in finem mundi; quin sancta ecclesia cantet et recolat illum ictum non sic de aliis ictibus ipsa se intromittit, et licet aliqui hystriones ictus predictorum cantent tamen hoc nichil est quia multa mendacia addunt.

> this was a handsome blow . . . A great deal is sung about Roland and Oliver and it is said that Roland smote his adversary upon the head so that he cut him down to the teeth, and that Oliver cut another in the stomach so that the lance passed right through. But this is all nothing because it is nowhere found to be true of Roland, of Oliver, of Charlemagne nor of Ogier the Dane that he made such a handsome blow [as St Martin] because there will be none such until the end of the world. Whence Holy Church must sing of the blow and call it to mind but does not concern itself with the other blows, and even if some minstrels sing of the blows of the aforesaid [heroes] that comes to nothing because they add many false things.

II f.40r From a sermon preached by 'a certain Dominican' at St Leufroy.

> ita quod quando cogitat de domino nullum penitus ibi saporem invenit . . . quando dicit unum pater noster vel Ave Maria nichil saporis invenit ita quod invenit cor suum sicut domus au jugleor ou a menestrere qui non invenit frigidiorem domum quam sit sua.

> so that when he thinks of the Lord he finds scarcely any taste within . . . when he says a *pater noster* or an *Ave Maria* he finds no taste there so that he finds his heart to be just as a house seems to a *jugleor* or *menestrere* who finds no house as cold as his own.

III f.49v From a sermon by the Dominican Johannes Agnellus for Christmas day, 1272, preached in the church of La Madeleine.

> Solet dici quod qui fecit parvum fecit joculatorem, quia delectabilius quod in terra posset videri est unus puer quando est bene gratiosus; quidquid ipse faciat, etiam si pocus et vitra frangat, non fit nisi ridere, unde etiam isti joculatores non libenter vadunt ubi sciunt talem parvum.

There is a saying that 'who gives birth to a boy gives birth to a minstrel',
because the most delightful thing that may be seen in the world is a
boy when he is excellently bred; whatever he may do, even if he breaks
cups and glass vessels, he provokes nothing but laughter, wherefore
minstrels do not readily go where they know such a boy to be.

IV f.186v From a sermon preached in the Ste Chapelle in 1273 by Pierre
de Limoges (Figure 2).

Homo quidam fecit cenam magnam et cetera. In principio rogabimus
dominum quod det nobis dicere et audire verbum suum ad honorem
suum et ad salutem anime nostre, et dicamus *Ave Maria* et cetera. *Homo
quidam* et cetera. Consuetudo istorum joculatorum quando fuerunt ad
aliquid magnum prandium est quod recitant mira que ibi viderunt et
audierunt. Ideo beatus Lucas. Qui fuerat ad illud magnum festum vel
prandium quod hodie filius Dei fecit apostolis suis et per consequens
toti ecclesie tanquam bonus joculator sancte ecclesie. Loquitur de hoc
magno cibo seu cena quod in gallico vocatur *soper*.

A certain man made a great supper (Luke 14:16) etc. At the outset we pray
God that He may grant it to us to speak and to hear the word of God
to His honour and for the salvation of our soul, and we say *Ave Maria*,
etc. 'A certain man' etc. It is the custom amongst minstrels, when they
have been at any great banquet, to recite the wondrous things which
they saw and heard there. Whence the text of St Luke. Anyone who
has been at the great banquet or dinner which today the son of God
has made for his apostles, and thence for all in the Church, is like a
good minstrel of Holy Church. The reference here is to the great meal
or repast which in French is called the *soper*.

V f.233r From a sermon preached by Nicholas de Caen in the church of
Saint-Antoine-des-Champs, 1273.

Isti joculatores, ut faciant homines ridere de suis canibus, amputant eis
aures et caudam, sic multi aures amputant sue orationis videlicet
principium, quia non orant propter deum, et caudam quia etiam in illa
oratione non perseverant, et sic de sua oratione canem joculatoris
faciunt.

Joculatores cut off the ears and tails of their dogs to make people laugh
at them, and in the same way many amputate the ears of their prayer,
that is to say the beginning, because they do not pray for the love of
God, and [they also amputate the] tail [of their prayer], because they
do not persist in that praying and therefore turn it into a minstrel's dog.

What is the view of minstrelsy in these passages? At first sight, it seems
a moderately differentiated one. The appearance of four different terms for
minstrels (*joculator, histrio, jugleor* and *menestrere*) suggests that distinctions of
function – and perhaps of status – may be implied. The choice of *histrio*
in extract I, for example, was surely a considered one, for this term never

shed its theatrical associations in the Middle Ages and was therefore an appropriate name for the singer-tellers of epic stories. The author of extract II breaks into the vernacular (*jugleor ou . . . menestrere*), but the force of his distinction between *jugleor* and *menestrere* remains unknown. What is clear, however, is that three authors out of five were content with a generalising terminology. The phrase *isti joculatores* (III, IV and V), 'these minstrels', is one in which *isti* obviously has a generalising force equivalent to modern English *these* in the same sense (compare Desdemona's plaintive reflection: 'O these men, these men').

In striking contrast to the imprecision of this terminology is the sharpness (and shrewdness) of eye with which these five preachers have observed minstrels at work. The remark that minstrels do not readily go where they know that they will find a gracious boy (III) is shrewd indeed, for the boys in question, who are so readily forgiven when they break cups and glasses, are probably to be identified with the pages of wealthy households whose tasks included carrying vessels and ewers for meals; as we shall see in Chapter 4, such *pueri graciosi* were highly valued at court and could be diverting company. Minstrels, it would seem, did not willingly compete with such boys. Again, the observation in extract II that a *jugleor* or *menestrere* finds no house colder than his own (that is to say that he is always travelling) is another mildly sententious one, verging on the proverbial.

Other passages reveal a similar and essentially dispassionate observation of minstrel behaviour. Pierre de Limoges comments that minstrels are accustomed to recount the wonders which they saw and heard at feasts and he does not seem to disapprove of this practice; indeed the context may imply the reverse. Nicholas de Caen describes a minstrel custom (the mutilation of a pet dog to raise a smile) that will strike many twentieth-century readers as a brutal one, and it is certainly a reminder that the trade of minstrelsy in medieval Europe encompassed the coarsest of fairground entertainment; Nicholas de Caen's view of it, however, remains unknown. The closest that we come to a condemnation of minstrelsy in these passages is the specific charge in extract I that the stories of Roland, Oliver and others contain many 'false things' as retold by *histriones*. This is a fairly mild rebuke, however, and one that reflects an increasing sense in the thirteenth century that historical veracity could only be achieved with literate techniques, with Latin, and with prose.[8]

These are the references to minstrelsy in almost three hundred folios of Parisian sermons in MS lat.16481. An examination of many other collections, both published and unpublished, produces nothing to change this picture in any of its essentials.[9] In the very places where conventional wisdom would lead us to expect virulent polemics against minstrels of all kinds, we find relatively little strong language but a good deal of close observation. This is not to deny that sermons exist in which *joculatores*, *histriones* and the rest are attacked in the most violent terms; it is merely to give a timely reminder of the mildness that we encounter in very many homilies.

A second test-case: treatises on the virtues and vices

The massive legacy of treatises on the Seven Deadly Sins provides us with many texts where some polemic against professional secular entertainers might reasonably be expected. This is because these are not academic works for the most part but pastoral ones designed to be reference manuals for preachers and confessors.

An association between professional secular musicians and deadly sin was present in the deepest stratum of patristic thinking known to the Middle Ages. It was a turbulent association which often identified these entertainers with Satanic forces. The roots of this lie long and deep. 'The sharp smell of an invisible battle hung over the religious life of Late Antique man', writes Peter Brown. To sin[10]

> was no longer merely to err: it was to allow oneself to be overcome
> by unseen forces. To err was not to be mistaken: it was to be
> unconsciously manipulated by some invisible malign power. The more
> strongly people felt about their ideas, the more potent the demons seemed
> to them.

In the eyes of the early Fathers of the Church (and especially those who wrote to combat the paganism of the Eastern Empire in the third and fourth centuries) there were few agents of this 'malign power' more deadly than the professional entertainers who enlivened games, banquets and theatrical shows.[11] By the thirteenth century, however, many churchmen were able to adopt a more tolerant attitude towards musicians than the early Fathers because the 'moderns' believed that Satan was now waging his war in a different way. Few of them believed – as many of the Fathers had done – that professional entertainers were in league with ancient gods and fighting to preserve an organised paganism; indeed the rarity with which *joculatores*, *histriones* and their fellows are associated in medieval documents with popular superstition or with magic of any kind is noteworthy.[12]

In the thirteenth century most of the imagery of Satanism and demonology used by preachers and theologians was directed towards something else: the public dances of young men and women (but especially of young women) called *caroles* in Old French and *c(h)oreae* in Latin. Many treatises on the seven vices and virtues were composed in the thirteenth century as an aid to preaching and confession, and it is common for these works to incorporate a section on *caroles* that may run to several folios or more.[13] Here the imagery of Satanism and the Black Mass is usually abundant:[14]

> Item in chorea habet diabolus sacerdotem cantantem et clericum
> respondentem et quasi omnes horas fecit cantari per vicos et plateas;
> et sicut sacerdos mutat vestimenta quando debet celebrare, sic isti
> quando debent choreas ducere ... et loco officii dei faciunt officium
> diaboli, ad quam conveniunt plures quam ad officium dei, et diutius
> expectant, quia prolixius est officium et quandoque tota nocte et amplius,

et magis devote et virilius serviunt diabolo quam deo . . . Item contra
sacramentum ordinis faciunt, quia tali servitium impendunt diabolo
quale clerici deo, ut habetur. Sed et per cantus earum cantus
ecclesiasticus contempnitur; quoniam enim deberent interesse vesperis
intersunt choreis.

In a *carole* the devil has a priest who sings and a cleric who sings the
responses, and he [the devil] causes almost all the hours to be sung
through the streets and roadways. And just as a priest changes his
vestments when he must celebrate, so they who lead *caroles* do . . . and
in place of the Office of God they celebrate the Office of the devil, to
which many more people come than to the Office of God and spend
more time there because the devil's Office is longer and at one time
or another can last the whole night or more. They serve the devil much
more devoutly and keenly than God . . . Again, they sin against the
sacrament of ordination, because they busy themselves in just such a
liturgy to the devil as clerics perform to God, as has been said. And
through the music of the women [who dance *caroles*] the music of the
Church is brought into disdain, for when they should be at Vespers they
are taking part in *caroles*.

Material like this can be found in many treatises on the sin of *Luxuria*, but
I find no comparable chapters *de histrionibus*.

Perhaps this should not surprise us. The demographic increase of the twelfth
and thirteenth centuries, together with the growth of towns and cities, had
created a large population of young women whose families often encouraged
them to attend the *caroles* in the squares and streets of the towns where husbands might be won on feast-days and fair-days. As we shall see in Chapter
5, the polemic which preachers and confessors directed against these dances
is characterised by a fervent demonology and a passionate misogyny – an
intoxicating combination that produces writing of a virulence that in earlier
centuries might have been directed against the *histrio*. Indeed the strength
of the misogyny which these texts reveal is impressive; they are driven by
the volatile combination of sexual disgust and envy which celibate men in
the clerical state felt for female display and for the female libido.

The minstrel as pauper

'If minstrels received no money, they would abandon their trade.' So says
the English casuist Thomas Chobham in his penitential of *c.* 1216. His is
a simple observation and a true one, for the services of a minstrel, be he
musician, actor, acrobat or whatever, were intangible, evanescent and often
unsolicited; there was no contract of hire. In theory, at least, a concerted
effort to starve the trade of minstrelsy out of existence by blocking every
route through which money travelled into it could not possibly fail. It was
widely believed that St Jerome himself had counselled the faithful to do exactly

this, warning them that 'to give to *histriones* is to sacrifice to demons': *histrion-ibus dare est demonibus immolare.*[15]

Any attempt to understand the place of minstrel and minstrelsy in thir-teenth-century thought eventually comes down to money. On one level, to concentrate upon the issue of legitimate earnings is to acknowledge the simple economic facts of the minstrel profession. On a deeper level, however, it is possible to recognise that throughout our period many writers were inspired to fresh reflection by money and by their attempt to assess the value, in terms of faith, of the mass of relatively new goods and services which possessed a monetary value.

Thomas Chobham did not wish that minstrels should be supplied with any money whatsoever. The very least that we can say to gloss his rigorously uncompromising view is that a great deal of medieval theology is not only opposed to the earnings of minstrels, it is also highly circumspect in its treat-ment of the very concepts of money and credit. There is no doubt that a great deal of sermon-literature is hostile in principle to moneylending with interest and even to the use of money as a means of reward and exchange.[16] To this extent, orthodox preaching tended to cherish an image of righteous labour and just reward which had always been dear to Christian tradition: an image of simple men at work on the land to secure food, shelter and clothing, the *necessaria*. Adam had lived in this way from the moment that the gates of Eden closed behind him; 'in the sweat of thy face shalt thou eat bread, till thou return unto the ground' (Genesis 3:19). Such pastoral labour, which exalted poverty and the simple dignity of unchanging daily duties, was deeply congenial to the monastic mind but it offered little comfort to men like merchants and minstrels who prospered by producing nothing (or nothing useful according to a severe notion of what *utilitas* comprised). In contrast to the farmer's harvest or the stockman's herd, the merchant's profits and the minstrel's entertainment were neither necessary nor salutary and there was no orthodox concept of honest toil that could accommodate them. In a great deal of Latin religious writing from the twelfth and thirteenth centuries, therefore, the merchant is treated with much the same vehement hostility as the minstrel. The colloquy by Honorius Augustodunensis quoted above does not simply deny salvation to minstrels; the prospect of eternal bliss is also denied to merchants:[17]

> *Pupil:* Do merchants have any hope of salvation?
> *Master:* Little, for they acquire almost all the things they have through
> frauds, lies and bribes.

There has been much discussion of the ways in which some churchmen of the thirteenth century came to terms with the money economy and with the commercial practices of the cities.[18] Attention has naturally been concen-trated upon the friars, whose urban convents and practice of relying upon alms provided (to a large extent) by wealthy merchants has inspired the theory that the preaching of the friars 'was one of a number of related responses to urban money-making'.[19] For the most part this issue lies outside the scope of this book, but the question of whether the growth of the money economy affected the minstrel's moral position in society is a crucial one. To present this financial, economic and urban growth as a specifically thirteenth-century phenomenon would be misleading, of course, for while the period 1150–1300 may be fairly described as the great period of urban expansion in northern France this was an aspect of a general economic revival experienced by the West whose origins lie in the eleventh century.[20] Nonetheless, the close attention which historians working in this field have paid to the Dominicans, to the Franciscans, and to the group of theologians who were influenced by Peter the Chanter (d.1197)[21] is a testimony to the special importance of thirteenth-century writing to an understanding of the relation between theology and economic development.

Let us begin with the obvious. A minstrel, whatever his trade, was a man, and all theologians acknowledged a distinction between payment for services rendered and alms given out of *caritas*. The minstrel, like other men, bore the likeness of God, the *imago dei*, with which his creator had freely endowed him, and it was therefore possible for some churchmen to countenance the argument that a minstrel deserved alms if he were poor and destitute like any other individual. Here is William of Auxerre in his *Summa Aurea* of *c*. 1220:[22]

> Ex predictis patet quibus danda est elemosina scilicet pauperibus in
> quibus est ymago dei et nostra, et quod eis damus quodammodo deo
> damus cum ipsi sint ymago dei et eis demus in quantum tales sunt.
> Sed cum in hystrionibus sit ymago dei videtur ergo quod dare ystrionibus
> non sit peccatum.

> From what has gone before it is plain to whom alms should be given,
> that is to say to the poor in whom is both the image of God and of
> ourselves. Whatever we give to them we give, in a manner, to God,
> since they are the image of God and we must give to them insofar as
> they are such. Because the image of God may be seen in minstrels it
> may be seen therefore that to give to minstrels is not a sin.

Such discussions about the legitimacy of giving alms in various contexts become increasingly common in thirteenth-century writings, especially in those pertaining to the conduct of confession (since the inappropriate giving of alms was at best an indiscretion and at worst a misdemeanour). The issue of alleviating poverty through alms and charitable acts was a recurrent concern of thirteenth-century writers in most fields of literary activity in Latin, and modern historians have devoted much attention to it. Mollat, among others, has shown how the century witnessed a renewed anxiety in northern Europe about the problem of poverty, and how this was a response, in part, to the growing crisis presented by the urban poor.[23] The cities inevitably attracted paupers and beggars in great numbers; city gates, chapels on bridges, market-squares, the portals of religious houses and the meeting-places of mercantile confraternities – all of these provided the homeless with a place to beg alms from passers-by.

Among them were some of the poorest and least-successful minstrels. Joinville, whose biography of St Louis is devoted to a king who made an exceptional attempt to alleviate the lot of the poor, had seen these pauper minstrels arriving to accept the king's charity and he noted the monarch's generosity to them. 'Every day', says Joinville, 'the king would give such great alms ... to poor minstrels who for reasons of old age or illness could no longer work ... that one could scarcely reckon the number [of beneficiaries]'.[24]

The scene which Joinville evokes conveys a truth about medieval minstrelsy which is easily forgotten. For many people who had failed in some other occupation minstrelsy was all that stood between them and a life of utter destitution at city gates or on the margins of the forest. A sermon by the Dominican Nicholas de Gorran (d.1295), prior and lector of the Parisian convent of St Jacques, has this revealing passage:[25]

> Cantabo Domino qui bona tribuit mihi. Ps.12. Solent pauperes cantare coram divitibus a quibus aliqua bona acceperunt vel accipere intendunt.

> 'I will sing unto the Lord, because he hath dealt bountifully with me.'
> Psalm 12 [AV 13:6]. Paupers are accustomed to sing in the presence of the rich from whom they have received, or hope to receive, some gift.

Who are these 'paupers' who sing before the rich? We can only answer that they must be minstrels of a kind, for what else was a man who went before a wealthy audience and sang in the hope of reward? The problem of such low-class minstrels worried the better-established members of the profession throughout the thirteenth century; any beggar who sang or scraped an instrument for money was effectively a minstrel and therefore liable to damage the image and the interests of more stable and successful musicians. The threat could come from almost anywhere. The anonymous *Dit des taboureurs* of the thirteenth century, for example, expresses the frustration of professional fiddle-players who find that they are losing the money to be earned in the towns because rustics from the villages and hamlets are taking all the trade with their tabors and wind instruments. The poet is firmly on the side of the fiddlers, but behind his satirical descriptions of rustics who make a tabor from a discarded sieve we may be afforded a glimpse of peasants striving to supplement the meagre income from a bad harvest or a herd of ailing cattle.[26]

It will never be possible to establish what proportion of the poor in thirteenth-century France possessed some kind of 'histrionic' skill which they could market if necessary, but a few scraps of evidence suggest that the dissemination of musical ability amongst both the urban and the rural poor should not be underestimated. Every minstrel who passed by and filled his purse with coins was an object lesson in a kind of self-help. An *exemplum* of the thirteenth century tells how a simple-minded man 'in a certain French village' became envious of a singer who earned a good deal of money for his songs and who asked the singer if he could buy the songs for himself. The musician promised to sell him a sackful, and duly appeared in the village square, where all the rustics were accustomed to gather, with a sack full of wasps whose humming was taken by the simple man to be sure evidence that the sack was indeed full of songs.[27] Another *exemplum* from the same manuscript tells of a certain very poor man named Robert who lived under the stairs of a rich and avaricious character in the town of Montpellier. 'This pauper had a fiddle', the story continues, 'and when he was tired of his work, he played it and sang songs therewith in a spirited fashion. When he had five or six *denarii* he purchased meat, made some sauces, and had a wonderful time in this manner.'[28]

The emancipation of musicians: Peter the Chanter and his circle

'I believe that anyone who gives to *histriones* because they are *histriones*, and not because they are men, sacrifices to demons.' So says Peter, elected chanter of Notre Dame of Paris in 1183. This stern pronouncement presumably means that in Peter's judgement it is legitimate to give alms to poor minstrels because they are men bearing the *imago dei*, but not to pay them for their minstrel services. Peter the Chanter may sound convinced, but as we shall see, his thought on this matter is not as plain as it seems. Nor was the thinking of many of his contemporaries, amongst whom St Jerome's dictum *histrionibus dare est demonibus immolare* was giving rise to some ingenious arguments:[29]

> quidam distinguunt dicentes: qui dat aliquid aliquibus ut hystriones fiant demonibus immolat, sed qui hystrionibus iam factis dant, non peccant dummodo non dent propter turpitudinem aliquam.
>
> some people make a distinction saying that whoever gives anything to anyone so that he may become a minstrel sacrifices to demons, but that whoever gives to those who are already minstrels does not sin, providing that he does not give to obtain any wantonness.

This is a remarkable piece of prevarication, and one that has all the sophistry we would expect of the university-trained clerics whom Peter the Chanter is probably evoking in his airy reference to *quidam*, 'some people', who hold the views expressed. No clerics, we may imagine, could possibly conclude that the above was Jerome's meaning unless they were keen to temper the severity and to limit the range of what he says. Indeed, this passage provides a timely reminder that the ideas which churchmen espoused in their conversations – and even perhaps in their lectures – may sometimes have been more circumspect than those which they expressed when their ideas took on a mantle of written Latin. The view which Peter the Chanter attributes to *quidam* here does not reappear anywhere else, as far as I am aware.

Despite Peter's firm ruling that anyone 'sacrifices to demons' who gives to a minstrel *because he is a minstrel*, his own sense of the legitimacy of at least musical minstrelsy was not so straightforward as this pronouncement may seem to suggest. He saw that there was some scope for regarding musicians as makers, *artifices*, whose product was intangible, but nonetheless important, because it gave pleasure and relief:[30]

> Videndum ergo, qui opifices necessarii essent Ecclesiae et qui non; qui tolerandi in ea et qui non. Necessarii sunt agricolae, sicut pes mundi. Vinitores autem propter infirmitatem nostram . . . Similiter pelliparii sutores, tannarii, carpentarii simplices; non daedalini, non sumptuosi fabri, textores simpliciter in materia operantes . . . pictores, historias, non vana, depingentes; artifices etiam instrumentorum musicorum, ut eis tristitia et taedium amoveatur, devotio non lascivia excitetur.

> It is therefore to be ascertained which kinds of artisan are necessary to the Church; which are to be tolerated within it and which not. Farmers are necessary like the soil of the land. Vine-dressers are necessary on account of the weakness of our natures . . . So too are tailors of skins, tanners and the carpenters who make basic objects, but makers of ornate and exquisite things are not necessary. Weavers who produce plain work with their material are, however, required . . . so too are painters who depict instructive narrative scenes, not vanities. Players of musical instruments are also necessary so that boredom and depression can be relieved by them and so that devotion, not wantonness, may be inspired by them.

This is an acknowledgement that players of musical instruments are necessary to the Church; their music can even inspire devotion. It seems that the Church is an ark upon a tempestuous sea and Peter the Chanter is listing the craftsmen who have been allowed into it. Only instrumentalists, we notice, have been admitted, apart from these, the *artifices instrumentorum musicorum*, all other entertainers are left to drown.

Many of the ideas expressed in Peter the Chanter's writings were subsequently developed by a set of theologians who show such an interest in the Chanter's teaching that Baldwin long ago described them as the Chanter's 'circle' at Paris.[31] Some of them had undoubtedly heard him teach in Paris, while others may not have had such personal contact with the Chanter but were so influenced by his work that the distinction between those who knew the master and those who did not matters less and less. The writers who developed the Chanter's views on the legitimacy of instrumentalists were Englishmen: Thomas Chobham in his penitential of *c.* 1216 (a highly influential work) and Robert of Courson in his *Summa* written between 1208 and 1212/13. A third author was the Franciscan Thomas Docking, by far the latest and most provincial member of the group, whose commentary upon Galatians, composed around 1265, owes much to the penitential by Thomas Chobham.

All of these writers, Peter the Chanter included, sense that it is necessary to draw a distinction between musicians and other minstrels. Each one of them perceives it as a simple contrast between two elements in minstrelsy.

On one hand are professional secular musicians; on the other are the enter-tainers whose activities pulled down the curtain of modesty which, for every medieval theologian, was essential to the dignity and control of the human physique. As expressed by these writers, this physical modesty is not a simple conception. In part, of course, it is a theological notion: a point of doctrine which can be interpreted in an objective and legalistic manner. The image of God, which all men bear according to the testimony of Genesis, should not be deformed or demeaned. More than that, however, there is a deep and almost morbid hatred in these four authors for all bodily movement without the modesty of carriage appropriate to virtue and without the dignity of a useful purpose:[32]

> Quidam enim cum ludibrio et turpitudine sui corporis acquirunt
> necessaria, et deformant ymaginem Dei.
>
> Some [*histriones*] earn the necessaries of life through wantonness and
> obscenity of their bodies, deforming the image of God.

This is Peter the Chanter in his *Summa de sacramentis*, expressing both doctrine and disgust. In the same way, and using a similar vocabulary, Thomas Chob-ham can barely use forms of the word *turpis* ('shameless/scandalous/disgust-ing') enough to express the strength of his meaning:[33]

> Quidam enim transformant et transfigurant corpora sua per turpes saltus
> vel per turpes gestus, vel denudando corpora turpiter, vel induendo
> horribiles loricas vel larvas, et omnes tales damnabiles sunt nisi
> relinquant officia sua.
>
> Some [*histriones*] contort and distort their bodies with shameless jumps
> or shameless gestures, or in shamelessly denuding their body, or in
> putting on horrible garments or masks, and all such are damnable unless
> they relinquish their trades.

Thomas Docking follows this almost word for word, save that he intensifies the use of *turpis* even further by closing his account of *histriones* with the assurance that 'they incite people to foul things' (*provocant homines ad turpia*).[34] Both Chobham and Docking react sharply against the nudity and immodesty of these performers and against their flamboyant physical movement. No attempt is made to draw a distinction between actors, dancers, contortionists and acrobats. Medieval Christianity acknowledged no licit form of physical display; it suffices that these performers, in their various ways, violate the dignity of the human physique and provoke wantonness.

This was not the only cause for concern. Thomas Chobham is also virulently opposed to the way some entertainers spread malicious gossip. They 'follow the courts of magnates', says Chobham, 'and say shameful and malicious things about those who are absent'. Indeed, Chobham states that this is the only trade by which these minstrels know how to live. The other face of calumny is flattery, and this is what Robert of Courson attacks in his *Summa*. For Courson, who had studied extensively in Paris, the outstanding vice of the *mimus* and the *joculator* (the distinction implied is unclear) is that they both stand too close to the empty flatterer, the *adulator*:[35]

> The same judgement is to be made with respect to an *adulator*, *mimus* or *joculator* who, if he dupes adolescents and simple people with his flattery, is obliged to return whatever he has earned. If, however, he flatters those who know themselves to be of sound judgement and willingly hold themselves out to be duped, and who may give to him what they can well spare, then the minstrel is not obliged to return what he has taken. But those who give to such minstrels sending them forth in their error commit a mortal sin, since perhaps they will be in a stronger position to work thereafter. Jerome says 'to give to *histriones* is to sacrifice to demons', unless perhaps someone gives with the intention of preventing the minstrels from accusing or defaming him in the presence of evil prelates and tyrants.

This passage implies that flattery and backbiting were such an important part of at least some minstrels' trade that Jerome's dictum *histrionibus dare est demonibus immolare* was giving rise to yet another piece of prevarication: it is legitimate to give money to minstrels if one does so 'with the intention of preventing the minstrels from accusing or defaming [one] in the presence of evil prelates and tyrants ...'. A desperate man, in other words, finding himself unable to control what a minstrel would say when he travelled far afield, could legitimately buy the backbiter's silence.

All four of the authors whom we have been discussing are agreed that musical minstrels stand apart from these actors, acrobats, dancers, flatterers and backbiters. This may seem surprising, for we might be inclined to suspect that singers and instrumentalists often contributed to the success of such entertainments as these; nonetheless, the distinction between musical minstrelsy and what might be called 'histrionic' minstrelsy was clear to Peter the Chanter, Thomas Chobham, Robert of Courson and Thomas Docking.

Peter the Chanter was the first. Having declared that it is legitimate to give something to a minstrel because he is a man, but not because he is a minstrel, he adds:[36]

> Item. Distinguendum est modicum in superioribus circa ioculatores. Quidam enim cum ludibrio et turpitudine sui corporis acquirunt necessaria, et deformant ymaginem Dei. De talibus uera sunt que diximus. Sed si cantent cum instrumentis, uel cantent de gestis rebus ad recreationem uel forte ad informationem, uicini sunt excusationi.

> Again, a slight nuance should be added to what has been said above about *ioculatores*. Some earn the necessaries of life through wantonness and obscenity of their bodies, deforming the image of God. As far as these are concerned the things which we have said hold true. But if they sing with instruments, or sing of exploits to give relaxation and perhaps to give instruction, their activities border upon being legitimate.

This is cautiously worded. As he separates musical minstrels from the rest Peter the Chanter says only that he is adding a 'slight nuance' to his previous, highly critical remarks, and he is only prepared to concede that the activities of musical minstrels 'border upon being legitimate'. However, there are also signs of tolerance. He seems prepared to allow vocal and instrumental music (*si cantent cum instrumentis*) for recreation, and although he envisages how such music might be of an improving character (*ad informationem*), he does not require it.

Thomas Chobham and Thomas Docking both felt the need to devise a specialised terminology to express the distinction between musical and non-musical minstrels. Chobham discusses entertainers in general under the term *histrio*, but he demands a terminological distinction for the musicians of whom he approves almost without reserve: those who sing and play instruments and sing of the deeds of secular heroes or of the lives of saints. These he calls *ioculatores*. His account of musical minstrels has been quoted many times, but it still deserves to be laid out in full. Having distinguished between (1) acrobats, contortionists and the rest and (2) backbiters who 'follow the courts of magnates', Chobham distinguishes a third category: singers and instrumentalists:[37]

> Est enim tertium genus histrionum qui habent instrumenta musica ad
> delectandum homines, sed talium duo sunt genera. Quidam enim
> frequentant publicas potationes et lascivas congregationes ut cantent ibi
> lascivas cantilenas, ut moveant homines ad lasciviam, et tales sunt
> damnabilies sicut et alii. Sunt autem alii qui dicuntur ioculatores qui
> cantant gesta principium et vitas sanctorum et faciunt solatia hominibus
> vel in egritudinibus suis vel in angustiis suis et non faciunt nimias
> turpitudines sicut faciunt saltatores et saltatrices et alii qui ludunt in
> imaginibus inhonestis et faciunt videri quasi quedam phantasmata per
> incantationes vel alio modo. Si autem non faciunt talia sed cantant
> instrumentis suis gesta principum et alia utilia ut faciunt solatia
> hominibus sicut dictum est, bene possunt sustineri tales . . .

> There is a third kind of minstrel using musical instruments to entertain
> people, but there are two varieties of these. Some go to public drinking
> places and wanton gatherings so that they may sing wanton songs there
> to move people to lustfulness, and these are damnable just like the rest.
> There are others, however, who are called *ioculatores*, who sing the deeds
> of princes and the lives of saints and give people comfort either when
> they are ill or when they are troubled, and who are not responsible for
> too much shamefulness as male and female dancers are and others who
> play in deceitful mummings and cause what appear to be certain
> phantoms to be seen through incantations or in some other way. If,
> however, they do not do this, but sing the deeds of princes and other
> useful things to their instruments to give comfort to people, as has been
> said, then such entertainers may be tolerated . . .

This looks black; Thomas abhors the haunts of secular musicians ('public drinking places and wanton gatherings'), he is disgusted by the sexual provocation associated with them and he is firm in his dismissal of minstrels who sing secular songs with voices and instruments. Yet there is a note of tolerance here and one which the pattern of surviving musical sources from the thirteenth century can easily obscure. Since most of the monophonic secular music that has come down to us from the period 1220–1300 is lyrical rather than narrative in character, there is a danger that we will mistake the implications for contemporaries of Chobham's ruling that lyrical repertoire of a secular character (*cantilenas*) is forbidden but that narrative song is not. This is a much greater concession than the negligible notated remains of narrative song repertoire would lead us to believe.[38] Chobham does not restrict his concession to the lives of saints; following the conventional medieval understanding of the purpose served by narratives of secular heroes he judges the 'deeds of princes' to be salutary material.[39] He is therefore instructing confessors to allow the activities of minstrels who performed a repertoire which, as we shall see, appealed to many social classes, including the highest, throughout the thirteenth century.

Thomas Docking, who follows Chobham closely, also favours musical minstrels with a terminological distinction: they are not *histriones* but *mimi*:[40]

> De hystrionibus sciendum est quod histriones dicuntur quasi hystoriones, eo quod corporum suorum gesticulacione representant hystorias aliquas turpes sive confictas sive factas, sicut olim fecerunt tragedi et comedi in theatris, et hodie fit in turpibus spectaculis et turpibus ludis, in quibus denudantur corpora ... De mimis autem cuiusmodi sunt cithariste et viellatores et alii utentes instrumentis musicis; si hac intencione utuntur labore et officio suo ut provocent homines ad ocium vel lasciviam, repellendi sunt et prohibendi a beneficio; si autem indigentes sunt et utuntur talibus pro victu suo adhipiscendo hac intencione ut faciant hominibus solacium contra iram, tristiciam, tedium et accidiam, vel contra infirmitates corporales, tanquam pauperes Christi ad beneficia sunt recipiendi.

> Concerning *histriones* it should be noted that they are called as it were *historiones* ('storytellers') in that they represent, with gesticulations of their body, various obscene, false or true stories, just as *tragedi* and *comedi* formerly did in the theatres, and as is done today in shameful shows and shameful games, in which people strip off their clothing ... Some *mimi*, however, are *cithariste* and *viellatores* and others playing musical instruments; if they spend their efforts, and exercise their trade so that they may provoke people to sloth or wantonness, they are to be shunned and kept apart from any benefit; if, however, they are poor, and use their trade to earn their food and with the intention of giving people comfort against anger, sadness, weariness or sloth, or against bodily infirmities, they are to be given benefits like the poor of Christ.

Robert of Courson also rules that musical minstrels may be allowed, and once again we notice a distinction of terminology: on the one hand are the *mimi, joculatores, histriones* and *adulatores*; on the other is the string-player, the *citharedus*:[41]

> Item queritur de mimis et joculatoribus et histrionibus et adulatoribus utrum possint de jure locare operas suas. Videtur quod non quia sic emolliunt et effeminant et sepe infatuant animos auditorum et ita emungunt subdole bona eorum; ergo non licet eis aliquid accipere intuitu talium. Quid ergo dicetur citharedo habenti uxorem et multos filios secum et viventi tamen ex canticis et cithara quod videtur ei licere cum David et Maria soror Moysi et multi alii timorati viri in liris in citharis et tympanis et psalteriis et organis et canticis commendentur.

> The question now arises of whether *mimi, joculatores, histriones* and *adulatores* may legitimately hire their services for money. It will be seen that they may not, for they soften, weaken and often dupe the minds of their hearers so that they somewhat deceitfully cheat them of their gifts; therefore it is not permitted to accept any service from them in respect of such things. What, therefore, will be said to a string-player having a wife and many sons with him, and living by his songs and his stringed instrument – which will be seen to be allowed to him, for David, Miriam the sister of Moses, and many other God-fearing persons have lent their lustre to *lire, cithare, tympana, psalteria, organa* and songs.

Musical minstrels are given an indulgence here. But what kind of musicians are they? For the most part they are string-players who also sing. The earliest of our authors, Peter the Chanter, is not explicit in the standard modern edition of his *Summa de sacramentis*, referring only to those who *cantent cum instrumentis*. This phrase might be translated 'should they sing with instruments' or 'should they play upon instruments', the former being preferable from an idiomatic point of view.[42] It is interesting, however, that a variant cited in the edition is more specific, for there the musicians are 'string-players or singing minstrels':[43]

> si sint simpliciter citharedi uel ioculatores canentes . . .

Thomas Chobham also has singer-instrumentalists in mind, although he does not specify what kind of instruments they play. However, a wealth of thirteenth-century evidence associates narrative song with a stringed instrument, usually the fiddle, or *viella*. It is a fiddle that accompanies *gesta* of Charlemagne in the *Karolinus* (1195–96) by Thomas Chobham's contemporary, Egidius of Paris:[44]

> De Karolo . . .
> Gesta solent melicis aures sopire viellis.

It is a *viële* which Gerard uses to accompany a *chanson de geste* in *Le Roman de la violette*:[45]

> 'Faire m'estuet, quant l'ai empris,
> Chou dont je ne sui mie apris:
> Chanter et viëler ensamble.'

> Lors commencha, si com moi samble,
> Con chil qui molt estoit senés,
> Un ver de Guillaume au court nes,
> A clere vois et a douch son :
> > *Grans fu la cours en la sale a Loon* etc

Since I have undertaken it I must do that which I am not at all good at : to sing and to play the *vïele* together. Then, as it seems to me, he began a laisse about of Guillaume au Court Nez, like one who was well-skilled in such matters, with a clear voice and sweet sound [a laisse of 22 lines follows].

Thomas Docking, as he adapts and reworks Chobham's passage, makes it clear that his minstrels are principally *cithariste* and *viellatores*, to whom are added 'others playing musical instruments'. Robert of Courson, for his part, defends instrumentalists with a reference to King David and other 'God-fearing persons' who have lent their lustre to musical instruments, including *lire*, *cithare*, *tympana*, *psalteria* and *organa*, as well as songs. This has the potential, at least, to be made into a comprehensive advocacy of all instrumentalists and singers; when it comes to the question of whether minstrelsy can provide a legitimate livelihood, however, Courson mentions only one kind of musician in explicit terms: the *citharedus*, or string-player.

> Quid ergo dicetur citharedo . . .

There is no positive evidence to suggest that any of these four authors is thinking of wind-players or percussionists when they make their concessions, but it would perhaps be an exaggeration to suggest that they have only string-players in mind. A more balanced assessment would be that all of them are sensitive to the musical climate of their times, for the thirteenth century seems to have been a period when the strings were regarded as the most subtle and artistic of all instrumental resources. As Johannes de Grocheio put it at the end of the century : 'in them there is a subtler and better difference of sound arising from the shortening and lengthening of the strings'.[46]

Why were singer-instrumentalists singled out by these four theologians for concessions and pardon ?

As first sight the assistance of the musical sources seems crucial here. We possess a great deal of courtly monophonic song produced in northern France during the last decades of the twelfth century; can it be a coincidence that the earliest concessions to musical minstrels are found within a decade or so of the first trouvères? Peter the Chanter was a contemporary of Conon de Béthune, the Chastelain de Couci and Gace Brulé; surely the Chanter's qualified acceptance of musical minstrels owes something to the emergence, within his lifetime, of the first repertoire of courtly vernacular song of which we have any written trace in northern France?

Perhaps it does, but it is equally possible that it does not. Peter the Chanter defines the legitimate state of pleasure in secular music as one in which we listen to[47]

> uersos iocundos de honesta materia, uel instrumenta musica ad
> recreationem sed nullomodo ad uoluptatem.

> pleasing verses dealing with some decorous subject, or musical
> instruments, for relaxation but by no means to enjoy wantonness.

This is a rather austere definition, and one that is perhaps unlikely to have encompassed the love-poetry of the trouvères, with its pervasive eroticism and its occasional moments of candour:[48]

> Or me lait Dieus en tele honeur monter
> Que cele u j'ai mon cuer et mon penser
> Tieigne une foiz entre mes braz nüete
>   Ainz que j'aille outremer.

> Now may God grant me that I may ascend to the high honour of holding
> the one who has my heart, and all my thoughts, naked once in my arms
> before I go overseas.

As for the Englishmen Thomas Chobham and Thomas Docking, it may be granted that an Anglo-Norman tradition of courtly song existed in England, analogous to the repertory of the trouvères and perhaps dependent upon it for models,[49] and yet this tradition has left little trace in English musical sources; if these are among the songs which Chobham has in mind when he attacks *lascivas cantilenas* then all that seems clear is that he loathes them; they cannot have been the basis of the tolerance he extends towards some musicians, and it is obvious from the rest of his remarks that they are not. This is not to propose that the surviving musical sources have no light to shed on this problem, but it is clear nonetheless that we must look elsewhere for the principal answers to the question of why instrumentalists (specially string-players) and singers achieved a degree of emancipation from their 'histrionic' colleagues.

The first place to look is into the confessional where so much of the twelfth-century's thought and theology was channelled into practical moral counsel. Peter the Chanter makes his concessions to musicians in the context of a discussion of penance;[50] Thomas Chobham is writing a manual for confessors, and so, in effect, is Robert of Courson.[51] Thomas Docking is commenting upon Galatians, but he is following Chobham very closely.

A major development in twelfth-century thought is explored and systematised in these and many other writings connected with penance and confession. It may be defined as a shift away from an essentially objective notion of sin as evil action deserving statutory punishments, and a corresponding move towards a concept of sin as evil intention fulfilled in circumstances to be explored by the confessor.[52] This is a complex change which owes as much to the initiatives of individual thinkers as it does to any concerted shift in sensibility. The *Ethics* of Peter Abelard (d.1142) proves an irresistible illustration in this context. As Michael Haren explains:[53]

> [Abelard's] chief contribution to moral theology in the *Ethics* is his
> definition of sin as a matter of consent, the thesis that action divorced
> from the intention which produces it is morally indifferent . . . It is the
> intention that determines the morality of an action and it is consent to
> what is known to be evil that . . . constitutes sin.

Abelard expressed (and refined) a twelfth-century insight; writers on confession and penance explored it in relation to the almost infinite variety of circumstances which sinful behaviour could present to a churchman with pastoral responsibilities.

Intentions had to be judged, and the results of action – the realisations of intention – had to be foreseen and assessed. Thus Peter the Chanter distinguishes three kinds of intention both in listening to secular minstrelsy and in making it: to enjoy relaxation (*recreatio*), to be pleasantly and profitably instructed (*informatio*) and to relish improper desires (*voluptas*). Thomas Chobham is also closely concerned with what is willed. He does not merely object that some instrumentalists go to taverns where wantonness abounds; he objects to them doing so because of what they wish to accomplish there:

> ut moveant homines ad lasciviam.

Chobham also looks to the results of minstrelsy where intentions are made manifest. Wanton songs result in wantonness, but songs about the deeds of heroes and the lives of saints are 'useful' things (*utilia*) in Chobham's judgement; they serve a constructive purpose by giving comfort (*solatia*). Thomas Docking, following Chobham's words some fifty years later, makes the issue of intention very clear. If instrumentalists ply their trade with the intention of arousing improper thoughts (*si hac intencione utuntur labore et officio suo*) then they are damnable, but if they do it with the intention of giving solace (*intencione ut faciant homines solacium*), then they may be received 'as the poor of Christ'. In a passage written by a Franciscan this last comment presumably means that a minstrel may be charitably received as if he were a friar seeking shelter. Writers on confession knew well enough that this kind of enquiry into the intentions and results of actions brought a new element of compassion, and even of indulgence, into the Church's confrontation with the individual sinner in the privacy of the confessional. In the words of Peter of Poitiers, it introduced a 'softening of the old medicines'.[54]

In part, the medicine was softened for musical minstrels because the new emphasis on intention and usefulness in the confessional mobilised a host of notions about the power of music which had never before been so closely or so soberly considered in relation to the daily needs and human weaknesses of ordinary people. The issue here is the relationship between felt experience, language and literary tradition. Throughout the Middle Ages every Latin author could produce a rhetorical set-piece about the powers of music – what

Cassiodorus, author of one of the most elaborate, calls a *voluptuosa digressio*.[55] Standard topoi included the influence of music over character and the emotions, the famous medicinal powers of harmonious musical sound, and the ability of music to inspire rapturous contemplation of heavenly joys. These set-pieces, common in Latin poetry, and often welcomed in Latin treatises on music theory,[56] generally have a static quality. To choose one example from a multitude, the music-theorist Johannes (fl. *c*. 1100) proclaims that the eight modes of liturgical chant appeal to different people in different ways: 'some are pleased by the slow and ceremonious peregrinations of the first . . . some are taken by the hoarse profundity of the second', while others 'are delighted by the austere and almost haughty prancing of the third', and so on.[57] These descriptions leave us rather bewildered, for a modern ear is not readily convinced that these qualities are present in the church modes to which Johannes refers.[58] His words are like an ambitious piece of wine criticism; we accept that he is trying to describe something that he sensed, but at the same time we doubt whether he sensed all (or even most) of the things to which his language lays claim.

When the confessors (or those, like Thomas Docking, heavily influenced by manuals of confession) write of the healing powers of music we enter a different realm. Thomas Chobham and his diligent follower Thomas Docking, for example, are not celebrating the power of music in rhetorical Latin so they do not bring an aesthetic reaction to music and a striving for imposing, metaphorical language together into a single, complex impulse of the kind felt by Johannes. When they speak of music's ability to heal, or of its power to give comfort, they speak plainly:[59]

> [If musicians] use their trade . . . with the intention of giving people
> comfort against anger, sadness, weariness or sloth, or against bodily
> infirmities, they are to be given benefits like the poor of Christ.

Here the language states the meaning but does not adorn it or seek to carry it into a higher realm. In these lines Thomas Docking has made a concession to human frailty, and as a friar, licensed to hear confession, it is his business to know something of human weaknesses and to weigh every concession that he makes to them. The quality of feeling in his words is certain. It was in pastoral writing of this kind, closely related to the pastoral ministry, that an ancient and rhetorical tradition of celebrating the 'effects' of music was transformed into pragmatic teaching of a plain yet vivid sort.

These are general considerations about the recognition of music's power over the mind. Can we speak in more precise terms and explain the emancipation of musical minstrels (and of string-players in particular) in terms of their repertoire? This approach has the sanction of at least one thirteenth-century source, for we remember that Thomas Chobham makes a distinction between singer-instrumentalists on the grounds of repertory (see above, p. 23). Indeed, Chobham's passage has led many historians to suggest that pious or profitable narrative repertoire of this kind played a crucial role in legitimising the activities of some musical minstrels. Geremek, for example, declares that amidst the general condemnation of professional entertainers an exception was made[60]

> for those who told stories likely to strengthen virtue and faith, who
> popularised the lives of saints, or told moral tales based on the actions
> and deeds of exemplary people. The Church was even ready to lend
> active support to such people, and this distinction led, little by little,
> to the recognition in practice of tumblers and singers.

This choice of words rather underestimates the breadth of content and appeal which narratives could possess if they dealt with the lives of saints and secular heroes. In thirteenth-century France this repertoire principally comprised the *chansons de geste*; around 1300 Johannes de Grocheio describes them in terms reminiscent of those used by Thomas Chobham :[61]

> Cantum vero gestualem dicimus, in quo gesta heroum et antiquorum
> patrum opera recitantur, sicuti vita et martyria sanctorum et proelia et
> adversitates quas antiqui viri pro fide et veritate passi sunt, sicuti vita
> beati Stephani protomartyris et historia regis Karoli.

> We say that a *chanson de geste* is a song in which the deeds of heroes
> and of the ancient Fathers are recited, such as the life and martyrdom
> of saints, and the battles and hardships which men in ancient times
> endured for faith and truth, such as the life of Saint Stephen the
> protomartyr and the history of King Charlemagne.

Grocheio, like Thomas Chobham, speaks of narratives about secular heroes and saints as if they were two aspects of the same kind of song. His reference to Charlemagne evokes many of the surviving *chansons de geste* (including the most famous, the *Chanson de Roland*); other epics deal with heroes such as Girart de Vienne (whom Grocheio mentions in another passage), Aymeri de Narbonne, Guillaume au Court Nez, and many more.

Geremek does not explain what narrative repertoire he has in mind when he speaks of the 'moral tales' performed by acceptable minstrels, but if he is thinking of the Old French *chansons de geste* then he has chosen a rather unhelpful phrase. While it would be possible to regard many of the surviving *chansons de geste* as 'moral tales' at bottom, we rarely find that any simple or confident notion of virtue is expounded in them; 'exemplary people' do not spring from the *chansons de geste* with the kind of vigour one might expect in a narrative repertoire which supposedly helped 'to strengthen virtue and faith'.[62] Indeed, the *chansons de geste* generally do their best to please and to divert in every way they can, offering luxurious descriptions of even more luxurious feasts, for example, and a liberal amount of 'gratuitous violence'. When Thomas of Chobham, for example, endorses 'useful' stories which deal with the lives of princes or of saints we should not imagine that he is condoning narratives of an overtly pious and purposeful character which only those who had disciplined their fondness for wilder material could hope to enjoy; the narratives which Grocheio describes as *gesta heroum* could encompass savagery like the following in which Raoul de Cambrai, hero of the epic that bears his name, burns down the nunnery at Origny on the Loire:[63]

> Li quens R., qui le coraige ot fier,
> A fait le feu par les rues fichier.
> Ardent ces loges, ci fondent li planchier;
> Li vin espandent, s'en flotent li celie[r];
> Li bacon ardent, si chiéent li lardie[r];
> Li saïns fait le grant feu esforcier,
> Fiert soi es tors et al maistre cloichier.
> Les covretures covint jus trebuchier;
> Entre .ij. murs ot si grant charbonier,
> Les nonains ardent: trop i ont grant brasier

> Count Raoul the proud-hearted had fire set to the streets. The dwellings
> burn and the wooden floors collapse; the wine is spilt, flooding the
> cellars. The hams are burning and the sides of bacon melt, the lard giving
> added fuel to the flames which leap up to the towers and the main belfry
> so the roofs have to fall. Between the walls there is such a blaze that
> the nuns are burned, so great is the fire.

The *chansons de geste* possessed a very wide appeal. Johannes de Grocheio is of the opinion that these stories of the *adversitates* endured by the great people of the past give consolation to old people, to working people, and to those 'of middle station', beset by their own trials. This may sound facile, and perhaps it is; we shall see in a later chapter that it is definitely not naive. For the moment let us recognise that it is probably a rationalisation of something which Grocheio had observed as he went his way in Paris. The epic stories were of passionate interest to the general populace. A Parisian sermon of the thirteenth century tells how minstrels would take up a position in the streets, or on the Petit Pont, and there recite stories of Roland and Oliver to such effect that the people standing round them were moved to pity and periodically burst into tears (see below, p. 177). At the same time, the existence of a knightly and aristocratic audience for these turbulent and violent epics can scarcely be doubted. A sermon by Evrard du Val-des-Ecoliers records that *homines militares* liked to hear the praises of Roland, Oliver and Charle-magne, while an anonymous sermon in MS Arundel 395 reveals how 'the excellent deeds of the ancients are customarily recited in the houses of nobles', and these *antiqui* may well be epic heroes like Grocheio's *antiqui patres*.[64]

The association between musical minstrels and narrative repertoire helps to explain why musicians – and especially the players of stringed instruments – achieved a degree of emancipation from other minstrels during the thirteenth century. As we have seen, the evidence favours the supposition that *chansons de geste* were principally associated with string-players, above all with players of the fiddle or *viella*, and a remarkable poem of the thirteenth century, entitled the *Dit des taboureurs,* reveals how closely the *chansons de geste* had become associated with the fiddlers' sense of professional pride and exclusiveness.[65] In this short poem a spokesman for fiddle-players sneers at the rustics and other low-brow musicians who are playing wind and percussion instruments like the *tabour, musele, fleustes* and *flajols,* and who are taking work away from the 'proper' minstrels, the players of the *viele.* The sense of a hierarchy of instruments, with the fiddle at the top and the winds and percussion coming a long way below, is strong in this poem. Most revealing of all is the stanza that inventories the fiddlers' repertoire; without exception, the material which these proud instrumentalists wish to be associated with is a narrative one, full of the names of heroes from the traditions of the *chansons de geste*:[66]

> Mès qui bien set chanter du Borgoing Auberi,
> De Girart de Viane, de l'Ardenois Tierri,
> De Guillaume au cort nez, de son père Aimeri,
> Doivent par tout le monde bien estre seignori.

> But they who know well how to sing about Auberi le Bourgoing, of Girart de Vienne, of Thierry l'Ardenois, of Guillaume au Court Nez and his father Aimeri, they are the ones who should be honoured throughout all the world.

The names of these heroes mean so little today that it is easy to miss the complex resonance of their stories in thirteenth-century France. In part, this resonance is an echo of real persons and events who had lived long before. The protagonist of *Raoul de Cambrai,* for example, whose deeds include the violent destruction of the nunnery of Origny (see above, p. 31) has a historical counterpart in the Raoul mentioned in the *Annales Flodoardi*; this Raoul did indeed have a battle with the sons of Herbert of Vermandois (d.943) as the epic of *Raoul de Cambrai* relates.[67] These events took place in the early 940s.

The case of Guillaume au Court Nez, mentioned in the extract above from the *Dit des taboureurs,* shows how readily *history* and *story* could merge in the traditions surrounding one of these heroes. Guillaume au Court Nez is William of Aquitaine, Count of Toulouse, who was canonised in 1066. His relics could be seen at St Sernin, Toulouse, and at the monastery of Gellone which was later named St Guilhem-le-Désert after him. Various aspects of William's story are told in more than half a dozen vernacular *chansons de geste,* many of which present him as a mighty warrior but also as a difficult man who often makes himself unpopular. This failing gives rise to many humorous situations – even after his decision to join a monastic community – which must have provided excellent material for minstrel narrators. The celebration of William's renown was not confined to the *chansons de geste,* however, for there is also a Latin *Vita Sancti Guillelmi* which has clearly drawn some of its material from vernacular narrative tradition.[68]

Here history and legend, hagiography and secular epic, are intertwined. We begin to appreciate why Thomas Chobham and Johannes de Grocheio speak of narrative songs about 'the deeds of princes' and about 'the lives of saints' in the same breath. It also becomes apparent that these epics were deeply involved with a sense of the past. The kernel of 'history' (as we understand the term today) in many of the epics is large enough to have given modern scholars a good deal of scope for discussion and research;[69] there are names, places and events in many of these epics, in other words, which correspond in various ways to details that can be disentangled from earlier 'historical' writings such as prose chronicles and annals. In the thirteenth century nobody had such comprehensive access to historical records as modern scholars now enjoy; furthermore, the authors of epics were sometimes inclined to claim a written source (an *escript*) in language that was designed to impress and must often have done so.[70] The issue of history and legend in the *chansons de geste* was therefore one that could scarcely present itself to the thirteenth-century mind in a sharply focused way. This is not to say that the century produced no educated men able to recognise the omnipresence in these epics of what we would call (using modern concepts of reading) an element of 'fiction'; in a sermon preached in Paris in 1272, for example, Daniel of Paris refers to the many 'false things' which *histriones* add to the stories of epic heroes such as Roland and Oliver.[71] Even here, however, the notion that minstrels 'add falsities' implies a basic structure of truth to which the additions are made. Daniel's underlying assumption – and it seems to have been one which most people shared – is that Roland, Oliver, Ogier the Dane and many others had once existed, and that at least the basic lineaments of their stories had been handed down for the instruction and edification of all.

When the issue is presented in these terms it begins to seem that at least some kinds of string-player were the bards of thirteenth-century France: a professional caste of musicians interpreting the past for a lay audience unable to consult any other version of it. We notice that all the epic heroes proudly claimed by the fiddle-players in the *Dit des taboureurs* belong to the Matter of France, what Jean Bodel, writing in the last third of the twelfth century, regarded as the most illustrious narrative material and the most truthful (*la plus voir disant*). This is the heart of the issue. Warriors like Charlemagne and Guillaume au Court Nez were not just great fighters of old; they stood shoulder to shoulder with the kings, warriors and saints whose crusades and feuds made up the warring past of France. The land of St Denis had risen to her position of strength and eminence because of – and in spite of – what these great men suffered. Johannes de Grocheio hits the mark when he refers to heroes like Charlemagne as the *antiqui patres*, the 'ancient fathers' of France.[72]

The views of the schoolmen: 1250–1300

I have suggested that during the first half of the thirteenth century we can detect an emancipation of musical minstrels from their 'histrionic' colleagues which is manifested in a certain qualified tolerance of musicians, and especially of string-players. Most of the sources for that enquiry were essentially pragmatic, being designed to teach or to offer guidance without pretensions to philosophical learning. Let us now turn to writings of a much more obviously academic kind, namely the treatises of the schoolmen. It was in these works that some of the most radical positions on minstrelsy and musical pleasure in general were developed. They are a rich seam of contemporary opinion, for the schoolmen, employing the usual scholastic method, assemble arguments *pro* and *contra* before offering a solution to any question, and their writings are therefore a unique record of contrasting ideas which cannot be found in any other kind of source.

The key text consists of a few words in the standard theological textbook at Paris, the *Sentences* of Peter the Lombard. In *Sentences* 4:xvi the Lombard follows Augustine word for word on the legitimacy of entertainments (*ludi* and *spectacula*) during a time of penance:[73]

> Caveat etiam ne prius ad dominicum corpus accedat, quam confortet
> bona conscientia; et doleat quod nondum audeat sumere quem multum
> desiderat cibum salutarem. Cohibeat sibi a ludis, a spectaculis seculi,
> qui perfectam vult consequi remissionis gratiam.

> Let the penitent be wary that he does not partake of the host before
> [confession], as shall be consonant with good conscience, and let him
> lament that he does not yet dare to partake of the life-giving chalice
> which he greatly desires. He who wishes the perfect grace of remission
> to follow will keep himself from entertainments and from worldly shows.

As interpreted in the thirteenth century this ruling that the penitent who wishes for true absolution should keep himself 'from entertainments and from worldly shows' raised questions not only about minstrelsy in the broadest sense but also about secular music. It was believed that Augustine himself had made this clear in his commentary on Paul's Epistle to the Romans that the Latin word *spectacula* encompassed the music of the *cithara*.[74] In the writings of the academics, however, it was the general sense of the term *spectacula* that attracted most attention, usually with results that are brief but revealing. Here as an example is the Dominican Master of Theology Pierre de Tarentaise, later Pope Innocent V, discussing the above passage in his commentary upon the *Sentences*, composed 1257–59:[75]

> spectacula omnia ad aliquam utilitatem instituta sunt, ergo non
> repugnant penitentie. Item in spectando non est peccatum nisi
> curiositatis; maior autem curiositas est in multis scientiis nec dicuntur
> impedire penitentiam. Item alia peccata graviora sunt quam spectacula
> et ludi, ergo magis deberent hec ab Augustino proiberi . . . Item videtur
> quod negociatio et milicia penitentiam non impediant quia sine quibus
> res publica non bene regitur.

> all entertainments have been instituted for some useful purpose, therefore
> they are not inimical to penance. Again, in giving attention to such things
> there is no sin but that of curiosity, and greater curiosity is involved

in many fields of rational enquiry and they are not said to impede
penance. Again, there are other, graver sins than entertainments and
worldly shows, therefore it is these that should rather be prohibited by
Augustine ... Again, it is clear that trade and military action do not
impede penance because without these things the state cannot be
governed well.

These remarkable lines can be read as an epitome of the major intellectual
achievements of the thirteenth century. First, there is a stern critical appraisal
of Patristic *auctoritas* which we recognise as the foundation of the scholastic
enterprise; Pierre de Tarentaise challenges St Augustine's ruling against *ludi*
and *spectacula* with the argument that there are worse things in the world
than entertainments but Augustine does not forbid them. Second, there is
an appeal to rational and scientific enquiry, a point of reference for judging
human enterprise that was newly vivid to men of the thirteenth century who
had begun to absorb Greek and Islamic science. Anyone who watches *spectacula*, Pierre de Tarentaise argues, is only guilty of the sin of curiosity, and
'greater curiosity is involved in many fields of rational enquiry (*in multis
scientiis*) but they are not said to impede penance'. The term *scientia* here
implies an intellectual quest whose rigour and dignity cannot be assailed,
while *curiositas* denotes an active interest in all phenomena presented to the
senses by Nature or by the handiwork of Man.

Third, and perhaps most important of all, is the consideration which Pierre
de Tarentaise puts first: usefulness, or *utilitas*. This has a familiar ring, for
usefulness was one of the considerations which occupied the confessors; we
remember that Thomas Chobham referred to minstrel narratives as *utilia*.
Men whose task it was to sort through human actions, judging their sinfulness
in terms of aims and intentions, necessarily gave close attention to *utilitas*.
During the second half of the thirteenth century, however, the interest and
importance of the concept of usefulness was immeasurably reinforced by
activities of a quite different kind: the close study of the works of Aristotle,
a philosopher whose thought is characterised by its persistent emphasis upon
final purposes and ends. 'All studies and undertakings are directed to the
attainment of some good', says Aristotle in his *Ethics*, translated in full by
Robert Grosseteste *c*. 1246, and this is clearly an argument which Pierre de
Tarentaise is prepared to apply to the question before him. 'All *spectacula*',
he proposes, 'have been instituted for some useful purpose'.[76]

Meditating upon the usefulness of human actions led many theologians
by degrees towards a kind of 'political' thought in the sense that the good
of the city or urban community was increasingly recognised as the supreme
criterion for judging usefulness. Such thinking was strengthened after the
1260s with the appearance of a complete Latin translation of Aristotle's *Politics*
by William of Moerbeke.[77] Pierre de Tarentaise, for example, rules that
trade (*negociatio*) and military action (*milicia*) are things which do not impede
penance because 'without these things the state cannot be ruled well'. The
word 'state' in this context is perhaps a slightly leading translation of the

Latin *res publica*, but the generalising force of Pierre's remark seems designed to declare a *principle* of government that demands a *conception* of government equally imposing and comprehensive.

In their different ways, trade and military action are both exhausting activities. How were the citizens to seek repose from such necessary labours? The answer was plain, and the theologians scarcely needed Aristotle's *Politics* to discover it for themselves: the citizens were to rest with the help of diversions as important to the maintenance of the *res publica* as the commercial and military activities for which such entertainments gave renewed commitment and vigour. Something recognisable as the modern concept of leisure, in other words, was rapidly emerging.

For the cause we look to the cities and the circumstances of urban living. Most of the theologians who explored these ideas had studied at Paris where a veritable 'monstre urbain' confronted them with the intense visual stimulus which is such an important element in the influence which urban living exerts over the psychology of those who experience it.[78] In virtually every street one could see craftsmen and artisans who were able to concentrate upon specialised manufacture because the surplus of food in the outlying fields – the foundation of the city's greatness – had freed them from agricultural labour. Released from the task of gathering the provisions which all men need, they could now set up in business to make the things which a few men want. They were the *deciarii*, the *compositores scacorum et alearum*, the *compositores toxicorum*, the *fabri balistarum* and many more whose names abound in Parisian documents of the thirteenth century. They produced objects in metal, wood, glass, leather and other materials to meet the requirements of an urban population in need of clothes, saddles, vessels, nails and other goods. When these sights were reinforced by the visible magnificence of Paris with its churches, bridges and enclosing walls, with its corners associated with special occasions (such as fairs or markets) which focused the life of the community, and with its streetnames which became as familiar in the mouth as the nicknames of close friends, it was possible to receive a deep impression of the *civitas* as a vast common enterprise that hallowed any work which contributed to its needs.

To say that these experiences pressed particularly upon the masters in the university is not to deny this kind of stimulus to the members of monastic orders. A monk could sometimes feel the texture of urban life well enough, for his monastery might well stand in the centre of a fortified *bourg* that had grown from a cluster of dwellings dependent upon the religious house.[79] His life might be circumscribed by the dormitory, refectory and church, but he was free to sense the benefits made possible by urbanism in the diversity and perhaps even in the delicacy of the food put before him, just as he could sense it in the flood of civic and mercantile visitors to the monastery and in the matters that preoccupied the officials charged with the financial affairs of his house. Nonetheless, it was part of his endeavour as a contemplative to distance himself from the city: to hold it in his mind as an ideogram, *urbs*, like the stylised rooftops and ramparts shown in miniatures of the twelfth and thirteenth centuries. It represented something which he had rejected, at least in his spirit, and from which he turned if he were moved to explore his religious life in writing. In contexts such as these, leisure (*otium, requies*) was apt to be regarded as at least potentially perilous because the work to which it provided an alternative was the perpetual work of God, *opus dei*. True and blameless *requies* was the perfect repose of wordless, contemplative prayer – not a break from the duties of life, but a culmination of them.

The theologians trained in the university cities tended to see things differently. As teachers, paid in cash for their teaching,[80] they were integrated into the urban economy whereby money was handed over for specialised luxury services which produced nothing strictly necessary according to the conventional definition of the *necessaria*: food, drink and essential raiment. The masters' learning was for sale and the urban university was their marketplace. They were too close to the daily realities of work and production to deny the importance of rest and diversion. Here is a late witness, the Dominican theologian Rainerus of Pisa explaining the importance of secular diversions in his *Pantheologia*, begun in 1333, a treatise which shares much of its material with commentaries upon the *Sentences*:[81]

> Ad omnia autem que sunt utilia conversationi humane possunt aliqua
> officia deputari et ideo etiam officium histrionum quod ordinatur ad
> solacium hominibus exhibendum non est secundum se illicitum.

> Some office may legitimately be established for all those things which
> are useful to human dealings, and therefore even the office of minstrels,
> established to bring some solace to men, is not illicit in itself.

This is a powerful antidote to the venomous attacks upon minstrels which have commanded attention for so long. Here are declarations both confident and comprehensive (*Ad omnia...*) reinforced by language that is bureaucratic and almost legalistic (*deputari ... officium ... ordinatur*). This is the cleric appointing himself as legislator for the laity, and we shall encounter him again.

A blameless state of judicious and moderate enjoyment inspired by some secular diversion: that is not a particularly exotic notion, and as early as 1159 John of Salisbury had approached it by condoning a sensation of *modesta hilaritas* as a perfectly reasonable response by a judicious man to any entertainment not calculated to violate decorum or good taste.[82] But it is a complex notion to express in a single word, however, and until it could be expressed, and in an authoritative form, it could not be completely disentangled from experience and laid out for study.

Aristotle provided the theologians with exactly the word that was required. In the Latin translations of the Philosopher's *Ethics* it appears as *eutrapelia*, and the eagerness with which theologians seized upon this term is a measure of their interest in the concept it conveyed. That concept can be succinctly defined. Aristotle argues that virtue in matters of pleasure and entertainment is achieved when the individual finds the mean between excessive indulgence on one hand and excessive restraint on the other. This mean condition is *eutrapelia*, a moderate and judicious delight. Let Aristotle define his own term as the theologians could read him in the complete Latin translation of Robert Grosseteste:[83]

> Virtus autem circa passiones et operaciones est, in quibus quidem superhabundacia viciosa est et defectus vituperatur, medium autem laudatur et dirigitur. Hec autem ambo virtutis. Medietas quedam ergo est virtus . . .

> Circa delectabile autem quod quidem in ludo, medius quidam eutrapelos, et disposcio eutrapelia.

> [Eutrapelia est] talia dicere et audire qualia modesto et liberali congruunt.

> Virtue operates in the field of feelings and actions, in which excess and deficiency are both blamed, while the mean is praised and used as a guide. These are both signs of virtue. Virtue is therefore a mean condition.

> Concerning pleasantness in social entertainment, the man who strikes the mean is *eutrapelos* and the disposition *eutrapelia*.

> [*Eutrapelia* is] to say and hear such things as are consonant with modest and liberal pleasure.

The concept of *eutrapelia* exercised many commentators in the second half of the thirteenth century, and most are clear in their minds that this state of judicious pleasure in a secular diversion is a *virtus*, a virtue. Durandus de Sancto Porciano, for example, argues that some secular diversions have the virtue 'that is called *eutrapelia*',[84] while the English theologian Richard of Middleton is similarly persuaded:[85]

> Ethica 4, c. penult: in ludis possit consistere virtus quae scilicet vocatur eutrapelia.

> In the *Ethics*, book 4, penultimate chapter: in social entertainments there can exist that virtue which is called *eutrapelia*.

It might be argued that all this does is repeat Aristotle, and that is true enough. But these writers do more. Inhabiting a world very different from Aristotle's Greece, they understand *eutrapelia* in their own way. The writer who has the most interesting things to say on this subject is perhaps the Dominican Albertus Magnus, an influential theologian whose commentaries upon the *Sentences* and the *Ethics* deal systematically with the concept of *eutrapelia*. Albertus knew well enough that *eutrapelia* is a mean state, and that the pleasure involved should be a 'liberal' one (*liberalis*). It is here that he parts company with Aristotle. For the Philosopher in Athens, a liberal pleasure is one that has been freed from the vice of servitude; for Albertus in Paris it is one that has been freed from the servitude of vice:[86]

> ludi liberales [sunt ludi] quibus homines virtuosi a liberi a vitiis utuntur, qui nullam habent turpitudinem et conferunt ad statum rei publice.

> 'liberal' social pleasures are those which men who are free of vice enjoy, which have no baseness in them and which contribute to the condition of the State.

Throughout the Middle Ages theologians were well able to understand, and indeed to reproduce, the class-consciousness inherent in the Ancients' concept of 'freedom' and 'liberal' art;[87] but for many the only true servitude before God was slavery to sin, and while Albertus would surely have maintained that the *homines virtuosi* to whom he refers in the above passage were most likely (and perhaps exclusively) to be found amongst students and masters, nobles and members of the higher clergy, the element of social class in his concept of a 'liberal' art is not as conspicuous as it is in Aristotle's writing.

Eutrapelia c. 1300: John of Freiburg and Johannes de Grocheio

Albertus Magnus and the other masters cited above were academics, and the hard word *eutrapelia* scarcely gives their books a welcoming appearance. Nonetheless, by the end of the thirteenth century the compilers of the confessors' manuals, who looked to the schoolmen for their pastoral theology, knew the word *eutrapelia* and were not afraid of it. Here, for example, is John of Freiburg in his *Summa confessorum* of *c*. 1297-98:[88]

> Qualiter circa ludos possit esse virtus et vitium sive secundum excessum sive secundum defectum sive alio modo . . . Unde philosophus enim .iiij. Ethicorum dicit quod in huiusmodi vite conversatione quedam requies cum ludo habetur et ideo oportet . . . ut iocus sive ludus sit conveniens secundum congruitatem persone, temporis et loci . . . et hec virtus secundum philosophum vocatur eutrapelia.

> How there may be in entertainments both good and bad either according to excess, or according to deficiency, or in some other way . . . Aristotle says in the fourth book of the *Ethics* that there should be a certain degree of rest and entertainment in the conduct of this life and therefore it is necessary . . . that the entertainment or game be fitting according to who indulges, at what time and in what place . . . and this virtue is called, according to Aristotle, *eutrapelia*.

The word *eutrapelia* seems at home in this manual designed to teach confessors to teach the laity.

Our final author, Johannes de Grocheio, does not use the term *eutrapelia*, but his treatise on music is so deeply imbued with the idea of constructive pleasure in secular music that it forms a fitting end to this chapter. Like many of the authors cited above, Johannes de Grocheio was an academic and a reader of Aristotle; he was apparently a Master of Arts in Paris around 1300.[89] Of Grocheio's pride in his city there can be no doubt; 'in our day', he claims, 'the principles of any liberal art are sought out in Paris diligently', and as far as the liberal art of music is concerned the modern historian can only agree that this was indeed the case. Nor is there any mistaking Grocheio's belief that music has a contribution to make to the smooth running of the city; indeed the very subject of his treatise is the liberal art of music 'as it is necessary for the use of [Parisian] citizens'.[90] Once again it is usefulness that is the criterion of worth.

Grocheio proceeds to classify the music of Paris, sacred and secular, monophonic and polyphonic, with comments (at least in the sections on secular music) about the contribution which each can make to the life of the *civitas*; trouvère songs in the best style teach the rich to be magnanimous; sprightly dance-songs keep the minds of the young from depravity, and so on.[91] To some extent, Grocheio's treatise may be interpreted as a systematic attempt to show how music can restrain the vices which the makers of sermons tended to associate with various social classes. Indeed Grocheio's willingness to specify the category of society where each kind of secular music does most good may owe something to the *sermones ad status* collections of the thirteenth century where preachers address a sermon to each social group in turn and discuss the failings of its members.[92] Like the preachers, Grocheio believes that kings and nobles have a tendency to shirk the magnanimity which is proper to their class, while the rich are prone to slide into luxury and depravity; young men and girls are prey to idleness and to lustful thoughts, while working citizens tend to complain of the state to which God has called them.[93] Music, Grocheio believes, can help to soften the deleterious effects of these ills.

We naturally turn to Grocheio's treatise for some sign of how contemporary ideas about *utilitas*, legitimate pleasure and the good of the *civitas* bear upon the status of minstrels. We find, in the event, that Grocheio's *De musica*, though concerned with what might be called the social morality of music, is lacking in any sense that the influence of professional secular musicians needs to be restrained or that their characters and offices need to be corrected. To the extent that they appear, they are explicitly or implicitly praised. Grocheio gives a lofty impression of their audiences ('the rich ... the wealthy in feasts and entertainments'),[94] and the only kind of secular musician specifically named in the *De musica*, the expert fiddler, or *bonus artifex in viella*, emerges with credit as a virtuoso to be admired,[95] just as he does from the *Dit des taboureurs*. The one minstrel whom Grocheio mentions by name, Tassin, is presented as a composer of a musical genre, the *estampie*, which requires a systematic and architectonic approach from the man who creates it, just as it demands concentration from the player who performs it.[96]

'*Joculatores*', declares Honorius Augustodunensis at the opening of this chapter, 'have no hope of salvation'. If the minstrel Tassinus had ever felt the barb of some cleric's remark *contra joculatores*, he would surely have taken comfort from Grocheio's teaching about the usefulness of the *estampie*, a primarily instrumental form which 'turns aside the souls of the wealthy from depraved thinking'.[97] What would Honorius have made of that?

CHAPTER TWO

MINSTRELS AND THE KNIGHTLY CLASS

The churchmen work against us; they shave us too close. I have captured in my lifetime at least five hundred knights whose arms, horses and caparisons I have taken for my own. If the kingdom of God is denied me for this reason, I can do nothing about it . . . Either the argument [of the priests and clerks] is false, or else no man may be saved.

Jean, *L'Histoire de Guillaume le Maréchal*[1]

In 1219, the Earl of Pembroke, William Marshall, feels death upon him. To prepare himself he clears his mind and speaks it. He makes no apology for having begun his chivalric career by doing the rounds of the tournaments, winning horses and costly harness, so if the priests and clerks condemn him for it, let them do so. Either their argument is false or no man may be saved. William's views on minstrelsy are not recorded in the poem, but we may suspect that they had something in common with his opinions about the tournament for the earl had an ear for music. He was a very acceptable performer of songs for dancing, and was overcome by a passionate desire to sing as he lay dying (this longing was assuaged by one of his daughters who sang him a vernacular song, a *rotruenge*).[2] From the vantage point of a magnate like William Marshall, minstrels possessed an appearance that churchmen like Thomas Chobham rarely saw. The clergy were almost completely incapable of exploiting the power of minstrels for their own pastoral purposes, but we can readily appreciate why William Marshall might have regarded a cleric who spoke ill of minstrelsy as yet another churchman trying to shave him too closely. Minstrels did not diminish a magnate's power and influence; as we shall see, they could increase it by spreading the news of his *largesse* or by telling of a young man's triumphs in the lists, helping him (in return for reward) to build a career just as William built his.

Munificence

Casagrande and Vecchio have emphasised that the itinerant minstrel escaped the ties of feudal obligation and loyalty that bound society together because the average *histrio* neither owned lands nor owed any fixed obligation to one who did.[3] There is little to quarrel with here, and we shall see that this is the view of minstrelsy presented in a thirteenth-century source which depicts the minstrel life from the inside. And yet the minstrel's function in aristocratic society was not as peripheral as this presentation might suggest. He participated, through the munificence of his patrons, in what might be termed an economy of honour and trust. The occasional, conspicuous display of generosity, or *largesse*, was expected of kings and their magnates. When great feasts were held then – as the preachers record in one of their favourite alliterating pairs – *largitas* and *letitia* went together. By appearing to squander his surplus wealth in an open-handed and public way a man of knightly stock displayed the magnanimity that distinguished him from the merchant whose thrift and prudence were (at least in theory) repellant to a man of great *estat*. Generosity was not perceived as merely a ceremony or a duty of greatness; *largesse* was a solace and delight, when the coffers permitted it, to men of exalted station. The twentieth century is more mercantile than chivalric, so it may be difficult to think ourselves back into the minds of magnates who gave away money and expensive gifts with an ardour that could border on a kind of lust. That was the strength of feeling involved, and the Parisian Master of theology Evrard du Val-des-Ecoliers is only one of many clerics to classify the giving of gifts as a form of *luxuria*.[4]

Minstrels profited greatly from aristocractic *largesse*. The tendency of younger men to spend lavishly upon tournaments and minstrels was almost proverbial in the thirteenth century. Earning one's fortune on the tourney field, as William Marshall had done, went hand in hand with generosity to minstrels. Caesarius of Heisterbach, in his *Dialogus miraculorum* (*c.* 1223), tells of a young nobleman in the area of Liège who gave himself over completely to tournaments and made lavish gifts to minstrels (*histrionibus larga manu sua tribuebat*).[5] Jacques de Vitry inveighs against magnates who squander their patrimony on minstrels in his *Historia occidentalis*, composed between 1221 and 1226.[6]

To some extent, the money and gifts which knights gave to minstrels were a payment in cash and kind for services closely connected with knightly interests. According to Evrard du Val-des-Ecoliers, knights made gifts to the 'minstrels or heralds who incited them to do battle fiercely in tournaments'.[7] Such incitement could be offered in various ways. A minstrel with the appropriate repertory at his command could sing the *chansons de geste* of Charlemagne and Roland which (again according to Evrard du Val-des-Ecoliers) the *milites* were so keen to hear and which set them such a high example of pugnacious virtue.[8] Or, perhaps, he might offer to compose and then to disseminate a laudatory song if his patrons were successful – the kind of *nova cantilena* which, according to Guido of Evreux, was usually composed when a great man gained some military success.[9] The frequency with which the heroes in the Old French epics reassure one another that 'no minstrel will ever make a bad song about this enterprise'[10] suggests the importance that the knightly class attached to such poems in an age when news generally travelled by word of mouth and when few people travelled more than the minstrel. Sometimes, however, more formal and official services may have been offered by minstrels to the men involved in tourneying; the gradual emergence of the office of the herald from the ranks of minstrelsy in the thirteenth century, chronicled by Vale and others,[11] suggests as much, and points to a long-standing and special relationship between some kinds of minstrels and the chivalric interests of *milites*.

When a great man gave gifts he obviously received praise in return; he spent his money *causa enim laudis*.[12] But in doing so he was buying more than the praise of those present at the tournament or feast to see what he had done; he was also bidding for the admiration of those in other regions who would only *hear* of his doings. For each knight, participation in chivalric culture rested upon the honour of a good name and a growing reputation for excellence, and in some measure the honour of a *chevalier* lay in the keeping of itinerant minstrels who had little or no chivalric status of their own but who commanded information and news that others were keen to hear. Once a minstrel had been given his money or gifts, in other words, there was an understanding that he had not yet completed the tasks for which he had been rewarded. When he departed, it was up to him to carry the report of his benefactor's honour and standing – his *estat* – further afield. Miscellaneous passages in several sermons allow us to glimpse this process. In a Latin homily which Pierre de Limoges preached in the Ste Chapelle at Paris in 1273 (Figure 2) there is an allusion to minstrels whose custom it is, when they have been to any great feast, to recount the wondrous things which they saw and heard there (*recitant mira que ibi viderunt et audierunt*).[13] A rich robe, or some other precious gift, was normally a guarantee of a good report, as Evrard du Val-des-Ecoliers had noticed:[14]

> Ego video quod isti hystriones et joculatores quibus isti divites consueverunt et vestes et alia exennia dare non cessant eos magnis preconiis commendare.

> I notice that *histriones* and *joculatores*, to whom rich men are accustomed to give both clothes and other kinds of gifts, never cease to praise them with great compliments.

It is in this context, I believe, that we should interpret many of the passages in clerical Latin literature which describe minstrels as flatterers and backbiters. Thomas Chobham, for example, attacks the minstrels 'who have no fixed abode, following the courts of magnates and speaking malicious and spiteful things about those who are absent'.[15] To some extent, the *adulacio* which clerical writers so often associate with minstrels is perhaps only the praise which a minstrel was expected to lavish on his secular patrons, both past and present, heard through the ears of clergymen whose burdensome task it was to speak ever in the opposite way, reminding lords of their sins and shortcomings.

There was more to a minstrel's loquacity, however, than eulogy. When a minstrel crossed the threshold of an aristocratic court he went amongst men who relied upon a lord for their lands and for the gifts that enhanced their status. Their environment was a competitive one where a single word or deed could set the network of favour and disfavour trembling again.[16] If a minstrel were seen to converse with people of waning influence for too long, or if he played for them in some corner of the hall while others in better grace were at chess elsewhere, then his prospect of reward could be damaged. In short, a minstrel needed a measure of political skill: a combination of shrewd judgement and a cunning tongue. The successful minstrel in an aristocratic or courtly context was therefore a *talker*: one who knew what to say and when to say it. Indeed, the minstrels whom we encounter in sermons and theological treatises are usually talking rather than making music. They appear as *joculatores loquentes*[17] whose characteristic vice is their *sermo*.[18]

The voluminous psalter-commentary by the Dominican Pierre de Palude, for example, mentions minstrels 'who live by their mouth because they do not know how to play a musical instrument',[19] a description which surely implies more than that the people in question are just singers. Pierre's contemporary Alexander of Hales expresses what must have been the aim of many minstrels when he defines 'minstrelish talk' (*scurrilitas*) as 'a courtliness or affability of speech',[20] while Thomas Lebreton acknowledges the risk which a minstrel took every time he opened his mouth (his theme is I Corinthians 13:1 'Though I speak with the tongues of men and angels, and have not charity, I am become a sounding brass or a tinkling cymbal'):[21]

> *Cymbalum tinniens.* Scilicet inutiliter me condividens et contendens alios delectans et mihi non proficiens. Unde tales qui sine caritate verbum proferunt similes sunt gulliardis et histrionibus quando verba virtuosa et delectabilia proferunt nec sibi proficiunt.

> 'A tinkling cymbal.' That is to say that it would be useless for me to parcel myself out and to stretch myself, delighting others and profiting nothing to myself. Whence those who speak words without love are like 'goliards' and minstrels when they say virtuous and pleasing things and get no profit thereby.

An essential art of courtliness was to speak both well and prudently, disarming and even gently manipulating those from whom one sought favour.[22] The minstrel's task was to steer a path through the thickets of court personalities and politics towards reward, flattering or deprecating the right people at the right moment. We must remember that a minstrel was rarely in the position of a modern professional musician who arrives, plays and then departs in expectation of an agreed fee. As we shall see, a minstrel was expected to supply not only good music but also – when it was sought – good conversation and company. It was not prudent for him to regard himself as released from his duties until everyone in a position to reward him had gone.[23] To begin an evening well, and then to damage his prospects for gifts and payments by a chance remark taken badly, was a disaster that constantly threatened him. If he saw that some members of the company would like him the better if he spoke ill of one who was absent, what could he do but to follow the direction which they set for him? He could not afford the nicety of conscience that the preachers and moralists expected him to display.

The sources used so far have been 'external' ones in the sense that they were not written by minstrels and therefore do not reflect the minstrel life from the inside. The purpose of this chapter, however, is to explore this relation between minstrelsy and court experience with 'internal' evidence, a Catalan poem of *c.* 1210 which is a disquisition upon the importance of courtly shrewdness to any minstrel who wishes to inspire courtesy in others and thereby to advance his own interests. It offers us a rare chance to get behind the language of the preachers and moralists and to sense the social context of the things to which they refer.

April was leaving and May was entering

This poem is Raimon Vidal's *Abril issia*, the work of a poet who had come too late.[24] By *c.* 1210, when Raimon Vidal composed it, the 'classic' period of troubadour poetry had just come to a close; Bernart de Ventadorn, Peire d'Alvernhe, Guiraut de Bornelh, Bertran de Born and Arnaut Daniel had all died within living memory. The magnate who features so prominently in the poem, Dalfi d'Alvernhe – a lord once famous for his liberality, his service of ladies, his court-displays and tournaments – is now an old man reclining by the fire in his hall.

Abril issia begins at the start of May. The narrator is walking in the town-square of Besalú in Catalonia when he sees a minstrel coming towards him dressed in an old fashioned way:[25]

> Sove.m que fo mati adoncx
> en la plassa de Bezaudun...
> E sel que totz fizels adzora
> volc e.m donet que.n eysa ora
> que ieu m'estav'aisi pessatz
> venc vas mi vestitz e caussatz
> us joglaretz a fort del temps
> on hom trobava totz essems
> justa.ls baros valor e pretz.

> I remember that it was morning then, in the town square of Besalú...
> And He whom every believer adores, willed and granted to me that at

that time when I was thus downcast, there should come towards me
a jongleur, dressed and shod after the fashion of the time in which valor
and worth were both found in the barons.

As the narrator and the minstrel fall into conversation it emerges that the
minstrel's choice of clothing is an emblem of a personal quest. His father
had told him stories of the Golden Age of the troubadours when lords were
courteous and generous, but now that Age has passed and the jongleur wishes
to know why. Like a monk in search of an order strict enough to satisfy
his conscience, he travels between courts in search of generosity to match
the old times which the narrator himself claims to have known when[26]

> . . . auziratz, si com yeu fi,
> als trobadors dir e comtar
> si com vivion per anar
> e par sercar terras e locx;
> e viras lay selas ab flocx
> a tans autres valens arnes
> e fres dauratz, e palafres

> . . . you would hear, as I did, the troubadours tell and relate how they
> lived by travelling and making the rounds of lands and places; and you
> would see there tasseled saddles and much other costly equipage, and
> gilded bridles and palfreys.

'Making the rounds of lands and places'; those are resonant words. The
'Lives' of the troubadours tell how Guiraut de Bornelh 'went among the
courts' during the summer months,[27] while Gaucelm Faidit, 'a glutton for
food who became grossly fat', went *per cortz* with a female jongleur.[28] With
the aid of Raimon Vidal's poem it is possible to clothe these bare words,
for the minstrel who speaks in the poem gives an account of the travels that
have brought him to the town-square in Besalú, producing in the process
a gratifyingly detailed picture of the minstrel life around 1200.

The jongleur's story opens in the province of the Auvergne one Saturday
morning during the Christmas season. The minstrel has been in Riom (see
map). Leaving that place by the main north–south route through the province
he journeys to Montferrand where Dalfi d'Alvernhe is holding court:[29]

> e si anc genta cort vi hom
> ni de bon solatz, si fo sela.
> Non y ac dona ni donzela
> ni cavayer ni donzelo
> no fos pus francx d'un auzelo
> c'om agues noirit en sa man.
> Aqui trobey senher sertan,
> [e] companha ben entenduda
> per qu'ieu laisi dans una muda
> a gran joys, si Dieu mi sal . . .

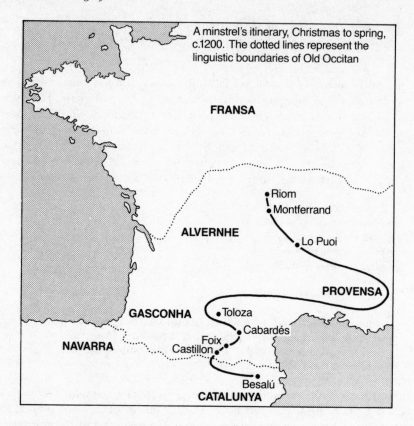

A minstrel's itinerary, Christmas to spring, c.1200. The dotted lines represent the linguistic boundaries of Old Occitan

venguem e fom, ses tot esmay,
a Monferran sus e.l palaitz;
e s'anc vis homes essenhatz
ni ab baudor, so fom aqui.
E la nueg si fo, co yeu vi,
mot tenebrosa apres manjar,
e.l solatz gran, josta.l foc clar,
de cavayers e de joglars
adreitz e fis e dos e cars
e suaus ad homes cortes . . .
E.l cavayer ses tot prezic
a lur temps s'aneron jazer;
car mo senher volc remaner
ab .I. companho josta.l foc.

And if ever anyone saw an agreeable court and good company, that was it. There was not a lady or damsel there, knight nor squire, who was not more gentle than a bird fed in one's hand. Here I found a perfect lord and a very well-bred company. Which is why I left hardship for a while with great joy, so help me . . . we came to and were at Montferrand, with no trouble, up in the great hall. And if you ever

saw well-bred and joyful men, that were we there. And the night, as
I saw, was very dark after dinner and next to the bright fire the company
was large, knights and jongleurs, clever and accomplished and amiable,
courtly and agreeable to courteous men . . . And the knights, without
any reminder, went to bed when they were ready, for my lord [Dalfi]
wanted to remain with a companion near the fire.

Here the minstrel enters the inner sanctum. Dalfi d'Alvernhe, Count of Cler-
mont and Montferrand from 1168–1234, was a troubadour himself (although
none of his poems is preserved with their music),[30] and his name is scattered
here and there in numerous troubadour pieces – most impressively, perhaps,
in Guiraut de Bornelh's *Leu chansonet'e vil* (Music example 2). Dalfi exchanged
stanzas with Peirol and Perdigon, and he appears as the judge in many poetic
debates, or *partimens*.[31] According to the 'Lives' and to the testimony of various
troubadour lyrics, he had contact with Peire d'Alvernhe, Peirol, Gaucelm
Faidit, Guiraut de Bornelh, Raimbaut de Vaqueiras, Perdigon and Pons
de Capdoill. Some of the information in the 'Lives' is probably derived from
Dalfi.[32]

Little remains of Dalfi's *palaitz* at Montferrand, but we see it much as
Raimon Vidal's minstrel would have seen it in the fifteenth-century sketch
of Montferrand by Guillaume Revel (Figure 3).[33] Located at the extreme
left of Revel's drawing, the *palaitz* comprises a massive quadrangular keep
that is equipped with corner-towers and placed within a curtain-wall also
reinforced with towers (six are visible in the drawing). This is presumably
the kind of place where Raimon Vidal's minstrel might be expected to perform
the troubadour songs he is proud to have in his repertoire. The remains
of the castle, Raimon Vidal's description of it, and the testimony of many
other sources, both literary and archaeological, permit us to reconstruct the
scene within the Great Hall in some detail.[34] At the end of the sixteenth
century, when the keep was already in a poor state, there were four great
and square rooms, one above the other, and each wall measured approximately twenty metres in length.[35] Raimon Vidal's minstrel would have been
led up a flight of external stairs to the second or perhaps the third of these
rooms (the first being used for storage of provisions, weapons and other
necessaries).[36] Dalfi and his followers are relaxing with minstrels and enjoying
their entertainment. It is dark outside and the scene within the hall is lit
by the flames of the fire whose brightness seems to be one of the jongleur's
keenest memories. In accordance with new French notions of comfort this
'bright fire' was probably a blaze dismissed to a corner of the hall and ken-
nelled in a wall-hearth and chimney, not a fierce conflagration on a stone
base in the middle of the hall. Nonetheless, every room, corridor, glass of
wine and bowl of fruit would have been touched with the perfume of wood-
smoke, even though (as contemporary preachers point out) it was nominally
one of the luxuries of the rich that their houses were *sine fumo*.[37]

Dalfi reclines upon a marble bench which is covered with samite and placed
by the fire. Around him are the *cavayers* in whom we recognise the knights

Example no. 2

Figure 3 *View of Montferrand, from the armorial compiled towards the middle of the fifteenth century by the herald Guillaume Revel. Paris, Bibliothèque Nationale, ancien Gaignières 2896, fr. 22297, number 31. Reproduced by permission.*

of the *estage*: the men who were required to garrison his castles, and to keep him company, for a fixed term before returning to their own lands.[38] Minstrels are in attendance and there is no mistaking the jongleur's pride in having been with Dalfi on that occasion. He boasts how 'we' were a good company if ever there was one to be seen. The magnate at the centre of things, introduced into the poem as Dalfi, has now become 'my lord' (*mo senher*), and the minstrel speaks of him with the kind of canine loyalty which must often have moved the hearts of jongleurs when they found themselves sure of reward and some creature comforts.[39]

The next day the minstrel leaves Montferrand having found in Dalfi some of the generosity that his father's tales of the Golden Age had brought him to expect:[40]

> E lo mati, vezen de tutz
> .I. dijous qu'ieu prezi comjat.
> E s'anc vis home ben pessat
> e de senhor, ieu ben o fuey.

> In the morning, a Thursday it was, I took my leave in the sight of everybody. And if ever you saw a man well taken care of, and by a lord at that, I was he.

Now, at the end of the Christmas season, the minstrel continues to follow the southward route that began a hundred kilometres or so from the border with France in Riom, and will end across the Pyrenees in the town-square of Besalú some four months later. He makes no mention of a mount, but there is no reason to suppose that a jongleur welcomed by magnates like Dalfi would have lacked what the 'Lives' call 'a minstrel's equipment, clothes and a horse'.[41]

From Montferrand the minstrel heads south-east. He passes through Le Puy and continues into Provence 'where I found many gay barons and the good count and the countess', Raymond Berenguer V and Beatrice of Savoy.[42] Next he sets off in the opposite direction. Turning westwards for a leg of the journey that even he, an experienced traveller, is forced to describe as 'very great', he makes his way to the lands of the Count of Toulouse. There he finds the Count 'and many gracious knights who are with him' and is given a suit of clothes:[43]

> E si be fon grans l'esdemessa,
> d'aqui m'en aney en Tolzan
> on atrobey ab cor certan
> mo senher lo comte premier,
> e mant avinen cavayer
> que son ab luy, e n'ayc arnes.

> And although the stage [of the journey] was great, from [Provence] I
> went to the county of Toulouse where I found, with a perfect heart,
> my lord the first count, and many gracious knights who are with him,
> and I was given an outfit of clothes.

Leaving the Count of Toulouse the minstrel travels south-eastwards to the region of Cabardès, perhaps to one of the four magnificent castles that still command the heights above the village of Lastours, due north of Carcassonne. There he might have found Pierre-Roger, Jourdain de Cabaret and other vassals of the Count of Béziers enjoying the autumn of their prosperity before the Albigensian crusade and the assaults of Simon de Montfort.

The next stage of the journey reveals the precariousness of the minstrel life in an age when great lords ruled by riding from one estate to another in order to consume produce, to administer justice and to negotiate with neighbouring seigneurs. If a minstrel wished to avoid the calamity of arriving at a magnate's castle and finding nobody there, he needed information about a lord's movements. Perhaps minstrels had some kind of grapevine for this purpose; on this occasion, however, this minstrel's source of information seems to have run dry, for after Cabardès he makes his way to Foix and finds that the count has gone:[44]

> E a Foys non trobey negu,
> que.l coms era ad Alberu.

> And at Foix I found no one for the count was at Alberu.

The jongleur pushes on to the west in the direction of Castillon, and finally,

'last Monday', he crosses the Pyrenees into Catalonia. At the court of Mataplana he is received by the troubadour Uc de Mataplana and finds in him
a lord who is 'gracious, frank, gentle and a ready critic to listen to all good
knowledge'.[45] Finally, he turns his steps towards Besalú.

This itinerary is a fiction, but a realistic one. As the map shows, Raimon
Vidal clearly knew central and southwestern France. Riom, Montferrand,
Le Puy, Provence, Toulouse, Cabardès, Foix, Castillon, Mataplana and
Besalú make a plausible journey, and the minstrel admits that the one major
detour (if that is the right term to use in this context) towards the lands
of the Count of Toulouse was a great undertaking. The timing of the journey
– taking in the season of Lent when minstrel entertainments at court were
sometimes suspended – is somewhat surprising,[46] but otherwise the logistics
of the minstrel's journey seem well planned. His travels occupy the four
months from Christmas to the end of April, and although many troubadour
poems present this as a time of frost and rain, *gel e plotge*, the season will
often have been mild enough in the Midi for going on the roads (and what
else could a travelling jongleur do when Christmas was over?). A period
of some 120 days would be enough for a mounted man who wished to cover
this distance, even allowing for the minstrel's sojourns at court and for the
difficult nature of the terrain (especially in the Massif Central between Montferrand and Le Puy). In 1819, for example, when the roads of France were
not exactly the *autoroutes* of the present day, a party of English travellers
journeyed by slow coach from Paris to Montpellier, stopping constantly to
visit monuments and to sketch beautiful scenes; it took them less than a
month, from the twenty-sixth of April to the fifteenth of May.[47]

Court experience

There is more to *Abril issia* than a vivid and plausible itinerary. The poem
also casts light upon what might be described as 'court-experience' viewed
from the vantage point of an itinerant minstrel. Court-experience in this
context denotes the nature of the life which a magnate shared with the members of his household who relied upon his favour for the gifts which enhanced
their prestige and which furthered their interests. In this context, courtliness
was not a form of silken dalliance but a subtle means of making the system
of dependence and favour work. As so often, it is the makers of sermons
who strip matters down to their essentials. 'When a man behaves in a courtly
manner towards another', says Guido of Evreux, 'he is more readily taken
into his service'.[48] A pleasing eloquence, for example, belonged to courtliness,
especially when it was combined with a youthfulness that made eloquence
seem fresh and precocious.[49] A resolutely affable manner helped to prevent
the outbursts of feeling which, as Norbert Elias has emphasised, are always
dangerous in a courtly context and become the more hazardous the further
down the ladder of rank one is placed.[50] In courtliness the medieval passion

53

for social behaviour governed by moral and aesthetic concerns of the highest order was combined with a frank recognition that reward depended upon a greater person's generosity and favour, not upon formal agreement and contract.

Raimon Vidal makes the point clearly enough. 'Above all be sure that your expressions and words are imitated from sophisticated men', says the narrator, 'so that, when you tell stories to people, you do not receive a meagre payment for it' :[51]

> e sobre tot
> gardatz que li dig e li mot
> vos venguan d'omes conoissens
> per c'al contar entre las gens
> no.us en sia vils pretz donatz.

The narrator requires that a minstrel should imitate the behaviour of the *conoissens*, a potent word in which the idea of a cultivated manner has become blended with a coarser virtue that is something like 'being in the know'. In another passage Vidal establishes the link between profit and a show of courtly virtue with more directness. 'God did not make this age so consistently bad', the narrator tells the minstrel, 'that an ambitious, clever and frank man cannot get gifts out of it in order to rise and make himself noticed if he knows how to be clever and has the right manner' :[52]

> ... Dieu no fes segle tan ver
> vas malvestatz, c'us homs curos,
> adreitz e francx, no.n traisses dos
> a se pujar e far valer
> si.n saup genh ni manieir'aver,
> ni l'art que se tanh, ni lo fait.

In these lines the richness of the language advocates virtue, affability and the shrewd pursuit of personal interest, but there is not the least sense in Raimon Vidal's words that this candid expression of what makes excellent behaviour is vitiated in any degree by the subtle rapacity of the motive. The ethical pitch is set very high; the implication is that a successful minstrel at court will be one who constantly maintains a vigilance bordering upon anxiety (*curos*), who is adroit, and who is *francx* – a term whose depth of colour cannot be copied with any one English word; it has shades of 'noble', 'open', 'affable', 'sincere' and more besides. To exploit these qualities well is a skill or stratagem (*art*), and in this case virtue is by no means its own reward; the aim is to win gifts.

In view of this lofty but shrewd conception of minstrel skills it is no surprise to find that in *Abril issia* the good minstrel who attends a court is not just the servant of the nobility but is also their judge. A minstrel travels from court to court and he therefore sees both the best and the worst of noble behaviour; he carries a fund of news and opinion along the network of aristocratic residences. A substantial part of *Abril issia* is taken up with the names of generous noblemen, strung together into a litany in which saints are replaced by worthy and generous lords. It is spoken by the narrator, but it endorses values of generosity and magnanimity so close to the minstrel's own heart that the distinction between the two speakers at this point becomes diaphanous; the words derive their authority from the implicit assurance that they embody the experience of a much-travelled man:[53]

> En Blacas no.y fai a laissar
> ni del Baus en Guillem lo blon,
> ni d'Alvernhe.l senher Guion
> ni.l comte Dalfi que tan valc;
> ni sai en Gasto a cuy calc
> may de pretz c'om non li conoys.
> E silh que venion per Foys,
> aqui trobavon .l. senhor
> adreg e plazen donador
> si com dizian totz le mons . . .

> En Blacas does not deserve to be left out, nor en William the Fair of
> Baux nor, from Auvergne, the Lord Guion nor the Count Dauphin,
> who was so worthy; nor, closer to us, en Gaston, who cared more about
> merit than is usually recognised. And those who came by way of Foix
> have found a lord who was courteous and a pleasant giver, as everyone
> says . . .

When a minstrel moved in circles such as these he was always the lowest in rank when he entered a room. As the narrator says in a passage of particularly plain speaking:[54]

> e s'eratz filh d'emperador
> no seriatz mas can joglar
> mentr'aisi.eus sapcha bo l'anar
> ni.l venir bos e saboros

> And if you were the son of an emperor you would still be no more than
> a jongleur as long as you enjoyed travelling back and forth and it was
> to your liking

A castellan and the members of his family, or a magnate like Dalfi d'Alvernhe, could send a minstrel packing at little cost to themselves. How should a minstrel conduct himself in this hazardous environment? We come now to the centre of our interpretation of Raimon Vidal's *Abril issia*. Historians have suggested that it is usually those of minor rank who become masters of courtly tactics because it is they who have most to lose. As Norbert Elias has written in his study of court behaviour at Versailles in the seventeenth century:[55]

> it is those of relatively low rank who become masters of the tactics of
> conversation . . . he is the one most at risk in such a conversation. The
> prince can always break the rules . . . he can, if he likes, break off the

discussion and the relationship for any reason he chooses without losing much.

The thirteenth-century minstrel at court was therefore required to cultivate one of the principal arts of courtly strategy: the ability to lead a person of higher rank in the direction that one wishes to go. As Elias explains:[56]

> To lead one's higher-ranking interlocutor almost imperceptibly where one wishes is the prime requirement of this courtly manner of dealing with people. Gestures pointing directly or indirectly to one's own cleverness, which may at times be useful in conversation between relatively independent and equal-ranking people . . . are strictly prohibited here. 'Never speak of oneself', one of Gratian's maxims is headed . . . This reflects the necessity to be always aware . . . of one's partner's general situation and its implications for the conversation . . . The art of what, with a characteristic narrowing of meaning, we call 'diplomacy', is thus cultivated in the everyday life of court society.

It is a measure of Raimon Vidal's engagement with these strategies of courtliness that the key episode in *Abril issia* is a conversation between the minstrel and the highest-ranking interlocutor that he could possibly have chosen at Montferrand: the Count, Dalfi d'Alvernhe. This is a delicate undertaking, and it is no surprise to find the minstrel admitting to the narrator that[57]

> . . . s'anc trobey bon cor ardit
> a ben parlar, si fis yeu lay.
>
> . . . if ever I found myself with a good heart eager to speak well, I did so then.

He has chosen his moment with some care. The convivial part of the evening is over; the knights have gone to bed and Dalfi is left lying on his couch by the embers of the fire, accompanied by just a few friends and the minstrel, who apparently cannot consider his duties over until the Count dismisses him or retires. Taking up a position next to Dalfi, the minstrel tells of his own father, an expert singer (*cantaire*) and narrator (*comtaire*) who had told him stories of the great generosity and luxury of the court of Henry II of England a generation or so before – a time when Dalfi himself was a young man. 'Because father described things to me thus', says the minstrel to Dalfi,[58]

> ab vostres motz me fis joglars
>
> I became a minstrel with your verses

These tantalising words presumably mean that the minstrel gave impetus to his newly chosen career by drawing some poems by Dalfi into his repertoire, either using the accepted tunes – none of which has survived – or by composing fresh ones himself (*see* Appendix). This was a fine start no doubt, but travels from court to court have shown him that the Golden Age described by his father seems to have gone forever. 'So I have come to ask you if you please,

Lord', he says to Dalfi, 'how such a misfortune has come about that the barons have thus lost merit and worth.'[59]

Dalfi pauses and then replies with a grace that is all the more sublime since it is not required of him:[60]

> Amicx, non es enquera
> a mon semblan tot ton saber.

> Friend, it seems to me that your knowledge is not yet complete.

Dalfi proceeds to tell the minstrel a story about two kings in Morocco, separated by some hundred years, each of whom was served by a fine knight. The first king presented his knight with a special head-dress and granted that it should be exclusive to him for ever; many years later, however, when a new king had come to the throne, the knight who served him was so presumptuous as to wear the head-dress and all were amazed 'that anyone who was not of the lineage dared in such a way to wear it...'. The knight was duly pardoned by his king and indeed his honour was enhanced by his bearing when upbraided, but there can be no doubt that Dalfi has given the minstrel a delicate illustration of the vice of presumption in one who is – whatever his special privileges – only a servant. As the knight presumed to wear the head-dress, so the minstrel, in speaking so directly and candidly to a magnate, has presumed too much.[61] Nonetheless, the minstrel's question about the decline of honour and valour is a valid one, and Dalfi responds to it with a speech stiffened with maxims about the most aristocratic of all the virtues and therefore the one most deeply involved in any loss of worth amongst the barons: the virtue of generosity. 'Giving brings merit and light and radiance to all sides'; 'a noble heart brings generosity'; the good man 'gives with good judgement'.[62] As Dalfi speaks the word *donar* rings like a bell in line after line.

Encouraged by the high moral tone of Dalfi's reply, and filled with new resolve by the veiled reminder that he has not yet fully mastered the arts of courtly tactics, the minstrel undertakes the itinerary described above, and which ends with him seeking out the narrator who is a *joglar* himself (he refers to 'our profession', *nostres mestiers*).[63] The narrator is to be understood as an expert on minstrelsy, and is presumably to be identified with Raimon Vidal himself, author of a treatise on the composition of troubadour poetry, the *Razos de trobar*. Having admitted, in effect, that he does not understand courtly procedure (*la manieira*),[64] the minstrel turns to the narrator for advice about the delicate matter of being a low-ranking success in a courtly context. Fortunately the narrator is generous with his counsel, and the poem proceeds to offer a remarkable insight into minstrel experience at court during the thirteenth century.

Above all, the minstrel must exercise self-control. When the boors at court roughly call him to sing, he should not be upset.[65]

'En joglar, e vos, com calatz?
Que non diretz una chanso?'
E vos, si tot non an sazo
lur dig, no vulhatz empeguir

'You there, sir minstrel, why don't you sing us a song instead of sitting
there saying nothing?' And, although their way of talking is out of place,
you should not be put out with them

The minstrel himself has left us in no doubt what these songs might be,
for he has barely met the narrator before he is proudly claiming that he
knows pieces by the troubadours Guiraut de Bornelh and Arnaut de Maroill.[66]
Sometimes, it would seem, a minstrel's audience might so far forget good
manners as to begin speaking the moment he had begun his song; once
again the advice is to treat them politely:[67]

Vos dic qu'entre.ls valens e pros
n'i a que son ses tot esgart,
e que.us diran a una part
e mest autrui que lur cantes;
e no.y gardaran nulh vetz
ni nulh temps ni nulha sazo,
e al ters de mot de la canso,
cal que digatz, ilh groniran
e josta vos cosselharan
o.s metran novas a comtar.
Anc Dieus sen non lur volc donar
ni fara ja, mon essien.
Aquels si tot no son valen
menatz al pus gen que poiretz;
car aital hom can vos etz,
cascu lo cuj'aver comprat . . .

I tell you that among the valiant and the worthy, there are those without
any consideration who will speak to you aside and ask you to sing in
front of everyone else; and they will not observe good manners nor time
nor occasion, and at the third word of the song, whatever you are singing,
they will grumble and begin to mutter to someone else, or begin to tell
a story. God never intended to give them any sense, nor will He, as
far as I can see. Although such people are worthless you should treat
them as courteously as possible; for everyone thinks that he has hired
a man such as yourself . . .

This is the kind of writing which makes *Abril issia* so exceptional. There
is surely no other source of comparable date that allows us to see the courtly
audience for troubadour song through the eyes of the performer, even to
feel what it is like to be there. Raimon Vidal is evoking that subtle feeling
of humiliation that all professional musicians who have performed intimate
music amongst the wealthy will know from their own experience. Across
nearly eight hundred years we sense the continuity of the most intimate feeling

generated by the life of a professional musician. At the same time the mechanics of the performing situation are open to view; the minstrel is taken aside by a few members of the company and asked to sing. Finally, and perhaps most vividly of all, there is that quality of shrewdness – indeed of psychological insight – which makes *Abril issia* such an effective primer for the tactics of courtliness. The reason for treating the grumblers 'as courteously as possible' is that in a courtly company every individual thinks of himself as the one who has hired the minstrel; offend nobody, therefore, for everyone nurtures a feeling within himself that a clever minstrel can foster until it bears fruit in gifts and coins.

This shrewdness is manifest in many other pieces of advice. Norbert Elias's observation that the courtly strategist should avoid 'gestures pointing directly or indirectly to one's own cleverness' is borne out by *Abril issia*. Indeed the praise and dispraise of others – something which clerical writers so often associate with minstrels – is presented in *Abril issia* as a two-edged sword to be wielded with exceptional care. 'Do not praise your skill to people', the narrator advises, 'even though it may be good and choice'.[68] A more subtle piece of counsel concerns a minstrel's references to previous patrons. 'Do not praise an honoured patron too highly', says the narrator; clearly, it was a very delicate matter to inspire one lord to magnanimity and generosity by praising the virtues of another. In a striking piece of counsel the narrator advises the minstrel not to speak ill of his competitors:[69]

> Autrui joglars ni las chansos
> dels trobadors non reprendatz
> qu'envejos e mal ensenhatz
> sembla qui son semblan repren,
> e cortes sel qu'en defenden
> vol razonar sos companhos.

> Do not criticise the jongleurs of others or the songs of the troubadours,
> for he who criticises his equal appears envious and uninformed, but he
> who, in defending his companions, excuses them, appears courteous.

The famous *sirventes* by Peire d'Alvernhe, *Chantarai d'aquestz trobadors* (the ultimate source for the statement that Bernart de Ventadorn was the son of a kitchen scullion) reveals that the troubadours and their jongleurs sometimes mounted vicious attacks upon one another. However, there is virtually nothing in Peire's poem that can be regarded as criticism of a *song*, and it is tantalising to learn that the conversation of minstrels and their patrons in the southern courts sometimes ranged over the qualities (good, presumably, as well as bad) of the lyrics of the troubadours.

Raimon Vidal's *Abril issia* is a powerful antidote to the attacks upon minstrelsy that we encounter in some kinds of Latin writings and which have attracted attention for so long. Vidal seems to be writing of minstrelsy, and of court experience, from the inside. His poem reveals how much skill and pride a professional musician travelling from court to court might possess.

No doubt Vidal's portrait of minstrelsy is idealised; it is certainly one that only depicts the more specialised members of the minstrel profession who sang courtly monody and who sought entrance to royal and aristocratic residences as a matter of course. Nonetheless, his sympathy for performers, and his keen understanding of the circumstances in which they were compelled to earn their living, make his poem unique among the writings of the Middle Ages.

CHAPTER THREE

MINSTRELS IN PARIS *c.* 1300: RULES AND REPERTOIRE

On Monday 14 September 1321, the feast of the Holy Cross, thirty-seven male and female minstrels, headed by Pariset *menestrel le roy*, asked the prévôt of Paris to ratify a statute of eleven articles which they had produced 'for the reformation of the profession [of minstrelsy] and for the common profit of the city of Paris'.[1] It is a brief document that covers only three pages in the printed edition, but it is a very suggestive one. The provisions that it makes, and the rules that it establishes, have often been discussed,[2] but it will be worth taking a fresh look at them in the light of what has gone before in this book. Accordingly, the purpose of this chapter is to make the statutes of 1321 the centre of an interpretation of the relationship between minstrelsy and authority in the thirteenth century, to be followed by a brief exploration of minstrel repertory, both written and unwritten.

In these Parisian ordinances some of the traditional concerns of the medieval trade associations are present in full or in embryonic form. Others seem to be implied. Their main purpose is to improve the security of the minstrel profession through the agency of a democratic governing body wielding an authority that is acknowledged and supported by the municipality. In doing so the statutes implicitly regard minstrelsy as a form of legitimate merchandise and they are closely concerned with the mercantile values of good professional conduct (behaviour that does not damage the interests of the confraternity) and basic 'quality control' (supervision of the commodities put on sale lest customer dissatisfaction should lead to loss of profits). The minstrels' street, the *rue aus jougleurs*, emerges from these statutes as an enormous shop for minstrelsy,[3] and an important purpose of the statutes is to prevent unscrupulous minstrels from circumventing the normal conditions of sale whereby those who desire minstrelsy walk into the *rue aus jougleurs* and shop for it as they might buy shoes from the cobblers in the *rue aus cordonniers*.

In addition to a rudimentary code of behaviour, the statutes provide for the exclusion of non-members in the sense that all minstrels who arrive in Paris must agree to abide by their decrees (the association does not function by being exclusive, in other words, but by being completely inclusive – at least in theory).[4] It would therefore be a mild exaggeration to say that this confraternity was designed to control a specific membership within a stipulated area of jurisdiction, like later minstrel guilds in both France and England, for no attempt is made in these regulations to restrict operations in Paris to those who are actually living in the city. The financial structure of the association also remains vague, for it does not appear from the statutes that the confraternity received payment from its members in return for professional and charitable benefits – the classic pattern of finance in such associations during the later Middle Ages.[5] The only specified sources of income are the fines levied upon offenders, half of which go to the king and half *au proufit de la confrairie du dist mestier*.[6] There are signs of an internal organisation, however, in the numerous references to masters and apprentices, although the regulations do not say how this system operated nor how long the apprenticeship lasted (which would have been a relatively meaningless figure, even if provided).[7]

These controls are achieved by establishing a hierarchy of jurisdiction which sets the minstrels on a ladder of authority rising to the Châtelet and ultimately reaching the presence of the king. It begins with the minstrels' own chief, the *prevost de Saint-Julien*, and those nominated 'masters' of the profession. Next come the prévôt of Paris and two or three *preudes hommes* chosen by the prévôt and his successors to ensure that the statutes are respected. They act in the name of the king.[8]

An alternative to courtliness

Now to examine these remarkable statutes in more detail. The following summaries contain the substance of each one (for the text see the Appendix).[9]

I No trumpeter (*trompeur*) of the city of Paris can enter into a contract at a feast for anyone but himself or his companion, nor for any other male or female minstrel of any other trade than his own. Some undertake to bring *taboureurs*, *vi[e]lleurs*, *organeurs* [i.e. members of the confraternity] and other minstrels with them, and then take their favourites [i.e. outsiders] from whom they receive money for the privilege. Thus people are deceived, for these minstrels are inferior and yet the trumpeters ask for full rates of pay for them and claim that they are other than they are.

II No trumpeters or other minstrels may leave a feast before it is finished.

III A minstrel who has been hired may not send a deputy except in the case of sickness, imprisonment or other necessity.

IV No male or female minstrel, and no apprentice, is permitted to go through Paris presenting himself or others for hire at feasts or weddings (*noces*).

V No apprentice minstrel who goes to a tavern may advertise himself nor any other minstrel, nor make any mention of his trade or praise it; he may, however, enter into contracts of hire for his own sons not yet married and for his daughters if their husbands are abroad or if they are estranged. If anyone makes an enquiry about minstrelsy he should say that the ordinances of his trade forbid him to hire anyone but himself, but if the potential customer will go to the *rue aus jougleurs*, he shall find good minstrels and apprentices.

VI   Those who come to the *rue aus jougleurs* should be allowed to hire whomsoever they please without interference from rivals until the point where negotiations break down and the purchaser walks on.

VII   The same rule applies to apprentices.

VIII   All minstrels, whether from Paris or not, must swear to obey the statutes.

IX   Any minstrel who arrives in Paris will be disciplined by *li prevost de Saint-Julien* (or by those who have been appointed as masters of the craft) unless he swears to observe the statutes.

X   No minstrel may allow himself to be hired through the agency of cooks.

XI   Two or three *preudes hommes* should be appointed who will punish offenders and levy fines upon them.

Despite the essentially urban and legalistic character of this document, there are points of contact between these ordinances and the utterly different world of the chivalric romances. As in Chrestien's *Erec et Enide*, for example, it is the great feasts and wedding celebrations (the *noces* of Statute IV) which provide minstrels with their most attractive employment,[10] and we also sense the nearness of such wealthy and noble patrons as dominate the services of minstrels in romance; the distinction between *les bonnes genz* and *li peuples* in the French text of Statute I shows that the Parisian jongleurs sought their work amongst the nobility and the most wealthy merchants as well as amongst the artisans and servants.[11] The power of trumpeters, so apparent in the first statute, also suggests that some of the masters served by the Parisian minstrels were either aristocratic or of wealthy stock with aristocratic pretensions. This ordinance shows that trumpeters could recruit other minstrels for a forthcoming engagement, presumably because trumpeters added such a lustre to banquets and other gatherings that anyone wishing to hire minstrelsy for a feast booked trumpeters first and left the rest of the hiring to them. Whatever the organists, fiddlers and other players of *bas* instruments might contribute, it was the trumpeters who added the element of ceremony.

A closer look, however, reveals a different picture, and one that leads away from the romances. In the Arthurian realm minstrels are generally itinerant performers living on gifts. The Parisian statutes, however, obliterate this form of minstrel life so clearly reflected in the romances and in Raimon Vidal's *Abril issia*. The generosity of lords was unpredictable and often left musicians in a poor state (Figure 4); in the statutes the minstrels work for

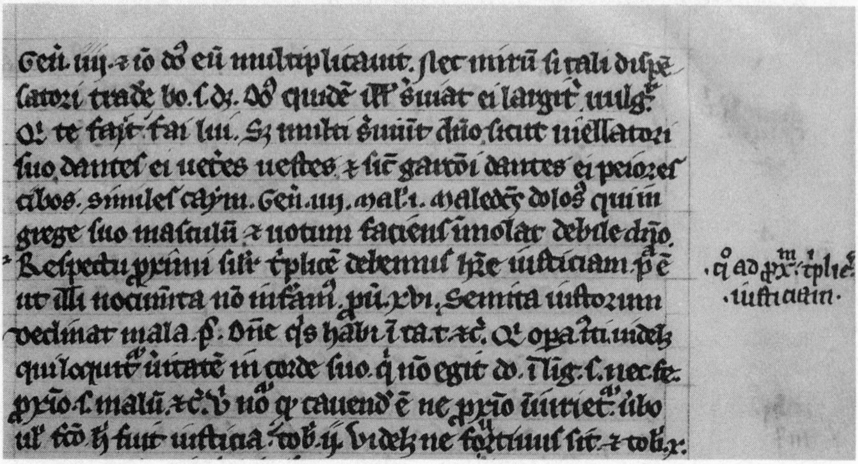

Figure 4 *A French preacher of the thirteenth century acknowledges the harsh plight of many minstrels:* Sed multi serviunt domino sicut viellatori suo dantes ei veteres vestes et sicut garcioni dantes ei peiores cibos *('But there are many who treat the Lord as they treat their fiddler, giving him old clothes and giving him inferior food as one would to a groom'). Cambridge, Sidney Sussex College, MS 34, f.9r. Reproduced by permission of the Master and Fellows.*

a fee (*salaire*). Furthermore, these Parisian minstrels are so disinclined to regard themselves as the guardians of courtly values that they are happy to appear in their statutes as artisans: *bons ouvriers*.[12] The status of these 'good craftsmen' seems to rest upon their capacity to earn and is reinforced by their adherence to quality levels set by the general standard of living and culture in their city; it owes little to 'courtly' considerations.

This professional view of the minstrel undermines the foundation of the itinerant jongleur's livelihood in one further way. In the judgement of Raimon Vidal's minstrel, for example, musical ability is nothing without certain ancillary gifts, shrewdness and a fluent tongue being chief among them. If the romances and *Abril issia* are any guide to the way minstrels behaved (and they are almost the only guides we have), then a good deal of the average minstrel's life was necessarily spent in boasting, more or less controlled according to circumstances. When a musician entered a residence he was often called upon to explain his minstrelsy both to the marshall of the hall, who admitted him, and to the company. As Guido of Evreux puts it in a striking *similitudo*, 'Not every minstrel who presents himself is admitted; it must first be determined what minstrelsy he has to offer' (*see* Appendix, p. 202). It is easy to imagine how such explanations required the vigorous selling that in modern experience is confined to the street market. Epics and romances contain many passages that offer a pastiche of these speeches:[13]

> Estrumens sui par droit non apielés,
> En paienie n'a nul tel menestrel;
> Ves ci me harpe, dont je sai bien harper,
> Et ma vïele, dont je sai vïeler,
> Et si sai bien et timbrer et baler.

> My name is 'Instrument' and it suits me well, for there is no such
> minstrel as me in all pagan lands; here is my harp on which I can play
> well, and my fiddle which I play in an accomplished fashion, and also
> I know how to play the drum (?tambourine) and to dance.

The first thing that Raimon Vidal's minstrel does when he meets the narrator
of *Abril issia* is to boast; he instinctively begins the conversation by advertising
his wares:[14]

> Senher, yeu soy us hom aclis
> a joglaria de cantar,
> e say romans dir e contar,
> e novas motas e salutz
> e autres comtes espandutz
> vas totas partz azautz e bos,
> e d'en Guiraut vers e chansos
> e d'en Arnaut de Maruelh mays,
> e d'autres vers e d'autres lays . . .

> Sir, I am a man inclined to the life of a minstrel, and I know how to
> tell romances and many stories and rhymed epistles, and other good
> and pleasing tales well-known everywhere, and verses and songs of en
> Guiraut (de Bornelh) and more by en Arnaut de Maroill, and other
> verses and lays . . .

Such boasting was to be expected from men who often relied upon gifts
rather than upon a *salaire* negotiated afresh for each 'engagement'. The Parisian statutes, however, free the individual minstrel from the need to provide
a voluble testimonial for himself every time that he seeks employment; admis-
sion to the confraternity provides him with credentials that will suit his urban
employers because they deal in the essentially mercantile terms of assured
value for an agreed price. Membership of the confraternity, in other words,
distinguishes the *bons ouvriers* from those who *sachent peu*.[15] These statutes
therefore modify the itinerant minstrel life evoked by Raimon Vidal in a
radical way and we begin to appreciate what they mean by a *reformacion*
of their trade. Statute IV, indeed, is designed to prevent musicians from
journeying in search of work within the walls of Paris; they must not make
their way through the streets offering themselves for immediate or for future
employment at any feasts or weddings that may be taking place. It is Statute
V, however, which offers the most drastic *reformacion* of all. We have already
noted that the establishment of this confraternity freed the individual from
the need to boast; the fifth statute actually forbids boasting, at least by probationary members. Apprentice jongleurs who go to taverns (a favourite minstrel

haunt, no doubt a useful place for gathering news, gossip and informal contracts) must not make any mention of their trade.[16] There is no longer any need for the fluent or roguish tongue which is associated with minstrels throughout Old French literature.

These ordinances undermine another principal factor in the life of itinerant minstrels: the solidarity within small groups of friends and associates that is now replaced by statutory loyalty to an elected governing body. Trumpeters are forbidden to take their favourite associates with them to feasts, while apprentices are told that they may only accept employment for themselves and for members of their family. Beyond that an apprentice may do no favours for any of his friends, and when approached by a customer he must direct the enquiry to the *rue aus jougleurs* in terms whose impersonality is deemed so important that the statutes fix it by breaking into direct speech:[17]

> 'Sir, the statutes of my trade forbid me to hire anyone but myself, but
> if you want minstrels or apprentices go to Minstrel Street and you will
> find good ones.'

Networks of loyalty and friendship within small groups had therefore to be suppressed; clearly, it was regarded as harmful to the *proufit commun* for a minstrel to *presenter aucun par especial*.[18] The complexity which these minstrel networks could assume is suggested by Statute X where, somewhat surprisingly, jongleurs are forbidden to allow themselves to be hired by cooks (*queux*). Presumably these were either resident cooks with friends in the minstrel business, or perhaps freelance cooks who were able to offer – as trumpeters were able to do – a 'package' deal in which they undertook to bring minstrels to a feast or wedding ceremony.[19]

The general thrust of the Parisian statutes may be simply defined. We meet in them, and perhaps for the first time, a view of the professional musician's responsibilities which has been so important in the musical life of Europe. According to this concept the musician is a kind of journeyman. Once his fee has been fixed (at a level as favourable to himself as possible), he arrives (as close to the required moment as circumstances will allow), he plays as agreed and then he departs as soon as he can. This last practice is regarded as an abuse in the statutes, and an attempt is made to correct it by requiring that no musician may leave a feast before it is over in order that he may play at another (Statute II).

The power of speech

Little seems to be left here of the aristocratic milieu for minstrelsy. There is no giving of gifts, no obligation to make good conversation and no duty to give a good report of a generous lord in all future travels. Why do the Parisian statutes 'dismantle the court' in this way?

The principal answer will surely be that the minstrels themselves wished it to be done. The statutes show that the initiative to 'reform' their trade came from the 'common accord' of the minstrels themselves, and the names of the thirty-seven protagonists are duly listed at the end of the document.[20] This initiative, I suggest, was born of a deep dissatisfaction and weariness which the traditional aristocratic milieu inspired in many entertainers. Raimon Vidal's *Abril issia* is both a eulogy of the conscientious court jongleur and an attack upon the avaricious lords who can make a good man's life hard. The 'gift economy' of honour functioned well in a time of bountiful patrons, but many a lord did not live up to his reputation for munificence and the jongleur was always at the mercy of a master's carelessness and caprice.[21] Gifts of robes might never materialise although they were promised;[22] presents might prove meagre (Figure 4). In *Abril issia* Raimon Vidal laments the passing of a system that relied so heavily upon the breeding and decency of both the minstrel and his host that it rarely worked to the jongleur's satisfaction.

The Parisian statutes offer a solution to this problem by refashioning the minstrel in the image of an honest journeyman with a responsibility reaching beyond himself, his family and his friends; he was entrusted with the good of his confraternity and beyond that with a part of the common good of his city. Indeed the Parisian solution is a distinctly urban one, for it obeys the tendency, so marked in the urban history of the thirteenth and fourteenth centuries, for matters of welfare and common profit to be regarded as the duty of public authorities and of confraternities based upon charitable sharing.[23]

These jongleurs got what they wanted, and it is possible to argue that they were not alone in doing so. There is a sense in which the formation of the Parisian confraternity was a victory for many of the clerics who had written about minstrelsy in the preceding century. About a hundred years before the minstrels of Paris presented their document to the prévôt, various theologians had been prepared to concede, with certain reservations, that the earnings of instrumentalists could be regarded as legitimate. The aspects of minstrelsy that these theologians could not tolerate – the flattery and boasting so important to minstrels relying upon *largesse*, for example – are identifiable in some respects with the very ones which the Parisian statutes seek to eradicate. Writers like Robert of Courson, Thomas Chobham and Thomas Docking would also have been satisfied with the proposition, implicit in the statutes, that instrumentalists are superior to other jongleurs, for the ordinances have nothing to say about any other kind of entertainer. It was instrumentalists, and them alone, that Robert of Courson was able to envisage as family men with wives and children, and in contemporary terms these were the ties that raised a man above the level of vagrants and low journeymen.[24] Here, once again, the ordinances have the effect of satisfying a certain kind of clerical opinion, for some of the minstrels in the confraternity were family men with *enfants à marier*,[25] and among the female minstrels who put their names to the Parisian statutes there are four married women.[26] Most of the minstrels with relatively long-term commitments to the confraternity were presumably persons of reasonable substance 'living in the city of Paris'.[27]

Thus it was that many of the theologians who wrote of minstrelsy in the thirteenth century, so often presented as the tireless enemies of professional secular musicians, could accept the same ends as the jongleurs themselves. Many theologians continued to attack musicians in their writings, and the members of the Parisian confraternity cannot stand for all European jongleurs (although the movement towards professional associations of 'municipal' minstrels shapes the history of urban minstrelsy in the fourteenth century).[28] Nonetheless, the changing relationship between theology and minstrelsy in thirteenth-century Paris has a general significance.

Above all, it reveals the churchmen's desire to control the jongleurs' power and especially their power of speech. A cleric engaged in a pastoral ministry had one powerful weapon to wield, and that was his voice. The sermons of the thirteenth century refer almost obsessively to this sacred faculty of speech; the words *vox, auris, predicatio, lingua, sonus, verbum* and *loquor* return again and again, their meaning enriched beyond all translation. It was by speaking the word of God in preaching and confession that a cleric with the cure of souls pursued his pastoral work. To the modern reader of medieval sermons it may seem at first as though this work only required the churchmen to apply the rules of Christian teaching as then understood to all manifestations of contemporary life and then to denounce what was found to be irregular. A closer acquaintance with thirteenth-century preaching, however, reveals that the preachers did not see themselves as schoolmasters of the conscience whose only hope of success lay with stern language and the constant threat of the rod. Their task was not only to proclaim like a trumpet, a *tuba per quem auditores percipiunt verbum dei*, but also to persuade and to speak with shrewdness and tact. The delicacy of this art emerges from a passage in a sermon preached at Paris in 1273 by Master Guillaume de Moussy le Neuf:[29]

> circumcisi in lingua . . . debemus esse et specialiter predicatores . . .
> Rectum debet esse suum verbum et quasi in scaceria ponderatum ut
> nichil dicat nisi edificarium nec quod videatur tangere aliquam personam
> specialiter, quia apparet quandoque quando non bene stringit verba sua
> quod propter aliquos loquitur qui sunt ad sermonem, et ideo debent
> sic esse circumcisus in verbo quod nullo modo putari possit quod de
> Gauberto vel de Martino loquitur, sed generaliter debet loqui ne dicatur:
> 'Audivistis quid dixit/Avez oi qu'il a dit? Sic fecit talis sicut ipse dixit.'

> we must be circumspect in speech, and this is especially the case for
> preachers . . . A preacher's words must be just and weighed, as it were,
> in the scales of an exchequer so that he may only say what is edifying
> and what is seen to touch no individual personally, because whenever
> he does not exercise rigorous control over his speech it will seem that
> he is referring specifically to individuals who are present at the sermon,
> and therefore he must be circumspect in his speech so that it may in
> no wise be thought that he is speaking about Gaubert or Martin. He

must speak in general terms lest they say: 'Have you heard what he
said? This person has done just as he describes.'

'A preacher's words must be just and weighed, as it were, in the scales
of an exchequer.' This is counsel that Raimon Vidal's minstrel would have
understood. He too knew the need for circumspect speech if his enterprise
were not to flounder. Even when we remember the wish of St Francis that
his friars should be the minstrels of God, it still seems an exaggeration to
suggest that preachers were keen to borrow the minstrels' techniques; however, they were certainly jealous of their success. As Evrard du Val-des-
Ecoliers remarks, and no doubt with some feeling, 'there are many who
would more willingly hear a minstrel than a good preacher'.[30] It was a constant
struggle for churchmen to compete, as speakers, for influence over laymen
who were constantly exposed to all the beguiling and shrewd talk of minstrels
– what Latin writers call their *adulacio* and *stultiloquium*. With the Parisian
statutes, however, the competition becomes rather more fair; these minstrels
have divested themselves of the power which a jongleur could wield in aristocratic society if he took the risk of relying upon *largesse* rather than upon
a contracted *salaire*. In becoming urban professionals who arrive and play
for a fixed fee, the Parisians have won a measure of security at the expense
of their old strength.

Minstrel repertoire I: the epics

Grocheio's *De musica* presents a comprehensive survey of sacred and secular
music, both monophonic and polyphonic, vocal and instrumental, as it was
in the city of Paris around the year 1300. This treatise is therefore a valuable
guide to the repertoire of at least the minstrels who were specialists with
the *viella*, or fiddle, for Grocheio describes the characteristic repertoire performed 'before the wealthy in feasts and entertainments' by the *bonus artifex
in viella*.[31] In the thirteenth-century French of scholars with a Parisian background the Latin word *artifex* ('a craftsman') was usually translated *menestrel*,
a word which could also mean 'a manufacturer or craftsman'.[32] Grocheio's
phrase might therefore be rendered in the vernacular as *bon menestrel de vièle*.

Grocheio associates three forms with a 'good minstrel' of this sort: the
High Style trouvère song, the *ductia* (a form of instrumental dance-music),
and the *estampie*. A wealth of evidence suggests that we should also add the
sung narrative epics, or *chansons de geste*, to this list, since this is certainly
the material which the Parisian minstrels would have needed when they
catered for *li peuples*.[33] Since Grocheio's remarks about trouvère song and
the *ductia* have been discussed elsewhere,[34] let us concentrate upon the *chanson
de geste* (which Grocheio calls the *cantus gestualis*) and then upon the *estampie*.

We have already seen that when the theologian Thomas Chobham distinguishes good instrumentalists from bad ones he does so on the basis of

their repertory; good minstrels chant of ancient heroes and men of the church; bad ones go to taverns and sing 'wanton songs'.[35] Such an unqualified reference to *lascivas cantilenas* would scarcely have satisfied Grocheio, a musician who was inclined to be indulgent to even such love-songs as were sung for *caroles*. Nonetheless, it may be significant that he begins his discussion of 'the monophonic music of the people' (*musica simplex vel vulgaris*) with repertory which is very close to the material that exonerated certain jongleurs in the judgement of Thomas Chobham – that is to say sung narratives 'in which the deeds of heroes ... and the lives and martyrdom of various saints are told'.[36]

It may be that Grocheio recognised such narratives to be the most readily defensible element in minstrel repertoire and began his account of secular monophony with them because of a desire to act as an apologist for secular music. From his description it is clear that these narratives are *chansons de geste* differing little in at least their form and their subject matter from the lengthy and 'literate' examples of the genre that have survived. These are poems about the greatest heroes of the French nation such as Charlemagne, generally cast in assonating or monorhymed laisses whose length within a single poem may vary considerably. The delicate question of whether these 'book' epics were sometimes sung as they survive, or whether musical performance was confined to 'oral' and partially improvised *chansons de geste*, is one to which we shall soon return. Grocheio's *De musica* is our principal source of information for the detail that in sung performances of epic every line in the laisse was chanted to the same melodic phrase.[37]

What was the audience for such songs in thirteenth-century Paris? According to Grocheio, epics ought to be performed for the old, for working citizens and for those of middle station because any story of the miseries and calamities endured by the ancient fathers of France made present work and hardship seem more bearable.[38] There is independent evidence that the minstrels of thirteenth-century Paris were able to exploit a popular interest in epics,[39] so Grocheio may be prescribing them for the people who did indeed enjoy *chansons de geste* in the city (although it is another question whether they relished them for the reasons that Grocheio gives).

What of the knights, the *milites*? Grocheio's declaration that epics were a comfort to working people should not lead us to underestimate the evidence for a continuing chivalric interest in these *chansons de geste*. Evrard du Val-des-Ecoliers, whose sermons contain so many references to Parisian life and customs, refers to knights and men of martial calling (*homines militares*) who love to hear stories of Roland, Oliver and Charlemagne.[40]

For the Parisian minstrels of *c.* 1300, did the *chanson de geste* form a written repertoire or an unwritten one? Was it both? We may be confident that the music was never written down; the musical idiom was so simple, and the tunes associated with particular stories were probably so widely known, that with very few exceptions the melodic material of the *chansons de geste* existed entirely in an oral tradition.[41] The question of the texts of these narratives, however, is more complicated than the issue of the music and it brings us back to the distinction between a 'book' epic and an 'oral' epic. The *chanson de geste* literature of twelfth- and thirteenth-century France is not the only corpus of medieval narrative poetry which scholars have investigated in relation to the oral traditions of professional entertainers. Some narrative poems in Old English, for example, and the Middle English tail-rhyme romances, are also written works that were probably brought into being by literate poets adopting the metrical forms and subject matter of illiterate minstrels to produce *texts*: relatively fixed creations which possess (or so the common argument runs) a sophistication supposedly made possible only by leisured composition at a desk as opposed to improvisation or composition without writing.[42] In the case of the Old French *chansons de geste* the problem of origins has been much disputed,[43] but many would accept that in the oral tradition of minstrels there were narrative songs whose characteristic metrical forms and subject matter are mirrored in the texts of *chansons de geste* in manuscripts of the thirteenth, fourteenth and fifteenth centuries.

The key issue is whether the words of the *chansons de geste* which Grocheio heard were derived from written texts, or whether they were extemporised (or perhaps composed without writing and then performed from memory) in the manner documented for the Yugoslav epic singers by Parry and Lord.[44] In simple terms, do we have the *actual* repertory of these minstrels, or only something *like* it? According to the theory of oral composition, developed both by Parry and Lord and by many subsequent scholars, the illiterate improviser of stories is a universal phenomenon;[45] singing to a musical instrument, he improvises a narrative poem by deploying formulas learned during his apprenticeship. These formulas are pre-set pieces of language that express a certain action or idea within fixed metrical constraints. The written *chansons de geste* contain a significant amount of language which is formulaic in this way;[46] the literate poets who produced these works were adopting an aspect of style from the oral tradition of minstrels.

What is Grocheio describing in his *De musica* – the performance of improvised (or at least orally composed) *chansons de geste*, or the performance of the written epic texts that have survived in manuscripts?

For an insight into the narrative repertory of Parisian jongleurs in the decades before Johannes de Grocheio's *De musica* we can turn to a sermon preached by the Dominican friar Daniel of Paris. In this sermon, dated 1272 and preached in the church of St Leufroy (by the Grand Pont), Daniel refers to St Martin who, with a 'blow' of his knife, divided his cloak with a pauper (for the original see Chapter 1):

> this was a handsome blow ... A great deal is sung about Roland and
> Oliver and it is said that Roland smote his adversary upon the head
> so that he cut him down to the teeth, and that Oliver cut another in
> the stomach so that the lance passed out beyond the other side of his
> body. But this is all nothing. Because it is nowhere found to be true
> of Roland, of Oliver, of Charlemagne nor of Ogier the Dane that he

made such a handsome blow [as St Martin] because there will be none
such until the end of the world. Whence Holy Church must sing of the
blow and call it to mind but does not concern itself with the other blows,
and even if some minstrels sing of the blows of the aforesaid [heroes]
that comes to nothing because they add many false things.

This carries us directly into the realm of Grocheio's *cantus gestualis*. The milieu
is a Parisian one, and the epic heroes mentioned are those whose stories
cluster around the figure of Charlemagne, the *rex Karolus* mentioned by
Grocheio. The performers are professionals, called here *hystriones*. This passage may also bring us close to something resembling the Oxford text of
the *Song of Roland*; Daniel of Paris has obviously heard minstrels performing
something like the formulaic (but none the less horrific) single combat scenes
that abound in the Oxford version of this famous epic:[47]

> [Rollant] le fiert tant vertuusement,
> Tresqu'al nasel tut le elme li fent;
> Trenchet le nes el buche e les denz.

> Roland struck [the saracen Grandonie] with great force, he split the
> helmet down to the nasal piece, cutting down through the nose, the
> mouth and the teeth.

Daniel's description of Oliver's blow also sets up many echoes of the Oxford
version of the *Song of Roland*. There may even be an allusion in Daniel's
Latin text to one of the many verbal formulas which the poet uses to describe
combat:[48]

Daniel of Paris	per medium ventrem *totum ultra*
Song of Roland	*tut* le fer li mist *ultre* (1286)
	tut le fer li mist *ultre* (1540)

We move closer still to a written text of an epic in Grocheio's reference
to a type of *chanson de geste* in which the last line of each laisse does not
have the same 'poetic concord' as the others (i.e. it does not rhyme or asso-
nate). As an example he cites the *gesta que dicitur de Girardo de Viana*. In the
only available English translation of his treatise these words are rendered
'the *chanson de geste* which is said to be by Girarde de Viana',[49] but the correct
interpretation is undoubtedly 'the *chanson de geste* which is about Girart de
Vienne'. Girart was one of the most famous heroes of French epic tradition
and he is the protagonist in a *chanson de geste* written by Bertrand de Bar-sur-
Aube, perhaps in the period 1205–25. The importance of this identification
is that the surviving text of Bertrand's epic shows exactly the feature which
Grocheio describes; each laisse ends with a line *ab aliis consonantia discordantem*.
A brief extract will show the manner:[50]

> Et qant ill ont la novele entendue,
> Einz ne veïtes gent plus fort irascue.
> Lors fu li oz de grant duel conmeüe.

Nus cele nuit n'i boit ne ne menjue,
N'a bon cheval n'i ot sele tolue.
Juq'au demein que l'aube est aparue
Firent baron grant duel et gent menue
    Por le roi Karlemene.

This correspondence between Bertrand de Bar-sur-Aube's epic and Grocheio's description of a narrative *de Girardo de Viana* suggests that Grocheio is referring to this very text and that the minstrels of Paris around 1300 who performed narrative repertory were singing all or parts of a written epic. When instrumental accompaniment was used in such performances, a minstrel would have needed to memorise his material, perhaps dividing it into key episodes that could be narrated in one sitting. There are many ways that a jongleur could gain access to such texts. Some members of the jongleur community were clerics who had dropped out of the educational system and who would have been better equipped to read a 'book' epic than many of the lay patrons whom they served. Others, although perhaps illiterate themselves, could presumably have the material read to them, and then store it with all the remarkable facility of memory which illiterates so often display.

Minstrel repertoire II: polyphony

In an important article, Lawrence Gushee has drawn attention to the way in which Grocheio's discussion of instruments and their repertoire is distinct from the section of his treatise devoted to polyphonic music.[51] The structure of his *De musica* might therefore be taken to imply that instrumentalists' repertoire did not normally encompass motet and conductus. This would be consistent with the fact that all of the music which Grocheio associates with the most esteemed kind of instrumentalist, the *bonus artifex in viella*, is monophonic.

The evidence on these points is delicate and contradictory, however, for a consideration of the social backgrounds of professional secular musicians suggests a different conclusion. The trade of minstrelsy absorbed individuals from many walks of life who, whether through failure in some other profession or through inclination, had decided to become professional musicians. Many of these men were clerics in the sense that they had taken a tonsure at some time in their lives and had perhaps also received a certain amount of education, *clergie*. The earliest detailed information that we possess about the social backgrounds of jongleurs is contained in the Old Occitan *Vidas*, or 'Lives' of the troubadours, and these documents reveal some of the patterns of social mobility that could cause a man of clerical condition to become a minstrel; they include a personal inclination to the jongleur's life, an insupportable boredom with studies and love for a woman.[52] Canon Law decrees of the thirteenth century confirm that clerics sometimes crossed the boundary into *jonglerie*. The *Liber Sextus Decretalium* (1298), for example, commissioned by Pope Boniface VIII as a supplement to Gratian's *Decretals*, rules that clerics who become *joculatores* are to lose all clerical privileges if they persist in that trade for more than a year.[53]

This decree suggests that it may be misguided to speak of a 'boundary' between *clergie* and *jonglerie*. The ruling in the *Liber Sextus* has the effect of allowing jongleur-clerics to continue in the trade of minstrelsy for twelve months before they forfeit the privileges of clerical status and their freedom from the jurisdiction of civil courts. It is not entirely clear, however, what sort of people the jongleur-clerics of the *Liber Sextus* may be. A tonsure, the outward sign of membership of the clergy, was easy to obtain for it indicated 'an inclination to the ecclesiastical condition' and little more;[54] indeed there were many thieves and criminals who had themselves tonsured in order to escape the civil courts, and in higher social spheres there were artisans and merchants who also took the tonsure.[55] In this sense the concepts 'cleric' and 'clerical condition' were flexible and generous in their inclusiveness; no doubt some minstrels were also *clercs* of this kind, enjoying (possibly on a temporary basis only), the privileges conferred by the tonsure.

There were other jongleur-clerics, however, who had acquired a measure of learning. They were *clercs* who had abandoned the clerical life or who had been driven out of it by circumstances. As mentioned above, the Old Occitan *Vidas* reveal these refugees in the process of fleeing, and the state of the employment situation for churchmen and university graduates in northern France was difficult enough to steer many clerics into unorthodox careers. Most of the young men who studied at the University of Paris, for example, were doing so with a view to office – a position within the university, a bishopric, a stall in a cathedral chapter, an archdeaconry or perhaps a pastoral cure – but such positions were not easily won because there was little growth or mobility in these areas. In theory, at least, new bishoprics could be created, but they rarely were. Membership of cathedral chapters varied little and after the twelfth century 'could show a downward trend, numbers in some parts being limited by law'.[56] The number of archdeaconries was also stable to the point of stagnancy and in many regions very few fresh parishes were created during the thirteenth century.

In one of his reminiscences about life in Paris *c.* 1200, the theologian and chronicler Jacques de Vitry reveals how the life of minstrelsy had found its place among the range of student ambitions as early as the first decades of the thirteenth century. In an *exemplum* he recalls how three Flemish students fell into a discussion one day about their reasons for studying. The first wished to become a master at the university, while the second, going to the opposite extreme, hoped to join the Cistercians. The third student, with ambitions of a different kind, declared his wish to become an *organizator*, *hystrio* and *ioculator*. Jacques reports that he was successful in achieving this aim and that he lived an itinerant life, 'thrusting himself up to the tables of others and refusing to do proper work'.[57] We can only wonder how many other students turned minstrels there may have been in thirteenth-century France. Such men would have possessed some reading knowledge of Latin, an ability to read at least plainchant notation, a good singing voice and perhaps (if this is what is implied by the term *organizator* in Jacques' account) some ambition in the direction of polyphony.

Minstrel repertoire III: estampies

Johannes de Grocheio reports that two of the principal forms which good fiddlers play 'before the wealthy in their feasts and entertainments' are *ductia* and *stantipes*. The *stantipes* is unique among the monophonic secular forms which he discusses because it can be admired for the same intellectual reasons as a motet or a polyphonic conductus. This is principally because of its complex structure, or in Grocheio's words, because of its 'difficult succession of agreements' (*difficilem concordantiarum discretionem*).[58] The complexity of the *stantipes* causes the *animus* of both player and listener to become rapt in a concentration that prevents depraved thoughts.

Grocheio describes the form of the *stantipes* and refers to some specific examples composed by a musician named Tassin (the *res Tassini*) fragments of which have survived. This information leaves no room for doubt about the form and the musical style of the pieces which he calls *stantipes*. The musical form is

$$\text{Ax Ay} \quad \text{Bx By} \quad \text{Cx Cy} \quad \text{etc}$$

where a change of capital letter signals a new melodic section, x stands for an 'open' ending and y for a 'closed' one. By a remarkable piece of good fortune, which has often been commented upon, Tassin is probably to be identified with the minstrel of that name who is listed in a roster of the household of King Philippe le Bel in 1288.[59] This Tassin would undoubtedly have spent periods of residence with the royal court at Paris which might explain how his music reached the ears of Johannes de Grocheio. Furthermore, three sections from the otherwise lost *stantipes* which Tassin composed, and which Grocheio admired, have been preserved as tenor parts in three motets in the Montpellier Codex where each bears the title *chose Tassin*.[60] In their form and musical style the Tassin pieces point directly to the *estampies royales* preserved as fourteenth-century additions to the Manuscrit du Roi (Music example 3). Brief though these pieces may be, they are long enough to give pause for thought. If Example 3 represents a difficult style of instrumental music, as Grocheio's account leads us to assume, then where does the difficulty lie? Like the supposedly difficult pieces by Tassin, *La quarte Estampie Royal* has seven sections, but as it stands it looks far from virtuosic. What was there in such music to provide strenuous exercise for what Grocheio calls the performer's *animus*, 'the rational mind'?

At this point the scholar must give way to the musician. To learn one of these *estampies* by heart, and then to set oneself the task of reproducing it exactly, is to discover where the element of *difficultas* lies. The musical

La quarte Estampie Royal

idiom of the Manuscrit du Roi pieces is highly controlled – indeed it is stereotyped – and a performer relying upon his memory must indeed exercise
his *animus* to ensure that no repeat be forgotten and that no section of the
music be inadvertently allowed to dissolve into another through the intermedi-
ary of shared melodic material. The open and closed endings, which look
as if they are ready to offer moments of relaxation and consolidation (like

the refrains of a lyric, for example), prove in performance to be only false friends; they do indeed allow the mind to relax, momentarily, in the performance of familiar material, but this can easily trip the player into muddling open and closed endings (since they both begin in the same way). When these pieces are considered in terms of performance it becomes possible to listen to them in an historical manner and to appreciate the artifice which Grocheio admired in them, and which prompted him to dignify the minstrels who played them with the title *artifex*: craftsman.

Visions of the city

The changing position of minstrels in Latin writings of the twelfth and thirteenth centuries can be explained in various ways. The emergence of the scholastic method certainly accounts for some of the change. As the Middle Ages knew it, the tradition of passionate harangue against professional entertainers was principally a legacy from the Church Fathers of Late Antiquity, so the schoolmens' determination to submit the writings of the Fathers to a dispassionate analysis, and to ascertain what guidance they could offer to preachers and confessors, was inevitably a force for change. The absorption of Aristotelian writings, and especially of the *Ethics* and *Politics*, brought Christian theologians into contact with an extraordinarily stimulating thinker who perceived the usefulness and dangers of music in terms both more urbane and more sophisticated than the terms of good and evil, godly will and perverse will, which defined the Judaeo-Christian heritage.

The elaboration of the scholastic enterprise and the study of the 'new' Aristotle in the twelfth century were both urban phenomena, the work of *magistri* in cathedral schools and the nascent universities. The changing position of minstrels between 1100 and 1300 owes a great deal not merely to the intellectual activities that were fostered in the urban schools, but also to the very fabric and appearance of urban agglomerations. It is the intense visual stimulus which cities offer to urban dwellers that sociologists have increasingly come to recognise as the one constant element in the many attempts which have been made to describe the consistent effects of urbanism upon human psychology.[61] Our attention naturally turns to Paris, home of many of the texts which have been cited in the last three chapters. There are many descriptions of Paris in medieval French sources, both Latin and vernacular, and like the fourteenth-century illustration reproduced here as Figure 5, they emphasise the major physical features of the city (such as bridges, market squares and gates) together with the extraordinary density of commercial activity visible on every side passing over, within or between the physical structures of the city. The description of Paris composed by Guido de Bazoches between 1175 and 1190 is typical of many in this respect. 'The Grand Pont', says Guido, 'is crowded, rich, ideal for buying, it swarms with people, it abounds with shops, with wealth, with innumerable commodities; it swarms with boats, it groans with goods, it abounds with things to

Figure 5 *View of Paris, the Ile de la Cité. The drawing shows a stylised view of the Ile with its two major bridges and crowded commercial life. On the Seine below three young men (students at the University?) sing from a music rotulus as they are rowed along by two boatmen. Paris, Bibliothèque Nationale, MS fr. 2090-91-92, f.99r (detail). Reproduced by permission.*

be bought and sold'.[62] Like many who contemplated Paris in the twelfth and thirteenth centuries, Guido is impressed by the diversity of the city. The goods are diverse, the purposes and wants which the goods imply are more diversified still, and the relations which trading establishes between people, essentially impersonal and yet to their mutual benefit, are infinite in their variety and extent. For Guido, as for many others who recorded their admiration of Paris, this sense of the city as a massive collaborative effort is not in the least abstract; it is so closely perceived in relation to the physical structure of the city (in this case the Grand Pont) that it seems to be an interpretation of the very stones.

The conventional Christian concept of work could not survive this intense visual stimulus without change. A monk, whatever his experience of a city might be, knew that it lay within his contemplative purpose to suppress all confused sounds and images, whatever their source, and to seek the prayerful peace which alone guaranteed true happiness. If he spoke or wrote, it was usually to other monks, whether in the present or in the future. Having no pastoral responsibilities, he had no need to diversify his understanding of how those outside the monastery lived and survived, and he was not required to address the problems of faith and conscience which lives vastly different to his own might present. It is in this sense that the great achievement of the thirteenth century can be described as unmonastic, for what happened in the Western Church between 1200 and 1300 was that many churchmen who lived outside the monastic cloister felt the need for an extraordinarily thorough, articulate and practical ministry in all areas of the pastoral calling.

The emergence of the orders of friars, licensed to preach and to hear confession, provided one answer to this need, and their ministry was specially directed towards the cities. As Humbert of Romans, one of the most eminent of the thirteenth-century Dominicans, records: 'in cities there are more people than in other places, and therefore it is better to preach there than elsewhere ... there are more sins there ... [and] ... lesser places which lie around cities are more influenced by cities than vice versa.'[63] It was impossible for this pastoral mission to develop in the cities – whether led by the friars or by others – without a keen sense of *the diversity of work*. Churchmen like Peter the Chanter and Robert of Courson knew that the city of Paris supported a huge number of small and specialised trades; it was generally obvious to them that their *civitas* was essentially a dense agglomeration of non-agriculturalists. They knew that there were many in the city of Paris whose labour did not help to produce what monastic theologians, with a severity befitting the strictness of their vows, had always regarded as necessities: essential food and raiment, and no more. Courson had confronted the confusion of small-scale manufacture in Paris, however, and to turn over the folios of a manuscript of his *Summa*, allowing one's eye to wander from the lines which deal with minstrels, is to become instantly lost in a throng of Latin words denoting the practitioners of small trades. There are makers of dice, makers of crossbows, compounders of toxic substances, dealers in white lead, and many more. Musical minstrels could now be regarded as merely one kind of tradesman among very many. For Peter the Chanter instrumentalists are *'artifices* instrumentorum musicorum', while for Johannes de Grocheio the expert fiddler is a 'bonus *artifex* in viella'. The Parisian instrumentalists call themselves 'bons *ouvriers*'. All these terminologies seem designed to draw instrumentalist-singers into the ranks of legitimate and skilled artisans. Within the intellectual context of Courson's *Summa*, and of Peter the Chanter's writings, the legitimacy of non-essential labour and craftsmanship is accepted in principle, for it supports the city's diversity, power and wealth. The questions which Courson asks about minstrels are therefore much the same as he chooses to ask about many other kinds of tradesmen. Is it legitimate for them to earn money from their trade? May some varieties be allowed to do so while others may not? The thrust of thirteenth-century reasoning on these questions was towards a special status for the instrumentalist, especially the string-player (trumpeters were clearly a special case), and it is tempting to believe that the institution of the Parisian minstrel confraternity in 1321, an association of instrumentalists, owed something to more than a hundred years of teaching in the confessional that instrumentalist-minstrels are a breed apart, to be distinguished from entertainers offering other kinds of minstrelsy.

CHAPTER FOUR

JEUNESSE AND THE COURTLY SONG REPERTORY

The previous three chapters have been concerned with professionals. This chapter is devoted to one of the most intriguing and enigmatic manifestations of musical life in medieval France: the activities of courtly amateurs. These amateur activities are intriguing, for they may have accounted for a good deal of musical performance at court, exploiting a repertoire that ranged from light and ephemeral dance-songs to multi-stanza trouvère lyrics of the kind preserved in the great chansonniers. The performances given by amateurs at court are also enigmatic, for archival documents reveal next to nothing about them (the performers were not paid, although they might be rewarded),[1] and the question of whether pictorial sources from the thirteenth century can advance our knowledge about music-making of this kind is still under discussion.[2]

However, the literary sources of the period are generously supplied with fictionalised references to the musical pursuits of courtly amateurs that have only recently been sorted and classified, albeit in a provisional fashion.[3] In particular, there are many narrative works in Old French that portray the musical life of large households during festivals and tournaments. The amateur musicians at court are usually young people such as *vallets, damoiseles, escuiers, bachelers* and *puceles*, and this chapter will therefore be closely concerned with manifestations of the ideal of *jeunesse*: a candid and insouciant disposition that was affected for the sake of mutual harmony and delight in court society. The evidence will mostly be taken from the epics and romances that cover the period from *c.* 1080 (the approximate date of the earliest epic, the *Song of Roland*), through to 1300, by which time the epic was almost moribund and new departures in narrative fiction (such as the emergence of the *dit*) were about to take place. These sources can be supplemented with other writings, but they are scattered and highly diverse in character; they are so varied, indeed, and the topic of amateur musicianship at court is such an elusive one, that this chapter cannot do more than present a few isolated extracts, from texts of various periods and places, in the hope of creating a suggestive context for them.

When the musical references in the Old French epics and romances are approached in this way it becomes clear that they form a pattern. In the earliest epics musical delight is often but an occasional episode in a general drama of pain; in many of the romances, however, it is associated with the insouciant bearing of the perfect *vallet, bacheler, pucele* or *chevalier*.[4] This is a contrast of tone and imagination; it can best be illustrated by comparing the way in which an epic and a romance treat the same narrative motif, and I have selected the motif of 'singing on horseback' for the purpose.[5] The epic of *Les Quatre Fils Aymon* (*c.* 1200) has an arresting passage where the four brothers of the title ride from the town of Montauban, singing as they go:[6]

> Or chevalchent li conte à joie et à baldor,
> Chascuns porte en sa main une molt bele flor.
> De Montauban issirent par la porte Foucon . . .
> Aallars et Guichars commenceront .i. son,
> Gasconois fu li dis et Limosins li ton,
> Et Richars lor bordone belement par desos;
> D'une grande huchie entendre les puet on.

> Now the counts ride with joy and high spirits, and each of them carries
> a beautiful flower in his hand. They leave Montauban by the 'Foucon'
> gate . . . Aallars et Guichars begin a song; the words are Gascon and
> the music Limousin, and Richars delightfully sings an accompaniment
> below them; one can hear them from a good way off.

This has a certain charm, but things are not as they seem. All four of Aymon's sons are riding here, yet only three are singing. A few lines later the fourth son, Renaus, rides into view sobbing and calling upon God. Bent under a weight of foreboding, he prays intently lest he and his brothers be murdered or cast into prison. Eventually, the poet shows why Renaus weeps as his brothers sing so gaily. They are riding into an ambush. The story of *Les Quatre Fils Aymon* is made of violent struggles such as this; every man is vulnerable to physical attack and to the mental torment of conflicting loyalties. Only by their prayers to a fearsome God and to his saints do men have the power to avert catastrophe or to mitigate its effects.

To examine the presentation of musical life in the twelfth-century epics is to discover how often music appears as a momentary consolation amidst violence and conflict. The mental landscape of the knights and aristocrats in the earlier epics is akin to the one that George Eliot depicted for the rural workers of the English countryside before the Industrial Revolution in *Silas Marner*:[7]

> . . . the rude mind with difficulty associates the ideas of power and
> benignity. A shadowy conception of power that by much persuasion can
> be induced to refrain from harm, is the shape most easily taken by the
> sense of the Invisible in the minds of men who have always been pressed
> close by primitive wants . . . their imagination is almost barren

of the images that feed desire and hope, but is all overgrown by
recollections that are a perpetual pasture to fear.

Whatever reservations we may have about 'the rude mind' as a historical
term, it is undeniable that this sounds like the terrain of the earlier *chansons
de geste*. The view of a warring military class 'pressed close by primitive wants
... their imagination ... almost barren of the images that feed desire and
hope' would seem to have been one of the chief attractions of the *chansons
de geste* for twelfth- and thirteenth-century audiences. These poems offer one
of the eternal pleasures of epic story: the chance to send one's imagination
into a past where an insufficiency of reflection makes action magnificent in
the performance but dire in the consequence. As an evocation of the historical
past in which many epics are set (the time of Charlemagne and the long
period of conflict following the collapse of his empire) the *chansons de geste*
have something to recommend them still. R. W. Southern, for example, has
dedicated an imposing chapter to the proposition that the earlier *chansons
de geste* record the mental and spiritual climate of Europe before the twelfth
century with considerable fidelity.[8] The tendency for God to be conceived
as a terrible judge who must be pacified by offerings, prayers and pilgrimages
– a tendency which Southern, in company with many other historians, regards
as a major characteristic of European spirituality before the twelfth century
– evokes *Les Quatre Fils Aymon* with some immediacy.[9]

Now let us follow the drift in literary fashion from epic to romance during
the second half of the twelfth century. Here is another instance of the 'singing
on horseback' motif, this time from *Guiron le courtois*, an Arthurian romance
in prose of *c.* 1235.[10] At this point in the story the knight Breuz is travelling
through a forest when he sees another *chevalier* coming towards him:[11]

> ... li cheualier estoit adonc montez sor vn cheual molt cointement . et
> en faisoit mener un autre en destre. li chequaliers dont ge uos cont uenoit
> chantant vn son nouel chant qui a celui tens estoit fait en la meson le
> roi artus . le cheualiers chantoit si halt et si fort . que toute la forest aloit
> retentissant la ou il aloit . et li uers qui aloit chantant si cestoit cest.

> En grant ioie ma amor mis
> Et de grant dolor ma hostez ;
> Malgrez trestuit mes henemis
> Sui ge si haltement montez,
> Que por son ami ma conte
> Cele qui passe flor et lys
> Et quant por son home ma pris
> Bien ai le monde sormonte.

> En tel guise com ge uos cont aloit chantant li cheualiers . si haltement
> que d'assez loing le peust l'en oir . a ce qu'il faisoit merueilleusement
> la forest retentyr . endroit soi . por la uoiz qu'il auoit fort . et halt . . .
> [Breuz] dist adonc a soi meesmes . que a merueilles chantoit bien li

cheualier . et se alcuns me demandoit qui estoit li cheualier . ge diroie
que ce estoit vn cheualiers de la meson le roi artus . gentill home . et
de grant afaire . et auoit nom messire yuains.

. . . the knight was mounted very graciously on a horse and was having
another led by his right. This knight of whom I am telling you came
singing a new song of his which at that time had been composed in
the court of King Arthur. The knight sang so loudly and strongly that
all the forest resounded as he went, and this was the poem he sang . . .
[poem follows]. The knight went along singing in the manner that I
am relating to you so that one could hear him from afar; he made the
forest resound around him with his loud and strong voice. Breuz [who
is listening] says to himself: 'The knight sings marvellously well, and
if anyone were to ask me who the knight might be, I would say that
it must be a knight from the household of King Arthur, and a noble
man of great account, named Sir Yvain.'

Here the clamour of battle, so clearly heard in the epic of *Les Quatre Fils
Aymon*, has subsided. Instead of four brothers trotting towards a catastrophe
and embroiled in a feud, the romance of *Guiron le courtois* presents a knight
who is fashioned for *courtoisie*. The almost exclusively masculine realm of
epic is far behind and Yvain rides with a lady as well as two squires, while
the song he sings – and the poet is glad to supply the text – is a delicate
love-lyric. In the best style of the trouvères it presents love as a kind of
joie (one of the most potent words in Old French lyric) and celebrates a
triumph over the backbiters who are the foes of every lover. Yvain's song
also expresses the view of love as a social and moral ascent which lies at
the heart of the trouvères' view of sexual passion. Of the song's courtliness
there can be no doubt, for it has the mystique of *la meson le roi artus* where
it has lately been composed. Furthermore, Yvain sings it in such a fashion
that Breuz identifies him at once as a knight from Arthur's retinue. It seems
that the gateway to Arthur's court leads into the capital of love-song in the
best trouvère fashion.

Les Quatre Fils Aymon is not the only epic where heroes sing to express
their good spirits immediately before some disaster overtakes them, nor is
Guiron le courtois the only romance in which singing is associated with an
unsullied and courtly bearing. This contrast suggests that between 1150 and
1200, when the genre of vernacular romance arose, French readers became
increasingly interested in stories where singing is portrayed as it is in *Guiron
le courtois*. Our sense that there is something here to be explored becomes
sharper when we discover that an astute and severe social commentator like
John of Salisbury could be disturbed by a sense that the ethos surrounding
secular song was changing. 'The singing of love-songs in the presence of
men of eminence was once considered in bad taste', he writes in his *Policraticus*
of 1159, 'but now it is considered praiseworthy for men of greater eminence
to sing and play them . . .'.[12] How did the imagery of romance give shape
and colour to the musical activities of 'men of eminence' – of courtly amateurs?

Music and courtliness

In the romances music is usually a gregarious and convivial pleasure to be enjoyed in the hall of some noble or in a royal palace.[13] The occasion is often a full court convened for a great holiday of the liturgical year or for a feast to mark an event in the court's own calendar (a royal wedding, for example).[14] Tablecloths being swept away, trestles being folded against the walls, *vallets* running forward with ewers and towels: these are the signs that music is about to be enjoyed in a lord's Great Hall.[15]

Viewed in this light, music at court seems to be inseparable from the sense of corporate indentity so important in the social life of the twelfth and thirteenth centuries. That was not an age when reasonable men valued solitude overmuch. Unless it were for the purpose of religious retreat, loneliness could be shameful and dangerous. Hermits might be alone for long periods, and so might the mad or destitute; but even these marginals gravitated towards highways and bridges where alms could be had, and within the body of feudal society most of the truly significant relationships were defined by obligations that were publicly owned and just as publicly discharged. A knight who wandered alone invited gossip and disdain; such a man needed heraldry on his shield to show where he belonged, and a household to join at the end of his travels. Even the Cistercian monks, building their monasteries in 'a place of horror and infinite solitude' as the book of Deuteronomy required of them, sought isolation within a communal life where their prayers, like the grain in their barns, could be heaped into a store of sustenance.

From the mid-twelfth century on, a close and complex relationship developed between the full courts convened by kings or magnates and the way in which such courts were portrayed in romance. Chivalry, a richly ethical conception of the mounted warrior's military duties and sportive inclinations, begins to find literary expression in the epics and romances of the 1170s;[16] it imposed many obligations upon the *chevalier*, but none was so easy to fulfil, and yet so charged with romance imagery, as the duty to be playful and festive during major court celebrations. These festivities would include both the full courts and also (as well shall see) the tournaments. The most ardent desire known to chivalry was the passion to win renown in a good lord's wars: to behave like a *proz e vasals* in contemporary terminology. But in practice this ideal could be compromised by political expediency, by brutish cruelty or by sheer cowardice. In contrast, the duty to be playful was easier to perform; it lay most heavily upon the *vallet, esquier* or *chevalier* at exactly the time when it seemed lightest: during some great festivity when presents flowed and when ladies were present in abundance 'exerting themselves to the utmost to be joyful'. For complete success the *escuier, vallet* or *chevalier* had only to suppress his personal anxieties beneath a show of carefree bearing, and that at a time when all things contrived to produce an intoxication of sense:[17]

> ert coustume que cele feste
> estoit si haute et si honeste
> que s'aucunz eust duel au cuer
> n'osast il mostrer a nul fuer
> que nuz s'en alast percevant.

> It was the custom for that festival to be so courtly, and to be conducted
> in such good faith, that if anyone had a sadness in his heart he dared
> not show it in any way so that none could perceive it.

During the thirteenth century one of the most striking developments in the romance portrayal of musical life affects courtly dance under the general name *carole*. Carolling, the performance of ring- and chain-dances, appears to have gradually become an acceptable pastime for young men as *vallets, bachelers* and *esquiers* showed themselves less determined to spend all their leisure with competitive and martial sports. In the romances of Chrestien de Troyes, for example, all of which are customarily dated to the 1170s and 1180s, the *carole* is a predominantly female diversion; amidst the entertainments which grace the Great Hall for the marriage of Erec and Enide, for example, *puceles querolent et dancent*.[18] There is no mention of young men here, and since the dances follow the entertainments offered by minstrels it may be that these *caroles* are being 'performed' by the girls for the pleasure of the onlookers.[19] Compare a passage in Chrestien's *Yvain* where it appears that the pursuits of the young girls and of the young men are again quite distinct. While the *puceles* dance[20]

> D'autre part refont lor labor
> Li legier bacheler qui saillent.

> In another place the sprightly *bachelers* renew their exertions and jump.

It is tempting to assume that Chrestien is witnessing a tradition of unfathomable age in these lines. As we shall see in the next chapter, the strictest churchmen of the Middle Ages never relaxed in their war against the *mulieres* and *puellae* who formed dancing throngs. Their enemy was an ancient one indeed. From King David's triumph through to Chrestien's *Perceval*, for example, it is possible to trace a tradition of women's dance-songs performed in honour of men for their victories in arms.[21] However, the potential of carolling to become an acceptable pastime for young men is latent in the lines from Chrestien's *Yvain* quoted above where the *bachelers* show their agility by leaping. *Bacheler* is a highly expressive word in Old French, denoting a man in his *jeunesse* with the fitness of body and the strength of will required for success in war and in adventure – qualities which are brought together in the favourite epithet *legier*, literally 'light'.[22] Gradually, it would seem, the concept of what made a man *legier* expanded to include a purely pacific display of physical address: the *carole*.

The process is at work in *Hervis de Metz*, an epic of *c*. 1250 whose relationship to developing ideals of courtliness has been described in a most illuminating way by Noiriel.[23] His view of the poem as one that reveals a new concern with courtly bearing is confirmed by the poet's attitudes to dancing. At one point in *Hervis de Metz* the *puceles* dance while the *legier bacheler* engage in the *bohord*, a contest involving equestrian display:[24]

> Behorder vont ci legier baicheler,
> Et ces puceles prandent a queroller.

> the *legier bacheler* engage in the *bohord*, and the girls begin to *carole*.

Later in the same poem, however, the young men are prepared to put their competitive sports aside:[25]

> Carolent i mescin et baceler,
> A l'escremie sont chil Breton alé

> young girls and *bachelers* go carolling there, while the Bretons go off to
> fence

While the *caroles* were sometimes an alternative to the joust, tourney or *bohord*, their ethos was often close to the festive but competitive spirit which prevailed at tournaments. Indeed there are many thirteenth-century narratives in which carolling is associated with the periods of evening celebration that separated the days of a *tournoi*. A striking example is provided by the biography of William Marshall (d.1219), Earl of Pembroke and Regent of England, which an otherwise unknown poet named Jean completed in 1226. In one episode William Marshall sings for a *carole* whilst he and his team are waiting for proceedings to begin at the tournament of Joigny (Yonne), held in 1178.[26] At this time the earl is a knight errant, thirty-one years old, unmarried, and so still in his *jeunesse* according to contemporary reckoning:[27]

> Aucuns a dit: 'Kar carolomes
> Dementiers que ci atendomes,
> Si nos en ennui [e] ra mains'.
> Lors s'entrepristrent par les mains
> Alcun[s] demande: 'Qui sera
> Si corteis qu'il nos chantera?'
> Li Marischa[l]s qui bien chantout
> E qui de riens ne se vantout
> Lors commensa une chansun,
> O simple voiz et o doz son.
> Molt lor plout a toz cels qu'i érent
> E bonement o lui chantérent.

> Someone said: 'Let us dance a *carole* while we wait here, that way we
> shall not be so bored'. Then they took one another by the hand and
> someone said: 'Who will be so courtly as to sing for us?' Then William

> Marshall, who sang very well and who never boasted of his
> accomplishments, began a song in his sweet and pure voice. It greatly
> pleased all those who were there with him and they graciously sang with
> him.

This passage may seem to be as *simple et doz* as William Marshall's voice, and yet there is no guarantee that this scene took place as the poet Jean describes it, writing a generation after the event. Furthermore, the tournament of Joigny is exceptional amongst those which Jean recounts because he signals the presence of woman there – a marked 'romance' touch; elsewhere in his poem the *tournoi* appears to be an exclusively masculine affair.[28] To sweep Jean's passage aside for these reasons, however, is to miss the point, for his debt to romance is what gives these lines their special interest. Jean has surely been reading a work like the *Lancelot*, an influential romance praised by Philippe de Novarre around 1265 for its 'fine and subtle matter'.[29] In the *Lancelot* the youthful hero is admired because[30]

> chantoit a mervoilles bien qant il voloit . . . qant il avoit raison de cui
> il deüst faire joie, nus ne poïst estre tant anvoisiez ne tant jolis.

> he sang marvellously well when he wished to . . . and when he had cause
> that he should be glad nobody could be so animated nor so delightful.

And in the *Lancelot* carolling is one of the diversions which *legiers bachelers* enjoy:[31]

> Qant vint aprés disner, si ne pot estre que mainz de ces legiers bachelers
> ne preïst talanz et envie d'els deporter et esbanoier . . . Li um joerent
> as tables et as eschas et li autre querolent et esgardent les dances des
> dames et des damoiselles.

> After dinner there was no stopping many of the *legiers bachelers* from
> conceiving a wish and desire to divert and entertain themselves . . . some
> played at draughts and chess, and others go carolling and watch the
> dances of ladies and young women.

Recent studies of chivalric narrative have stressed the way some romances like *Lancelot* were regarded, in part, as models for excellent behaviour by contemporary readers.[32] As Philippe de Novarre admired *Lancelot* for its *biaus diz et . . . soutis*, so William Caxton could still call English knights to read 'the noble volumes of Saynt Graal, of Lancelot, of Galaad, of Trystram . . . Ther shalle ye see manhode, curtosye, and gentylnesse'.[33] Putting aside the question of whether William Marshall did indeed sing for a *carole* at the Joigny tournament of 1178, it is certain that his biographer, writing between 1219 and 1226, believed that to put such a scene into his poem would do honour to the memory of the Earl of Pembroke and Regent of England. The insouciance of the scene (knights and ladies are whiling away the time before a tournament) catches the tone of many references to music in romance. How many other knights were influenced by the kind of romance imagery

with which Jean invests his historical hero at this point? It is a short step
from here to the *caroles* which took place at the tournament of Chauvency
(Meuse) in 1285,[34] and to the *caroles* of the celebrated tournament at Hem
(Somme) in 1278, where so many of the noble families of Vermandois and
of the surrounding region acted the part of characters from Arthurian legend.
As the poet Sarasin records in his versified account of the tournament at
Hem:[35]

> De toutes pars puet on vëoir
> Vins et viandes metre as tables;
> N'i oïssiés romans ne fables
> Mais parler d'armes et d'armour.
> Les caroles dessi au jour
> Durerent.

> On all sides one might see wines and meats put on the tables; you might
> hear no romances or tales there but conversation about love and arms
> instead. The *caroles* lasted until the dawn.

To dance in a *carole* during a tournament or full court was not merely to
pass the time; for those whose imaginations inclined them thus, it was also
to act in a romance scene of one's own making. The fallen present dissolved
into the brilliant past of Arthur. Life was sensed, for an instant, to be like
a text, and the texts in their turn became more verisimilar in their presentation
of the *carole* until literature and life were easily confused in the exhilaration
of the moment.

The bachelers *and the* carole

How did carolling become so closely associated with the ideal bearing of
the young knight or knight-to-be, the *vallet* or *bacheler*? Part of the answer
to that question may lie with the urban renewal of the twelfth and thirteenth
centuries. In Chapter 5 we shall see that carolling was a prominent feature
of urban life, and various chronicles suggest that *caroles* were judged to be
an adornment to major civic events. Amongst the greatest occasions were
the royal or aristocratic 'entries' which could inspire the whole citizenry to
celebration with music and dance. The early thirteenth-century annalist
Nicholas de Braia describes such a royal entry in his Latin verse-chronicle
the *Gesta Ludovici VIII Francorum Regis*. He reports that when the king entered
Paris to a rapturous welcome in 1223, 'young men in festive mood, and the
excited girls led their *caroles* through the fields and through the broad cross-
roads'.[36]

Many of the Old French romances (and some of the later epics) describe
fictional entries whose details match those given by Nicholas de Braia point
for point: the same banners in the streets, the same throng of minstrels,
and so on. These entries, together with other kinds of civic show and

procession, rarely failed to excite the authors of narrative poetry and prose alike. In common with some of the Latin sermons to be examined in the next chapter, these narratives often convey the impression that a crowd of girls carolling in the square was one of the first sights a visitor saw upon entering a city in festive mood:[37]

> Et en la place querolent ces pucelles.

In the romance of *Meraugis de Portlesguez* (*c.* 1200–20), by Raoul de Houdenc, the carolling girls issue forth from the city gates as part of a splendid civic procession to meet an approaching party:[38]

> De la cité qui bien fu close
> Voient par mi la porte issir
> La gent et la terre covrir
> Dou pueple qui fors s'en issoit.
> N'i remaint dame qui n'i soit
> Venue, et totes vont chantant.
> Les puceles dont i ot tant
> Vienent chantant et font caroles
> Si granz qu'onques as maieroles
> Ne veïstes greignors; devant
> Vienent li chevalier corant
> Sor les chevaus isneaus et forz.

> They see the citizens issuing out of the gate of the city that was securely surrounded by walls. They cover the land. There was not one lady that did not come, and they all went forward singing. The girls, of whom there were so many there, come forth singing and making *caroles* so large that you never saw the like at the May celebrations; before them come the agile knights on their swift and powerful horses.

There is a similar description of an entry in the romance of *Jehan et Blonde* (*c.* 1270–80) by Philippe de Remi, Sire de Beaumanoir. This time the dancers are *vallets*, presumably the young men in the royal retinue, but also, perhaps, the boys and youths of the town:

> A tant es chevaus remonterent,
> Ne de chevaucier ne finerent
> Devant qu'il entrent en la vile,
> Ou il avoit plus de dis mile
> De bourgoises bien acesmees,
> Qui les routes ont saluëes
> Le roi leur signeur, la roïne.
> La oïssiés maint buisine,
> Mainte moïnel et maint tabour
> Et maint grant cor Sarrazinour,
> Mainte cytole et mainte muse.
> N'est mervelle se on i muse
> C'as courtines c'as estrumens

C'as autres apparillemens
C'as trompes que devant aus vont
C'as danses que li vallet font.

They remount their horses and do not stop riding until they enter the
town where there are more than ten thousand townswomen who have
adorned themselves to greet their lord the king and the queen along the
streets. There might you have heard many a trumpet, many *moinel* [?],
many tabors, many great Saracen horns, many citoles and many
bagpipes. It is no wonder if one is fascinated there by the hangings,
by the instruments, by the other adornments, by the trumpets that go
before them and by the dances of the *vallets*.

Sermons and devotional treatises of the thirteenth century suggest that many
different social classes mingled in the urban *caroles*. Ceremonial entries –
and the festivals which followed them – could draw many social groups
together: the girls and young men of the town, local knights, townsmen
and townswomen, the *serjens, escuiers* and *vallets* of the magnate's retinue and
the sons and daughters of any local nobles in residence in their town-houses.
The reference to *vallets* in the lines above suggests that the festive splendour
of these entries and processions could easily create circumstances in which
pages, young knights, and men aspiring to be knights would find themselves
drawn into a *carole*. Several texts suggest as much: the romance of *Floriant
et Florete* (*c.* 1250), for example:[40]

Ensi vers Palerne s'en vont;
Quant en la cité entré sont
Voient les rües portendües
De courtines a or batües;
Ces dames et ses damoiseles
Courtoises, avenanz et beles,
Ces varlés et cil bacheler
Dancier, treschier et caroler.

[King Loth and King Baudemagus] make their way towards Palerne;
once they have entered the city they see the streets adorned with hangings
of beaten gold; ladies and young women, courtly, fair and beautiful,
vallets and *bachelers* dance and go carolling.

Or again, perhaps, in the mid-fourteenth-century epic of *Godefroid de Bouillon*:[41]

Les borjois et les dames . . .
Véissiés en ces places trescher et caroler.
Esquiers et serjans et puceles canter,
N'i a maison, ne rue c'on i puisse trover
Qui ne soit portendue de paile et de cender.

You might see the townsmen and the ladies carolling in the squares,
squires and *serjans* and young girls singing; there is no street and no
house to be found there that is not adorned with hangings of gold and
silk.

References such as these suggest that urban customs and practices may have influenced the prevailing conception of what was *legier* about a *legier bacheler*. The emergence of carolling as a festive activity for young men during full courts and tournaments, reflected in thirteenth-century narratives, might therefore be interpreted as an opening of masculine, martial decorum towards the festive culture of urban centres when seigneurial retinues were united in celebration with the townspeople amongst whom they lodged. It is impossible to say for certain when this process occurred; the romances cannot be expected to map changes in social custom with any precision. It seems likely that the change was taking place throughout the twelfth century, especially during the second half when both urban expansion and demographic increase were moving towards their peak.

Jeunesse de cuer

The ability to sing for a *carole* in an acceptable way, like the ability to dance in one, was probably widespread amongst the nobility of thirteenth-century France. A *carole* was a relatively informal affair so it seems unlikely that an excellent voice was required (although some, like William Marshall, could sing unusually well). The dance was not a musical performance but a shared experience of sound and movement: spontaneous, gregarious and informal. What then of the surviving trouvère songs, mostly High Style *grands chants*, that did require special gifts? What courtly amateurs (if any) performed these songs, and under what circumstances did these performances take place?

The answers to these questions, insofar as we may hope to answer them, may best be sought amongst the young men and women of the household. As we have seen, a recurrent theme in the romance imagery of festivity is *jeunesse*: a candid and insouciant bearing which was especially gratifying in the young who needed little nurture to make them what they already were by nature. The constant preoccupation of both medieval romance and trouvère song might indeed be described as 'young' love as the Middle Ages understood it: the infatuation which a man was free to feel for any woman until he married, the contract which put an end to his *jeunesse* for ever.[42] It is therefore particularly instructive to examine the role of the young men and boys to whom contemporary writers applied the terms *bacheler* and *vallet*, for these were the individuals whose position at court was particularly susceptible to the influence of romance imagery.

We begin with one of the most celebrated of all the epic heroes: William, Count of Orange. In the two redactions of *Le Moniage Guillaume*, composed during the later twelfth century, this celebrated warrior joins the monastic community at Genevois, having been told by an angel to enter a monastery. When the abbey lands are threatened by robbers William is asked to undertake the hazardous journey which is necessary if fresh provisions are to be fetched. He agrees to go, and sets off with two pack-horses and a young groom (*vallet*) to lead them. As they make their way, William decides that he wishes to enliven his journey with song, so he calls upon the *vallet* to sing:[43]

> Li quens Guillaumes met son vallet devant
> Et si li dist: 'Biaus amis, or entent . . .
> Se sés canchon, par amors, di nous ent,
> Si en irons un poi plus lïement.'
> Li valleś l'ot si respont erraument:
> 'Sire', dist il, 'par le cors saint Vincent,
> Est chou a certes, ou vous m'alés gabant?'

> Count William bids the groom to go before him and then says to him:
> 'Fair friend, listen: if you know any song then I pray you sing it for
> us, thus our journey will be more pleasant.' The groom hears him and
> then replies at once: 'Sire', he said, 'by the body of Saint Vincent, is
> this serious or are you joking?'

The groom, who knows that the hills are full of robbers, has no wish to draw attention to himself by singing. William persists, nonetheless, and the young man eventually begins to sing a narrative song.[44] At first he is timid and Count William finds that his singing is too soft. Just as the *vallet* feared, the robbers hear the song. 'That sounds like a minstrel', says one of them to his companions, 'who has come out of some town, village or city where he sings in the square.'[45]

This episode is designed to reveal William's boldness in the face of danger and to do so with a certain humour. But this does not lessen the interest of the relationship between Count William and the groom whose only acknowledged duty on the journey is to lead the pack-horses. In the twelfth century the obvious way to speak of the relationship between a magnate and a groom attending upon him was to regard the *vallet* as if he were a servant in the lord's household; the second redaction of *Le Moniage Guillaume* makes this clear by calling the groom William's *famle*, a term derived from latin *famulum* (compare *familia*, 'household') and denoting a domestic servant.[46] It seems to come naturally to a count like William to request a song from his servant in this way.

This passage from *Le Moniage Guillaume* highlights an important theme: the theme of service. At a time when most social relations of significance were dominated by the hierarchical structures of feudalism there may often have been occasions when a performance by a gifted amateur was perceived as a form of service: the due which a young man owed to his elders, for example, or the many informal services which every landless and unmarried young man performed in the hope of favour.

As early as *c.* 1000 it is possible to discern the mechanism which drew promising boys into court service, at least in England and Germany. The *Vita* of Bishop Bernward of Hildesheim, composed around 1000 by Thangmar, tells how Bernward used to gather skilled young men to himself and lead them to court when business required him to be there. Some of these young men, Thangmar relates, were scribes, while others were painters, smiths or jewellers.[47] Can we doubt that some of them were also musicians? The various *Lives* of the Englishman St Dunstan (d.988) show how young men with musical talents might be taken to court in the tenth century. A gifted scribe, painter, and 'player upon that instrument which we call "harp" in the native tongue',[48] Dunstan's talents were noticed by a bishop who introduced him to the court of King Athelstan. Indeed, Osbern's *Vita Sancti Dunstani* (*c.* 1090) relates that Dunstan used to play for Athelstan when the king was exhausted by his worldly cares.[49] In the light of these stories we begin to understand why the sons of noblemen were so keen to study stringed instruments at the Abbey of St Gall with the gifted monk Tuotilo (d.915);[50] such talents, if they caught the eye of a bishop who made regular visits to court, could help a young man of good family to preferment in royal or aristocratic service.

Old French literature of the twelfth century shows many signs that young men with musical talents could obtain a privileged position within a royal or noble household. Let us glance at the royal entourage, the *familia regis*.[51] In the twelfth and thirteenth centuries the royal household included chamber-lains whose task was to ensure the security of the king and of the treasure kept near him.[52] They were therefore required to 'sleep before him', exorcising his fear of the dark. At the French royal court these chamberlains were gener-ally drawn from the ranks of the king's unmarried and unlanded retainers, the *juvenes*.[53]

These *juvenes* of the royal chamber make several striking appearances in epics of Charlemagne.[54] In *Aye d'Avignon*, probably composed around 1200, a young member of the royal household named Garnier has enjoyed the privilege of being raised by Charlemagne and his queen; he is currently a young page in the king's household.[55] His main duty, it seems, is to attend the king when he goes to bed and to sing for him before he sleeps:[56]

> Quant le roi veut dormir, Garniers est au couchier,
> E dit chançons e sons por le roi solacier.
> Jamés n'orrez tel honme por gent esbanoier.

> When the king wishes to sleep, Garnier is there when he is bedded,
> and he performs songs and melodies to relax the king; there never was
> such an entertaining man.

As he emerges from boyhood Garnier earns a rich reward for his services as a singer in the royal chamber; when he reaches the age when he may bear arms the Emperor knights him and appoints him to the office of senes-chal.[57]

In *La chanson d'Aspremont* the figure of Charlemagne's retainer-musician is given more circumstantial detail. This time the young man is called Graelens – a significant choice of name, as we shall see:[58]

> Né de Bretagne, parent fu Salemon;
> Deduitor Karle, estoit de sa maison

Et l'ot nori petitet valeton ;
Ne gissoit mais se en sa cambre non.
So siel n'a home mels vïelast un son,
Ne miels desist un bon ver de cançon.
Icestui fist le premier lai breton.

[Graelens] is a Breton, a relative of Salemon ; Charlemagne's
entertainer, he was a member of his household where the king had raised
him from the time that he was a little boy ; he sleeps nowhere if not
in the king's chamber. There is no man under the skies who could fiddle
a melody better nor who might sing a song in a more accomplished
fashion. He it was who composed the first Breton *lai*.

Graelens does not seem to be a minstrel ; the poet calls him a *deduitor* ('enter-tainer'), and this is a rare word in Old French despite the abundance of references to minstrels in both the epics and the romances of the period 1100–1300.[59] Like Garnier in *Aye d'Avignon*, Graelens is connected with the royal bedchamber for he invariably sleeps there. The poet intends us to understand that this young man has been placed in Charlemagne's household as a young boy to perform small services ; at the same time he would be trained in stablecraft, swordplay and the other skills so often mentioned in connection with the raising of young men (Figure 6).[60]

To this extent the figures of Garnier and Graelens are similar. Yet the poet of *La chanson d'Aspremont* has gone further with Graelens, for this *petitet valeton* also plays the fiddle. Furthermore, Graelens is a composer : 'he it was who composed the first Breton *lai*'. This is perhaps the most revealing detail of all, not only because Graelens is presented as a kind of trouvère, but also because the poet has immersed him in the imagery of the new romances. To say that Graelens composed the first Breton *lai* is to swathe him in the mystique so powerfully evoked in the *Lais* of Marie de France, the celebrated collection of narrative poems produced in the third quarter of the twelfth century.[61] In contrast to the earlier epics like the *Song of Roland*, the *Lais* of Marie tell some brief but notable stories in which love is often the most important theme. Furthermore, Marie gives these stories of love a mystique by claiming that the original events happened in *Bretaigne* – Britain before the coming of the English.[62] Marie also says that the events she recounts inspired the musicians of ancient *Bretaigne* (including Tristan) to produce commemorative instrumental compositions.[63] This mythology endowed instrumental playing with a romance aura which it was to retain – at least as a motif in chivalric narrative – well into the fifteenth century.[64] Graelens, a fiddle-player, takes his name from the title of a poem by one of Marie's imitators.[65] By calling this *valeton* Graelens, and by making him not only a composer of *lais* but also the originator of the genre, the author of *La chanson d'Aspremont* associates him with the mystique of a figure like Tristan. As we read in Marie de France :[66]

Tristram, ki bien saveit harper,

Figure 6 *The coronation and celebratory banquet for Henry, son of Henry II of England. At the bottom right-hand of the picture a musician, clearly a young boy, sits and plays the harp. His hair is held back by an elegant headband, and in accordance with general usage at this time he secures the harp on his lap by wrapping the base of the instrument in its bag. From the Becket Leaves. London, British Library, MS Loan 88, f.3r. English, thirteenth century. Reproduced by permission of the owner and of the British Library.*

En aveit fet un nuvel lai;

Tristan, who knew well how to play the harp, made a new *lai* about it [i.e. the event narrated in Marie's *Chevrefoil*].

Official documents and chronicles reveal so little about amateur music-making at court that we can scarcely hope to trace the historical counterparts of Garnier and Graelens in their pages. Nonetheless, we may glimpse a musician of this kind in one of the thirteenth-century *Lives* of St Louis (reigned 1248–54). Emphasising the piety of the king, the author reports that King Louis did not sing secular songs (*les chançons du monde*) and never permitted the members of his household to sing them; however, there was a squire in the king's retinue who had sung such things excellently *el tens de sa joenece*, and the king told him to give them up, teaching him instead a Marian antiphon and the 'hymn' *Ave maris stella* 'which was a very difficult thing to learn'.[67] This is a suggestive story, for in his youth this squire would have been a *vallet*, like Garnier and Graelens, and he had clearly acquired a reputation for excellence in the performance of secular songs. This reputation seems to have lingered about him into later life and caused the king to single him out for genial correction – indeed for special favour, since the biographer goes on to relate that the squire and St Louis sometimes sang these plainchant items together.[68] To judge by *La chanson d'Aspremont*, it was already possible by *c*. 1200 for such activities to be endowed with a sense of history – or rather, with a sense of *estoire*: an awareness of the dignity and exhilaration that could derive from imagining the present in terms of the distant past as revealed in narratives.

Music and eloquence

The fundamental sense of the Old French word *vallet* appears to have been 'a young male individual';[69] a *vallet* might therefore be a male child newly born, a boy or an adolescent not yet knighted. The main current of meaning, however, tended strongly towards the semantic area 'young boy, youth'. Thus in Gautier de Tournai's *Gille de Chyn*, a valuable record of social life in Picardy and the Walloon area, a *vallet* is mentioned who is fifteen years old and the son of a German count; 'he was not yet a knight'.[70] In the epic of *Doon de Maience* a *valleton* (the diminutive is perhaps an affectionate one) is seven years old.[71]

The aristocratic courts of twelfth- and thirteenth-century France incorporated a population of *vallets* being trained, above all, in the use and maintenance of horses and arms.[72] Several texts suggest that musical skills were much appreciated in any young person who possessed them. The late thirteenth-century romance of *Sone de Nansay* tells how the hero, born to an aristocratic family, begins his education at an early age. He learns letters, becomes accomplished at chess and draughts, acquires mastery over the dogs and birds used for hunting and becomes a fine swordsman – all by the age of twelve.[73] Board-games and hunting, however, are not the only arts of peace in which he excels:[74]

> Sonez avoit. xii. ans passés,
> Plus biaus enfes n'estoit trouvés
> Ne nus enfes mieus ne cantoit.

> Sone has now reached the age of twelve; a more handsome child was
> not to be found nor did any child sing better.

Despite the hyperbole, there is nothing unbelievable in the presentation of a boy who is praised for his singing at twelve years old, and some romances (and later epics under the influence of romance) suggest the importance of such *vallets* in keeping the festive energy of a household alive. Time and time again it is the *vallets*, together with the young girls of the court, who enliven the household on greater occasions. In *Guillaume de Palerne* (*c*. 1300), for example:[75]

> La peussiés oir grant joie
> Chanter vaslès et damoiseles.

While in *Jehan et Blonde* by the famous legist and romancer Philippe de Remi, Sire de Beaumanoir, a courtly party enters a city enlivened by the *danses que li vallet font*.[76] In *Les Quatre Fils Aymon*, Charlemagne's court gathers for Pentecost in Paris, and[77]

> Grant joie i ot le jor el palais honoré,
> Assez i ont vallet et chanté et joé.

There is a wealth of evidence in the romances to reveal the qualities that were expected of the *vallet*.[78] As we have seen, the physical alacrity which he would require as a knight were displayed as he danced *caroles* with the young women of the household; ideally, he should be a boy *qui le corps ot legier*. It was even more of a credit to his masters if – as Jean Renart says of one young man – he was a *vallet . . . qui de chanter avoit le los*.[79]

These were not the only virtues expected of a *vallet*, however. There was also that quality of wisdom expressed in (moderate) eloquence of speech, *sagesse*,[80] and here we begin to approach the trouvères and their love-songs in the High Style. In the year 1203 the trouvère Conon de Béthune was conducting delicate negotiations at Constantinople on behalf of the Crusaders; he was chosen for this task because he was 'wise and most eloquent' (*sages et bien emparlez*).[81] This is the only contemporary comment we have on the personal qualities of a trouvère relevant to his poetry and to the way in which his art was appreciated. There can be little doubt that contemporaries would have regarded Conon's love-songs in the High Style as a manifestation of his scrupulous judgement and the considered eloquence of his speech when the occasion demanded. In trouvère songs, does the lover not generally address his lady with the delicacy of an ambassador newly come to court?

The qualities attributed to Conon de Béthune – that he was *sages et bien emparlez* – are exactly those which seem to have been valued in these young attendants. We hear of a *vallet* who is *bien . . . emparlés* and who is assigned the task of carrying letters,[82] while in Jean Renart's romance of *Guillaume de Dole* (1228), Lienor, sister of the hero Guillaume, seeks a *valles* who is *plus sages* so that she may find a messenger fit to carry a letter to court. 'I have one', replies a knight, 'and he is handsome and gracious.'[83] In the Anglo-Norman romance of *Waldef* the task of carrying an important missive is entrusted to a *vaslet* who is *sage . . . et bien parlant*.[84] The task of carrying a letter, of course, required a *vallet* to be much more than a mere courier. When he arrived at his destination he had to make a favourable impression upon those who saw him, and he was required to explain his purpose before the letter was opened and to receive any reply that was to be given. In short, he had to be – like Conon de Béthune – an ambassador and negotiator, speaking both well and to the point. Such missions will not have been entrusted to mere boys, but the eloquence of a *vallet* was especially pleasing in one who had barely emerged from adolescence.

The social position of *vallets*, and the imagery with which they were surrounded by their elders, may often have made those who could sing well seem ideal as performers of courtly song, both of the informal, impromptu kind used for dancing and of the High Style variety as cultivated by the trouvères. Fortunately, Jean Renart's romance of *Guillaume de Dole* contains a passage which suggests that this is exactly what happened. Renart has a sharp eye for the good qualities of these young attendants and more than once he draws attention to a *vallet* 'who was praised for his singing'.[85] The most striking scene occurs when a *vallet* performs a High Style song by a noted trouvère, the Vidame de Chartres (Music example 4). The emperor of Germany, a single knight and a minstrel named Jouglet are present:[86]

> [li bons rois] onques n'ot conpegnon ne per
> q'un sol chevalier et Juglet,
> s'oïrent chanter un vallet
> La bone chançon le Vidame
> de Chartres . . .
>
> *Quant la sesons del douz tens s'asseüre . . .*
>
> [The good king] never had any friend or companion with him other than a single knight and Jouglet; and they heard a *vallet* singing this fine song by the Vidame de Chartres . . .

As I have argued elsewhere, this is one of the most convincing descriptions of musical performance in Old French literature.[87] The quietness – almost domesticity – of the scene, the routine character of the performer (a young household servant), the citation of a specific song by a named trouvère: all of these details suggest that the passage may be rooted in contemporary practice. Such performances might be expected of any *vallet* in a household *qui de chanter avoit le los*.

Many passages in *Guillaume de Dole* help to clarify the status and function

Example no. 4

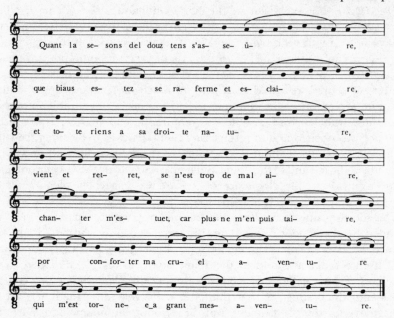

Quant la se- sons del douz tens s'as- se- ü- re,

que biaus es- tez se ra- ferme et es- clai- re,

et to- te riens a sa droi- te na- tu- re,

vient et ret- ret, se n'est trop de mal ai- re,

chan- ter m'es- tuet, car plus ne m'en puis tai- re,

por con- for- ter ma cru- el a- ven- tu- re

qui m'est tor- ne- e_a grant mes- a- ven- tu- re.

of *vallets* in Jean Renart's poem. Apart from carrying important letters, one of their principal tasks is to bring the towels and basins of water to table at the end of a meal. They are sometimes called upon to search the household for courtiers who are required in any place (to 'page' them, indeed; the etymology of this word is not far to seek). One of the *vallets* who performs this service is the son of a count.[88] When guests are lodged away from the main court complex the duties of the *vallets* include laying out fruit and wine in an upper room for when the guests return from festivities with their host; in church, a knight's *vallet* may be expected to carry his master's offering to the altar.[89]

Jean Renart's passage takes us directly to the trouvère chansonniers. But what of the motet manuscripts? Are there any indications that *vallets* sometimes had expertise in polyphonic music? Unfortunately, this is not a question that the literary sources can answer for the most part. References to polyphony are rare in Old French literature; indeed they are hard to find in any medieval writings apart from the highly specialised treatises devoted to that very subject.[90] It is difficult to understand why the Old French authors, who were otherwise so keen to refer to the social and festive aspects of music, should have deliberately filtered a musical phenomenon out of their works if they knew it to be common; it is therefore tempting to conclude that the rarity with which poets and narrators mention polyphony is a true reflection, in general terms, of the content of contemporary secular music-making in aristocratic circles.

For a sign that things may sometimes have been different amongst the *vallets* we must advance almost a hundred years beyond Jean Renart. The early fourteenth-century poet Jean de Condé describes in his poem *Li dis dou levrier* the education of a young *vallet* (also called *damoisaus* and *escuyers*) at the hands of a cleric.[91] Not yet twenty years of age, he is the son of a knight. He speaks well (he is *boins amparliers/Pour parolles moustrer en court*) and is regarded by all as precocious in his good sense and wisdom because he is *moult saiges de son tans*. The cleric teaches the young boy some Latin, and instructs him how to read both script and plainchant notations (*lire et bien canter*).[92] However, the musical element in his lessons goes further than plainchant:[93]

> Quintier, doubler et descanter,
> S'aprist lais, contes et rommans,
> Les fais d'amours et les commans
> Mainte cançon et mains biaus dis . . .

> He learned to 'fifth', to 'double' and to descant, he learned *lais*, stories
> and romances, the deeds and requirements of love, many a song and
> many fine *dits* . . .

This seems a very comprehensive preparation for the task of making oneself pleasant at court. It is presumably a somewhat idealised account of the education which the sons of wealthy knights received from their clerical tutors. Nonetheless, the presence in this passage of at least two terms which definitely imply some polyphonic practice, *quintier* and *descanter*, is most arresting. *Descanter* may imply the ability to take part in polyphony and perhaps even to compose or to improvise it. *Quintier*, as Sarah Fuller has argued, probably denotes the ability to sing an improvised, note-against-note counterpoint beginning on a unison or octave and then stepping into parallel fifths with the main melody (returning to a unison or octave at the ends of phrases according to set patterns that were described in 'fifthing' treatises and which could be learned by heart).[94] The meaning of *doubler* cannot be established with certainty; it may mean 'to sing in octaves' perhaps with added decorations of the material being 'doubled'.[95]

Very few pieces of French secular polyphony survive from the time of Jean de Condé to elucidate what kind of music may be implied by this reference to a *vallet* who can *descanter*; indeed it is the occurrence of Jean's reference at this crucial but obscure moment in the history of the polyphonic chanson that makes these lines so tantalising. Despite this uncertainty, however, a two-part piece included in the seventh book of the *Speculum musice* (c. 1330) by Jacques de Liège may resemble the kind of music which Jean de Condé has in mind when he speaks of *quintier*.[96] The beginning is shown in Music example 5. The poem of this piece is a *pastourelle* whose text is cast in a form of meridional and macaronic romance, and the text-setting is in a note-against-note style where the words (only supplied for the lower part in the manuscript) are surely to be sung in both parts. The texted sections are followed by hocketing passages. In some places (the opening bars, for example) the polyphonic texture of this piece is little more than a set of parallel fifths as produced

by the technique of fifthing, and it may be legitimate to regard *A l'entrade d'Avrillo* as a tidied version of an unwritten practice. The hocket sections, of course, with their careful planning of notes and rests, are another matter.

Puceles *and chaplain-tutors*

Vallets, however, were not the only young persons whose presence helped to give the major phases of court life a festive tone. Many romances suggest that young girls – *damoiseles* and *puceles* – were just as conspicuous. For the most part these girls were the daughters of the lord and of men currently fulfilling a term of military or administrative service in a way that allowed them to be accompanied by their families. Until they married there was often little for them to do, for they were not expected to serve an apprenticeship in the stables, to hunt with dogs, to fence or to carve at table. However, they were expected to acquire certain gentle arts in readiness for a summons: a call to open a book and recite some romance of Thebes, perhaps, or to sing and thus while away a few moments which their betters would otherwise have found heavy. Indeed the romances of the thirteenth century acknowledge the importance of music in the contemporary ideal of womanhood with more candour than they treat of anything comparable in the deportment of men. Here, for example, is a young girl named Fresne in the early thirteenth-century romance of *Galeran de Bretagne*; in spite of what she imagines to be her low birth, Fresne finds herself to be a person of courtly tastes:[97]

> Mon cuer, madame, si m'aprent
> Que je ne face aultre mestier
> Le jour fors lire mon saultier
> Et faire euvre d'or ou de soie,
> Oÿr de Thebes ou de Troye,
> Et en ma herpe lays noter,
> Et aux eschez autry mater,
> Ou mon oisel sur mon poign pestre:
> Souvent ouÿ dire a mon maistre
> Que tel us vient de gentillesse . . .

> My heart, my lady, directs me to do no other office than to read my
> psalter and to embroider with gold threads or with silk, to hear romances
> of Thebes or of Troy, to play *lais* on my harp, to checkmate another
> at chess or feed my hawk on my wrist; I have often heard my master
> say such behaviour springs from nobility . . .

At first sight this passage seems almost too good to be true; here are nearly all of the female accomplishments which we have come to associate with a romanticised Middle Ages when aristocratic ladies supposedly span in their bowers. However, this is not merely a nineteenth-century romanticism; it is also a medieval one, for as early as 1228 a poet like Jean Renart could evoke an ancient time in which women had been thus. When the hero of Renart's *Guillaume de Dole* asks his mother to sing, she replies with a smile:[98]

> Biaus filz, ce fu ça en arriers
> que les dames et les roïnes
> soloient fere lor cortines
> et chanter les chançons d'istoire!

> Fair son, it was in olden times that ladies and queens used to sing *chansons
> de toile* as they worked on their embroidery.

Nonetheless, Fresne's account of her aristocratic tastes in *Galeran de Bretagne* clearly contains an element of realism, for her belief in the gentility of music, board-games and embroidery is directly confirmed by thirteenth-century manuals of deportment addressed to women. The author of an adaptation of Ovid's *Ars amatoria* has this advice for young girls:[99]

> Chanter est noble chose et bele,
> especiäument a pucele . . .
> Metre doiz ton entencion
> a sonner le psalterion
> ou timbre ou giterne ou citole.

> Singing is a fair and noble thing, especially in a girl . . . You should
> apply yourself to playing the psalterion, the timbre, giterne or citole.

This is a little too close to Ovid for comfort, perhaps,[100] and we may feel
more at ease with the following passage from *Le chastoiement des dames* by
Robert of Blois, a poet whose works are dedicated in one manuscript to
Hue Tyrel, seigneur de Poix (1230–60), and to his son Guillaume (1260–
1302):[101]

> Se vos avez bon estrument
> De chanter, chantez baudemant.
> Beaux chanters en leu et en tans
> Est une chose molt plaisanz.
> Mais saichiez que par trop chanter
> Puet on bien beaul chant aviler.
> Por ce le dient mainte gent:
> Beaux chanters ennue sovant . . .
> Se vos estes en compaignie
> De gent de pris et l'on vos prie
> De chanter, nu davez laisier,
> Por vos meïsme solacier.
> Quant vos estes priveemant,
> Le chanter pas ne vos desfant.

> If you have a good singing voice, sing gladly. In the right place at the
> right time, beautiful singing is a most delightful thing. But you should
> know that one can spoil good music by singing too much; wherefore
> many people say that good singing often tires the ear . . . If you are
> in the company of courtly people and you are asked to sing, you should
> not refuse simply for your own convenience. I do not forbid you the
> pleasure of singing when you are alone.

Here Robert of Blois not only anticipates that woman will sing for their
own pleasure but also that they will be asked to perform before *gent de pris*.
Above all, it would seem, young women were expected to motivate and
enhance the most conspicuous of all court festivities: the *carole*. In the telling
phrase used around 1280 by Gerard d'Amiens, a large company of 'young
girls trained in making festivity'[102] was a great asset to any occasion when
the noble families of a region were gathered together for a full court. The
Arthurian romance of *Escanor*, from which I have taken those words, is particularly rich in references to the role of *dames, damoiseles, meschines et puceles* on
such occasions, and in these passages we surely find a reflection of the festive
decorum that surrounded Edward I of England and his wife Eleanor of Castile
for whom the romance was composed. In this poem the girls and ladies may
dance *caroles* alone to entertain the squires and knights wounded in the day's
jousting,[103] while on another occasion they lead the young men to the dances
with their 'gracious white hands' and exert themselves as much as they can
to ensure that the festivities will be a success.[104] On these occasions the *dames*

and *puceles* were required to sing or to lead the simple refrains that are so liberally quoted in *Escanor*.

A magnate like William Marshall could require his daughters to sing for him when he chose; it was their duty to enter silently when called, to sing, and then to accept any criticism that the listeners felt inclined to offer them. In this way a group of *dames qui le renon/avoient d'estre bien chantanz*[105] at court was a reserve of musical talent and free entertainment to supplement the activities of the minstrels whose demands upon attention (and upon the purse) were not always in season.

Several romances suggest that young women with good voices could gain a reputation for their musical skills. Among the most striking is *Guiron le courtois* of *c*. 1235.[106] This time the expert performer is no less a person than a relative of King Arthur himself, the damoisele Orgayne, 'who sang better than any lady in the world and who most delighted in it'.[107] Her reputation is such that Gawayn, who knows that a new song has come to court, asks her if she can learn it somehow and then teach it to him.[108] Later, Orgayne sings by the riverside where she is clearly the centre of attention. The passage is worth quoting at length since it provides an admirably detailed description of a courtly singing-party:[109]

> Or dit le contes que apres mengier celui ior estoient les dames et les damoiseles as loges . ces loges estoient de fust et estoient droitement faites sor la rivere de lombre . entrels estoit la reine de scoce . . . poi auoit de cheualiers . entrels auoient vn harpeor qui lor harpoit vn chant que vn cheualiers de norgales auoit fait . tant nouelement . la damoisele qui orgayne estoit apellee disoit le chant. et cil larpoit.

> Now the story relates how that day, after the meal, the ladies and the girls were in the loggias made of wood and placed directly on the riverbank in the shade. Among them was the Queen of Scotland . . . and there were a few knights. In their company was a harpist who was harping for them a song that had just been composed by a knight from north Wales. The girl who was called Orgayne sang the song while the man harped.

Here are all the usual images of musical life in ancient *Bretaigne*: the harps, the talk of new songs, and the constant reminders that the story is set in the Celtic realms of ancient Britain ('the Queen of Scotland . . . a knight from north Wales . . .'). Nonetheless, this passage may reflect the circumstances of informal music-making during full courts, and the important place of women in performing the songs of the trouvères.

A second romance can be approached with more confidence. Once again we turn to the Anglo-Norman biography of William Marshall, Earl of Pembroke and Regent of England. The most striking musical scene in the *Histoire de Guillaume le Maréchal* takes place during William's last days in 1219 – a recent memory when the poem was composed. The details of the following events were probably transmitted to the poet from the eye-witness account of the Marshall's great friend, Jean d'Erly.[110] William, now infirm and near death, is lying in his chamber. He divests himself of all his worldly responsibilities: his high office of state, his lands and his garments among them. At one point he calls Jean d'Erly to his bedside and says: 'I shall tell you something extraordinary: I have a great desire to sing.' 'Sire, sing', says Jean, 'and throw your heart and mind into it; if it comforts you then it will be well done.'[111] But the spirit of the nightingale, which helped William to sing so well at the tournament of Joigny many years before, is soon put to flight by the spirit of the owl. 'Quiet John', says William with a sudden change of heart, 'such singing would not be good for me; the people here would think me mad'.[112] This was neither the time nor the place for the Earl of Pembroke to sing. His appetite for music has not been quelled, however, by the sobering realisation that he now lies on his deathbed, so Henry Fitzgerald, standing nearby, suggests that William should order his daughters into the chamber to sing for him. 'They were summoned, and they came, for they willingly obeyed his every command.'[113] Maheut is told to sing first, then Joane:[114]

> ... el n'en ot talent,
> Car molt esteit sa vie amére.
> Mès le commandement del pére
> Nevolt el mie trespasser.
> Lor[e]s comença a chanter,
> Car a son pére voleit plère,
> E el le saveit molt bien fère,
> E dist uns vers d'une chanson
> O simple voiz et o doz son.
> 'Joane, chantez, com qu'il prenge.'
> Un vers dist d'une rotruenge ...

> ... She had no desire [to sing] for she was full of distress. Nonetheless
> she did not wish to disobey her father's command in the least degree.
> Then she began to sing because she wished to please her father and she
> was skilled in the art. She sang a stanza of a song with a sweet, direct voice.
> 'Joane, sing, as the mood takes you.' She sang a stanza of a *rotruenge* ...

The *rotruenge* is not a well-represented genre, nor are its formal characteristics entirely clear; however, the use of a recurrent refrain may have been one of the diagnostic characteristics of the form (Music example 6).[115] It is also possible that by this time *rotruenge* was a somewhat old-fashioned term for a courtly monophonic song of any kind.[116] Be that as it may, there can be little doubt that the author of William Marshall's biography has carried us directly to the realm of trouvère monody as we know it from the surviving chansonniers.

How did William Marshall's daughters gain access to such pieces? Did they own written copies of them, and was there already a written tradition of trouvère monody *c.* 1220? These are wide-ranging and controversial ques-

Example no. 6

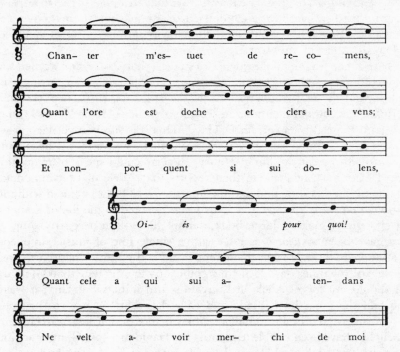

Chan– ter m'es– tuet de re– co– mens,

Quant l'ore est doche et clers li vens;

Et non– por– quent si sui do– lens,

Oi– és pour quoi!

Quant cele a qui sui a– ten– dans

Ne velt a– voir mer– chi de moi

tions which cannot be treated here in anything like the fashion they deserve.[117] Nonetheless it may be said that several literary sources of this period suggest that there may well have been some kind of written tradition by *c.* 1220. In the prologue to *Guillaume de Dole* (1228) Jean Renart leaves us in no doubt that the lyric poems inserted into his narrative (including songs by noted trouvères such as the Vidame de Chartres) were intended to be sung when the person reading the romance aloud reached them.[118] Unless the songs were very well known in Renart's circle – which is conceivable – then musical notation would have been required for them. There is none in the single surviving manuscript of *Guillaume de Dole*,[119] yet Renart seems to be alluding to the presence of notation in his own authorial copy when he says that he has 'caused beautiful songs to be notated' in his romance (*fet noter biaus chans*;[120] there seems to be no other plausible translation of these words). Renart clearly regards his practice of interpolating lyrics into a narrative as an innovation for which he can claim the credit; was it also an innovation, at this date, to record the music of trouvère songs using the plainchant notation employed in almost all of the trouvère sources and which had been mastered by every household chaplain and confessor worthy of his office? We cannot say, although it seems clear that Renart's own assessment of what is new about his work lies in the fact that the songs are interpolated into a narrative, and not that they are recorded in writing. And even though there is no music in the surviving manuscript of *Guillaume de Dole* (an omission whose significance is hard to judge) we may be sure that an author of 1228 in north-east France – the best place for a connoisseur of French courtly monody – could consider the possibility of putting written forms of trouvère songs, both words and music, into a literary work.

There is one fragment of evidence to suggest that aristocratic women sometimes commissioned books containing musical notation, and it carries us back well beyond the first trouvères. In his *Estoire des Engleis* (*c.* 1139) the Anglo-Norman poet Gaimar mentions an account of the life of King Henry I (reigned 1100–35) produced by a certain David.[121] This was surely a vernacular work in verse, for Gaimar calls it a *chançon* and further says that if he, Gaimar, also wished to treat the life of Henry, then he could speak of many things passed over by David.[122] He then reports that Adele of Louvain 'made a great book' of this song and had the first stanza (? laisse) notated with music (*Le primer vers noter par chant*).[123] This song, devoted to the life of a king and big enough to make a large book, cannot have been a courtly song, and may have been a *chanson de geste* with a single line of music supplied for what appears to have been the accepted method of performance (at least in the time of Johannes de Grocheio, significantly later in date than Gaimar).[124] We should not forget Adele of Louvain's own initiative in this; it was she who had the great book made and caused the first 'verse' to be notated with music – and this almost half a century before the earliest trouvères.

Scholars have been unable to identify the David to whom Gaimar attributes this song on the life of Henry I.[125] He was surely a cleric and may well have been a chaplain in Adele's household. Be that as it may, we may suspect that such domestic chaplains played a crucial role in developing a young person's musical talents to the point where they might perform the courtly song repertory of the trouvères. It is well-known that these chaplains were often entrusted with the task of teaching the young persons of a household – and especially the girls – how to read and write; who else was there in the *mesnie* with the time and the ability to discharge this duty?

Literary works, and especially the romances, are our principal source of information about the accomplishments of these chaplains and about the content of their teaching during the twelfth and thirteenth centuries. One of the most striking accounts appears in the anonymous romance of *Galeran*, probably composed *c.* 1220 and formerly attributed to Jean Renart.[126] Here we encounter a monastic chaplain named Lohiers who is assigned the task of educating the young persons brought up in the care of the abbess. He is the image of courtliness:[127]

> Il ot la bouche bien apperte
> A bien chanter et a bien lire . . .
> Si s'en savoit bien entremectre
> De trouver layz et nouviaux chans;
> Moult fu de biaux deduiz trouvans
> Et en françoys et en latin . . .

He was well trained in the arts of singing and reading aloud . . . and
he knew how to compose *lais* and new songs; he often composed
delightful things in both French and Latin . . .

No doubt there is an element of hyperbole here, and yet the figure of a
chaplain whose interests include the composition of songs in French and
Latin is quite believable and finds a historical counterpart in a man like
the thirteenth-century theologian Henri Bate.[128] Such chaplains, if competent,
were literate and able to read the neumatic notation which was used both
for plainchant and for the repertory of trouvère song when it first makes
an appearance in writing in the second half of the thirteenth century. What
could be more natural than for a chaplain with an interest in courtly monody
to pass on the requisite skills to a promising young pupil?

CHAPTER FIVE

THE *CAROLE*, THE PULPIT
AND THE SCHOOLS

The first chapter of this book showed theologians coming to terms with one
of the Church's ancient enemies, the professional secular musician. This
chapter is devoted to another adversary: the women who participated in
the public dances called *caroles* (Latin *c(h)oreae*). These entertainments, often
depicted in the visual arts of the thirteenth century (Figure 7), were popular

Figure 7   *A carole. London, British Library, MS Egerton 1151, f.47. Reproduced by
permission.*

throughout the Middle Ages. The rulings of ecclesiastical councils, sermons, and narrative sources are full of references to them, for the ecclesiastical authorities generally regarded them as an abomination – an evocation of the Israelite's blasphemy as they danced before the golden calf, and of Salome's wickedness in Herod's palace. The testimony of Christian history, therefore, from God's first unfolding of his purpose in the wilderness, through the advent of Christ, to the present struggles of the Church Militant showed that *caroles* were evil. For many churchmen the women in floral crowns who danced in *caroles* bore the terrible curse of Isaiah 3:16–17: 'the daughters of Zion are haughty, and walk with stretched-forth necks and wanton eyes . . . Therefore the Lord will smite with a scab the crown of the head of the daughters of Zion.'

As we shall see, the expansion of the European population between 1150 and 1300, together with the changing shape of cities all over France, made these dances a familiar spectacle in fields, streets, squares and cemeteries that lay within the city walls. Many opposed the *carole*, but in the thirteenth century others began to take a more tolerant view. These men, who possessed the intellectual and spiritual energy to overcome a millennium of monastic hostility to dancing, were generally university-trained theologians, and the collision of views between these schoolmen and their traditionalist colleagues reveals the owl and the nightingale in their most warlike aspect. To compare what the schoolmen have to say about the *carole*, for example, with what the travelling preachers and confessors write on the same subject, is to gain a vivid sense of what the coming of scholasticism meant to the way literate men looked at the musical life around them.

This chapter explores the abundant evidence which sermons and other works of religious instruction, mostly unpublished, provide about the social context of the *carole*. These enable us to form a picture of a social experience involving the form of music which, as I have emphasised elsewhere,[1] simply *was* secular music as far as many contemporaries were concerned. Preachers and theologians – even those active in Paris – say little about motets or conducti, but on the subject of carolling they are almost unstoppable. Who took part in these dances, and when were they held? What was their significance to the people who enjoyed them? Why do the preachers spend so much energy denouncing *caroles*? How did court culture and popular culture interact in the *carole*? These are some of the questions which this chapter will address.

Sermon-materials, for the most part still unprinted or unedited to modern standards, are a fine source of information about the *carole*. These include not only sermons themselves, many of which include *exempla* which mention the *carole*, but also the treatises upon the vices and virtues that were compiled in great numbers during the thirteenth century, often as a preaching aid.[2] Some of these manuals are of truly encyclopedic scope and it is not uncommon for them to incorporate entire chapters on the *carole*. In addition there are books of stories for use in the pulpit. Some of these stories, no doubt, are old concoctions whose ingredients had lain simmering in what Tolkien has called 'the cauldron of story' time out of mind, while others have a known origin in the Bible or in the writings of the Fathers. *Exempla* of this kind have little to reveal. The intensive preaching ministry of the friars, however, produced many new *exempla* of the first interest to social historians in that they relate events within living memory, complete with named places and (sometimes) dates.[3]

These stories include some intriguing references to carolling. Here as an illustration is a cautionary tale preserved by the Dominican friar Thomas of Cantimpré in his collection of stories entitled the *Bonum universale de apibus* ('A Universal Profit Extracted From [the study of] Bees'), completed in 1263. It reveals the kind of material that many *exemplum* collections preserve, but also shows how information bearing upon the social history of music in the Middle Ages is often to be found in literary sources where it is least expected. The mere title of Thomas's work makes it seem an unlikely source of information about the *carole*, but the location of the material within the book is more surprising still, for it appears in a section on clairvoyance:[4]

> Exemplum . . . de medico qui puellam suaviter canentem mox morituram praedixit.

> Quod etiam homines sagaci ingenio futura prevideant, tali exemplo probabo. Comes Lossensis in confinio Brabantiae, Ludowicus nomine, physicum expertum valde in comitatu habebat. Qui cum per villam quandam iuxta choream haberet transitum, puella quaedam pulcra facie cum mira suavitate vocis chorizantibus praecinebat. Quam quidem Comes per horam nimis intuitus diligenter cum familia pertransivit, et cum stupentem videret physicus: Miraris, inquit, o Comes, vocem et pulchritudinem praecinentis, magis iam miraberis morituram. Vix verba complevit physicus, et clamor validus in villa sublatus est, cognovitque directis nunciis dictam praecentricem morte subita corruisse.

> An *exemplum* of a physician who predicted that a girl singing sweetly was about to die.

> By means of this *exemplum* I shall prove that men of great skill can predict the future. There was a count of Loosbroek in the province of Brabant, named Ludwig, who had a highly expert physician in his household. One day, when his passage through a certain town led him by a *carole*, a girl with a beautiful face and a wonderful sweetness of voice was leading the dance. The count crossed the town with his retinue and admired her excessively for an hour. When the physician saw him in this reverie he said: 'You marvel, count, at the voice and the beauty of the woman who leads the dance. You should rather marvel that she is about to die.' These words were scarcely out of the physician's mouth when a mighty wailing went up in the town, and he learned, having sent messengers there to find out, that the girl had suddenly collapsed and died.

It scarcely matters whether this event really took place. We can accept the plausibility of the basic circumstances without committing ourselves to faith in every detail, and Thomas would not have told this story if it made no sense to show a count of Loosbroek riding out one day and being struck by the beauty of a girl in a *carole* as he passes by. Indeed the realism of stories like this one helps us to reconstruct the world of events and sentiment that sustained the imagery of contemporary dance-songs and *pastourelles*; it is possible to recognise how encounters such as this could have nourished the 'popular' ethos of so much courtly poetry with its chance meetings in an outdoor setting:[5]

> L'autrier en une praele
> trouvai pastore chantant;
> mult fu avenant et bele
> et cortoise et bien parlant.
> Trestout maintenant
> descendi jus de ma sele
> et li dis: 'Ma damoisele,
> m'amor vos present
> jolivetement.'

> The other day in a meadow I came across a shepherdess singing; she was very fair and beautiful, courteous and gracious of speech. Immediately I got down from my saddle and said to her: 'My young lady, with a gay heart I offer you my love.'

Caroles *and city limits*

It is an English theologian of the early fourteenth century, the Dominican friar John Bromyard, who records one of the most revealing stories about the *carole* (although there is no reason to believe that he invented it, nor even that it is necessarily an English story).[6] In his manual for preachers, entitled *Summa predicantium*, Bromyard tells how some saintly men approached a certain city:[7]

> viderunt daemonum in muro civitatis, et interrogantibus cur solus ibi sederet, respondit non indigeo alicuius auxilio, quia tota civitas nobis obedienter est subiecta, et intrantes civitatem invenerunt homines in maxima dissolutione, videlicet choreizantes, aliis diversis ludis occupatos. Ipsi vero timentes exierunt de civitate illa.

> they saw a demon sitting upon the ramparts of the city, and when he was asked why he sat there alone he replied: 'I do not need the help of anyone, because all the city is obediently subject to us [the forces of the Devil].' Entering the city they found the population in a state of the greatest dissoluteness, that is to say dancing *caroles* and occupied with diverse other entertainments. Terrified, they left that city.

This is a long way from the civic humanism which allowed Bromyard's Italian contemporary Ambrogio Lorenzetti to depict a *carole* within the walls of Siena as one of the effects of good government.[8] In northern Europe around 1300 only an exceptional awareness of civic pride and identity – such as we shall discover in the Parisian theorist Johannes de Grocheio – had the power to overcome orthodox moral objections to urban carolling. For all their intellectual and spiritual differences, however, Bromyard, Grocheio and Lorenzetti attest together to an association between carolling and city-life. In northern France this reflected a close and developing relationship between the *carole* and the process of urban expansion reaching a peak during the period 1150– 1300. Until the eleventh and twelfth centuries the traditional boundaries of many cities and towns were those established by the encircling walls that had been built, for the most part, during the later ninth century as a protection against Norman invasion and attack.[9] The area enclosed by these ninth-century walls was often quite small, even in the case of important cities such as Rheims.[10] Between 1150 and 1300, many towns were equipped with larger walls that engulfed some of the cemetery churches which had originally lain *extra muros*, in accordance with pagan and Gallo-Roman custom, like 'great dormitory suburbs of the dead'.[11] The result, in many cases, was a large community enclosed within the massive physical and symbolic presence of new walls and gates, and one which contained within itself many open spaces – cemeteries, certainly, but also land left open within the walls for future expansion.[12]

It was to these open spaces, and especially to the land around cemetery churches, that the dancers tended to go for their entertainment. The author of the Harley treatise on carolling attacks them for choosing a place dedicated to saints,[13] while Guillaume Peyraut, author of the most elaborate of all the tracts against carolling, declares that dancers do grave offence to a saint when they dance in a place dedicated to him.[14] An anonymous treatise on confession, now in the Bodleian Library, confirms the suspicion that these places 'dedicated' to saints were often the cemetery lands around churches, for here the author inveighs against *caroles* performed 'around the bodies of the dead'.[15] We shall return to the significance of this peculiar choice of venue for a convivial company dance.

The texts say little about the choreography of *caroles* and there was perhaps no one way of dancing them. To judge by scattered references in sermon literature the dances might be convened in various ways: by a minstrel playing a wind instrument, by a girl (*una garcia*) beating a drum,[16] or by the appointed leader calling out through the streets *a la touche de karoles*![17] Bromyard mentions a minstrel whose trade (*opus*) is to accompany *caroles*.[18]

Once convened, the dance could take various forms. No doubt the place chosen for the carolling was a decisive factor in establishing the actual shape of the dance. There is abundant evidence, for example, that *caroles* were sometimes danced through squares and streets. A common location, often mentioned by the moralists, is a public square (*platea*),[19] and the Harley chapter on carolling locates these dances in the 'thoroughfares and squares'.[20]

This explains why an anonymous preacher in MS Royal II B.iii adorns his section on the *carole* with Ecclesiasticus 9:7, 'do not look around you in the streets of the city'.[21] On these occasions it would often have been impractical to dance in a ring and we may therefore understand why Guillaume Peyraut refers to the 'procession of the carole',[22] and the Harley manuscript to the *processio diaboli*,[23] suggesting that *caroles* were sometimes performed in a line as narrow medieval streets would often have required.

When the place chosen was a churchyard, however, or a town-square,[24] the *carole* often took the form of a ring. The sermon materials are explicit about this detail. According to Peyraut, whose *Summa de vitiis et de virtutibus*, completed before 1249/50, is by far the richest source of information available, the dancers often moved 'in a circular motion' (*motu circulari*).[25] The basic position was for the dancers to hold hands (whence the call *a la touche de karoles!*), a detail which moralists such as Peyraut found particularly disturbing. This touching of hands (*tactu manuum* is Peyraut's explicit phrase;[26] *manibus ... ducendo* says the author of the collations in the Birmingham manuscript),[27] constituted one of the formal categories of sin which carollers committed: a sin of physical contact. However, it is clear that the clasping of hands was sometimes released for clapping, accompanied by stamping (whence Peyraut's use of Ezekiel 25:6, 'because you have clapped with your hands and stamped with your feet').[28] The circular motion of the dance, which led to the left,[29] could also be interrupted, to judge by Peyraut's reference to dancers 'that go back and forth and to the right and to the left'.[30]

On great feast-days of the church year the dance could become a major public event, and the preachers attack the way that women preened themselves for the occasion. The amount of detail in their polemics is extraordinary. Girls adorn themselves with wigs made from the hair of dead women;[31] they paint their faces;[32] they accept garlands from their 'gallants'.[33] Some even wore pearls, according to Jacques de Vitry, and those unable to adorn themselves in this way looked on with jealous eyes, blushing with shame and envy.[34]

It would be a mistake to present the *carole* as an entertainment restricted to the young; the social meaning of these dances was more comprehensive than that. Sermons and treatises on the Seven Vices (where *caroles* are often discussed under the heading of *Luxuria*) reveal that old women sometimes took their place beside the young.[35] Usually, however, the *carole* was too strenuous for them. The English Dominican author John Bromyard reveals that old women were usually content to lead the girls to the dance, just as old knights lead young squires to the field,[36] while the chapter on *caroles* in the Harley manuscript confirms this picture, adding that these 'wrinkled old women' lend their dancing-clothes to the young girls (see below). Presumably these clothes were more traditional than they were fashionable, and it is tempting to believe that many other details of the *carole*, including the music, were traditional in the same way.

Court and city

The traditions of carolling appear to have been remarkably democratic. The evidence suggests that people of virtually all social classes took part in the dances to which the vernacular name *carole* or the Latin equivalent *chorea* might be readily applied. As we saw in Chapter 4, vernacular romances of the thirteenth century show that carolling was a favourite pastime during the large festivities, or 'full courts', convened for the great holidays of the liturgical year, and Old French writers show no reluctance to use the term *carole* for the urban dancing of the bourgeoisie. To some extent, perhaps, the ubiquity of the words *carole* and *chorea* in thirteenth-century writings can be explained by the imprecision of both terms (meaning, perhaps, little more than 'a festive company dance performed in a line, ring or chain')[37] and by the protean nature of the choreography employed in *caroles*. However, the meaning which I have assigned to *carole* and *chorea*, if the correct one (and it seems to be supported by a large number of texts in which contextual detail is provided) is not very imprecise, and writings of the period 1200–1300 leave a strong impression that the 'festive company dance performed in a line, ring or chain' was enjoyed at almost all levels of society.

This is suggested by a passage in the *Sermones ad status* ('sermons to each stratum of society') by the Dominican Humbert of Romans, compiled *c*. 1266–67. In this collection Humbert assembles preaching material for members of his order to employ according to the social class and calling of the persons amongst whom they find themselves. Of the *carole* Humbert has this to say:[38]

> Ad iuvenculas sive adolescentulas saeculares
>
> Sicut opus est commendabile in Christo predicare pueris, ut supra ostensum est, ita charitatis est instruere huiusmodi puellas cum occurrit opportunitas, vel in scolis, vel in domibus, vel alibi circa ea que pertinent ad salutem. Notandum igitur, quod huiusmodi puelle, maxime quando sunt filie divitum, debent libenter addiscere . . . ex hoc enim convenit eis quod sciunt tempore opportuno dicere psalterium, vel horas de Beata Virgine, vel officium pro mortuis , vel alias orationes Deo dicendas . . . Item debent cavere a levitatibus que fiunt in cantilenis, in choreis, et similibus.
>
> To young or adolescent girls in secular life
>
> Just as it is a commendable work in Christ to preach to boys, as has been shown above, so it is a work of love to instruct young girls of this kind when the opportunity arises in schools, private houses, or elsewhere, concerning what pertains to salvation. It is therefore to be noted that girls of this kind, especially when they are the daughters of the rich, should learn willingly . . . and on account of this it befits them that they should know how to recite, in a fitting time, the psalter, or the Hours of the Blessed Virgin, or the Office of the Dead, or other prayers

> which are to be said to God . . . Furthermore, they must beware of the
> trifles which are committed in songs, in *caroles*, and in things of this kind.

This seems almost deliberately vague. Humbert envisages that this advice will sometimes be given to 'the daughters of the rich', but otherwise he does not attempt to distinguish social classes amongst carollers. He apparently intends that counsel against the *carole* should be given to all girls who are young enough to need it. On the greater festivals *caroles* appear to have become populous events; 'the more the merrier', says a preacher in MS Arundel 395.[39] There may have been some social snobbery and segregation in these dances, but the moralists and preachers – whose favourite target is female vanity – do not give any impression that this was the case.

If this is an accurate picture then the *carole* may have formed the principal point of contact between the musical culture of the villages, towns and courts. The words of Humbert of Romans certainly suggest as much. Since (as we shall see) carolling was closely associated with holidays granted for the feasts of the most important saints of a region, and since the *caroles* often seem to have taken place in an urban environment, it is possible that many different social classes came together in them: the daughters of peasant families in town for the holiday and middle-class women with husbands among the burgesses. Did the daughters of local nobles take part also? A passage in a sermon by the Franciscan Nicholas de Bayard suggests that the daughters of good (indeed noble) families did not join the *caroles* in the towns, but rather stayed at home, busy with their private devotions:[40]

> Item canis nobilis, aliis lutentibus per villam, pacifice stat in domo et
> tacet; sic nobiles puelle, filie summi regiminis, aliis canentibus in chorea,
> remanent in domo sedentes et orantes.

> A noble dog, while others fight in the town, will sit at home peacefully
> and remain silent; so noble girls, daughters brought up in the most
> respectable fashion, will stay in the house sitting and praying while
> others sing in a *carole*.

This is clear, and yet it is hard to believe that the behaviour of noble girls was always so devout and exemplary. It seems likely that carolling with a full court at Christmas or Pentecost was a way for noblemen and their families to enliven their visit to a magnate's household with a luxurious version of a pleasure they enjoyed back on their estates. When the full court dissolved, many of the 'courtiers' returned to their lands, or to their town-houses, and thus to the gradual round of seasonal festivities: celebrations of local saints, May dances, summer games, harvest suppers, and many more seasonal diversions of the festive calendar.[41] Once we begin to ventilate the romances with the brisk draught of sermons and treatises on the Seven Vices we begin to feel fresh currents of doubt about how much meaning the terms 'courtly' and 'popular' actually possess in the context of the *carole*.

The social mobility of the *carole* phenomenon is perhaps the most striking and significant aspect of these remarkable festivals. There is evidence that, in accordance with the popularity of these dances at virtually all levels of society, *carole* verse and music were able to cross many of the boundaries which historians of medieval music are accustomed to treat – no doubt quite rightly – with some reverence: the boundaries between court and city, and between monody and polyphony, being chief amongst them. Let us consider the following brief lyric quoted in the romance of *Guillaume de Dole*, by Jean Renart:[42]

> C'est la jus desoz l'olive,
> Robins enmaine s'amie.
> La fontaine i sort serie
>   desouz l'olivete.
> E non Deu! Robins enmaine
>   bele Mariete.

It is clear from the context that this poem is sung for a dance (*les puceles et li vallet/ront la carole commenciee*). However, there may be little reason to describe this as 'courtly' poetry save in the obvious sense that in Jean Renart's romance it is sung by young, well-born people. The evidence of sermons, for example, allows us to give some substance to our suspicion that poetry of this kind could also serve for non-courtly *caroles*, defined more closely as the dances which took place in urban communities and which probably attracted participants of many different social classes and callings. A sermon preached in 1272 at the church of St Gervase in Paris, by Daniel of Paris, reveals that conventional figures like Robin, Marion and Enmelot were instantly recognisable to Parisians as figures from the dances which they joined on religious feast-days. Daniel of Paris, attempting to counter the suggestion that it is legitimate for the faithful to sing *caroles* at Christmas because the angels themselves sang at Christ's birth, rounds upon his audience and declares:[43]

> tu non cantasti sicut angeli; non eis ibant ad coream propter cantandum de marion ne de robecon.

> you have not sung like the angels; it is not with them that you went to a *carole* to sing of Marion or of Robin.

These conventions had their charm for the clergy as well, to judge by several passages in Gauthier de Coinci's *Miracles de Nostre Dame*, begun *c.* 1218 and probably completed (as far as the narrative part of the work is concerned) in 1231. Gauthier leaves no doubt that the clergy were fond of what he calls *chans de karoles*; his call to his fellow clerics is[44]

> De Tybregon et d'Emmelot
> Laissons ester les chançonnetes.

> Let us give up the ditties of Tybregon and Emmelot.

This provides a suggestive link not only with the *carole* traditions of Robin,

Marion and Enmelot, but also with the traditions of the motet. Gauthier de Coinci's point is that songs about Robin and his rustic fellows were performed when *gens letrees* – that is to say learned clerics – were gathered together, and these were doubtless also the occasions when motets were sometimes performed; Johannes de Grocheio's famous reference of *c*. 1300 to the festivities of the *litterati* as the best occasion for the performance of motets suggests as much. The kinds of occasion envisaged (disapprovingly) by Gauthier would have been ideal for the performance of motet poetry such as this:[45]

> Entre robin et marot
> s'en vont oir le douz chant dou rosignol,
> godefroi s'en vet apres qar mout li plot
> de marion le solaz . . .

Example no. 7

It will never be possible to ascertain how much of the lighter verse in the vernacular motet repertoire is designed to echo, or even to quote, contemporary *caroles*.[46] A link between many items in the motet repertoire and the *carole* in terms of literary tone and content – and perhaps even in terms of some musical material – seems a distinct possibility however. The importance of these dances in thirteenth-century Parisian society is clear; as we shall see, the *caroles* held outside the walls at St Germain brought the young women and the young men – both *li cler et li lai* – together in an atmosphere of festivity, and the passage of music and verse from *caroles* to motets would have been a natural process, especially given the ebullient spirit of so much of the earlier vernacular motet verse, leaning towards what might be described as the '*pastourelle* register' with its imagery of pastoral insouciance and of Robin and Marion.

Caroles *and the marriage market*

Many of the manuals that were written for the use of confessors reveal the Church's battle against carollers from the front line. These handbooks sometimes give lists of questions (Figure 8) which confessors may wish to put to penitents during confession; these are some of the very words which laymen in the cities and villages heard as they knelt to be shriven – the pleasures of the *carole* seeming very remote, perhaps even dreamlike, in the awesomeness of the moment:[47]

Concerning Pride

> [Enquire whether the penitent] will have celebrated *caroles* which may
> have been done in many ways: in assembling together, in buying fine
> clothes, in disturbing young girls, and in doings of this kind.

Caroles come into view a second time when the confessor turns to the sin of Lust. There, amidst questions about visiting prostitutes and courting widows, there are these pointers to a confessor's catechism:[48]

Concerning Lust

> [Enquire whether the penitent] will have polluted himself with a
> prostitute, deflowered a virgin or visited a widow. [Enquire whether the
> penitent] will have taken part in *caroles* much, or in spectacles of this
> kind, and delighted in others.

In the eyes of many churchmen the *carole* was a daily enactment of Man's fall, and to see the *carole* from within the dance, so to speak, it may seem imperative to leave the preachers and look elsewhere. Yet in the event it is these same writers who reveal much about the funtion of songs like *Main se levoit Aaliz* (Music example 8).

Many *exempla* in sermon-collections reveal that *caroles* were almost as popular with young men as they were with young women. An *exemplum* in the Birmingham manuscript of collations shows (and perhaps without great exaggeration) how far some parents were prepared to go to prevent their young sons from being seduced into *caroles* that passed by in the street:[49]

> Exemplum quod quidam fuit iuvenis coreisator maximus. Unde volebat
> omnibus coreis interesse. Quia igitur ad paupertatem deveniant parentes
> sui, in alto carcere incluserunt. Eadem hora in platea ducebatur corea
> in qua quidam iuvenis omnino ei similis erat rector, et hic dyabolus.
> Tunc parentes putantes iuvenem de carcere exuisse currunt ad carcerem.
> Ibique eum reperiunt vinculatum. Stupefacti igitur irato veniunt ad
> coream suscitantes a iuvene quisnam esset; qui cum dicere recusaret
> coegerunt ipsum. Tunc ille: 'Ego sum dyabolus, cuius vester filius

Example no. 8

Main se le– voit A– a– liz,

J'ai non En– me– lot.

Biau se par– ra et ves– ti

Soz la ro– che gui– on.

Cui lai– rai ge mes a– mors

a– mi– e, s'a vos non.

servicium faciebat, et quoniam ipsum tenetis vinculis alligatum, cum
meum non posset facere servicium quod modo sedule faciebat, facio
ipsum pro ipso et me.' Et hiis dictis, dyabolus ab oculis ipsorum evanuit.

A story tells that there was once a certain young man who was the most
devoted of carollers. For this reason he liked to take part in every *carole*.
Since his parents were in danger of being brought to poverty by this
they shut him up in a high chamber. In that same hour a *carole* passed
through the street, and the young man leading it was in every way like
their son. It was the Devil. The parents, thinking that their son must
have broken out of his captivity, ran to the chamber where they found
him, chained up as before. Astonished, they came angrily to the *carole*
calling out to the young man that he reveal his identity, and since he
was reluctant to speak they coerced him. Then he said: 'I am the Devil,
whose liturgy your son used to perform, and since you hold him bound
in chains so that he can no longer conduct the liturgy he was wont to

celebrate with such keenness, I am doing it for him and for myself.'
With that the Devil vanished before their eyes.

Strange though it may seem, some parents encouraged their children to attend
caroles. Peyraut tells how mothers adorned their daughters and led them to
the dance, while the treatise on carolling in the Harley manuscript shows,
with a striking simile, that old women lent their best clothes to the girls
who went dancing:[50]

> Et sicut milites quando non possunt ad bella personaliter accedere
> infirmitate gravati et alia causa detenti mittunt sibi arma sua per alium
> ne sint in forisfactione, sic faciunt vetule rugate seniles . . . ad tripudium
> non habiles vestes suas puellis commodantes.

> And just as soldiers who cannot go personally on a campaign because
> of illness, or any other reason, lend their arms to another lest they be
> forfeited, so old wrinkled women do . . . unfit for dancing, lending their
> dancing-clothes to young girls.

Special clothes, floral garlands in the hair, the generous application of striking
facial cosmetics – these and other such details recorded in the sermon literature
suggest that *caroles* could function as a marriage market in which young girls
of marriageable age could be shown to potential suitors. To judge by a passage
in a thirteenth-century adaptation of Ovid's *Ars amatoria*, in which Ovid's
teaching is ingeniously adapted to the urban milieu of Paris, the holiday
atmosphere of the *carole* was ideal for young men looking for lovers:[51]

> Ja se tu estais a Paris,
> Mar iras en autre païs,
> Por amer dames ne puceles . . .
> Dire porras par uerité,
> Soz ciel n'a si riche cité,
> La ou tantes puceles sont
> et la ioie de tot le mont . . .
> 'Quel part?' 'Vers s.Germain des prez.'
> 'Or me dites, se uos sauez,
> Porquoi g'irai.' 'Et ge porquoi,
> Gel te dirai, entent a moi!
> Illue[c] les puceles quarolent
> Qui uolentiers d'amors parolent.'

> If you have been in Paris you will find it hard to go anywhere else to
> love women or girls . . . you will be able to say truly that there is not
> such a rich city under the skies where there are so many girls and where
> there is all the pleasure that the world has to offer . . . 'To what part
> shall I go?' 'Towards St Germain des Prés.' 'Tell me, if you know,
> why I should go there.' 'I will tell you why you should, listen to me!
> It is there that the girls dance their *caroles* who willingly speak of love.'

The author of the treatise on carolling in the Harley manuscript has a passage
which seems to hint at the matrimonial purpose of at least the more populous

and festive *caroles*. Conscious of biblical echoes, he recalls how the sons of Benjamin stole wives for themselves by snatching girls from a dance (Judges 21:19–25); the 'young demons and young girls' of his own day apparently behaved in a similar fashion:[52]

> Sed audi quod legitur Iudic. ultimo quod filii Benjamin lat[ita]verunt in vineas et quandoque viderunt filias ad ducendas choreas exierunt et rapuerunt eas uxores; sic faciunt demones iuvenes et iuvenculas in choreis.

> But hear what may be read in the last chapter of the book of Judges, how the sons of Benjamin hid themselves in the vines and when they saw the daughters [of Shiloh] come out dancing *caroles* they sprang out and snatched them as wives for themselves; thus young demons and young girls do in *caroles*.

In this context it becomes easy to understand why the moralists place such an emphasis upon the youthfulness of the girls taking part, and often mention their clothes and make-up. Whence also the flirtatious behaviour – the beckoning, and the choosing games, for example, which emerge so clearly in Caesarius of Heisterbach's story about a band of devils who appear to students at the University of Toledo:[53]

> ... in puellas speciosissimas se transformantes, choreas circa illos ducebant, variis anfractibus iuvenes invitantes. Ex quibus una forma ceteris praestantior unum ex scholaribus elegit.

> [the devils] transform themselves into surpassingly beautiful girls and dance *caroles* around them, inviting the young men with their many lithe movements. One of them, more beautiful than the rest, chooses one of the scholars.

The link with marriage, once discerned, only increases the flirtatious humour of much *carole* poetry. So far from allowing the purpose of the dance to surface, many *carole* poems attack marriage as hard as they can, and the writings of the preachers show how this assault on marriage could dominate a contemporary view of these dances:[54]

> Contra sacramentum etiam matrimonii fit, quia maritis in multum detrahitur [quibus dicitur *Povre mari, fi*! et cetera] et multi incitantur ad faciendum contra matrimonii fidem; aperte etiam contra matrimonii legem ibi predicatur, ut cum cantatur quod pro pravo [marito] uxor non debeat dimittere quin amicum faciat.

> [A *carole* is an offence] against the sacrament of marriage, because husbands are often betrayed there, of whom it is said *Povre mari, fi*! etc., and many are tempted there to do things that contravene the law of marriage; the *carole* openly involves preaching against the contract of marriage such as when the song says that a wife should not refrain from taking a lover on account of a vicious husband.

This is astutely observed, for the author has spotted the favourite antithesis between the woman's husband and her *ami* in much of the lyric poetry of the thirteenth century that probably has connections with company dancing. The fragment of French text that Guillaume Peyraut quotes echoes many *refrains* and is the kind of poetry that would later receive the attentions of Adam de la Hale.[55] The dance was all the more flirtatious for the laughing face that the girls turned towards adultery.

Hymen, however, was not the only deity honoured in the *carole*. There were also local saints of parish, estate and town. The preachers were horrified by the carollers' tendency to dance on saints' days.[56] Such *caroles* were a way for a community to honour a saint: indeed we shall see in Chapter 8 that the tendency of the *carole* to be seen as a kind of popular liturgy does much to explain the way in which the Latin moralists present it. The tendency for the dances to be located in sacred places – including churchyards, and therefore perhaps near an altar, relic or chapel of relevance – may be significant in this context. A saint had power over hearth and home; to honour him was to help towards a good yield of crops, perhaps, or towards a safe return from a journey about to be undertaken. In parishes or communities which enjoyed some kind of 'professional' relationship to their saint (as when fishing villages or ports chose St Peter, for example) it is possible to imagine how the *caroles* on the vigil of the feast might express a sense of communal identity in a highly effective way.[57]

Above all, perhaps, the place of *caroles* in the festive calendar contributed to an awareness of passage. This was not only a passage through the events of Christ's life and the festivals of His saints, the stages of the liturgical year; it was also a movement through the seasons with their changing patterns of work, warmth and sunlight. The principal season for carolling ran from Easter to Autumn;[58] it therefore began in early spring and continued through to the harvest, making the most of the long, light evenings and turning many a saint's vigil into a true night-watch. *Caroles* mattered. By the mid-thirteenth century there were learned men prepared to defend them in spite of everything that was said in the pulpit.

Caroles *and the schools*

Many churchmen in the Middle Ages knew the vexation caused by a simple melody that lingers in the mind, refusing to go away. Travelling preachers like the friars, for example, were often exposed to infectious tunes like *Main se levoit Aaliz* (Music example 8) and driven to distraction as a result. 'Secular songs echoed continuously in his ear and brain', says one thirteenth-century friar of another, 'and they gave him no pleasure, as they had done before, but rather vexed him a good deal'.[59] A famous story told by Gerald of Wales reveals that the refrain of one *carole* 'to which the singers often returned', proved so contagious that a priest inadvertently sang it to his congregation instead of the customary benediction *Dominus vobiscum*.[60] Songs like that were as dangerous as they were distressing, for anyone who heard a *carole* and forgot to mention their experience in confession incurred no less than eighteen days of punishment in purgatory;[61] thus could a few moments of music trick the soul into more than four hundred hours of exile from God.

It is no wonder therefore if the preachers went to war against the *carole* with such determination. From our distance we can watch their strategy unfolding and see them rally to the fanfare that sounds in the pages of just one book: the *Summa de vitiis et virtutibus* (b.1249/50) by the Dominican friar Guillaume Peyraut.[62] This dramatic call deserves to be heard in its entirety, for it summoned the preachers into the field against a new and dangerous army: the throng of academics in the universities, especially Paris. In this intense civil war the academics took a much more indulgent view of carollers than their fellow clerics out preaching in the world.

We can explore this contrast by laying Guillaume Peyraut's chapters on the *carole* beside those of his contemporary, and fellow Dominican, Albertus Magnus. Peyraut employs a truly homiletic manner: fervent, literary, and prone to passionate exaggeration. It is a style for preaching to the masses, and especially to the large congregations of the towns and cities. Its opposite is the rigorous and discursive language that we hear in the chapters on carolling by Albertus Magnus. When he writes about carolling he does not incline to the homiletic style; he employs the scholastic manner of men with a university training. It is objective and it eschews metaphor. Like two trees planted side by side, the homiletic and the scholastic manner are rooted in a common soil which is the Christian view of history; from certain corners of the field they seem to be tangled together, while from others we see that each one stands in its own measure of ground.

The roots of the homiletic manner lie in Christian asceticism. Peyraut, for example, is ready to warn that the only counsel for those wishing to lead a good Christian life in a fallen world must be a harsh one. 'Let us be warned by the example of Christ', he cries, 'Because three times we read that he wept; we never read that he laughed.' This is the spirit of Peyraut's chapters on the *carole*; indeed, it is almost the letter of them, for this chastening reminder that Christ never laughed is immediately followed by a cross-reference to the section of Peyraut's book concerning the *carole*. Some medieval readers literally marked his words (Figure 9). In the densest and most fervent part, Peyraut compares the dancers to the locusts who swarm from the reeking pit in the Apocalypse (for the text see the Appendix):

> The smoke rising from the bottomless pit is the stench and heat of lust which has darkened the sun, which represents the company of priests whose task it is to light the Church, and the air, which represents the company of monks, to a large extent. Out of the smoke come locusts, that is female singers and dancers, not governing themselves in a sane way but advancing in chaos and as if they were brute beasts. These

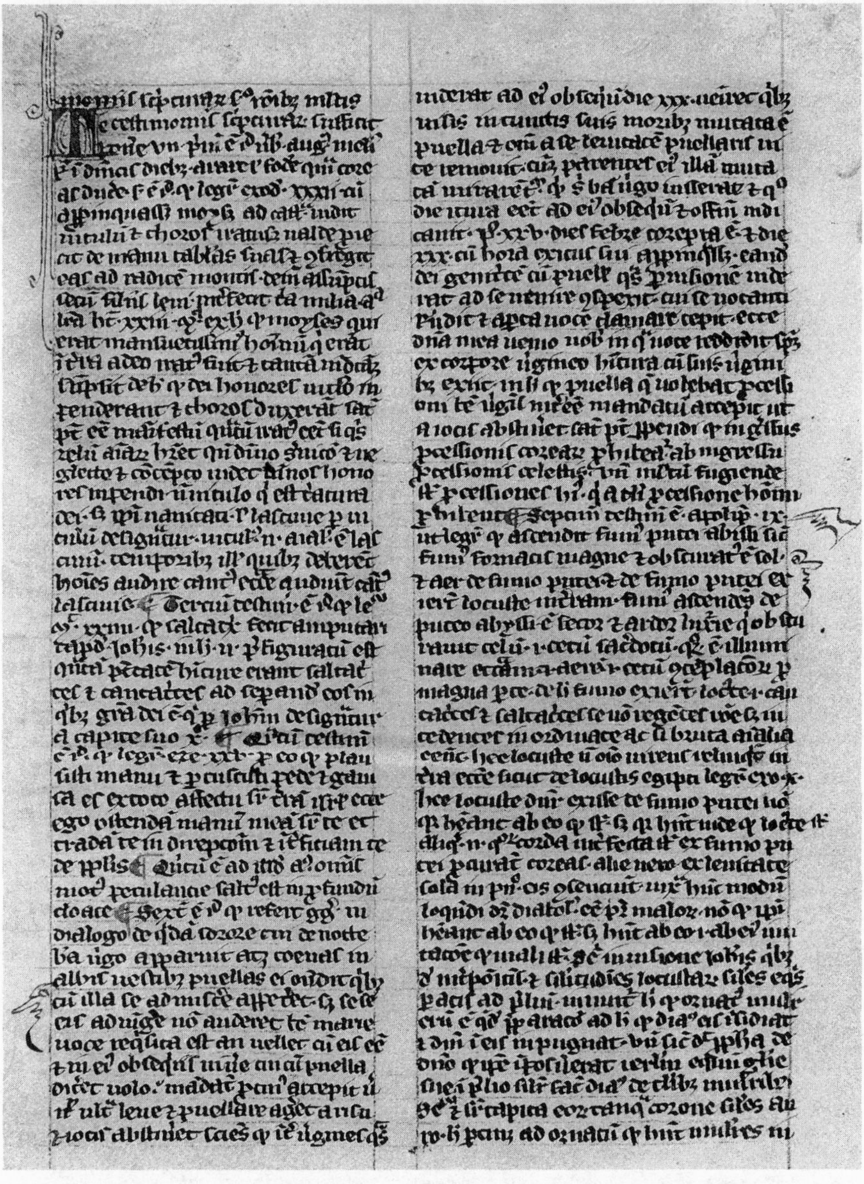

Figure 9 *A page from the influential treatise* Summa de vitiis et virtutibus *by Guillaume Peyraut. The long discussion of* caroles *in terms of the locusts of the Apocalypse begins in the right-hand column at the point marked by a medieval reader. Cambridge, University Library, MS Ii.4.8, f.18r. Reproduced by permission.*

locusts have left *not any green thing* in the land of the Church, as may
be read of the locusts of Egypt in Exodus 10 . . .

After several more verses the vision of St John continues: *And the shapes
of the locusts were like unto horses prepared for battle.* This signals that the
adornments of these women are a kind of preparation for the manoeuvres
which the Devil is planning to make with them . . .

Then follows: *and on their heads were, as it were, crowns of gold.* This relates
to the adornment which such women have on their heads, and it implies
that the adornments which they bear on their brows, and which they
have acquired from their gallants, are like crowns of manifold triumph
that the Devil has won through them over the sons of God. In like
manner hardy knights are accustomed to put garlands on the heads of
their horses in tournaments.

Now follows: *and their faces were as the faces of men.* He says *as the faces
of men* on account of the women who paint themselves, whose visages
are like masks beneath which they conceal their natural faces which God
gave them, and which are pallid. The remark of Jerome pertains to these
[painted] countenances: 'with what assurance', he says, 'they raise
skywards faces that the Creator does not recognise'.

Then follows: *And they had hair as if it were the hair of women.* The text
says *as if it were* on account of those who bear away hair cut from dead
women, which is not the hair of women because it does not belong to
the dead from whom it has been cut, nor to those who bear it away,
any more than grapes belong to thorns even though they might be tied
to them. And it is a wonder how these women are not afraid to bear
away the hair of the dead and wear it on their heads at nights. But
it is probable that the Devil inspires this boldness in them, and a token
of this is that they would fear to bear away the smock, or any other
item of clothing, from a dead women, yet they do not fear to carry off
the hair, which should be more frightful still . . .

Then follows: *and they had mail-shirts of metal.* This represents their
incorrigibility, just as one ring of a mail-shirt cannot be separated from
another, so they cannot be persuaded to lay aside a single one of their
ornaments.

And the sound of their wings was as the sound of many horses running to battle.
And just as a great army sometimes puts its foe to flight and conquers
simply by its tumult, and through its clamour makes flying birds fall,
so the diabolic army of carollers conquers the virtuous, with only its
mockery and clamour, and brings down those who may have the feathers
of the virtues from the sublimity of the life to come . . .

Then follows: *and their power was to hurt men five months.* This may be
referred to the fact that *caroles* principally injure the Church from Easter
until Autumn. Just as kings are accustomed to go to war during this
season, so that they can bear away the things which their enemies have
produced by labouring during the winter, so the Devil, as soon as it

is Easter, musters an army of carollers and carries off what the Church
has produced during Advent and Lent.

There is a disturbing mixture of passion and cunning in this. Peyraut is
appalled by an ungodly thing and he yearns for his hearers to share it in
full measure. He is summoning us to the love of God, for a retreat from
the ungodly must be an advance towards Him. Yet there is cunning here
also as Peyraut shows, with unrelenting determination, that the apocalyptic
imagery of St John's locusts can be treated as a kind of extended simile
and then becomes laden with figurative but precise allusions to daily experience and customs. This is the 'homiletic' manner adopted by one of its
most influential practitioners. The relation to sermon technique is plain, for
like any homilist Peyraut takes a biblical text and expounds it. There is
no argument, for Peyraut has nothing to prove.

Albertus Magnus : pro and contra

To leave Peyraut and to turn to the schoolmen is to encounter writers whose
very method forced them to rethink many questions of social morality. They
took a question, such as 'whether entertainments are a mortal sin or not',
and then they began to examine the contrary propositions which the question
implied (in this case 'entertainments are/are not a mortal sin'). Next, the
schoolmen assembled passages from the Bible or the Fathers into two groups
according to the propositions which they seemed to endorse. The result was
two sets of passages that contradicted one another, and the task was then
to clarify them. Since the authors of the biblical books, like the Church Fathers,
were regarded as writers who 'by their nature cannot err, contradict themselves or deceive',[63] it followed that when their words seemed to contradict
one another in truth they did not; it had to be the understanding of them
which was at fault. The schoolman's project was therefore to study the texts
which he had gathered in the hope that they would untangle themselves
as his understanding of each one became more precise and particular. When
the passages in question related to social or moral issues, his aim was to
define the special patterns of conduct, intention and circumstance to which
each one referred.

We see this process in a discussion of *caroles* by Albertus Magnus.[64] The
chapter appears in Albertus's commentary upon a work that often drew forth
the schoolmen's most 'advanced' views on questions of social morality: the
Sentences of Peter the Lombard (1150/4–7). Albertus became a Master at Paris
in 1245 and worked on his commentary until 1249. From the musical point
of view, the passage of outstanding importance in the Lombard's work
is the brief injunction which we encountered in Chapter 1: 'Let him who
wishes for the full grace of remission keep himself [during time of penance]
from games and worldly entertainments.' This is a single sentence, but

Albertus Magnus needs five columns to clarify the issues which it raises. As the following paraphrase shows, he begins by gathering passages from the Bible and the Fathers which suggest that *ludi* and *spectacula*, forbidden to penitents by Peter the Lombard, are indeed mortal sins:

1. It says in I Corinthians 10:7 that an entertainment is a lascivious gesturing in *caroles*; there we read 'Neither be ye idolators, as were some of them: as it is written: The people sat down to eat and drink and rose up to play (*ludere*).' And according to this it may be seen that *caroles* may be a mortal sin.

   Further, this may be proved by four more arguments of which the first is this: that lewd gestures are performed in this entertainment, and signs of lewdness are mortal sins for they inflame concupiscence by degrees; therefore this kind of entertainment [the *carole*] is a mortal sin.

2. The second argument is that a *carole* is said to have been danced before the first idol [Exodus 32:19] and it is obvious that idolatry has no other purpose than to inspire men to greater lewdness. Therefore it may be seen that [the *carole*] may be a mortal sin.

3. The third [argument] is that in Isaiah 3:16 and 17 the Lord has expressly threatened this kind of entertainment, saying: 'Because the daughters of Zion are haughty, and walk with stretched-forth necks and wanton eyes, walking and mincing as they go, and making a tinkling with their feet. Therefore the Lord will smite with a scab the crown of the head of the daughters of Zion.' All of these things are done in *caroles* and dances. Therefore it may be seen that [carolling] can be a mortal sin.

4. The fourth argument is taken from the text of St Paul, I Thessalonians 5:22, which says: 'Abstain from all appearance of evil'. It is plain to all that entertainments are a kind of evil, in which lecherous persons stimulate one another to lust, and this is chiefly done in *caroles*.

Despite the numbered arguments and the constant assurances in the language that something is being proved (*ergo . . . ergo videtur quod*) the reasoning here is more casual than it may seem at first. The passage from I Corinthians cited in section 1 says nothing about dancing, and only when we consult the Bible do we discover that St Paul, in his turn, is quoting; his source is Exodus 32 which is soon to appear as a separate item of evidence in Albertus's section 2!

Next, Albertus compiles the authorities that sanction a more positive view of the *carole*. He begins with Miriam and her sisters dancing in Exodus 15:20-21, praising the Lord for bringing His people out of bondage in Egypt and for parting the Red Sea. 'By this it may be seen', says Albertus, 'that the act of carolling is not evil in itself.' Then comes Psalm 68, verses 25-26: 'The singers went before, the players on instruments followed after; among them were damsels playing with timbrels.' Albertus concludes in the same positive way: 'here it may be seen that, according to the letter of the text, the psalmist speaks of *caroles* and does not reprehend such signs of rejoicing'. Finally there are these mighty words from Jeremiah 31, verse 4:

> Again I will build thee, and thou shalt be built, O Virgin of Israel:
> thou shalt again be adorned with thy tabrets (*tympanis*), and shalt go
> forth in the dances (*in choro*) of them that make merry.

The academic mind does not always anticipate obvious objections to a detailed case it is striving to build; Miriam may have danced in praise of the Lord, but Miriam was an exceptional girl.[65] There is also a learned air to Albertus's use of that favourite academic ploy, the argument from silence. Peyraut deals with biblical passages that trumpet their meaning but Albertus is struck by King David's reticence; he mentions carolling but says nothing against it.

Here are two piles of conflicting authorities. As Albertus tries to reconcile these discrepancies the grandeur of the scholastic enterprise emerges. In contrast to Peyraut, who believes that only a powerful feeling – contrition – can save Mankind, Albertus assumes that much can be achieved by sound judgement; it is the rational mind that ponders the usefulness of every action. The *carole*, in this view of things, is not Peyraut's horrifying dance of women-faced locusts; it is a pursuit that is not evil in itself but can be turned to evil ends through a permission of the will.

At this point we see Albertus in a particularly revealing light, for now he undermines the authorities he has marshalled against the *carole*. He glosses St Paul's passage from I Corinthians ('The people sat down to eat and drink and rose up to play') with the claim that carolling is not inherently evil, and that Paul must be referring to circumstances in which, by a perversion of will, it has become so. Next is the passage from Exodus where the Israelites dance before the golden calf: here Albertus offers what amounts to a historical speculation: since the victory dance of Miriam (Exodus 15:20–21) happened before the calamity with the golden calf, he proposes that such dances may have been more often associated with Divine praises than with idolatry amongst the Hebrews.

Having cleared the ground in this way, Albertus establishes circumstances in which carolling may be allowed. The dance can be held only when there is legitimate cause for celebration: a marriage, a victory in battle, the liberation of a man (or a homeland), and the return of a friend from a distant country. The second requirement is that carolling should be done *cum honestis*, that is with persons who do not use the dance as an excuse for lechery, and the third is that clerics should have nothing to do with it. The fourth is that the dances must be performed in a decorous way, without 'excessive gestures', while the fifth and final relates to the music and poetry which the dancers use. The words should be of an improving kind (*de moribus*), says Albertus, and as for the melody, there is no need to legislate, for a *carole* must have a light (*levis*) tune that suits carolling.

Glancing at these conditions, we must resist the temptation to make Albertus more of a liberal than he is. At first sight, his list of circumstances in which carolling may be permitted seems a lenient and empirical one, yet it owes more to the Bible than to bounty. If Albertus allows dancing during victory celebrations it is surely because of Miriam in the book of Exodus, while the case of a friend coming home from a far country sounds very like the prodigal son of Luke 15:25 who returned to hear a *chorum* in his father's house; the terms *chorus* and *chorea* were often synonymous.[66] Yet it is obvious that Albertus differs from Guillaume Peyraut in his approach to the *carole*. Albertus is more indulgent towards the human need to play and the wish to fix the high points of life in the memory with festivals. He does not regard the *carole* as an evil traceable to the weakness which drives all women to repeat the calamity which took place beneath the Tree of Knowledge.

Carolling and confession

How did Albertus's lenient views become possible, and what influence did they have? These are the questions raised by his *questio de choreis*. We have already framed one answer for the first; the scholastic method of gathering 'conflicting' texts from the Bible and the Fathers required the schoolmen to draw fine distinctions of intention and circumstance, for it was only by refining their interpretation of each passage in these terms that they could explain the apparent conflicts between texts which could not, in the final analysis, be regarded as contradictory since they embodied divine truth.

There were many who disputed the position adopted by Albertus (never, however, citing him by name, and often, no doubt, taking his ideas at second- or third-hand). The English Franciscan Alexander of Hales allows that there is kind of delight, *delectatio naturalis*, that is neither good nor bad, and which manifests itself in the pleasure given by disciplined music, yet he cannot allow a view of entertainment (*ioculatio*) that fails to point the finger at the weakness of women; in his scheme of things the *carole* is 'a choreographic entertainment of lascivious women': *ioculatio chorealis mulierum lascivarum.*[67]

There was a channel for carrying the views of Albertus into the ears of the laity, however, and it was provided by confession. Let us glance at the influential *Summa confessorum*, a manual for confessors by the Dominican John of Freiburg, begun *c.* 1290 and completed in 1298. Pondering the issue of whether it is a sin to dance *caroles*, John immediately refers his readers to Albertus's commentary upon *Sentences* IV:16 and his discussion of carolling. He then follows Albertus almost to the letter. *Caroles* are not evil in themselves, he proposes, but can be made so by bad intentions (especially by the intention of inspiring lust) and clerics must therefore shun them; they can also be corrupted by those who persist in dancing them at inappropriate times: the proper circumstances are a wedding, a time of victory, the liberation of a man, and so on. We recognise the list for it has been taken verbatim from Albertus. Like his master, John concedes that the melody of any *carole* must be *levis*, or light and tripping, so there is no need to legislate on that matter.[68] Such is the message of this influential book, a manual to teach those who teach the laity. Its teaching, on this count at least, was formulated in the schools and lecture-rooms of Paris, and it now becomes a little easier to understand how the music-theorist Johannes de Grocheio felt able to write these audacious words in Paris around 1300:[69]

> Ductia vero est cantus levis et velox in ascensu et descensu, quae in choreis a iuvenibus et puellis decantatur, sicut gallice *Chi encor querez amoretes*. Haec enim ducit corda puellarum et iuvenum et a vanitate removet, et contra passionem, quae dicitur amor vel eros, valere dicitur.

> The *ductia* is a melody that is light and brisk in its ascents and descents, and which is sung in *caroles* by young men and girls, like the French song *Chi encor querez amoretes*. It influences the hearts of young girls and men and draws them from vanity, and it is said to have power against that passion which is called love or 'eros'.

THE MASTERS OF ORGANUM: THE STUDY AND PERFORMANCE OF PARISIAN POLYPHONY DURING THE EARLY THIRTEENTH CENTURY

The plainchant of the liturgy was not intended for 'performance'. The extrovert and self-conscious activity that we associate with that term did not mean much to monastic singers – except, perhaps, in relation to certain solo portions of the chant. Gathered in the choir for the conventual liturgy, these singers heard, but they did not exactly listen; they sang, but they did not exactly perform. Performance requires vanity, but liturgical chant demanded humility, each singer being required to submit his voice (just as he submitted the rest of himself) to a discipline imposed by a common rule. The greatest desire was for the choir to achieve a placid unison in which their chant became a communal prayer, addressing to God (as prayer was supposed to do in its purest form) the words that He had spoken or caused to be written in the Scriptures.[1]

The singing of polyphony, however, could be a very different matter. In *The Owl and the Nightingale* it is the sober owl who represents the ideals of plainchant, proudly claiming that she sings in a mild and even fashion (*efne*).[2] Such singing was in harmony with the ultimate goal of the monastic life, a holy simplicity, *sancta simplicitas*. The nightingale, in contrast, is a performer, and inventiveness is the essence of her art; she chatters, warbles and sings in 'many kinds of ways'. In these respects *The Owl and the Nightingale* echoes a dispute about the legitimacy of inventive and individualistic singing in the liturgy which began in the twelfth century and was to lose none of its vigour in the thirteenth.[3] That a man like John of Salisbury should have wished to make a vehement contribution to this debate in his *Policraticus* of 1159 is a measure of the feeling that this dispute aroused. John was not a monk, and was therefore free from the passion for a particular kind of liturgical propriety which membership of an order could bring. When he inveighs against liturgical singers whom 'neither the nightingale nor the parrot can rival' he is showing a concern such as any sensitive man might share, if so inclined.[4] And there were many who did share it, especially in the ranks of those who had gone further than John and committed themselves to the life of the cloister. In that context life could develop like a Bible in the scriptorium, spiritual riches slowly accumulating in layers for the man who could surrender to the serene and self-effacing work required of him. The choral execution of plainchant was such a task as this, and many could not endure to see its dignity impaired. To choose one example from the many that present themselves, the treatise *De claustro anime*, attributed to Hugh of St Victor (d.1142), attacks the singers who produce elaborate ascents and descents with 'breaking' of the voice.[5]

It was the Cistercians, however, who fought the hardest of all against the individualistic impulse in the performance of chant. Their campaign reveals how profoundly the issue of chant decorum was influenced by two of the most powerful forces in ecclesiastical life during the twelfth century: the revival of the strict monastic spirit on the one hand, and the secularising impulse on the other. It is well known that the desire of the Cistercians was to recover the 'authentic' form of monastic life described in the Rule of St Benedict, and in their quest for this experience they attempted to reform the chants which they inherited. The reforms of the 1140s, supervised by St Bernard himself, tailored the chants until the melodies became as chastening, and as levelling, as the white habits which the Cistercian brothers wore.[6] By divesting their plainsong of everything which seemed either to be corrupt or to be vainglorious, and by trimming the melodies until they fitted the patterns of the church modes and obeyed the psalmist's injunction to praise the Lord 'on a psaltery of ten strings', the Cistercians hoped to produce a form of chant which was more authentic in the sense that it gave better help in the traditional monastic quest for *sancta simplicitas*.[7]

Just as the Cistercians associated their own enterprise with the recovery of authenticity in plainsong, so they associated corrupt chanting with the clerics whose style of life was furthest from their own. These were the secular clerks holding prebends and other benefices in the secular cathedrals. The shift of musical and scholarly energy from the monasteries to the secular cathedrals in the twelfth century is familiar to historians of music, for they have a striking example of it in the rise of the polyphonic repertoires associated with the secular cathedral of Notre Dame in Paris. However, in a Cistercian document like Caesarius of Heisterbach's collection of miracle tales, the *Dialogus miraculorum* (*c.* 1223), this shift seems too vivid and particular in its implications to be familiar, and we sense it as something which is in the very process of happening and of causing alarm. Caesarius of Heisterbach speaks of the secular canons as they were spoken of in stories passing along the Cistercians' international network of news and gossip. He notices their indifference to Christ's example of poverty, and evokes the chapter of Notre Dame of Paris in a story about a canon 'who lived most luxuriously because he had many benefices'.[8] He also records how the canons of an unspecified secular church performed their chant in a vainglorious, noisy way that expresses the undevout nature of their lives:[9]

> Tempore quodam clericis quibusdam in ecclesia quadam saeculari
> fortiter, id est, clamose, non devote, cantantibus . . .

> One day certain clerics in a certain secular church were singing strongly,
> that is to say loudly, not devoutly . . .

We may be sure that Caesarius is not trying to be discreet when he alludes to 'a certain secular church'; he employs general terms because he believes himself to be describing a general phenomenon of the seculars' existence, and indeed the cushioned life of the secular canons was attacked not only by writers who had chosen the hard bench of the Cistercian rule, but also by many others.[10] They did not like the turn which the religious life had taken around the bishops. In the later eleventh century it became the custom for the canons to be given cash payments and supplies when they were so scrupulous as to attend the services (and thus to perform the duties) for which the benefices had been provided in the first place.[11] This was anathema to many men in the clerical state, for it was a common understanding that the wealth of clerics should be corporate, serving to found new houses or to further the aims of the community in some other way, but that it should never be private like the wealth of the *publicani* denounced by Christ.[12] The other privileges of the secular canonical life – the banquets, the bonus payments on special feast-days, the fondness for minstrelsy, for example – also attracted scornful comment,[13] and it must be conceded that for many seculars the words 'double feast' meant a celebration that was twice as lucrative as well as twice as solemn. The list of 'distributions' from the cathedral of Amiens, for example, which records many thirteenth-century endowments, reads like a household account for the purchase of stores, so business-like are the swift contractions of words, so dense are the figures, and so abundant are the references to *solidi* and *denarii* together with payments in fish, wine, salt, beer and other goods:[14]

> In Annuntiatione B. Virginis habet unusquisque canonicus ii sol. et
> divid. scilicet in vesp. vi den., in matut. xii den., in missa vi den., in
> secundis vesperis pro omnibus vi den., et de additione Bernardi Epi.
> xl sol.: pro offerenda *Ave Maria* quilibet capellanorum habet xii sol. Et
> vicarii viij. Et sic restant canonicis xx sol.: Et de novo cuilibet canonici
> x sol.

An *Ave Maria* at Amiens Cathedral could cost twelve *solidi* for each chaplain taking part in it. Even a senior member of the secular hierarchy like Peter the Chanter, elevated to the rank of canon at Notre Dame in 1183, could be ill at ease with this situation, as the following passage from his *Verbum abbreviatum* reveals:[15]

> *Vos autem non sic. Hoc enim faciunt et ethnici et publicani.*

Item : Ad hoc detestandum valet exemplum clericorum in alea
ludentium, ad vesperas confugientium inordinate et indecenter, cum
audirent nummos vespertinos vesperis decantandis adfore, et prius in
ecclesia eos distribuendos esse.

Item : Exemplum praelati petentis in ecclesia a choro festum S.Stephani
duplex fieri in sericis et canticis ecclesiasticis, sed non impetrantis, nisi
cum pastum et refectionem annuam clericis promitteret, insuper
nummos matutinales illius noctis duplicandos ; ut sic celebrarent potius
festum nummi duplicati, quam festum S.Stephani.

You however are not thus ; thus pagans and tax-gatherers do [Matt.18 :17].

There is a further and detestable *exemplum* of this, concerning clerics
playing dice ; vespers being over, they came running in a rowdy and
indecorous fashion having heard that the vespers coins were about to
be distributed to those who came to the church first.

Again, there is the *exemplum* of a bishop seeking to have the feast of
St Stephen celebrated in his church by the choir as a double feast with
candles and liturgical chants ; he did not succeed in his request until
he promised an allowance of food and an annual meal, and until he
promised furthermore that the matins coins should be doubled for that
night. Thus they celebrated the feast of Doubled Penny rather than the
feast of St Stephen.

The second of these two *exempla* reveals how the canons of a secular cathedral
could bargain with their bishop when there was a prospect of raising the
rank of a liturgical feast. In Peter the Chanter's story a prelate who wishes
to elevate a feast has first to negotiate with the clergy in order to put a
price on the new duties that the elevation will entail. The secular clergy
had become, in effect, purveyors of liturgical services for money, and as
a cordwainer would charge extra if asked to make a shoe with ornamented
buckles, so the seculars required more for their attendance during an ornamented liturgy.

Polyphony and the University of Paris

It was often the case that canons of Notre Dame were masters in the university,
and the question arises of whether the notation and techniques of the new
polyphony associated with the names of Leonin and Perotin were integrated
in any way into the arts curriculum. Some modern historians seem to be
convinced that they were. According to Nan Cooke Carpenter there is 'over-
whelming evidence ... for the study, cultivation and practice of music as
science and art at the great French university',[16] while Anderson claims that
the teaching of music 'held an important place' in the university of Paris.[17]

Mathiassen even alludes to 'university lectures' which, according to his account, were devoted to polyphonic music.[18]

It is difficult to investigate these claims, or to challenge them, since there is nothing stronger to bring against them than an argument from silence: the silence of the university curriculum, as far as we know it, which makes no mention of polyphony, or the silence, for example, of the *quodlibete* and other records of university disputations, none of which has yet been found to mention polyphony, as far as I am aware.[19] Furthermore, it can be granted at once that a great deal of polyphonic music, both sacred and secular, was sung in thirteenth-century Paris, and there seems no reason to doubt that some of it was composed and performed by individuals who were following a recognised course of study or even directing one. That being said, however, it is another matter to assume that polyphonic music was a university subject – an assumption that commits us to believing in courses of lectures and in the study of prescribed texts leading to formal examinations on passages taken therefrom. May we picture a group of Parisian students leafing through their pages of notes on Peter the Lombard's *Sentences*, let us say, to make space for material on modal notation?

The search for an answer to that question, insofar as we can hope to provide one, begins with the seven Liberal Arts. For many centuries the relative positions of grammar, dialectic, rhetoric, astronomy, geometry, mathematics and music had remained relatively stable like heavenly bodies in a constellation. Towards 1200, however, the pattern of stars changed in a way that was both rapid and portentous. *Theologia* moved to the centre (at least when viewed from Paris), and all the other studies in the system either faded or grew bright according to their proximity to her. The study of the Latin language and of its literature, *grammatica*, almost disappeared from view in Paris despite the efforts of conservatives like the grammarian Johannes de Garlandia, and with the gradual recovery of Aristotle's philosophy the course in 'Arts' (the term was a misnomer by 1220 or so) came to be dominated by logic. This was generally regarded as a preliminary training – an important preliminary to be sure, whence the great size of the Arts faculty – but a preparatory study nonetheless, and one that was often treated in a perfunctory fashion. By the time a student reached his twenty-first year, he could expect to have completed his course in arts; if he had done well (and if funds were forthcoming) he would proceed to one of the higher faculties of Theology, Law or Medicine where a lucrative career would at last come into view after his years in the schools.

The study of music had only a small place in this system. The university statutes of 1215, drawn up by Robert of Courson in his capacity as the papal legate and as an experienced Master of the university,[20] allow for the study of quadrivial subjects on feast-days, but on these occasions music would have been forced to compete for attention with the other books and subjects which Courson recommends for these occasions: the writings of philosophers and rhetoricians, the *Barbarismus* (i.e. the third book of the *Ars maior* of Donatus), the *Ethics* of Aristotle and, if the students wish, the fourth book of the Philosopher's *Topics*.

As far as it is possible to discern, the study of music at Paris was conducted with the *De institutione musica* of Boethius and with that work alone. A book-list produced by the English scholar Alexander Nequam some time before 1213, and probably reflecting the content of Parisian studies in arts subjects, recommends the *musica Boecii* to students seeking a thorough grounding in the arts.[21] More reliable than this list, however, is a manual for arts students at the University of Paris, compiled between 1230 and 1240/45, now in the Archivo de la Corona de Aragon in Barcelona. This handbook specifies the set texts for each subject in the arts course, gives a very general guide to their contents, and then provides specimen questions for the examination. These are accompanied by model answers (Figure 10). The section on music, in which we can almost smell the straw in the Rue du Fouarre where the examinations were often held, is entirely devoted to the *De institutione musica* of Boethius who is the only author mentioned.[22] It will be worth dwelling upon this document, for its value as a guide to the officially recognised contents of the arts course in music around the time of Johannes de Garlandia can scarcely be exaggerated.

It is quickly said that the students of Paris 'studied the musical treatise of Boethius'. However, anyone who reads the *De institutione musica* today, following not only the Latin prose but also the many sums contained therein, will discover that the book is not as rudimentary (and not as brief) as sometimes supposed. The syllabus in the Barcelona manuscript reveals that the students of Paris concentrated upon the first two books of the five, for 'in these two ... the author manifests the means of knowledge of all the things which are at issue'.[23] This assessment is not entirely just, but it is correct insofar as Books I and II incorporate most of the general matter that a medieval scholar without a specialist interest in *musica* might wish to possess. Book I broaches some major themes in the medieval understanding of *musica*, including the ethical effects of music and the union of body and soul according to harmonic relationships; it also includes fundamental matters such as the basic physics of vibration, the classification of music into *mundana, humana* and *instrumentalis*, and the numerical ratios which produce the octave, fourth and fifth. Book II is more mathematical in character, and from there the students would learn further about forms of ratios, the classification of intervals, and semitones both major and minor, *inter alia*. At the end of Book II, it would seem, the masters and students of Paris generally chose to stop, and the author of this Parisian manual seems to have only a diaphanous notion of what Books III–V of the *De institutione musica* actually contain.[24]

The specimen questions, and the answers given for them, are most revealing. They avoid mathematics and concentrate upon general issues of classification. For example, there is a question about the integrity which music can claim for itself given that one of its categories, *musica mundana*, cannot be heard by the human ear.[25] Another casts doubt upon the right of music

Figure 10 *A page from a thirteenth-century curriculum for students studying the Arts Course at the University of Paris. The section concerning music begins in the middle of the left-hand column. Barcelona, Archivo de la Corona de Aragon, MS Ripoll 109, f.135. Reproduced by permission.*

to be regarded as a free-standing discipline independent of arithmetic. Other questions are designed to check on basic knowledge of a kind that could be derived from that universal encyclopedia, the *Etymologiae* of Isidore of Seville, or from countless digests (the etymology of the terms *musica* and *diapente*, for example, or the story of how Mercury invented the lyre). In short, this curriculum provides no evidence for Mathiassen's 'university lectures' on polyphony, and at one point it wanders so far from polyphony as to claim that it is not the province of the student of music to examine time: *musicus de tempore non habet determinare*! What would Johannes de Garlandia have made of that?

This neglect of the practical aspects of music in formal university study may not require a complex explanation. The objective of a basic musical training in the thirteenth century was an ability to read plainchant notation and to sing certain chants, often used as prayers, from memory. These goals were usually accomplished in boyhood. The university course in arts took these attainments for granted and therefore paid little attention to the knowledge which liturgical observance required; the course was designed to equip students for lucrative and responsible posts in church administration or government where they would not exactly require to have their antiphoners by their elbow. The higher education of the thirteenth century therefore tended to leave neumes and staves behind. This emerges clearly from the sermon-notes which the Dominican Master General Humbert of Romans (d.1277), who read the arts course at Paris, compiled for the use of preachers wishing to address those engaged in studies. Beginning at the bottom of the ladder, as it were, the first two sermons are addressed to students of grammar and then of chant, described as 'boys in their infancy', *pueri in infantia sua*. Next come the young men who have entered the university to study in the Faculty of Arts; finally there are the members of the higher faculties: the physicians, the lawyers and the theologians.[26] Humbert has now climbed so high in the cathedral of knowledge that nothing remains but a vault of silence where study gives way to contemplation. The students of chant are a long way below.

What of the claim, often made by medieval authors, that some knowledge of music is necessary to the study of theology? There was some disagreement on this point. Roger Bacon believed that 'in many ways musical matters are necessary to theology',[27] but his contemporary Jacques de Vitry took a different view. In a sermon addressed to the students of Paris he declared that grammar, dialectic and rhetoric can contribute to the *scientia pietatis*, the combination of grace and erudition that allowed a cleric to interpret scripture. But he did not believe that the same could be said of geometry, arithmetic and music:[28]

> Sed de quadrivialibus, licet contineant veritatem, non tamen ducunt ad pietatem ... Geometria autem et arithmetica et musica habent in sua scientia veritatem, sed non est scientia illa pietatis.

> But as far as concerns the arts of the quadrivium, although it may be granted that they reveal truth, they do not lead to piety ... Geometry, arithmetic and music reveal their own truths when they are investigated, but it is not the *scientia pietatis*.

It is difficult to predict what a systematic search through works by Masters trained at Paris would reveal about the musical knowledge and interests of these men, all of whom will have read the course in arts. At present, no such survey had been undertaken, and the enormous quantity of material which waits to be sifted, most of it unpublished, is daunting to say the least. Having examined about fifty major works (and a much greater number of sermons) produced by Masters who taught and studied at Paris, I have scarcely been able to find any acknowledgement that polyphony existed, let alone that it was systematically studied through textbooks and university lectures. Now and then an author may express admiration for liturgical polyphony in general terms,[29] and one theologian even shows that he is familiar with the words *triplum* and *quadruplum*. The author in question there, however, is William of Auvergne (d.1249), bishop of Paris, who must have heard organum in Notre Dame on many occasions; furthermore, these two technical terms from the parlance of *organiste* appear only once in William's voluminous theological works, and in that single instance the subject that he is pursuing is not liturgical polyphony but (strange to relate) the music of a complex bagpipe.[30]

To assess the kind of musical learning which a theologian like William of Auvergne could deploy in his theological work we can turn to William's extensive theological writings, especially the *De universo*. There we find many deposits from the great centuries of Bible-commentary between Augustine in the fifth century and the first *magistri* such as Anselm of Laon in the twelfth. They include allegories involving musical instruments: 'What is the *cithara* if not a heart made deep and hollow with humility', and so on.[31] There are also many musical *similitudines*: comparisons in which an aspect of faith or doctrine is likened to some aspect of musical life. These bring random observations such as 'it is the custom of magnates to call wind-players after their meals to bring on sleep', or 'a skilled player of the *viella* can sing and play at the same time'.[32] Other passages inveigh against the misuse of music:[33]

> Sic et de amatoriis carminibus, vel aliis operibus, quae propter amorem mulieris stulti et decepti facere consueverunt . . .

> So it is with love songs and with other things which fools and the misguided were accustomed to make for the love of a woman . . .

The musical references in William's work which seem to reflect some formal study of music can all be traced to the treatise of Boethius, or to the general medieval understanding of certain fundamental issues in the study of music which Boethius did so much to build. In a passage of the *De universo*, for example, William ponders upon the aesthetic effect of music; endorsing the kind of academic investigation that Boethius expects from the true *musicus*, William suggests that it is not the audible sounds which give pleasure in music but rather the numerical relationships that they convey and which are subliminally perceived:[34]

> Non immerito vero perscrutandum est quid sit quod delectet animas nostras in vocibus musicalis seu melodiacis, et forsitan videatur alicui

The structure of musical learning and observation in the theology of
William of Auvergne

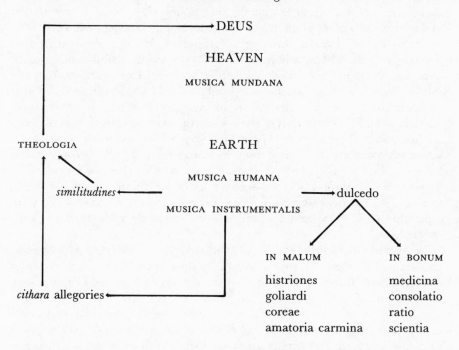

non irrationabiliter, quod non voces ipse delectent eas, sed magis
numeri, et proportiones musicae, qui nullatenus audiuntur, sed interius
solummodo cogitantur. Indicium autem huiusmodi non leve est,
quoniam videmus aliquos absurdissime canentes et iniucunda
percussione aures audientium offendentes, suis cantibus non mediocriter
delectari.

It would not be otiose to study what it may be in musical or melodious
notes that may delight our minds, and perhaps it will not seem an
irrational suggestion to anyone to propose that it is not the notes which
may delight our minds but rather the numbers, and the proportions of
the music, which are not audible and are only perceived within us. It
is not easy to proceed with such studies, for we see some who are not
a little delighted in their music and who nonetheless sing in an absurd
way, and who offend the ears of those who listen with an unpleasant,
jarring sound.

Listening to sermons, reading commentaries upon the Bible, glancing at
the musical chapters in Isidore's *Etymologiae* – that was enough to provide
a theologian with all the musical learning that he required in his 'professional'
life, providing that he had studied his Boethius. Why should the preparatory
course in Arts have included more?

The Masters of organum

If there is no solid evidence that the techniques of polyphony were taught in the University of Paris, then how were they taught, and by whom?

Let us begin with the performers themselves. It has long been evident that the performers of polyphony at Notre Dame during the thirteenth century were not usually members of the chapter but were rather drawn from the shifting body of clerics, beneficed and unbeneficed, who shouldered so much of the musical burden of the liturgy in that cathedral (as they do in most English cathedrals to this day). These were the *clerici* and the *clerici chori* who are mentioned as performers of polyphony in the Obit register of Notre Dame where endowments for liturgical services are recorded.[35] The sum set aside for each of these polyphones is invariably six *denarii*. They were principally drawn from the ranks of the unbeneficed 'clerks of Matins', the *clerici matutinorum*, of whom there were (at least in theory) sixteen, but polyphones were especially likely to be found among the six senior clerks of Matins, called the *machicoti*.[36]

The position of all the clerks of Matins at Notre Dame, polyphones or no, was highly insecure. Although many of them were former choirboys who had been sent through the university at the expense of the chapter, they were all unbeneficed, and they are sometimes referred to in Notre Dame documents as the 'poor clerics', the *pauperes clerici*. Each year they were required to resign *en masse* to be appointed at the discretion of the chapter.[37] Like the lay-vicars of so many great English cathedrals in the later Middle Ages, these singers presented the authorities with many problems arising from their indiscipline, their sexual misdemeanours and other kinds of malefaction.[38]

Here we have something truly remarkable: a body of singers in Paris, many of them quite youthful, and including singers expert in performing polyphony, yet with no long-term security and, we may presume, in constant competition for places with new men who had freshly graduated from the university and who were keen to win a position. It was in the nature of university education in the thirteenth century – and especially education at Paris – to make every form of clerical expertise into a lucrative science that could be made so, and an ability to perform polyphony was no exception – especially after the massive polyphonic enterprise of Leonin. Indeed it is from Leonin's contemporaries in Paris that we first gain a sense that organum has become tinged with the excitement of student ambition. We have already seen how Jacques de Vitry recalled meeting a student in the university whose ambition was to become an *organizator*,[39] and Ranulph Ardens, a Master at Paris who taught there until 1215, describes how the heavenly virgins who sing before the throne of God are said to be blessed 'because they are appointed as new *organiste* in the heavenly court' – a comparison which may have its roots in the more terrestrial blessings of an appointment, however brief, at some great church.[40]

The payment which *organiste* could hope to receive was not lavish, for their status within the Notre Dame hierarchy was a lowly one. Those who had been appointed faced the constant danger that their term would not be renewed when the time came, and those who were still hopeful of a place had to plan for the eventuality that they would be unsuccessful. What could they do but diversify their activities, perhaps by setting themselves up as teachers?

This is speculation, of course, but this hypothesis begins to look much stronger when we introduce a passage from a work which has not received the attention it deserves. This is the *Summa* of Robert of Courson, compiled during the period 1208–1212/13. Courson taught in Paris from *c*. 1200 until he became a cardinal in 1212, and both as an academic and as a papal legate he was deeply involved with the affairs of the university. His *Summa* considers many questions of social morality (we have already examined his discussion of minstrelsy in Chapter 1) and is especially concerned with the circumstances in which it is legitimate to earn money from professional services (*locare . . . operas*). In one section Courson reveals how, at a time when Leonin's *Magnus liber organi* was still new, organum had indeed become a 'lucrative science'. Having considered the work of scribes who hire themselves at fairs, he turns to 'Masters of organum', *magistri organici* (see Frontispiece):

[1] Si queras de operis minorum puta de scriptoribus in nundinis qui locant operas suas et scripturas feneratoribus cambiatoribus, dico ut supra quod tenentur ad restitutionem omnium eorum que a feneratoribus receperunt.

[2] Similiter dicimus quod illicite sunt opere magistrorum organicorum qui scurrilia et effeminata proponunt iuvenibus et rudibus ad effeminandos animos ipsorum,

[3] tamen locare possent operas suas in licitis cantibus in quibus servitur ecclesiis.

[4] Si autem prelatus lascivus lasciviis talibus cantatoribus det beneficia ut huiusmodi scurrilia et lascivia audiat in ecclesia sua, credo quod lepram symonie incurrit.

[5] Si tamen in aliqua sollemnitate pro consuetudine terre decantent aliqui in organis, dummodo scurriles notule non admisceantur, tolerari possunt.

1 If you ask about the labours of small traders, such as the scribes at markets who hire themselves and their writings to money-changing usurers, I say, as I said above, that they should be charged to return all of the things which they have got from usurers.

2 In the same way we say that the services of Masters of organum who set minstrelish and effeminate things before young and ignorant persons, in order to weaken their minds, are not licit;

3 however they can sell their services with respect to licit chants insofar as they are of use in churches.

4 If, however, a wanton prelate gives benefices to such wanton singers in order that this kind of minstrelish and wanton music may be heard in his church, I believe that he becomes contaminated with the disease of simony.

5 If, however, some sing any organa on a feast-day according to the liturgical customs of the region, they may be tolerated if they avoid minstrelish little notes.

There seems no reason to doubt that these 'Masters of organum' are performers of vocal polyphony; there is very little support at this date for the suggestion that they are organists,[41] and it is quite clear from section 4 that they are singers (*cantatores*) who perform (among other things) liturgical chants, as revealed in section 3.

In attempting to interpret this document it is essential to remember its early date. Even allowing for the uncertainty about the period when Leonin was composing the organum for the *Magnus liber organi* (or when Perotin was revising it), we violate no conventional opinion by regarding Courson's *Summa* as a work written at a crucial period in the development and dissemination of the Parisian repertoire.

The first conclusion to be drawn from this passage is that performers of organum formed a group defined by the earning capacity of its members, directly comparable to that of the jobbing scribes who are discussed immediately before them. Courson may not have regarded the Masters of organum as members of a profession as such, but he clearly does think of their activities as professional in nature. In this context the term *magistri* needs delicate handling. During the thirteenth century, as is well known, the word *magister* included amongst its many senses 'the possessor of a university degree', but it was also widely used to denote a cleric who had mastered any art of moment to the Church and was equipped to teach. As early as *c.* 1100 the music theorist Johannes was freely referring to teachers of chant as *magistri*, long before we can speak of university 'degrees' as such.[42] At the same time, the fundamental sense of *magister*, 'one who has *mastered* any craft and who teaches', remained strong throughout the Middle Ages, and it was standard practice to refer to craftsmen as *magistri*. 'A *magister* is anyone who is concerned with anything . . . to a greater extent than other people' says one famous legist; 'the teacher of any skill can be called a *magister*'.[43]

The second clear implication in Courson's passage is that the Masters of organum are clerics of lowly status who do not necessarily enjoy any kind of benefice (section 4), and whose talent is purchased, as it were, by members of the senior clergy who wish to incorporate the music which these singers can provide into the liturgies of their churches. Insofar as Courson's passage refers to Parisian circumstances – and there is no city which Courson knew better, and none where he had more legislative authority – then these Masters of organum are surely to be identified with the singers amongst the *clerici matutinales* of Notre Dame who formed a shifting body of polyphonic talent. There may even be an echo of the disciplinary problems which these *clerici* so often caused in Courson's angry reference to the wanton and seductive nature of some of their music (section 2).

At this point it is perhaps advisable to stand back for a moment. Courson's reference to the doings of these *magistri*, while most suggestive and probably unique at this date, is nonetheless very brief, and there is always a danger that we may be led astray by tendentious or strained interpretations of his text. Indeed, it may be that general agreement about the implications of his words will never extend much further than the few preliminary deductions which I have offered (together with any others which I have failed to make). That being said, however, I believe that we may proceed a little further.

Courson's overriding concern is not with the legitimacy of liturgical polyphony *per se*, but with the legitimacy of certain *performing styles*. Some Masters, he remarks, 'set minstrelish and effeminate things before young and innocent persons', and some 'wanton' prelates (the vocabulary of sexual indulgence is abundant here) buy this 'minstrelish and wanton music' into their churches by offering the singers some kind of benefice. However, Courson judges that it is legitimate for the Masters to earn money by performing 'licit chants in so far as they are of use in churches', duly regulated according to the liturgical customs of the place concerned, providing they do not corrupt their performances with 'minstrelish little notes' (*scurriles notule*).

At bottom, this is the debate between the Owl and the Nightingale all over again: the continuing dispute in the twelfth and thirteenth centuries between those who could reconcile highly elaborate and soloistic singing with their sense of conventional liturgical propriety, and those who could not. For Courson, the key issue is whether the performances by the Masters incorporate 'minstrelish little notes', and in any attempt to clarify this expression it must be borne in mind that he is using a well-worn convention when he elects to stigmatise an irruption of soloistic singing into the liturgy with vocabulary derived from the world of minstrelsy; for many centuries clerics had resorted to the terms associated with the classical theatre (*scurra, mimus*, etc) for purposes of this kind, and Courson's use of the adjective *scurrilis* belongs in that tradition. His meaning is that the music which uses these 'little notes' sounds (at least in his ears) excessively secular, implying a primarily aesthetic purpose, not a devotional one, and also implying a measure of exhibitionism on the part of the performer.[44]

The most plausible interpretation of these *notule* is that they are to be identified with the improvised embellishments which, according to Anonymous IV and Jerome of Moravia (among others), were used by performers of the two-part organum that would have formed the basic liturgical repertoire of any Master of organum when Courson wrote his *Summa*. These embellish-

ments included the *longa florata* ('a long adorned with flowers'), *floratura, florifi-
catio vocis, reverberatio* (defined by Roesner as 'a short, rapid, appoggiatura-like
ornament that approaches the main note from below'),[45] the *flos harmonicus*,
vibratio, the *nota procellaris* ('the agitated note'), and more besides. All of these
embellishments, insofar as we can now reconstruct them, ornamented one
note by adding more – sometimes many more – shorter notes. In other words,
they introduced *notule*.[46] By the time of Jerome of Moravia (*c.* 1300), these
ornaments had become acceptable both in polyphony and (which seems more
surprising) in plainchant. Courson, who wrote at a time when Leonin's
Magnus liber organi was far from superseded, seems to be describing a situation
in which the great polyphonic enterprise of Notre Dame has been accompanied
by a new cult of vocal virtuosity whose excesses were causing concern to
some.

Were the Parisian Masters of organum involved in the performance of
secular polyphony? Courson's accusation that they 'set minstrelish and effeminate things before young and ignorant persons', and the implied contrast
with 'licit chants' used in churches, suggest as much. The charge of effeminacy
is one that the moralists of the thirteenth century consistently levelled against
the secular music of minstrels, both vocal and instrumental.[47] It is obvious
that the Masters often performed liturgical organum in a way that sounded
overtly secular to men of strict conscience like Courson, and an audience
of 'young and ignorant persons' suggests a secular context. If the Masters
were indeed performing secular polyphony then the music in question is
presumably to be identified with the very earliest vernacular motets, it being
uncertain how much an audience of 'ignorant' persons would have gained
from listening to the often highly elaborate and learned Latin poetry of the
conductus. This is an intriguing possibility, and one which invites us to ponder
the conventional view that the Ars Antiqua motet was a serious genre for
the *litterati*. This view owes a great deal to Johannes de Grocheio's description
of the motet, written *c.* 1300 and therefore on the verge of the Ars Nova,[48]
but it is far from certain, however, that Grocheio's words can be taken as
a reliable guide to the milieu of the vernacular motet in the time of Courson,
approximately three generations earlier. Furthermore, the chronology of the
early motet is obscure; it is far from certain whether the polytextual motet
had been invented by the time of Courson's *Summa* (1208–1212/13), and it was
polytextuality, we may presume, that gave rise to much of the 'difficulty'
which Grocheio perceived in the form.[49] It is possible that a significant proportion the vernacular motets known in Paris when Courson wrote his
Summa consisted of works in two parts of the kind found so abundantly in
the tenth fascicle of the Notre Dame manuscript W2. In these, as in the
monophonic tradition, a single text is declaimed in a forthright manner,
but here with an accompanying, textless part. Moreover, when the texts
of many of these vernacular two-part motets are viewed in relation to contemporary monophonic songs, including those of the trouvères, it can be
seen that the verse of early motets often displays a lightness – even a

cultivated triviality – not to mention a fondness for the *pastourelle* form with its imagery of rustic encounters.[50] The Parisian students and girls who went to the *caroles* at St Germain des Prés – very much the sort of people whom Courson is likely to have regarded as 'young and ignorant persons' – would surely have found some vernacular motets quite appealing (Music example 9).

If some of the Masters of organum in Paris were involved with the performance of secular music then that accords with the highly insecure nature of the life which they were compelled to endure. They were members of a junior clerical body that was forced to resign *en masse* each year to be reappointed at the discretion of the chapter, and they did not enjoy generous benefices. What could they do but diversify their activities in any way that would increase their income? Let us not forget why Courson turns his attention to their activities in the first place: it is because they earn money. If these deductions are correct, then we have in the *magistri organici* a body of singers performing secular motets to young students and their friends in Paris for cash in hand.

A closer look at Courson's passage, however, shows that he does not think of the Masters as a specifically Parisian phenomenon. Indeed he does not mention Paris at all, although there are good reasons for believing that in many respects his *Summa* principally engages with Parisian conditions. In his eyes the Masters are closely connected with the *dissemination* of the music which they perform. He says that they may sing 'licit chants in so far as they are of use *in churches*' (we note the plural), and that they may perform suitably decorous organum 'according to the liturgical customs *of the region*' (a wide, even an international context seems to be implied). All this springs from what Courson discerns to be a demand for the music amongst prelates who wish to have organum performed in their liturgies; he thus confirms the theory, advanced by Wright and others,[51] that the dissemination of Parisian organum owed much to the initiatives of senior clergy returning from a period of study or teaching at Paris to their own ecclesiastical foundations; such men knew that this organum carried the prestige of Paris, and that every means of raising the rank of a liturgical feast was an invitation to benefactors who might wish to endow a new feast or elevate an established one.

Craig Wright, challenging the work of Husmann, has recently argued that it is mistaken to imagine the history of Leonin's *Magnus liber* in terms of the gradual expansion of an early, Leonian repertoire.[52] He proposes instead that the contents and interrelations of the three so-called Notre Dame manuscripts (F, W1 and W2) can better be explained by the hypothesis that singers actually *reduced* the *Magnus liber* of Leonin, gradually sifting the repertoire and extracting what could be used in the rites of other churches.[53] This interpretation throws Courson's description of the Masters into sharp relief, for he is surely describing the very people who did this work, and moreover his description dates from a crucial period, for it may well have been while Courson was writing his *Summa* that Perotin was busy making an *abbreviatio*

Example no. 9

of Leonin's great collection of organum. The aim of the Masters, as Courson shows, was to *locare operas suas*, to 'sell their labours', and it was therefore directly in their interests to work on the Parisian repertoire bequeathed by Leonin in order to disentangle from it a repertoire lacking in what Wright calls 'liturgical specifity';[54] this adaptable repertoire could be sung in churches where the Masters were inevitably required to sing *pro consuetudine terre*, as Courson has it. Viewed in this light, the *Magnus liber* repertoire as it appears in W2, for example, with much of the liturgical specifity removed,[55] can be seen as the result of an essentially commercial exploitation of Leonin's legacy by a mobile body of singers working on a professional and essentially opportunistic basis.

The English theorist Anonymous IV gives us some impression of how these Masters of organum pursued their careers. Writing *c.* 1285, and so looking back over a century or more of Parisian organum, he recalls various *magistri* who made a notable contribution to the art.[56] Few of these men have been traced, and some of the earliest may have belonged to the very generation of *magistri organici* which Courson describes. Two of Anonymous IV's *magistri* are said to be composers: Leonin, described as *organista* (a common term in the treatise) and Perotinus, described as *discantor* (a term which Anonymous IV uses once only). Robertus de Sabilone is praised for his 'extensive' teaching (which included the *tempora*, the bases of mensural organisation) and for his fine singing. Petrus was a celebrated music-scribe (*notator*), and Thomas de Sancto Iuliano was also a *notator*, although he did not notate according to the way of the moderns. Johannes called 'the first', who may perhaps be identified with the theorist Johannes de Garlandia,[57] is also described as one involved with the craft of notation.

This summary is correct as far as it goes, but it misses a certain amount. A closer look at Anonymous IV's text suggests that it is impossible to draw a firm line between the singing, teaching and notating of these *magistri*; indeed, it is probable that some of them were busy in all three occupations. Here, for example, is a famous passage in which Anonymous IV describes how Perotin worked on the legacy of organum bequeathed by his famous predecessor, Leonin:[58]

> Sed abreviatio erat facta per signa materialia a tempore Perotini Magni
> et parum ante, et brevius docebant, et adhuc brevius a tempore magistri
> Roberti de Sabilone, quamvis spatiose docebat. Sed nimis deliciose fecit
> melos canendo apparere ... Post ipsum ex documento suo fuit magister
> Petrus optimus notator, et nimis fideliter libros suos secundum usum
> et consuetudinem magistri sui et melius notabat.

> But an edition was made by means of written notation from the time
> of Perotin the Great and a little before, and they used to teach more
> briefly, and hitherto more briefly from the time of Master Robert de
> Sabilone, although he used to teach extensively. But he rendered the
> melody extremely delightfully in his singing ... After him Master Petrus
> was the best notator, as may be seen from the material that he has left,

> and he notated his books very faithfully according to the use and custom
> of his master, and even better.

From this passage it appears that Perotin, and others, used to teach (*docebant*),
so it would seem that Perotin was more than a composer. The account of
Robertus de Sabilone reveals that Robertus was a distinguished singer but
he also *taught* extensively. Furthermore, 'after him Master Petrus was the
best *notator*', a phraseology which might be taken to imply that Robertus
de Sabilone was also an expert music-scribe. It seems probable, therefore,
that the 'Masters' mentioned by Anonymous IV as the key figures in the
elaboration of Parisian organum and its notation, were musicians whose professional expertise encompassed the arts of singing, teaching and notating.

There is one activity, however, with which Anonymous IV never associates
these Masters: not one of them is mentioned as having written a treatise.
Indeed, Anonymous IV seems to possess only a very faint awareness that
treatises might have played a role in this developing tradition of performance,
notation and teaching. The only text on measured music that he mentions
is Johannes de Garlandia's *De mensurabili musica*, but he does not seem to
know who wrote it, for he does not give Garlandia's name (he identifies
the work by its opening words).[59] He seems convinced that the *antiqui* (see
diagram) had not yet completely succeeded in making their art into a fully
literate and scientific one. This seems to have been basically correct. To
judge by the treatises which survive, it was during the period 1270–1300 that
the great incursion of discursive literacy into the musical practices of Parisian
polyphony took place, for it was in those decades that Franco of Cologne,
Jerome of Moravia, Lambertus, Johannes de Grocheio and indeed Anonymous IV himself produced their treatises. The state of affairs in the early
thirteenth century, however, is much less certain, and the description which
Anonymous IV gives of the situation amongst the *antiqui* is consistent with
the view that it was an essentially bookless time as far as theory was concerned.
In the view of Anonymous IV the *antiqui* did not know how to explain (*narrare*)
all the rules which they used, and their teaching therefore rested upon demonstration and imitation: 'You may listen to us and remember', the teachers
among the *antiqui* used to say, 'and sing it this way'.[60] It seems implausible
that practical musical teaching of this kind was associated with formal instruction in the university, but it is much easier to imagine how it could have
flourished amongst Courson's Masters of organum.

There is one final, and tantalising possibility which Courson's description
of these Masters seems to raise. Might these singers have been directly
involved in the creation of the vernacular motet and then in the dissemination
of the repertory? As paid singers of Parisian liturgical polyphony they would
have known a large number of discant clausulae, the matrices of the motet,
and would have learned many of them by heart.[61] It is only necessary to
sing these pieces today to feel the presence of the latent secular songs which
musicians in the early thirteenth century seem to have sensed for themselves.

The precedence of Masters according to Anonymous IV (all datings hypothetical)

ANTIQUI   MODERNI

1000   1100   1200   1225   1250   1260   1270   1280

[Guido]
inter alia

Master Leoninus
'and very many others'

Master Perotinus
'and his predecessors'

Master Robertus
de Sabilone

Master Petrus
(? pupil of the above)

Thomas de Sancto Iuliano
'a Parisian of old times'

Iohannes
[? de Garlandia]
'called *the first*'

Master Franco the first
Master Franco of Cologne
Master Theobaldus
Master Symon de Sacalia
A Master from Burgundy
Master Iohannes le Fauconer
A certain other good singer

153

These clausulae often use isoperiodic phrases, short-range and conspicuous patterns, open and closed phrase-endings, and their modal rhythms must have resembled, in certain respects, the rhythms of popular dance-songs or *caroles* (Music example 10).[62] What could be more natural than that singers who were trying to make a living from their voices and from their polyphonic expertise should have seen an opportunity to *locare operas suas* in a secular context by the simple device of adding vernacular words to clausulae, performing the results before a secular audience – one which a moralist like Courson was all too ready to dismiss as a collection of 'young and ignorant persons'?

CHAPTER SEVEN

PLAINCHANT AND THE BEYOND

It is surprising to see how happy the founders of those religious houses have been in their choice of situations, all the world over.

Smollett

It was probably around the year 1200 that Master Humbert of Balesma preached a sermon before the Masters and students of Paris. This was the essence of his message to them:[1]

> Tua enim fides non debet esse fides demonum vana sine argento moneta.

> Your faith must not be the faith of demons which is empty without silver coin.

These words are designed to cut into the very roots of university learning. Amongst the Masters of Paris who were paid for their services, and amongst the students who laboured in the hope of lucrative office, an observer of strict conscience could easily find signs that *sapientia* was being bought and sold, even though it was nominally a free gift from God. As we saw in the last chapter, it is in this context that Robert of Courson draws attention to the Masters of organum, singers who earned money with their expertise in polyphonic music. Many opposed this kind of commerce in knowledge,[2] and it is no surprise to find that the unique manuscript of Humbert of Balesma's sermon about *fides . . . sine argento* was once the property of the Cistercians at Cîteaux and may well have been compiled there.[3]

In the culture of the twelfth and thirteenth centuries it is hard to discover a more vivid contrast than between the severe, communal life of the Cistercians and the careerist outlook of the schoolmen. The contrast is a familiar one, of course, and can easily be overdrawn, for there were Cistercian theologians who made their mark in Paris, as there were schoolmen (Abelard amongst them) who turned to the life of the cloister; nonetheless, it is inescapable. As manifested in liturgical music, and as seen through the eyes of the Cistercians, the contrast took the form of an opposition between the reformed simplicity of the White Monks' liturgy on one hand, and the various excesses of the secular clerics and of the Cluniacs on the other. We have already heard the Cistercian Caesarius of Heisterbach describe the clerics of 'a certain secular church ... singing strongly, that is to say loudly, not devoutly',[4] and the White Monks were also inclined to speak in this way of the Cluniacs. In the *Dialogus inter Cluniacensem et Cisterciensem Monachum*, probably composed around 1180, the representative of the Cistercians makes his view of the Cluniac liturgy very plain:[5]

> Talibus vocibus cum novis et lascivis melodiis in novis et usurpatis festis vestris ultimini contra veneranda canonum decreta.

> With such voices and with new and wanton melodies in your new and improperly constituted feasts you go beyond what is stipulated in the venerable statutes of canon law.

The Cistercians' own ideal of the plainness of plainchant is proclaimed in a statute of the Order, promulgated in 1134:[6]

> Viros decet virili voce cantare, et non more femineo tinnulis, vel ut vulgo dicitur falsis vocibus veluti histrionicam imitari lasciviam. Et ideo constituimus mediocritatem servari in cantu, ut ad gravitatem redoleat, et devotio conservetur.

> It befits men to sing with a manly voice, and not in a womanish manner with tinkling, or, as it is said in the vernacular, with 'false' voices, as if imitating the wantonness of minstrels. We have therefore stipulated that the mean should be adhered to in chant, so that it may exude seriousness and devotion may be preserved.

The Cistercians set themselves against every secularising impulse in chant, whether it sprang from the musical luxuries of the secular clergy in a cathedral like Notre Dame at Paris, from the liturgical elaborations of the Cluniacs, or from the wantonness of minstrels. What were the consequences of their resistance? Much of this book has been concerned with the spread of a certain tolerance – even of a certain Humanism – in the twelfth and thirteenth centuries. This chapter is different, for its theme is the persistence of a debilitating superstition that tortured the monks who built their houses, as Deuteronomy asked of them, 'in a place of horror and of infinite solitude'.

A good deal of evidence has survived about the experience of plainchant in Cistercian monasteries, and above all about the state of mind induced by the daily performance of plainchant in a Cistercian context of rigorous isolation from the world. Most of this evidence takes the form of prose texts, of Cistercian origin, in which the detailed reminiscences of White Monks are recorded, some of them relating to supernatural experiences in choir. They include: the *Liber de miraculis* by Herbertus, composed *c.* 1178 at Clairvaux;[7] the *Liber revelationum* of Richalm, Abbot of Schöntal (d.1220),[8] and the *Dialogus miraculorum* (*c.* 1223) of Caesarius of Heisterbach.[9] In comparison with the materials employed in the previous chapter, these Cistercian documents establish a contrast between the rational and the irrational. The activities of the Masters of organum, for example, are revealed to us in a document which places them in a wholly rational context of professional service and monetary exchange. In the writings of the White Monks, however, the choral performance of chant has given the Cistercian choirstalls the aspect of the sky in a rapid storm, darkened by a fear of diabolic power one moment and radiant with joy the next. Their stories are permeated by a sense of wonder at the thinness of the partition between this world and the next; thinner even than the thread of life that is broken in death, the partition could fall down many times during the life of a monk, either to exhort him to virtue or to frighten him from sin.

Paradise and the serpent

Throughout the Middle Ages monastic authors chose to portray their monasteries in terms reminiscent of the biblical description of Paradise in the second chapter of Genesis. Such language was the inheritance of every monk, but as Constable says, 'some of the most sensitive descriptions of the natural beauty of monastic sites, and those reminiscent of contemporary descriptions of paradise, were written by Cistercians'.[10] It suffices to recall the names of their abbeys: the Court of God, the Fountain of Salvation, 'as well as innumerable shining, bright, beautiful, good, and golden valleys, springs and meadows'.[11] Walter Daniel, for example, described the Cistercian abbey of Rievaulx as 'another paradise of wooded delight', surrounded by 'streams softly sounding in a gentle murmur and joining their sweet notes in delightful songs'.[12]

But the monastery was not quite Paradise on earth. Until he fell, Adam had been free from all but the lightest toil; for the monk, however, there was work to be done that could often seem arduous to him in his fallen state. It was the *opus dei*, 'the work of God', performed day after day in the liturgy. The metaphor of work was an appropriate one, not only because the White Monk's exertions in choir were integrated into a day that took him (at least in theory) into the fields with hoe and scythe, but also because the successful performance of choral chant depended upon the kind of obedience necessary for efficient teamwork in field and grange. The musical idiom of choral plainchant, in which the assembled voices of the monastic community sang the same melody with as much unanimity as they could achieve, demanded humility, and monks in all orders were forbidden to ornament the music or to show off by pitching it too high.[13] The stylistic ideal of smoothness in chanting demanded a surrender of will: a surrender required not only by the performance of plainchant but also by love.[14]

The reward for humility in the choir was an experience which some could regard as an anticipation of heaven. Indeed, according to a common medieval simile, the choirstalls resembled heaven. As the monks stood on opposite sides of the choir before the altar steps, so in time would the blessed stand with the angels before the Throne.[15] Theologians even pondered the question of whether the heavenly praises offered by the blessed in Paradise would be genuinely vocal, and they asked whether voices would ever become hoarse there.[16] Many believers accepted that a quasi-physical continuity of choral praise bridged the chasm of death, and it was widely held that the angels themselves attested to this continuity by delighting in the chants which earthly choirs offered to God:[17]

> Cantica divinae laudis, et Ecclesiastici Officii, si cum devotione cordis et mentis attentione fundantur, delectant etiam angelos, sicut cantus et harmoniae hominum dicitur delectare delphinos ... Unde etiam Basilius dicit quod psalmodia daemones fugat, et angelos in adiutorium salutis invitat ... cantica divinae laudis valeant ad sublevandum taedium vitae praesentis ...

> The music of Divine worship, and of the Church Office, delights the angels also if it springs from a devout heart and an attentive mind, just as the music and harmony made by mankind is said to delight dolphins ... Whence also St Basil says that chant puts demons to flight, and calls angels to the aid of salvation ... divine chants also have the power to relieve the tedium of this present life ...

It scarcely matters that these are the words of a fourteenth-century Dominican, Johannes de Sancto Geminiano. Such lines could have been written at virtually any time during the Latin Middle Ages. They make a fine encomium of plainchant, but Johannes may be altogether too idealistic when he claims that plainchant alleviates the 'tedium of this present life'. To judge by the testimony of a wealth of literary sources, the sheer boredom and repetitiveness of life in the cloister, the *tedium claustri*, weighed heavily upon the spirits of many monks, and to some the obligation to sing plainchant day after day was the most onerous task of all. In the dialogue between Soul and Reason composed by Adam of Dryburgh (d.?1212), Reason asks Soul what things irk her, and Soul replies:[18]

> *Soul*: De modo psallendi et cantus in choro.
> *Reason*: Quomodo a te in choro celebratur divinum officium?
> *Soul*: Nimis tractim, nimis morose; et illo denique modo, qui mihi valde onerosus et taediosus est.
> *Reason*: Nescis, O anima mea, quia inter omnia, de quibus te intromittis sanctae religionis exercitia, hoc specialiter opus Dei est. Hic namque Deo sisteris, hic ei praesentaris, hic etiam cum eo loqueris ... Quam sapienter nihilominus illa, quibus eum alloquaris, verba et corde meditari, et ore te deceret proferre
> ...
> *Soul*: Bene mones et dicis

> *Soul*: I am irked by the manner of singing plainchant in the choir.
> *Reason*: How do you celebrate the Divine Office in choir?
> *Soul*: In an excessively protracted fashion and too slowly, and

> therefore in such a manner that it is very burdensome and
> tedious.
>
> *Reason*: Do you not know, O my soul, that of all the tasks which the
> practice of holy religion requires you to undertake, this is the
> work of God above all other things. For here you present
> yourself to God, here you are exhibited to Him, here also you
> speak with Him . . . Those words which you address to Him
> should be meditated in your heart and uttered by your mouth
> as wisely as possible . . .
>
> *Soul*: You speak and admonish me well.

In this colloquy Soul is a complex creature, privileged above all other faculties
in her loving relationship with God and yet the most prone to weakness.
Her objection to the task of singing plainchant is that it does not lighten
'the tedium of this present life', and Reason responds to the challenge by
sounding the very depths of the monastic tradition of meditation. Chant,
he replies in effect, is like the spiritual exercise of reading Scripture, *divina
lectio*, because it absorbs all the principal faculties. The mind meditates upon
the meaning of the words while the mouth pronounces them.[19] Let it never
be done inattentively. This colloquy suggests that when Johannes de Sancto
Geminiano praises the chant because it lightens tedium he is more concerned
to record the unchanging counsel of Reason than the vacillating feelings of
Soul.

His claim that plainchant can brighten the dullness of life is only one
of two partial truths in this passage. There is also his succinct and confident
declaration that chant puts demons to flight. How could this be true? When
a monk described his monastery as a mirror of Paradise he did not forget
the literary masterstoke which follows the description of Eden in Genesis:[20]

> Sed et serpens erat callidior cunctis animalibus terrae.

> But the serpent was more artful than all the creatures of the earth.

To describe the monastery as an earthly paradise was to admit that a monk
was not alone as he passed to and fro amongst the buildings that circumscribed
his life; like his first father, Adam, he had a maleficent shadow in Satan.
In making the claim that chanting puts devils to flight, Johannes de Sancto
Geminiano is repeating a wisdom culled from the philosophical traditions
of the Greeks and from the demonology of the Hebrews. At bottom, this
wisdom rested upon a belief in the medicinal power of music; as Pythagoras
cured a raging man by calling upon a lyre player to change the mode he
was using,[21] so the harping of David had drawn a demon out of the breast
of Saul (figure II).[22] Yet in spite of the authority of this teaching, the thirteenth
century brings literary evidence that there were many, both within the cloister
and without, who did not believe that plainchant – or any other kind of
music – provided a secure protection against diabolic assault.

The schoolmen were sceptical about this after their own fashion. They
did not question the power of Satan, of course, nor did they doubt the power

Figure 11 *David arrives before Saul, his harp neatly wrapped in a bag on his back, and then expels the demon from him with his music. From the Tickhill Psalter. English, fourteenth century. New York, Public Library, Spencer Collection, MS 26, f.9v. Reproduced by permission.*

of music to alleviate the consequences of his malice. Their interest was in *how* such alleviation took place. One of the most illuminating discussions is provided by the English theologian, Richard of Middleton, who devoted a *quaestio* to the issue of 'whether herbs or harmonies are capable of preventing a demon from afflicting mankind' during a quodlibet (a debate on 'whatever you please') at Paris in 1287.[23] Richard is determined and systematic. He concedes that music can mollify the effects of bodily sickness, and that it can influence human disposition. But can it influence a diabolic disposition? Certainly not, Richard argues, because a demon, being a malign spirit, is exactly what its name implies; a spirit that has no body to be prevailed upon by sensations such as those produced by musical sound. Furthermore, he argues, a diabolic intrusion into the life of an individual arises from a Divine or Satanic command, and such commands cannot be averted by chants, by special herbs, nor indeed by any means under human control.[24] His general conclusion is both rational and irrational, sceptical and credulous, in a way that makes the study of the scholastic mind so fascinating. It is that music can soothe a man's feelings and thus give him extra strength to endure diabolic vexation, but the music cannot work upon the demon:[25]

> Quaestio. Utrum herbae vel harmoniae possint impedire daemonem in vexando homines . . . [Solutio]: Possunt, sed in vexatum a daemone, non autem in ipsum daemonem agendo.

> Question: whether herbs or harmonies are capable of preventing a demon from afflicting mankind . . . [Solution]: they can, but by reacting upon him who is afflicted by the demon, not by acting upon the demon itself.

Amongst the Cistercians there were many who had reached the same conclusion as Richard of Middleton, but by a more arduous route. Their experiences in choir had shown them that plainchant often provided little protection when the curtain between the present world and the horrors of the next fell without warning. An eloquent text in this regard is Richalm's *Liber revelationum*, written at the Cistercian abbey of Schöntal sometime before 1220. This compilation allows us to overhear the conversation of Cistercian monks as they discuss their fears of the supernatural. The text opens as a group of monks come together to talk (although that word does not catch the urgent, personal and frightened tone of what they say). Their exchanges evoke a landscape in which everything can be infected with supernatural evil. These monks fear the trillings of birds, because demons sometimes speak in birdsong:[26]

> Per voces etiam avium sibi mutuo loquuntur . . .

> They talk to one another through the voices of birds . . .

For them, as for T.S.Eliot, the thunder speaks:[27]

> audivi voces ex tonitru . . .

> I heard voices in the thunder . . .

Greatest of all horrors: it is never possible to be sure that a man whom one meets is actually *alive*:[28]

> Daemones nequam tenent subinde hominem, qui jam dudum obiit, in
> motu aliquo, quasi vitali, per unum, aut duos, aut plures dies, et ut
> non putetur mortuus . . .

> Sometimes vile devils hold a man, recently dead, in a state of movement,
> as if he were alive, for one, two or more days, and in such a way that
> he will not be thought to be dead.

In this enclosed world every sound is suspect. A novice, newly arrived from the outside, may not realise it, so any sign of slowness or scepticism on his part must be crushed:[29]

> Richalm: Audistis sonum illum?
> Novice: Video, quod fricatis vos inter scapulas vestras.
> Richalm: . . . Sonus est daemonis.

> Richalm: Do you hear that sound?
> Novice: I see that you are scratching yourself between your shoulders.
> Richalm: . . . It is the sound of a demon.

It was not just the external world that was darkened by the shadow of Genesis: 'cursed is the ground for the sake'. The Cistercians of Richalm's *Liber revelationum* live in constant fear that their bodies will be invaded by demons. This fear is almost second nature to them and they have learned to speak of such infestations in practical terms. One monk, for example, explains how he would dispose of his vomit if a *spiritus malus* induced nausea in him: 'I would put it in a piscina, and if there was none, in some vessel, and if I did not even have that, I would put it in my habit'.[30] The fear of losing the mastery of one's own body ran deep, and it is touching to read of the terror that afflicted one Cistercian for no better reason than that he had noticed the sound of his own digestion:[31]

> Jam cum sedi ad scribendum, audivi tanquam inter meum ventrem
> sonum, quasi bufonum, et hoc saepius. Et plane timeo, ne forte aliquid
> simile intra me habeam.

> Recently, while I was sitting down to write, I heard what seemed to
> be a sound in my stomach, like that of a toad, and this has often
> happened. I am wholly frightened lest I may by chance have some such
> thing inside me.

Fear that the privacy of the body might be violated forced the monk to contemplate a vile physical prospect of vomiting, dizziness and other horrors; it also offered an affront to his will by threatening his sovereignty over his actions. Such fears became particularly intense when the monk entered the choirstalls for the conventual liturgy and the performance of its chant. It was clear to all Cistercians that when they approached the choir they came out of their camp, as it were, and challenged Satan in the open field. The devils inhabited the monastery like a shadow community, coming and going about their daily *opus diaboli*, and like the monks they regarded the Mass as the centre of their work; a monk in the right place at the right time could overhear the devils as they rebuked one another in a diabolic parody of an abbot calling brothers to their duty:[32]

> Unde cum essem in calefactorio, audivi dicentes daemones ad alios
> daemones: quid vos inertes, ac debiles huc curritis, et hic otiosi
> occupamini? Quare non estis ad Missam?

> When I was in the calefactorium one day, I heard demons speaking to
> other demons saying: why are you idling, running around like fools,
> occupying yourself worthlessly here? Why are you not at Mass?

In the choirstalls the invasion of the precincts of the body could take various forms. There was no bodily infirmity so mild, and none so transient, that minds reared upon the intense contemplation of the unseen could not see a malign influence in it. The devils might induce fainting:[33]

> Hodie impeditus sum ab eis malignis spiritibus quod non potui
> celebrare; quia tantam mihi capitis vertiginem fecerunt.

> Today I was beset by these malignant spirits so that I could not officiate;
> they gave me such dizziness in the head.

They could induce coughing fits that threatened to disrupt the liturgy:[34]

> Sicut scitis, ego frequenter in choro soleo excreare; et hoc praecipue
> solebam ante non multos dies, ad quas excreationes faciendas compulit
> me quasi suboriens nausea quaedam, inarctans me in gutture, et

constringens, et quasi conglomerata in faucibus, ita, ut nisi excreassem
in aliquod indecens, quod aut vomitus, aut vitium esset vomitui, quasi
prorumpere in ipso choro cogerer.

As you all know, I often cough in the choir; this happened to me
particularly not many days ago, and producing these coughs pressed in
on me with what seemed a kind of nausea rising inside me, constricting
my throat and squeezing it, and so gathering there that unless I spat
in an indecorous way I should either vomit or go through the motions
of it, and be compelled to rush out of the choir.

With the subtlety of spirits, the demons could enter a monk's throat and
make his voice hoarse so that he could not sing the chants:[35]

Eadem nocte ad vigilias audivi, quod dixit iterum unus daemon ad
alium, ut faceret mihi vocis raucedinem.

On the same night at prayers I heard one demon say again to another
that he would make my voice hoarse.

If it had been the case that devils were abroad in the monastery and persecuting
whomsoever they chose, then there would have been a modicum of relief.
A threat of that kind could be regarded as an intermittent one. The reality,
however, induced a fear without respite, for each monk had his own private
demon:[36]

praeterita die steti in aestuario, et alii sex fratres mecum, qui omnes
cantaverunt, sed ego adhuc cantaturus eram. Et ecce! meus daemon
ivit ad illius daemonem, qui juxta me stetit, et valde supplici voce ait
ad eum: Esto mecum, hodie, obsecro, in missa, ex quo expeditus es.
Quae verba sic intelliguntur: adjuva me ad impugnandum istum, qui
adhuc cantaturus est, ex quo cantavit iste, quem tu impugnas . . .

the other day I stood in the aestuarium, six other brothers with me,
who had all sung, and I was still to sing. And behold! my demon went
over to the demon of another who stood near to me, and said to him
in the most suppliant manner: 'Be with me, today, I implore you, at
the Mass, for which you have no duties assigned'. Those words are to
be interpreted thus: 'Help me to fight against this monk, who has still
to sing, since you battle against one that has already sung'.

The speaker here registers no surprise that he should have been standing
with a group of fellow monks and become aware of a group of demons,
shadowing each man, conversing in a part of the aestuarium. The monks
shared the monastery – as they were sometimes forced to share their very
skin – with their enemies. The presentation of the evil spirits as a horrific
parody of the monastic community (as a crucifix hung upside down parodies
the crucifixion) affects the way that these Cistercians imagine the conversation
between the demons. In their own way the demons are dutiful, diligent and
even courteous, one delicately reminding another that since he has no duties
assigned for the Mass he is free to help his diabolic colleague. With such

demonic forces abroad it was sometimes impossible to complete a liturgical celebration without constant recourse to exorcisms performed as almost automatic gestures, one monk doing it for another as a man might brush a spider from the clothes of his friend :[37]

> Unde iste talis frater cum heri cantaret Invitatorium, defectum illum, quem habuit in voce, sicut audistis, daemones fecerunt. Et ego, sciens hoc, feci crucem illuc, versus gradum ad eundem fratrem; et reliquos deinde versus statim, ut audistis, explevit. Unde et ego irrisi eos, quod tam impotentes fugerint crucem, quamvis indignati sint multum. Item cum Evangelium lecturus idem aliquando Frater deficeret, feci crucem, et exinde vocem coepit recuperare.

> When a brother should have sung the Invitatory yesterday the demons produced a defect in his voice as you heard. I, knowing this, made the sign of the cross in that place towards the step at this same brother; at once he completed the remaining verses, as you heard. I laughed at them because they were so weak that they must flee the cross although it enraged them greatly. Again, when the same brother failed when he was about to begin the Gospel, I made the sign of the cross and from that moment on he began to recover his voice.

Coughing fits, hoarse voices and dizzy spells may seem to be rather trivial manifestations of Satanic malice, although there is no sign in these Cistercian writings that the monks thought them so. For stories of more spectacular assaults upon the monks, however, we can turn to the *Dialogus miraculorum*, composed *c*. 1223 by Caesarius of Heisterbach. As its name implies, the *Dialogus* is a colloquy between two members of a Cisterian community, a monk and a novice, about miraculous happenings which took place for the most part within monasteries of White Monks. The fifth section of the work is entirely devoted to diabolic manifestations. As they stand in the choirs and naves of their churches the monks and lay brothers of the *Dialogus miraculorum* do not simply see devils; they are assailed by a succession of dire marvels and the church becomes a theatre for diabolic shows of an intensely vivid kind. At Matins on the feast of St Martin, a demon enters the choir in the form of a rustic stonecutter; he is clearly seen and just as clearly described. With a broad chest, high shoulders and a short neck, the hair on his brow is shaven and the remainder of his hair hangs down 'like ears of corn'.[38] On the eve of St Kunibert's day a simple monk sees two demons enter the presbytery; they pass so close to him that he could have reached out to touch them, and he sees that one has a woman's face and wears a black garment on its head.[39] As in many of these stories, the meaning of the vivid but seemingly arbitrary details of the vision are obscure and are all the more sinister for remaining so.

In many of Caesarius's narratives it is the animal world which breaks into the choir. As the protean demons assume whatever shapes they please, a nightmarish world of fur, horns, bristles and claws is brought into the choirstalls, evoking the wild country beyond the monastery walls or the filth of the farmyard within it. A bear materialises in a presbytery, crying out in a human voice as it staggers to and fro, looking at the brothers who stand gaping;[40] monkeys and cats are espied sitting upon the backs and shoulders of the singers;[41] Satan himself is seen slithering out of the choir in the form of a serpent, doing so in the full light of the lamp 'lest his departure might be concealed from any onlooker'.[42]

One of the effects of such apparitions is to turn certain chants into a kind of conjuration so that a monk never knew what dire effect might be produced by the words he was pronouncing. Caesarius of Heisterbach tells several stories in which an apparition is a response to the sense of the words being sung. One takes place on the vigil of St Columbanus:[43]

> Alio itidem tempore, in vigilia, ut puto, sancti Columbani, tunc eo exsistente Priore, cum chorus Abbatis inciperet primum matutinarum Psalmum, scilicet: *Domine, quid multiplicati sunt qui tribulant me?* daemones in choro adeo multiplicati sunt, ut ex illorum concursu et discursu mox in eodem Psalmo fratres fallerentur. Quos cum chorus oppositus conaretur corrigere, daemones transvolaverunt et se illis miscentes ita eos turbaverunt, ut prorsus nescirent quid psallerent.

> On another occasion, in the same way – I think it was the eve of St Columbanus, the Prior being present – when the choir on the Abbot's side should begin the first psalm of Matins (that is to say *Lord, how are they increased that trouble me?*) the demons in the choir increased in number so much that, because of their bunching together and their running up and down, the brothers soon failed in their singing of this same psalm. When those in the choir opposite attempted to correct them, the demons winged across and mingled themselves with the brothers to the point where they put them into a turmoil so that they scarcely knew what they were chanting.

This story suggests how potent such supernatural beliefs could be. Caesarius of Heisterbach sees a diabolic influence in one of the most common accidents of medieval chant performance: the breakdown of psalms sung by the divided choir.[44]

Talismans of Mary

Standing in the choir provided the monks with little protection against diabolic attack. The standard repertoire of liturgical chant, performed day after day in a choral context, was only an incitement to their ancient enemy. With certain items, however, the situation was rather different. These were chants, many of them para-liturgical, in honour of the Virgin Mary. The Cistercians' exceptional devotion to the Virgin was freely acknowledged by the members of other religious orders, and since the intercession of Mary accounted for many of their miracle stories it was inevitable that contemporaries should have regarded the Cistercians' devotion to Mary as a catalyst for supernatural reactions. The Dominican friar Thomas of Cantimpré probably expresses the majority view when he writes that 'many miraculous things are recorded as having taken place within the Cistercian order whose members are exceptionally devoted to the Virgin'.[45]

The willingness to regard certain chants in honour of Mary as items with a life and usefulness independent of such place as they had in the liturgy reflects a medieval conception of devotional Latin song and poetry which is easily overlooked. Edmund Rich expresses it well in the early thirteenth century when he speaks (in disparaging terms) of those who pray 'with words arranged in rhythmic form or composed in curious poetry'.[46] The chant texts, both with and without their music, that tended to be used in such private devotions as Rich describes were often metrical ones; many of them were known to have originated within recent generations and were therefore felt to be distinct from the more sacrosanct (and more obviously liturgical) material in the ancient 'Gregorian' heritage. The sequences of Adam of 'St Victor' provide an example.[47] The poems of such pieces were often copied into miscellanies. Adam's sequence *Salve mater salvatoris*, for example, appears in a miscellany formerly belonging to Cîteaux itself (Figure 12). A passage from the *Dialogus miraculorum* suggests a context for miscellanies of this kind and reveals how such poems could be used to heighten prayer with eloquence and devotion with delight. A saintly priest named David in the Cistercian convent at Himmerod takes a new novice under his wing; a bond forms between the two, and they recite sequences and other chants together:[48]

> Venit illuc quidam adolescentulus multum devote et humiliter petens ingressum; susceptus autem, sine querela conversatus est. Hunc vero venerabilis sacerdos David, de cuius sanctitate mira dicuntur, specialiter amabat . . . Cui iuvenis idem sequentias et quaeque dulcia cantica de Domina nostra versa vice recitavit, quibus sanctam illius devotionem saepius excitavit.

> There came to that place a certain young man, very devoutly and humbly seeking admission into the order; once received, he became one of the *conversi* without demur. The venerable priest David, of whose sanctity many wondrous things are said, held him especially dear . . . The young man would recite to him sequences and other sweet chants about Our Lady with alternating verses, with which he often inspired him to holy devotion.

There is an echo here of the court practice, discussed in Chapter 4, whereby a junior and essentially probationary member of a community (a *vallet*, for example) was expected to divert his elders with song.[49] The verb *recitavit* in the passage above presumably implies only recitation, however, and a miscellany giving just the text of a Marian sequence like Adam's *Salve mater salvatoris* would have been ideal for use in such an intimate situation where the preference was clearly for *sequentias de Domina nostra*, not only because such poems enhanced private devotions of various kinds but also because of their beauty; they were *dulcia cantica*. Simply to learn such poems, and thereafter to possess them, was to be strengthened as the words released

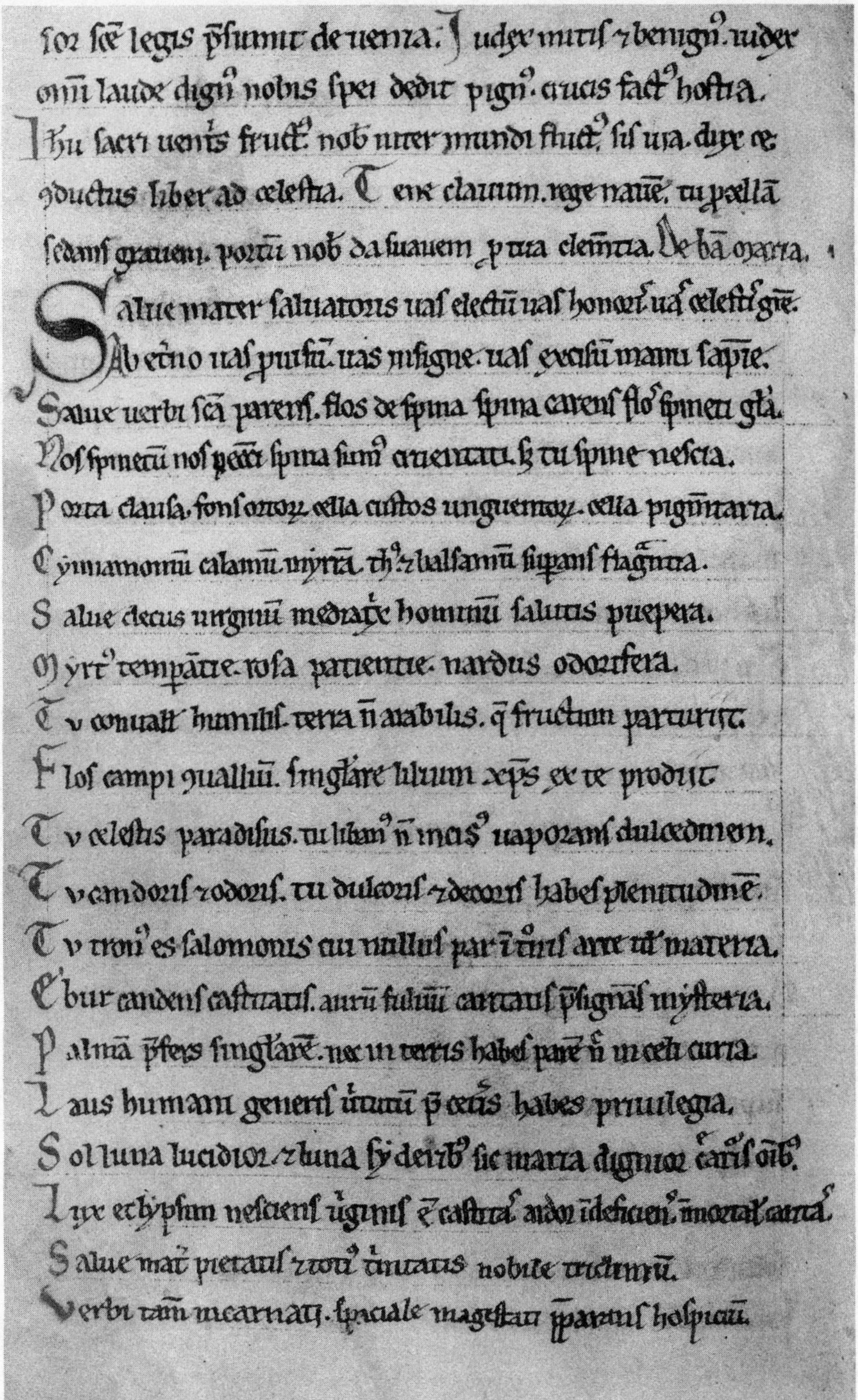

...for sc̄e legis p̄sumit de uenia. Judex mitis ⁊ benign̄. iudex
om̄i laude dign̄ nobis spei dedit pign̄. crucis fact̄ hostia.
Jhu sacri uen̄is fruct̄. nob̄ int̄er mundi fluct̄. sis uia. dux cē-
⁊ductus liber ad celestia. T̄ ene clauum. rege nauē. tu puellā
sedans grauem. portū nob̄ da suauem p̄ t̄a clem̄tia. De bā oȳata.

Salue mater saluatoris uas electū uas honor̄ uā celestī grē.
Ab et̄no uas p̄uisū. uas insigne. uas excisū manu sapīe.
Salue uerbi sc̄a parens. flos de spina spina carens flo̅ spineti glā.
Nos spinetū nos p̄ccī spina sum̄ cruentati. ⁊ tu spine nescia.
Porta clausa. fons ortoꝛ. cella custos unguentoꝛ. cella pigm̄taria.
Cynamom̄i calam̄ myrrā. th̄ ⁊ balsam̄ sup̄ans fragntia.
Salue decus uirginū mediat̄ce hom̄iū salutis puepera.
Myrt̄ temp̄āt̄e. rosa patiēt̄e. nardus odorif̄a.
Tu conuall̄ humilis. terra n̄ arabilis. q̄ fructū parturit.
Flos campi ꝗuallū. singlare lilium xp̄s ex te prodit.
Tu celestis paradisus. tu libanꝰ n̄ incis̄ uaporans dulcedinē.
Tu candoris ⁊ decoris. tu dulcoris ⁊decoris habes plenitudinē.
Tu troñ es salomonis. cui nullus par ī troñs arte uł materia.
Ebur candens castitatis. aurū fuluū caritatis p̄signans mysteria.
Palmā p̄fers singlarē. nec in t̄ris habes parē n̄ in celi curia.
Laus humani generis. uirtutū p̄ cet̄is habes priuilegia.
Sol luna lucidior ⁊luna syderib̄ sic maria dignioꝛ car̄ oībꝰ.
Lux eclypsim nesciens uiginis ē castitas. ardor idefciens immortal̄ caritas.
Salue mat̄ pietatis ⁊totī trinitatis nobile triclinium.
Verbi tam̄ incarnati. speciale magestati p̄parans hospiciū.

Figure 12   *A text of the sequence* Salve mater salvatoris *by Adam of Notre Dame (formerly 'Adam of St Victor'). From an anthology of the late twelfth century formerly in the library of Cîteaux. London, British Library, Additional MS 15722, f.53v. Reproduced by permission.*

their nourishment. To repeat them from memory as a form of prayer was to ruminate upon them (a favourite monastic image) 'like some clean animal chewing the cud'.[50] Sometimes, it would seem, such prayer might involve the melody as well as the words of a chant. Caesarius of Heisterbach tells how a certain Daniel, instructor of the boys at the monastery of St Crisantius, was accustomed to enter the crypt of the church every day, to kneel before the altar, and then to sing the Marian sequence *Ave praeclara maris stella*. The structure of such strophic poetry served a purpose when it was used as prayer, for a pause between verses, or between the versicles of a sequence, afforded an opportunity for meditation or for the performance of some ritual action of personal moment. The *magister puerorum* named Daniel in Caesar of Heisterbach's story always stands when he reaches the versicle with the words *ora Virgo nos illo pane coeli dignos effici*.[51] In another story from the same collection a Cistercian nun is told by the Virgin to recite the sequence *Ave dei genitrix* 'and seek forgiveness at each of the verses'.[52]

This view of a Marian chant as a treasured possession was accompanied by a readiness to regard such chants as a measure of protection against diabolical forces. Both impulses can be clearly felt in another story told by Caesarius of Heisterbach. A priest in the diocese of Trier is received by the *conversi* of a Cistercian monastery, and during his stay there he confesses his special affection for the Cistercians. 'I have received many benefits from your order', he tells the lay-brothers, 'and I have that glorious antiphon *Salve regina misericordie* from it'.[53] These words do not reveal whether the Cistercians gave the priest a written copy of the antiphon or whether they simply taught it to him. What seems clear, however, is that the process which produced the intense and predominantly Marian lay-devotion of the later Middle Ages is taking place in this story, and right in front of our eyes. This was the process whereby Marian texts and devotional commonplaces spread to the laity through the medium of parish priests and confessors. The story goes on to reveal why the priest is so pleased to know the antiphon. One day, as he crossed an open field to visit a certain hermit, a mighty storm arose. The priest fled into a church, quaking with fear as the blows of the thunder fell about him, and prostrated himself before the altar, beseeching Mary to quell the storm. This she blithely did at his request, 'because you have gladly and freely sung the antiphon *Salve regina misericordie* on many occasions'.[54]

A similar story is told by Thomas of Cantimpré. He relates that on one occasion the monks of a Cistercian monastery were beset by dense clouds and flashes of lightning; they immediately fled into the conventual church, 'seeing that their native land, and especially their own cloister, must be in imminent peril'.[55] There they began to sing the antiphon *Salve regina misericordie*, and when they came to the place where the words say 'turn your merciful eyes towards us', a wind blew from the west with such a tremendous clap of thunder that the glass windows of the church broke asunder. The priest of the convent fell to his knees and began the antiphon again, singing the words 'reveal blessed Jesus to us, the fruit of your womb, after this exile', and at once an image of Christ crucified opened its eyes 'contrary to nature', and the storm subsided.

Why is there record of such intense diabolical activity in these Cistercian documents? They are not the only writings of the twelfth and thirteenth centuries to reveal this intense and active fear of supernatural evil, but why are the Cistercian texts so concerned with it? Those are questions for the next and final chapter of this book; for the moment, let us consider the explanations that suggest themselves immediately.

Many of the apparitions can be explained as the feverish dreams of monks just woken from sleep, or of lay brothers who, exposed to a liturgy in a language they did not understand, were unable to resist the soporific effects of a hard day's manual work.[56] The Cistercian documents themselves acknowledge this, although they do not seem to attach much importance to the distinction between dreams and reality.[57] Many other apparitions can perhaps be explained as the tortuous superstitions of rustics whom the Cistercians recruited as lay brothers. Since the Cistercians rejected (at least in theory) the possession of churches, altar offerings, tithes and manorial rents, they relied heavily upon their estates for their incomes; accordingly, they recruited huge numbers of workers, chiefly from the peasantry, to become lay brothers. It would be rash to suggest that a peasant of *c.* 1200 was more superstitious than the reeve who collected his tithes or the count who owned his lands, but the harsh realities of flood, drought and disease have always surrounded agricultural work with a host of beliefs in spirits, both good and evil, and we should not underestimate the influence which the presence of the lay brothers exerted upon the tone of the Cistercian life. One can only imagine the state of mind of such *conversi*, sent in groups to work in the lonely granges and required to celebrate some kind of nocturnal liturgy in the chapels with which these granges were sometimes provided.

Frustration of appetite, whether for food or for sexual satisfaction, is easier to comprehend, and the Cistercian authors provide important signs that diabolic visions were connected in some way with the rigours and deprivations of their strict monastic regime. Quite apart from the passages where such sexual temptation is made explicit,[58] modern psychoanalysis could probably make something of the constant animal imagery in these visions – the pigs, boars and bears, for example, for most of the creatures in the animal kingdom have been chosen by writers at some time or another to express what is sensed as a brutishness in the sexual drive, be it animal or human. The beasts of Iago's sexual imagination, 'prime as goats, as hot as monkeys, as salt as wolves in prides' belong in this erotic menagerie. However, it is possible to exaggerate the importance (especially in our century) of the erotic element in the monks' common psyche. The devils rarely choose to take the form of alluring women, and there is hardly ever a suggestion that the demons in the monastery are trying to exploit the monks' celibate condition in a systematic way.[59]

To some extent, perhaps, the ubiquity of diabolic manifestations in these Cistercian writings can be viewed as an expression of a favourite theme of the White Monks: the importance of the spiritual experience of the simple man. As Lawrence has pointed out, Cistercian writers attached considerable importance to stories in which simple or illiterate people 'scaled the heights of contemplative prayer',[60] and the purpose of many apparition stories is to demonstrate the ability of simple men (and especially of the lay brothers) to experience supernatural events, which are a token of grace, within the context of the Cistercian life and liturgy. Caesarius of Heisterbach tells how a certain Henricus, who is a master of a grange, has the special gift from God that he can see demons in diverse forms at night, but especially in the choir.[61] He is a 'good and upright man, mature in years and a virgin', and he is a lay brother, no doubt of modest (or even of peasant) extraction. His gift of seeing evil spirits is greatly envied by the Abbot who has no such powers, and yet he is a 'nobleman of high birth and blood'. The moral of this story could scarcely be more plain.

Above all, perhaps, the Cistercians welcomed all news of apparitions within their walls because such diabolic attacks were a token of monastic success. In this respect their belief in the supernatural was central to their life of the spirit, and it would be quite unjust for us – who enjoy the privilege of living in an age when the burden of anxiety about the unseen has been lightened – to regard their fears as foolish or primitive. They were neither. This dread of what an evening prayer calls 'the perils and dangers of this night', was shared by men of great learning and spiritual depth. As the book of Deuteronomy seemed to require, in a passage that resonates throughout the monastic reforms of the eleventh and twelfth centuries, the monastery should not only be a place of infinite solitude; it should also be a place of horror. The greatest father of monasticism, St Anthony, had been beset by devils in the desert, and the Cistercians were surely inclined to regard the intense diabolic activity within their walls as a sign that their own enterprise was succeeding; Satan was desperate and afraid, just as he had been many centuries before when Anthony became a hermit. An intense fear of supernatural evil was a penalty that had to be paid by those who withdrew from the world of the twelfth and thirteenth centuries. They resisted – with great fervour – its tendency to secularisation, and turned their backs upon its new tolerance of some human weakness. Yet they did not go thereby to the periphery of religious and political concerns in the twelfth and thirteenth centuries; as we shall see in the next chapter, their achievement was to retire and yet to place themselves in the very centre.

CHAPTER EIGHT

INVENTING THE STATE

'Too great an attention to detail generates disgust and turns many away from the knowledge of truth.'[1] So saying, Johannes de Grocheio dismisses what many of his contemporaries regarded as the very substance of rational thought about practical music: the rules of measured notation. Grocheio is content to leave a detailed treatment of longs, breves and the rest to 'the treatises of others', for his aim lies elsewhere. It is a bold aim: to classify the musical forms, both sacred and secular, that are employed in Paris, and to show how they contribute to the stability of the *civitas*. As one who had pursued the Arts course in the University of Paris, Grocheio will have known the value of stiffening a work with references to standard authors. When he is concerned with the general theory and philosophy of music he cites Plato, Aristotle, Galen, Boethius and others; when the subject is Parisian polyphony, he dutifully mentions Johannes de Garlandia, Franco of Cologne and Lambertus. The section on secular and popular music – what Grocheio calls *musica vulgaris* – presented a problem, however, for there were no authorities. How could there have been? There was no Latin tradition of writing about trouvère songs, dance-songs, instrumental pieces or *chansons de geste*, for example, and no vernacular tradition of doing so, at least in France.[2]

Unable to consult a book, Grocheio consulted a colleague:[3]

> Dicamus igitur, quod formae musicales vel species contentae, sub primo membro, quod vulgare dicebamus, ad hoc ordinantur, ut eis mediantibus mitigentur adversitates hominum innatae. Quas magis particulavimus in sermone ad Clementem exaquiensem monachum.

> We declare, therefore, that the musical forms or types subsumed under the first category, which we have called [*musica*] *vulgaris*, are ordained for this purpose, namely that through their mediation the innate contrarieties of men are mitigated. Which things I have itemised in a discourse to Clement, a monk of Lessay.

This is an enticing picture; a secular Master, trained amidst the noise of Paris, offers his thoughts about the power of secular music to a monk in a remote corner of Normandy. Perhaps Grocheio wanted the views of a contemplative, it being a duty of all Benedictines to reflect daily upon the significance of the *adversitates hominum* which are mentioned in the lines above; or perhaps Grocheio was communicating with an old friend or Master from his native land, western Normandy, where the life of Paris, set well away to the east, could be viewed with detachment.[4] Whatever the truth may be, Grocheio's consideration of secular music, and Clement's part in it, have a wider significance than either of the two men can have realised. Grocheio is a literate cleric fluent in Latin – a *literatus* in contemporary terminology – and it comes naturally to him to legislate for the laity: trouvère songs of middle style *should* be performed before young people to keep them from idleness, and so on. He does not make any such comments when the subject turns to the secular polyphony of the clerical *literati*, the motet and conductus. Grocheio only writes in this authoritative way, and with the presupposition that those to whom he refers display vices which music can cure, when his subject is the music of the laity. As he legislates for them, he employs the terminology which appears in countless thirteenth-century discussions of good government (*bonum regimen*)[5] and the State (*civitas*).[6] The life of a Benedictine and the life of a Master in the university tended to impose different views of the world, but the passage quoted above shows that Grocheio chose to send a version of his thoughts about the function of music in secular society to a monk. When the task was to devise regulations for the laity – even if they were regulations that would never be enforced – the clerical *literati* were of one mind whatever form of life they had chosen.[7]

Grocheio's treatment of secular music may seem unpretentious enough, but in his pages we feel the forces which helped to produce the State in twelfth- and thirteenth-century France – which helped to produce France, indeed. As a cleric with a university training, Grocheio belonged to the class which supplied princes with their advisers and provided the whole of France with the principal agents and beneficiaries of bureaucratic power. As Murray explains:[8]

> The growth of the University of Paris must . . . be seen in a French
> political context. Their country's political expansion offered students
> jobs. They in their turn backed up the political conquerors with an army
> of intellectual colonists. French ascendancy can be seen from this aspect
> as that of a Paris-trained national élite.

In his *De musica* Grocheio is certainly an 'intellectual colonist', defining the boundaries of laymen's music as he sees fit and imposing value judgements upon it in line with clerical concepts of social good. We should not overlook the political nuances of Grocheio's treatment of secular music. It is there in the vocabulary, for as the passage quoted above clearly reveals, Grocheio made a discourse to Clement on the subject of why secular musical forms are 'ordained', *ordinantur*, as if those forms were regulated by a central authority charged to issue ordinances for their control. These are the powerful overtones of the word *ordinantur*, for such concepts resonate through the Latin vocabulary of 'ordaining' for the State during the twelfth and thirteenth centuries. They became louder still with the study of Aristotle's *Politics* and *Ethics*. This is Albertus Magnus:[9]

> Delectationes autem quidem sicut cantoria, viellatoria, tripudia,

saltatoria, tragoedia, et comoedia, et hujusmodi, quas oportet politicum
sufficienter praeordinare, ut omnis civis jucundus apud civem in
delectabilibus liberalibus inveniatur . . . Saltatoria autem virtutes motivas
preparans, civem facit velocem.

Delights include singing, playing the *viella*, springing, dancing, acting
and the recitation of epics, and such things as these which the politician
should regulate in adequate supply, so that every citizen may be found
to be happy in 'liberal' pleasures [i.e. pleasures that are free from sin]
in the city . . . Dancing nurtures the motor faculties and makes the
citizens agile.

Such thinking owes a great deal to the Parisian tradition of lecturing upon
the *Sentences* of Peter Lombard, discussed in Chapter 1. Indeed, these lines
are essentially an expansion of the kind of dictum which Albertus would
have known from such lectures in Paris, both as a student and as a Master:
'those things which maintain the State cannot be impediments to virtue'.[10]
Albertus uses these sentiments in a way that anticipates Grocheio's emphasis
upon the contribution which secular music makes to the *civitas*, and he does
so in language that implies centralised authority. It is up to the 'politician'
to 'regulate' secular music (*praeordinare*) so that contentment will be guaranteed
for all citizens.

The writings of Albertus do not merely seem to anticipate Grocheio's *De
musica*; at one point they virtually call upon him to undertake it. In his
commentary upon Aristotle's *Politics*, probably composed *c.*1262–63, Albertus
recommends that musicians should study the ways in which the musical forms
they employ may exert an influence upon *disciplina* – in this context surely
civic conformity and discipline for the sake of common welfare:[11]

. . . musicam videmus distinctam per melodiarum formam et per rythmos
diversos, et quod oportet in omnibus his invenire quam unumquodque
potentiam habeat ad disciplinam. Deinde, quia sunt multi musici
praesentis temporis, committit illis per singula quaerere de his.

. . . we may see that music has many distinct forms according to the
form of melodies and the various kinds of poems, and that it would be
fitting to discover what contribution each one may have to make to
education. Since there are many authorities on music at the present time
it can be entrusted to them to investigate these things in detail.

Grocheio fulfils the terms of this open letter to musicians. To borrow the
terms employed by Albertus, Grocheio discusses the 'form of melodies' (*melodiarum formam*) and the various kinds of poems (*rythmos diversos*) used with
them, and he also considers how each musical form may exert an influence
upon *disciplina*. In Albertus's sense of the term – if not in ours – Johannes
de Grocheio is a politician.

'The invention of the State', writes Cheyette, 'is the story of how [a] small
minority of literate men slowly imposed upon the non-literate their special
ways of thinking about politics and law.'[12] To suggest that these ways of

thinking were invariably designed to further the special interests of this 'small minority' would be to display an excessive scepticism. The concept of the State which theologians and legists espoused rested upon an earnest conviction that Man in his fallen condition must be a social and political animal for the sake of common welfare on earth, and that the State is the natural way for this necessity to be met.[13] Theology and the politics of centralised authority were therefore difficult to disentangle, and were often inseparable. As Grocheio's contemporary, Bartholomaeus de Pisa put it: all questions of practical morality are questions 'of the common good of the Church or of the State' (*communis utilitatis ecclesie vel rei publice*).[14] That being said, however, there is still a persuasive argument to be made that the elaboration of canonical controls during our period, whether in manuals for confession, in moral imperatives issued through sermons, or in statutes for the condemnation and persecution of heretics, Jews and lepers, does indeed represent what R.I.Moore has recently described as 'the dark underside of the revival of the twelfth century'.[15] Let us look more closely at this proposition.

Confession and coercion

The manuals of confession, whose evidence was particularly important in Chapter 1, are open to interpretation as elaborate and influential forms of coercion. The proliferation of such manuals during the thirteenth century has often been regarded, no doubt correctly, as a response to a decree issued by the Fourth Lateran Council in 1215 that all the faithful of either sex should be confessed at least once a year,[16] and in this context it is worth recalling some of the other decrees promulgated by that same Lateran Council. The last three rulings, for example, require that Jews be distinguished from Christians in their dress, that they be prohibited from holding public office, and that any of those who convert to Christianity be forbidden from observing any of their former rituals. It is yet more striking that[17]

> the Lateran decrees opened with a declaration of faith. It was clearly
> and precisely formulated in a manner calculated to repudiate the tenets
> of the Cathar heresy which in the last two generations had been
> establishing itself rapidly, particularly in the Languedoc, Provence and
> Lombardy. This creed was followed by the third and longest canon,
> which anathemetized 'every heresy that raises itself against the holy,
> orthodox and Catholic faith', and prescribed detailed measures to
> extirpate them.

The flood of manuals for confessors in the thirteenth century was therefore released by a Council closely concerned with establishing systematic control over subversion: subversion by Jews, regarded as sexually profligate, blasphemous and prone to alliances with Satan, and subversion by heretics. The manuals themselves, which often raise issues that the lawyers also discuss, and in very similar terms,[18] are an attempt to achieve a systematic control over the bearing, contrition and penance of the laity, and there is no difficulty in seeing them as part of the process whereby a 'small minority of literate men' slowly imposed their conceptions upon the non-literate. The manuals were an extension of authority into the minutiae of pastoral work, paralleling the expansion of legal controls in the twelfth and thirteenth centuries. In both urban and rural communities 'kings, popes and nobles extended governmental institutions of new force, permanence and intimacy . . . [establishing] . . . networks of permanent officials to do their justice, raise their taxes and enforce their will'.[19] The confessors were the travelling justiciars of a Catholic Church newly conscious of the efficacy of concerted, centralised action, and they worked in the same way as their secular counterparts: by systematic inquisition. The legal resonances of all this were loud; in contemporary terminology, the confessor's task was to investigate *cases* of conscience.

During the twelfth and thirteenth centuries the canonists strove to elaborate a definition of legal infamy: the notion that certain forms of behaviour and ways of life are so demeaning to the individual that they imperil his legal status.[20] The manuals of confession enforce a theological equivalent: a kind of behaviour so useless, or so corrupt, that it imperils the individual's right to the sacrament that reconciles him to his Creator. 'When prostitutes or minstrels come to confession' says Thomas Chobham, just before elaborating his threefold classification of minstrels, 'they are not to be given the sacrament of penance unless they completely abandon their trades, because otherwise they cannot win salvation.'[21]

This was an extension of a quintessentially *literate* authority. Through the manuals of confession, the laymen of thirteenth-century Europe were to be brought to book in every sense of the phrase. A work like Thomas Chobham's penitential, composed almost immediately after the Lateran Council of 1215, represents a crushing use of literacy. The difference between Chobham's voluminous review of human sinfulness and the penitentials of the Carolingian period with their simple tariffs of punishments for offences – a difference that has often been emphasised – is primarily a contrast between memory and written record. The Carolingian lists had to be memorised by barely literate priests in their pastoral work; Chobham's *Summa* is a comprehensive handbook which unburdens the memory and allows its subject to ramify in a way that only a written treatment of a matter, where memory is thus unburdened, can hope to do. It is literacy, therefore, and the authoritarian wish to provide trenchant legislation for all instances, which brings the classification of *histriones*, *scurrae* and the rest into works such as Chobham's.

But why make concessions to any of these entertainers? Part of the answer lies with the 'naturalness' of the State which was so clearly sensed by theologians and canonists of the twelfth and thirteenth centuries.[22] Since the natural, primitive society of mankind before the Fall had passed away, it was held to be consistent with the will of God and with natural law that human beings should form a State. Reflecting upon this naturalness, numerous theologians and canonists recognised that there were some human weaknesses which were also natural in a lower sense, and that therefore the State could not exist without tolerating them. In the early fourteenth century, for example, Nicholas de Lyra was prepared to countenance prostitution within the *civitas* as a measure to preserve public order,[23] and to some extent the tolerance extended to instrumentalists was a concession of a similar kind. It was recognised that the pleasure which their music gave appealed to an appetite inseparable from Man's gross physical nature, a 'delectatio *animalis*'.[24] In their willingness to concede that some comfort was necessary to mitigate the sadness of human life, the *tristicia huius seculi*, or to enliven its dullness, the *tedium huius vite*, the theologians recognised the salutary powers of music while continuing to acknowledge that Man's crippling weakness since the Fall was responsible for all *tristicia* and *tedium*.[25]

The question of why clerical administrators were prepared to look favourably upon at least some of the narrative repertoire performed by minstrels is a wide-ranging one. The signs of their favour are clear, not only in Thomas Chobham's approving reference to accompanied songs of the deeds of princes and of the lives of saints, but also in Johannes de Grocheio's description of *chansons de geste* in virtually the same terms. It is a useful hypothesis that the importance of such narrative repertoire was related to the increasingly urban context of instrumental minstrelsy. The gifts of clothing which minstrels received in great households, both lay and ecclesiastical, did not constitute a particularly portable or divisible form of wealth, nor was the supply of such things either predictable or regular. The wider range of coin available in the twelfth and thirteenth centuries, accompanied by a growth in the money economy, furnished minstrels with a more effective form of wealth, and it is no surprise to find a reference (in a sermon of the early fourteenth century) to minstrels who only wear the robes given to them for a few days; soon after that they sell them for cash.[26] In the countryside the supply of money varied considerably according to the season. At harvest time, when many agricultural workers were paid for the year, and when the makers of agricultural equipment did most of their trade, the supply of coin in rural areas could be abundant, but during the rest of the year the use of money often remained 'in a minor key'.[27] In the cities, however, the supply of coin was much more regular. The fiddlers of the *Dit des taboureurs*, so proud of their epic repertoire, are out to earn the *argent du commun*, 'the silver of the town'. Their complaint is that agricultural workers – whose supply of money could be so tenuous – are earning it with their tabors made from converted sieves.[28]

The best place for minstrel instrumentalists, therefore, was a city, a town, or at least some reasonably complex agglomeration where a density of trading and artisanal manufacture kept the supply of money alive. In the epic of *Le Moniage Guillaume* (second redaction), some robbers in the countryside overhear a young man singing a song which, in the first redaction of the poem, is a *chanson de geste* about Guillaume au Court Nez himself. 'If you ask me that is a minstrel', says one of the robbers, 'and he must have come from some *borc*, *vile* or *cité* where he has sung in the square.'[29] The very least that *borc* and *vile* can imply is some kind of substantial and probably fortified agglomeration around a monastery, perhaps, or a seigneurial residence (Figure 3).

An urban context for the performance of *chansons de geste* by minstrels is also suggested by a passage from a thirteenth-century sermon, presumably preached in Paris, although not exclusively there:[30]

> Cum voce joculatoris, in parvo ponte [var: in plateis] sedentis, quomodo
> illi strenui milites antiqui, scilicet Rolandus et Oliverius, et cetera, in
> bello occubuere recitatur, populus circumstans pietate movetur et
> interdum lacrymatur.

> The voice of the minstrel sitting on the Petit Pont [variant: 'in the
> streets'] tells how the mighty soldiers of long ago, such as Roland, Oliver
> and the rest, were slain in battle, then the people standing around them
> are moved to pity and periodically burst into tears.

This offers a precise picture of minstrels performing *chansons de geste* in the streets of Paris or on the Petit Pont (Figure 5). We notice the powerful impression that such narratives could make upon the populace; even allowing for the existence of a 'tears' topos in this passage it is striking to be told that the listeners periodically wept. The sermon reveals some of the epic subjects that had the power to induce this flood of feeling, and to the stories of Roland and Oliver mentioned there we may add the various epic heroes claimed by the fiddlers in the *Dit des taboureurs*: Auberi le Bourgoing, Girart de Vienne, Thierry l'Ardenois, Guillaume au Court Nez and Aimeri. All of these are protagonists in the Matter of France, the cycle of stories concerned with feuding magnates who lived (insofar as they are historical) between *c.* 750 and *c.* 1000, the period which the Old French poets took as their Heroic Age. It is a matter of pride to the fiddlers of the *Dit des taboureurs* that each item in their narrative repertoire should be what another text calls '*un son ... de la terre des francs*'.[31] It is still possible to appreciate why these stories of treachery, feud, murder and wanton cruelty had a powerful effect upon the urban populations of the twelfth and thirteenth centuries. These dwellers in cities and towns, living in communities that were predominantly settled and mercantile, could find in the *chansons de geste* an evocation of a tumultuous past dominated by headstrong warriors who all but live on horseback, who think not of wealth but of treasure, and who have the grandeur to regard mercantile thrift and prudence with contempt.

Charlemagne, of course, is one of the greatest figures of the Old French epics, but many of the surviving *chansons de geste* show him as a weak king or as one who mistakes stubbornness for strength. They also portray clerics as liturgical celebrants who are good for very little outside the church. So it may seem surprising that the clerical *literati* were sometimes prepared to endorse such stories (while reserving the right to denounce their wilder fictions, the *mendacia*). The lofty disdain which many *chansons de geste* reveal, both for the cleric's literate intelligence and for the merchant's cunning, was a scorn for some of the principal forces in the expansion of economic life and centralised power during the twelfth and thirteenth centuries.[32] But that is precisely why the clerical *literati* were able to approve them. Many of the epics provided listeners in settled urban communities with a view of how things had been before that great expansion took place. It is a terrible picture of lawlessness and treachery. Despite endless variations of theme and treatment, the message in many of the epics seems to be a simple one: before there was central governmental control under a supreme monarch – before there was France, in effect – there was only feud and conflict. The lesson for the *populi* as they stood around the minstrel on the Petit Pont was clear: learn from the sufferings of the great ones in the past and see that present trials are comparatively light. This seems to have been exactly the way in which the *chansons de geste* were regarded by Johannes de Grocheio, who must often have passed the minstrel narrators at work as he crossed the Petit Pont:[33]

> Cantus autem iste debet antiquis et civibus laborantibus et mediocribus ministrari, dum requiescunt ab opere consueto, ut auditis miseriis et calamitatibus aliorum suas facilius sustineant et quilibet opus suum alacrius aggrediatur. Et ideo iste cantus valet ad conservationem totius civitatis.

> This kind of music should be performed for old people, for working citizens and for those of middle station, so that, hearing the miseries and calamities of others, they may more easily sustain their own and may perform their work, whatever it may be, with greater willingness. By these means this kind of music has the power to protect the whole state.

Parisian sermons from Grocheio's lifetime leave no doubt whom he means by 'working citizens and ... those of middle station'. These are the small artisans and craftsmen, such as carpenters and blacksmiths, whom contemporary clerics could lightly call the poor, the *pauperes*, because they conformed to a contemporary sense of that word in being powerless.[34] These *carpentarii* and *fabri* were rarely wealthy; a Parisian sermon of 1273 assures us that 'such men who win their daily bread with their hands are not usually very rich', and they were powerless in that their power could only be shown by civil disobedience.[35] At first, Johannes de Grocheio's remarks about the social influence of *chansons de geste* may seem somewhat naive. It is surely not so.

As Thomas Chobham's discussion of minstrels opens, one word tolls in line after line: 'office', *officium*. Opening a brief and general discussion 'of offices in general', for example, Chobham instructs confessors that 'it is necessary to ask the penitent what his office may be'.[36] In total, the word appears seven times in only twice as many lines. On one level, the close attention to duties and callings which is found throughout the theological writings of the twelfth and thirteenth centuries reflects a fundamental development in the social thought of theologians. As the century progressed, more and more trades came to be accepted as legitimate means of livelihood, if not necessarily praiseworthy in themselves.[37] This concern with *officia* is perhaps one of the most characteristic developments of our period, for it involves a gain in stability – even a gain in dignity – by the intrusion of written regulation and statutory control into human relations. To speak of a trade as an *officium* was to regard it as a fulfilment of all the written, statutory obligations which were automatically laid upon anyone who practised it. In Cheyette's phrase, it was to draw 'the crucial distinction between person and office – the person of flesh and character, the office as an abstract category of law'.[38] Such *officia* conferred a measure of dignity, and one which many minstrel instrumentalists deeply desired.

The history of the word *menestrel* suggests how deeply they desired it. One of the major meanings of *menestrel* in the twelfth and thirteenth centuries was 'craftsman'.[39] In Latin, this was an ancient usage; as early as *c.* 800 it was possible to refer to blacksmiths, tailors, carpenters, soapmakers, brewers and many others as *ministeriales*,[40] and in Old French this usage flourished. In 1268, for example, the Parisian prévôt Etienne Boileau used the term *menestreus* (in various spellings) to denote any kind of master artisan as distinct from an apprentice or a mere unskilled assistant.[41] In some thirteenth-century texts, indeed, discussions of artisans and the tools of their trade mention *menestrels* and their *instrumens*, and yet the sense is still a general one; musical minstrels are not specifically meant.[42]

How did the term *menestrel* come to acquire the specific sense of 'an entertainer, generally an instrumentalist', side by side with its other meanings, including 'a craftsman'? The answer is probably that minstrels working frequently in an urban context, and wishing to acquire the status of legitimate and approved artisans, began speaking of themselves as craftsmen, *menestrels*, abandoning the older and less respectful word *jongleur*.[43] In a revealing passage from *Huon de Bordeaux* (1216–29) the hero meets a skilled instrumentalist, and when he asks the musician what he is the narrator reveals in advance of the musician's answer that he is a *jougleres*; but when the musician speaks of himself he says 'there is no better *menestrel* than me'.[44] The way is open here towards the Parisian minstrel statutes of 1321 wherein the instrumentalists of Paris make their trade into an 'office' by devising statutory controls for it, and by proclaiming themselves to be good craftsmen, *bons ouvriers*. Johannes de Grocheio is sensitive to this development and he carefully describes the most skilled kind of fiddler as a *bonus artifex in viella*, 'a good *craftsman* on the fiddle'.

Minstrelsy is not the only kind of professional musical activity which comes to light in the thirteenth century as theologians concerned with the sacrament of penance began sifting through the *officia* of their day to separate the licit ones from the illicit. There is also the activity of performers of polyphony, the Masters of organum. Once again, the purpose of the writing in question, this time Robert of Courson's *Summa*, is to identify a service that is discharged for money and to bring it under statutory control. The very appearance of such Masters of organum who 'hire out their services' (*locare operas suas*) represents a divorce between the sacred and the secular of a kind whose importance to the social and intellectual history of the Middle Ages has been emphasised by Peter Brown.[45] In Courson's day there was no longer a supposition – as there had been in the time of Guido of Arezzo – that a singer of liturgical polyphony will be one devoted to the monastic life; indeed, there is no supposition in Courson's discussion of these Masters that such singers will be committed to any form of religious life whatsoever beyond such minimal membership of the clerical state as the tonsure and minor orders would confer. With Courson's *Summa* we are probably seeing the culmination of a development whereby the performance of composed liturgical polyphony gradually passed into the hands of specialists as the skills required to perform it began to diverge from those required for the standard conventual plainchant. The commodification of this skill, whereby a monetary value was placed upon it, manifests the overwhelming direction of twelfth-century economic life towards monetary payment for the proliferating results of artisanal manufacture, just as it reflects the practice of providing cash payments for participation in liturgical services to canons and lesser *clerici* with choral duties in secular churches.

By recognising that the work of the Masters of organum constitutes an *officium*, Courson objectifies it and makes it susceptible (at least in theory) to the intervention of clerical authorities in the form of prelates of good conscience who judge that the *officium* is not being conducted according to the guidelines that Courson's *Summa* provides for it. We should not miss the powerful concept of centralised ecclesiastical authority that contemporaries who understood Courson's purpose and importance would have sensed in his work. Courson was the papal legate to France and a Master of Theology from the University of Paris. In the year 1215, he and the Masters of the university produced a set of statutes 'that would secure the corporate achievements and complete the programme of educational reform begun years before when Courson himself had been teaching in Paris'.[46] Courson was therefore identified with the highest clerical authority and with a powerful organisational enterprise in a city whose university was rapidly becoming the training-ground for Europe's bureaucrats. His lines about the Masters of organum are an internal memo for circulation within a huge edifice of ecclesiastical and civil government. They provide the first evidence that we have of the career structure for singers and composers of polyphonic liturgical music which was later to be of such importance in the history of Western music.

Fear of the Ancient Enemy within

In the previous section I have suggested that the general history of minstrelsy before *c.* 1300, and the emergence of the Masters of organum, both reveal an impulse characteristic of the twelfth and thirteenth centuries, but especially of the thirteenth. This might be defined as the desire to secure stability and moral cleanliness within the *civitas*, felt to be the natural form of social organisation in a fallen world, by imposing centralised and literacy-based controls. So far, however, we have only considered writings arising from a clerical reaction to subversion of a fairly immediate and tangible kind: the *histriones* whose lascivious gestures appalled Peter the Chanter and Thomas Chobham, for example, or the Masters of organum whose occasional use of 'minstrelish figures' disturbed Robert of Courson. But these were by no means the only forces that threatened the common welfare. There were others, much more insidious, which brought the Church into daily conflict with the Devil.

The clerical culture of the twelfth and thirteenth centuries was marked by an increasingly neurotic fear of pollution from groups of individuals collaborating with dark powers to further Satan's influence in the world.[47] A story, first told on the threshold of the Middle Ages, may serve as an illustration. In Constantinople there was an image of the Virgin in a certain house. When a Jew visited the house and heard whose portrait it was, he snatched it from the wall, took it to a privy and defiled it in every possible way. The filthy image was later discovered by a pious Christian, and once it had been cleaned and re-placed it began to secrete a miraculous oil. This is a straightforward story, and when it was told by Adamnan (d.704), Abbot of Iona, the subsequent fate of the Jew was of no interest. 'What the Jew did afterwards', says Adamnan, 'how he lived, or how he ended his life, is unknown.'[48] When the story came to be retold in the thirteenth century, however, by the poet-composer Gauthier de Coincy and by the music-theorist Aegidius of Zamora, the fate of the Jew had become clear. 'His body and soul were snatched by the Devil', says Gauthier,[49] 'he was taken off by an evil spirit', says Aegidius.[50]

During the twelfth and thirteenth centuries the Jews were surrounded by rumours of sexual immorality, intense blasphemy and child-sacrifice. The same kind of neurosis characterised the official clerical view of two problems that became increasingly pressing in the twelfth century: leprosy, and the spreading contagion of that even more hateful disease, heresy. As R. I. Moore, who has written magnificently of twelfth-century persecutions, explains:[51]

> there was a special link between the Devil and the Jews, sexually bonded
> and characterised by the seduction of Christians into the Devil's service
> by means of Jewish wiles. Jews were also held to resemble heretics and
> lepers in being associated with filth, stench and putrefaction, in
> exceptional sexual voracity and endowment, and in the menace which
> they presented in consequence to the wives and children of honest
> Christians . . . The images and nightmares are not always consistent,
> but they always feed the same fear. For all imaginative purposes heretics,
> Jews and lepers were interchangeable. They had the same qualities, from
> the same source, and they presented the same threat: through them the
> Devil was at work to subvert the Christian order and bring the world
> to chaos.

In his discussion of persecution, Moore asks why it is that this disgust for Jews, lepers and heretics, together with the vindictive behaviour which ensued, should have taken such a systematic and institutionalised form in the twelfth and thirteenth centuries. His answer is that the specialisation and professionalisation of government made possible by the talents and initiatives of the clerical *literati* produced a situation in which the clerics who occupied the vast number of different positions of bureaucratic power which existed for clerics to fill began to react sharply against influences which threatened the spiritual or legal power of the clergy. Popular heresy, for example, 'represented, not exclusively, but more than any other single force, the assertion of collective values and communal independence against the subordination of religion first to seignurial and later to bureaucratic power'.[52]

This provides a suggestive context for the virulent polemics against the *carole* examined in Chapter 5. What would it mean to say that many churchmen regarded the *carole* as a form of popular heresy? To consider the term 'popular' for a moment, it is noteworthy that the polemics against the *carole* invariably refer to dances in what might be loosely described as an urban or village context. The dancers move through a street or a square, a *vicus* or a *platea*, but never through an aristocratic hall, an *aula*. In the minds of the authors who wrote these polemics there seems to have been little or no connection between the Latin works that they were writing and the courtly milieu for *caroles* which is so abundantly attested in the vernacular romances. Guillaume Peyraut's attack on *caroles*, for example, contained in a book that was a mandatory volume for every Dominican reference library,[53] would have principally been heard in the urban context to which Humbert of Romans called all the preachers of his order, 'because there are more sins in cities',[54] and in the towns and villages. It is uncertain what exposure it would have received from preachers and confessors employed in aristocratic residences.

To describe the *carole* as 'popular' creates few uncertainties, for there can be little doubt that the *carole*, at least in city, town and village, is virtually the only form of popular music from this period of which we have any direct knowledge. It seems a much less obvious choice of words, however, to describe the *carole* as a 'heresy', or to say that contemporary clerics regarded it in much the same way as they regarded heresy (even if they did not think of participation in a *carole* as a heretical act of an officially punishable kind). To clarify this idea, let us attempt a rudimentary and no doubt selective definition of a popular heresy in the contexts of twelfth- and thirteenth-century neuroses about pollution and subversion of the established Church. Firstly, a popular heresy must be an assertion by its adherents that they are in some significant measure independent of the controls which the ecclesiastical authorities are entitled to exert over their beliefs and their behaviour. Secondly, a popular heresy must possess a degree of initiative, reinforcing the independence which its adherents claim by incorporating some way of solemnising the religious festivals it respects in competition with the liturgy of the established Church or as ancillary observances to it. Thirdly, the heresy must pose a sufficiently grave threat that the clerical imagination is excited into deploying a conventional but still nightmarish imagery of sexual corruption, blasphemy and Satanic power.

The *carole* met all of these conditions. The Latin polemics against it repeatedly stress that *caroles* threaten the liturgy of the Church by drawing members of the congregation away on major feasts, by disturbing the liturgy with their noise, and by establishing an alternative way for a community to celebrate holy days within the very physical spaces – the *loca sancta* – claimed by the Church for its own use, principally the cemeteries. In this way the *caroles* of a community that was focused by a village, by a small town or by an urban parish or quarter, represented an 'assertion of collective values and communal independence' analogous to the popular heresies which inspired such anxiety and disgust in the clerical authorities.

The imagery of sexual corruption is ubiquitous in the polemics against *caroles*. There are constant references to the lascivious influence of the young girls who figured so prominently in the dances, and these seem to betray a deep-seated fear of enhanced female attractiveness brought to a game where women could at least pretend to be sexually predatory. This language of sexual disgust is compounded with a virulent demonology. Time and time again the polemics refer to the *carole* as an unholy parody of the Church's liturgy: as priests sing to God with their acolytes singing the responses, so carollers sing to the Devil, the dancers 'replying' to the leader of the dance; as the priest dresses himself in special vestments for the Mass, so the carollers put on special clothes for what some polemics explicity call the 'Devil's liturgy', the *officium diaboli*. The nightmare culminates in the protracted horror of Peyraut's chapters on the *carole*, where female carollers become the human-faced locusts of the Apocalypse. With a lion's teeth, a scorpion's tail, and with deafening wings, they fulfil the prophecy of the first of the great woes to be brought upon the earth by the blast of the fifth trumpet.

Plainchant and the supernatural

As early as the eleventh century there are signs that an almost indiscriminate disgust for heretics, Jews, women and the Devil who seduced them could inspire the monastic mind, reared upon the contemplation of the unseen, to horrific visions of Satan and his ministers. After centuries of apparent quiescence, in which it is hard to find signs of any systematic persecution of Jews or heretics in the West,[55] the first decades of the eleventh century bring a change signalised particularly by Raoul Glaber, a Cluniac monk of St Leger-de-Champeaux, near Dijon, whose *Five Books of History* were principally written to illustrate the apocalyptic prophecy that 'Satan will be released when a thousand years have passed.' Writing during the second quarter of the eleventh century, Raoul tells of condemnations and burnings at Milan (1028), and mentions various other heretics. We also hear of a burning for heresy at Orléans in 1022. In Raoul's mind this resurgence of heresy, such as it was, is associated with an indiscriminate fear of the wiles of women, Jews and heretics. In one of his chapters, 'Concerning the discovery of heresy in Italy',[56] Raoul tells how a certain castle was filled with people 'stained with the defilement' of heretical beliefs. They even made sacrifices to heathen idols in the company of Jews. Nearby was a Christian house where a knight lay ill, and one day he received a visit from one of the heretics, a woman. As she walked into his chamber he noticed that she was accompanied by an innumerable army dressed in black and with the most terrifying faces. This 'army' is a diabolic apparition, of course, and just the sort of conspicuous evil that Raoul associates with *mulieres*, *Judaei* and *heretici*. Sometimes, however, the evil is much more conspicuous. The ministers of Satan are abroad with such vigour, and with such boldness, that they break into daily experience. Raoul reports that he actually saw devils on several occasions, once as he lies in bed in his cell:[57]

> Erat enim, quantum a me dignosci potuit, statura mediocris, collo
> gracili, a facie macilenta, oculis nigerrimis, fronte rugosa et contracta,
> depressis naribus, os exporrectum, labellis tumentibus.

> As far as I could discern, he was of medium stature with a thin neck
> and a thin face, with the blackest eyes, with a shrivelled and twisted
> forehead, with low lying nostrils, with a distended mouth, with swollen
> lips.

A firm belief that the pungent odour of Satan's presence could be detected nearly everywhere was inseparable, in the twelfth and thirteenth centuries, from an equally intense and rational determination to frame legislation, to define formally constituted bodies and to govern for the common good. Satan was the ultimate subversive. It therefore follows that the rational and systematising impulse so abundantly displayed in our period were accompanied by an increase in the incidence of demonic encounters – by a constant reminder, as it were, of what was being fought against and suppressed. Such visions intruded especially into the lives of those who taunted the Devil by their otherworldliness. These were the monks who, like St Anthony, went out 'into a place of horror and of infinite solitude', above all the Cistercians.

The intensity of the demonic experiences endured by Cistercian monks of the twelfth and thirteenth century, especially when they were standing in the choir to perform plainchant, can be interpreted in various ways. To some extent, no doubt, the tendency of these monks to regard trivial or natural happenings as warnings, or as the work of vindictive supernatural agencies, arose from the infinite number of ways in which the monastic life could arouse remorse of conscience. We must also consider the confined nature of monastic experience. The monks were convinced that their purpose was a momentous one, but unlike the great military campaigns which provided the contemporary mind with its clearest understanding of what a momentous purpose was, the monks fought their great battle without travel, without any variation of visual stimulus, and without any tangible objective. The momentousness of their enterprise was therefore inevitably expressed in habitual sights – the choir, the infirmary, and so on – suddenly illuminated by beautiful or by terrifying glimpses of what was normally unseen.

It is also possible to argue that the demonic experiences of the Cistercians represented a form of willing sacrifice, for it was the Cistercians who, by the way of life that they had chosen, took the full force of what ensued from the contemporary belief in immanent justice: the power of natural and accidental events – a thunderstorm, a strong wind, a fire – to warn and to punish. It would be mistaken to regard the Cistercian mentality in this respect as being somehow 'primitive' for its time, and Radding is surely guilty of anachronism when he argues that in the twelfth century '*intellectuals* saw fire, rain and lightening where their *predecessors* saw the miraculous intervention of God or the saints, and instead of devils they saw flies, wind and the chance misfortune' (my italics).[58] If that view is to be accepted then it becomes difficult to understand why there should ever have been a European witch-craze beginning three centuries later. The proliferation of Latin treatises of an objective and 'scientific' kind during the thirteenth century, for example, should not be too readily interpreted as testimony to an evolution from an essentially superstitious view of the natural world to an objectified and rational one. If there is a significant change in our period in this regard it is that the prevailing belief in the ubiquity of demonic presence becomes *more* intense between 1100 and 1200, and not less so. This was inevitable, for the Devil was increasingly perceived by the centralised Church as the controller of an infinite number of subversives: Jews, heretics, clerks abusing their intellectual powers by enquiring into occult sciences, and a monstrous regiment of women. In this battle with the supernatural, the Cistercians in their choir, performing the ritual which was the centre of their monastic life, placed themselves in the front line.

The freedom of the court

The hypothesis presented above has been that many of the Latin writings which reflect the musical life of 1100–1300 can be interpreted in terms of the special interests and the religious convictions of the clerical *literati* who played a major part in the invention of the State. It is some confirmation of that hypothesis that when we turn to the Old French narratives, where the interests and convictions of the chivalric aristocracy are uppermost, then the picture of musical life which we receive seems to change out of all recognition. The neurosis about the heresy of the *carole* completely disappears. It is replaced by a vision of a milieu in which the dances of the court, and the *caroles* in the city squares encountered by travelling retinues, are regarded with delight. The Latin polemics against *coreae* often reveal a deep loathing for female attractiveness – especially when enhanced in some way – and for the playful energy of young males; but in the romances the hated *juvenes* and *mulieres* of the polemics are replaced by *vallets* and *puceles*, terms which imply an essentially pragmatic view of young persons at court as a welcome source of impromptu, unpaid entertainment and of festive energy. At the same time, minstrels of all varieties are welcomed, an enthusiasm which is merely one aspect of the almost completely unshadowed enjoyment of feasts and great court occasions which the romances reflect.

APPENDIX

A brief conspectus of some major types of sources

The purpose of this Appendix is to provide a brief conspectus of the major kinds of source material used in this book, and to present freshly edited texts and translations of key extracts which are not readily accessible, either because the works in question have never been published or because they are only available at present in manuscripts or in early printed editions. The editions are based upon manuscript sources, but no attempt had been made to produce critical editions (which, in the case of a text like Guillaume Peyraut's *Summa de vitiis et virtutibus*, would require a lifetime's work). Annotations have been kept to a minimum, being mostly confined to indications of the biblical passages which the authors quote or echo. The orthography is generally that of the manuscripts. In one case, the Parisian minstrel statutes of 1321, the text is given here (taken from Faral, *Les jongleurs*) even though it is not hard to come by, for ease of reference.

'Many non-medievalists', writes David d'Avray, 'are under the impression that sources for the Middle Ages are scarce. This is half-true of the twelfth century, fairly true of the period before, and fairly untrue of the period after. From the thirteenth century on the study of many topics suffers from the same embarrassment of riches as, say, the study of the First World War'.[1] That is well said. The quantity of written material that has some bearing upon the musical life of the twelfth and thirteenth centuries is enormous, and most of it remains unpublished. There are many thousands of sermons, for example, any one of which may reveal some vivid detail,[2] and a very large number of manuscripts survive which contain sections on the Seven Vices where references to musical life are often to be found in the chapter on *Luxuria*.[3]

Sermons

Sermons are a major source of information about the life and predicament of minstrels. The sheer quantity of the homiletic material which survives, and which remains unpublished for the most part, is unnerving,[4] but a preliminary sampling suggests that the most useful sermons for the present purposes are those which make extensive use of the *similitudo*, or extended simile (Figure 13). These similes often reveal small pieces of information about professional entertainers and musicians (for some examples see p. 200). Many preachers were probably attracted to the *similitudo* for the dimension of ingenuity that it could accommodate, comparable in some respects to the wit required for the conceits of the English metaphysical poets who also loved to extend similes to the limits of acceptability and coherence. As with the metaphysical

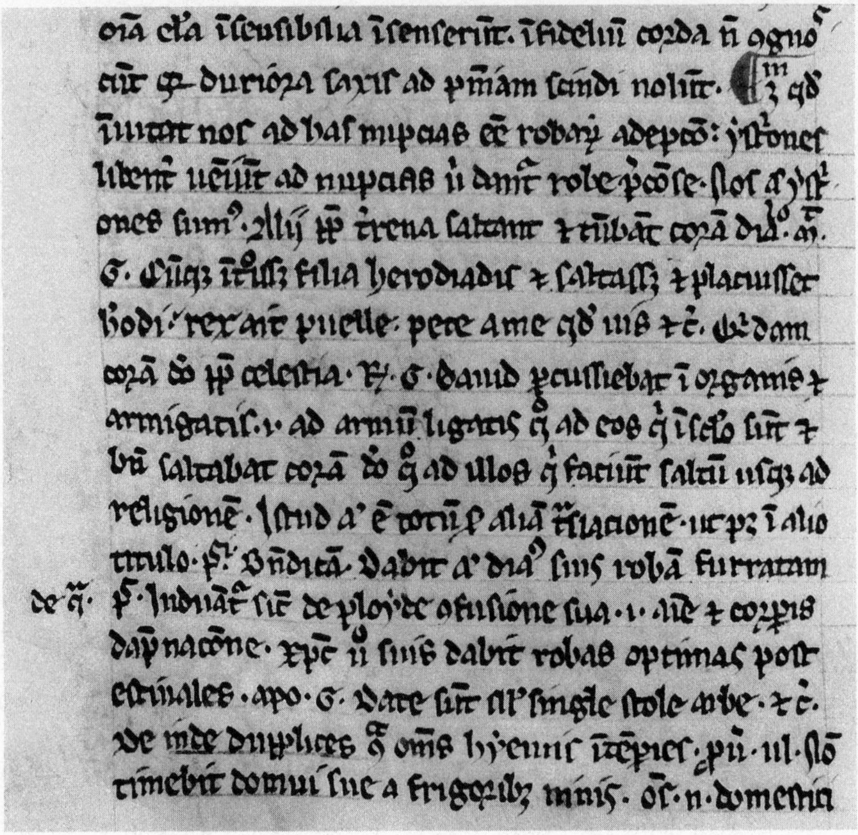

Figure 13 *A* similitudo *concerning the minstrels employed in great households. Cambridge, Gonville and Caius College, MS 52/29, f.158v. Reproduced by permission of the Master and Fellows.*

conceit, the thirteenth-century *similitudo* required a firm basis in observed reality, often made explicit by common phrases that are used to introduce them : *sicut videmus* ('just as we may see') *consuetudo est* ('it is the custom') or *ego video* ('I notice').

Exempla

Exempla are illustrative stories intended for use in the pulpit. Many of them are based upon literary sources much older than the period under consideration here, but the intensified preaching associated with the new orders of friars in the thirteenth century produced a fresh and vigorous stream of *exempla*, and these were often channelled away from the sermons in which they were used and collected into anthologies for ease of reference. The *Bonum universale de apibus* (1263) by the Dominican friar Thomas of Cantimpré, for example, contains several stories which describe *caroles* that took place in Brabant, for the most part. In one of these *exempla*, a woman who habitually leads the *caroles* in her region is killed;[5] another tells how demons appeared at Koningsthorpe in the year 1258, dressed as Cistercian monks (!) and dancing a *carole*.[6] Stories such as these sometimes contain an element of the fantastic, and indeed of the grotesque, but many of them provide an insight into the social circumstances in which *caroles* took place. One of Thomas's stories mentions carolling at weddings, for example, a link with court practice.[7] Virtually all of these *exempla* reach beyond the confines of court experience and take us into the towns and villages. They often display the passionate mysogyny which accounts for much of the clerical polemic against the *carole* at the same time as it points to the exceptional importance of women – and especially of young women – in giving these festive *caroles* their distinctive character. An imagery of wanton beauty, blasphemy and death surrounds the *carole* time and time again in the *exempla*, making these stories one of the most striking refractions of musical life to be found anywhere in medieval literature.

Manuals for confessors

In 1215 the Fourth Lateran Council decreed that all Christians of both sexes should be confessed at least once a year, and as a result manuals were compiled for the use of confessors. It is increasingly recognised now that these manuals are a valuable source for the social and intellectual history of the Middle Ages.[8] By emphasising the importance of the confessor's own judgement in assigning penance, and by seeking to guide that judgement, many of the manuals provide an intimate guide to the moral psychology of the period. The religious life of the thirteenth century was stirred from beginning to end by a passion for pastoral care. The determination to mount and then to sustain a new pastoral effort, both in the confessional and in the pulpit, produced a great deal of writing for preachers and confessors, and the urban background of many of the clerics involved in this work ensured that the pastoral impulse would be joined to an appropriately complex notion of what human labour and recreation could entail. The legitimacy of minstrelsy, and the nature of minstrel entertainment, are subjects often discussed in these manuals; they reveal much about the gradual (but never total) emancipation of musical minstrels from the taint of sin and corruption which marked dancers, acrobats, actors and other such entertainers. Above all, perhaps, the treatises on confession and penance enable us to identify a conduit whereby the ideas of academic theologians, as formulated within the universities, could be diluted and then poured to the laity.

Distinctiones

It is a measure of the extraordinary importance of the *carole* in thirteenth-century French life that the Latin equivalent of Old French *carole*, namely *c(h)orea*, is sometimes included in alphabetical compilations of terms and concepts of moment to preachers. No other kind of secular music – indeed no other kind of music whatsoever – is treated in this way. A list of *distinctiones* drawn up by Pierre de Limoges (known to musicologists as the owner, around 1300, of the only complete surviving manuscript of Jerome of Moravia's *Tractatus de musica*) provides an example both of the need which theologians felt to take notice of these dances and of the information which they gathered (Figure 14).[9] As a consideration of these and other sources will show, the term 'dances' seems hardly sufficient to describe a festivity which was impregnated

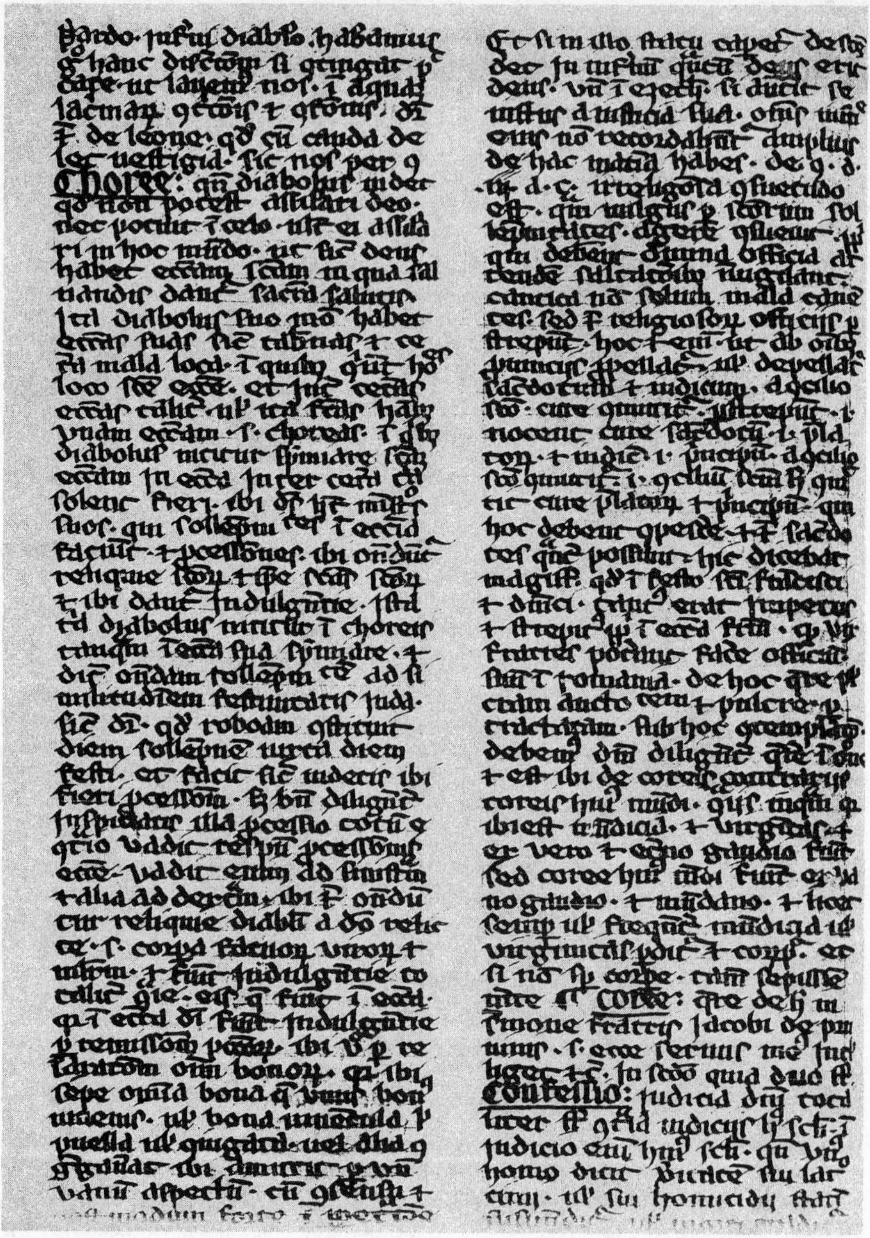

Figure 14 *Pierre de Limoges on* chore[a]e (caroles). *Paris, Bibliothèque Nationale, MS 16482, f.15v.*

with the very savour of time as it was sensed in an age when days were only held together in sequence by the rosary of saints to be remembered, and when a year was experienced as the life of Christ from Advent to Advent, and as the life of the crops from autumn to autumn.

Treatises on the virtues and vices

Treatises on the virtues and vices are an especially valuable source of information about the *carole*. These texts were often devised for the use of preachers and a very large number of them have survived.[10] Most are still unpublished. They range from brief notes, covering a page or so, to encyclopedic treatments in which the virtues and vices are divided and subdivided in scholastic fashion with abundant illustrative references to contemporary customs and abuses. In the sections devoted to Lust (*Luxuria*), we sometimes encounter whole chapters on the *carole* (Figure 9). The amount of social and incidental detail in these manuals is extraordinary, although much of it clearly became conventionalised at an early stage and is repeated from text to text. All the evidence suggests, however, that the single source for almost all of the material on *caroles* is the *Summa de vitiis et virtutibus* of Guillaume Peyraut.

Prose narratives

Virtually all of the extended narrative sources in Latin employed for this book appear in Chapter 7, devoted to an aspect of the Cistercian experience of liturgy. Most modern studies of plainchant, whatever their subject, impose a rational filter between the reader and the experience of chant in the twelfth and thirteenth centuries. Studies of particular neumes, or of the filiation of chant manuscripts, for example, all help us to colonise plainchant and to bring it within the pale of rational consideration and enquiry. However, various White Monks of the twelfth and thirteenth centuries have left narrative writings which shed light on what might be loosely called the 'experience' of chant – the full psychic consequence of singing the liturgy day after day in a Cistercian context of strict isolation from the world. These writings, the principal one among them being Richalm's *Liber revelationum*, are replete with stories that circulated along the Cistercians' international network of news, and they have much to reveal about the mentality of the monks. These stories have the power to 'defamiliarise' plainchant almost completely for any modern reader who chooses to linger over them. They evoke an experience in which the aura of candlelight above the antiphoner recedes into shadow where horror begins. Everything in the world bears the taint of supernatural evil, and even the noises of digestion or hunger issuing from the stomach can make a monk believe that he is sharing his very skin with the Ancient Enemy.

The Old French epics and romances

With the Old French epics and romances we turn to sources of a very different character. In recent years the question of whether the literary works of the past can legitimately be regarded as a reflection of the social reality within which they were produced has become a central issue amongst literary critics interested in all periods.[11] A situation has now arisen in which anyone who attempts to use medieval narrative sources in this way runs the risk of being regarded by many literary critics either as an incurable Victorian romantic or as an historian, it being uncertain which is worse. The charge of Victorianism is an interesting one, since it might well be possible to argue that current scepticism (in some quarters) about the 'historical' content of literary works is directly related to the decline of narrative poetry on historical subjects, so popular in Europe during the nineteenth century but now hardly written anywhere (although there are some recent signs of a revival). When it was fashionable to write long narrative poems on such subjects as the battle of Waterloo, or the siege of Acre, it was not considered a critical indecorum to regard such a poem as 'a relation of facts [that] may be resorted to for grave historical information'.[12] That view has not survived now that ambiguity, compression, irony and verbal game-playing are the qualities most admired in poetry. In the twelfth and thirteenth centuries the life of a historical magnate like William Marshall could be written in verse, combining a wealth of verifiable information with many conventions borrowed from contemporary epic and romance; in the same way, a prose chronicle like *La Conquête de Constantinople* could be strewn with verbal tags and hyperboles borrowed from the vernacular epics.[13] To regard the evidence of such texts as inadmissible would be to cut away the foundations of much modern scholarship based upon the narrative sources of the Middle Ages, be they 'fiction' or 'chronicle'.

In interpreting the vernacular narratives it is advisable to be guided by two principal assumptions. Firstly, that the material must be read in bulk, taking in as many texts as possible, and that the musical references must then be sorted into genres to provide a control upon the interpretation of individual passages.[14] Secondly, that a passage in an epic or romance cannot prove anything by itself, although it may possess a kind of metaphorical realism whereby contemporary interests and preoccupations are brought onto the stage of the narrative in the garb provided for them by the story-materials and conventions available to the narrator.

Texts and manuscripts

Since the manuscripts of any given text are likely to be scattered in libraries all over the world, it is necessary to make some use of early printed editions. When the opportunity arises to check a print against the text of one (or more) manuscripts the print will often stand up very well. It should be remembered, however, that little work has been done on the textual history of many of the works used here and it is therefore rarely possible to be confident that the best text of a medieval work will be the one contained in any medieval manuscript which happens to be accessible; there may be a better text in prints of the sixteenth (or even of the seventeenth) century whose manuscript sources are unknown. What is certain, however, is that Renaissance printers generally treated theological texts of the kind listed in this conspectus with a great deal more respect than Martin Gerbert was prepared to accord to treatises on music in his famous collection of editions published in 1784. The massive library of Migne's *Patrologia Latina* is still the backbone of modern work on medieval religious and intellectual life up to the early thirteenth century although many of the editions that Migne reprints date from the seventeenth century. The problem remains, however, that many texts cannot be cited from modern critical editions (since no such editions exist in these cases) and it is therefore rarely possible to be certain that the texts represent the exact words and syntax which the original authors used. (The same might be said about any medieval work existing in a number of manuscripts and presented in a modern critical edition, of course; the modern editor makes his choices.) It may be assumed, however, that passages extracted from thirteenth- or early fourteenth-century manuscripts can be considered as legitimate evidence of a medieval stance relative to an issue within our period, even though the place which these passages occupy in the textual history of the works in question is not known.

The problem of dating is also delicate. Some works can be securely dated; others are dateable within limits (sometimes no better than a *terminus ad quem* established by the author's death). Many cannot be dated in a precise way. The issue of provenance raises similar considerations. A substantial number of texts in all the Latin genres mentioned above can be traced to Paris (some of the commentaries upon the *Sentences* of Peter the Lombard, the *De musica* of Johannes de Grocheio, and some sermons, for example), while a few texts (such as Guillaume Peyraut's *Summa de vitiis et virtutibus*) were so widely disseminated in their own day that the question of their provenance loses much of its importance, so extensive was their influence.

Documents

The following selection of documents presents some illuminating texts which are not readily accessible.

before 1302 John of Erfurt: *Summa de Poenitentia*

Source: Oxford, Oriel College, MS 38, f.102v
From Book I:6:25 (concerning generosity and the giving of alms)

Sunt autem prodigi, ut dicit Tullius *De officiis* liber .ij., qui in epulis ludorum venacionumque apparatu pecunias profundunt; ludi apparentur coree qui in epulis solent fieri et gesticulaciones hystrionum et usus instrumentorum organi-corum. Chorea autem quedam est lauda, velut quando fit ad honorem dei
5 ut Maria soror Moysi sumpsit timpanum et duxit choreas transito mare rubeo, vitupera vel prava quando fit propter lasciviam et dissolucionem. Hic tamen potest fieri sine mortali si 4 concurrant: si fiat in tempore non prohibito, scilicet in quadragesima vel in pascha [vel] quando tempus communionis est; quod modus chorizandi non sit lascivus nec ad libidinem provocativus; [si fiat] sine
10 lascivia id est sine mala intencione; [si fiat] a persona non prohibita secus si fiat a persona religiosa . . .

De histrionibus . . . De citharedis autem et aliis qui utuntur instrumentis musicis. Nota secundum Johannem quod licite potest homo ad talibus dare et potest talia instrumenta audire vel tangere de modo ob iusticie causam faciat, scilicet
15 ob laudem dei ut David, et Samuel qui dixit adducite mihi psalten, et beatus Franciscus cui dedicanti melodiam cithare angeli citharizabant.
Potest etiam hec melodia audiri vel tangi causa recreacionis si debilis vel infirmus est, vel propter aliquam causam honestam vel consuetam, vel propter nupcias, vel quia militavit, vel quia triumphavit, vel de peregrinacione longa venit,
20 vel propter aliquam causam in qua communiter fieri consuevit. Unde utens

instrumentis musicis ex causa justa et honesta potest communicare. Iniusta non potest nisi velit resistere.

1 Cicero, *De officiis* 2:16. *5* Exodus 15:20 *7–11* the scribe has muddled the syntax of the text here in a remarkable way; I have attempted to clarify the sense. *13* Who is this Johannes? Or is it St Jerome? The latter interpretation seems to fit the MS contraction better, but I find no such attitude espoused in the writings of Jerome. *15* 4 Regum 3:15 [*AV* 2 Kings 3:15] *16* Thomas of Celano *Vita Secunda*, chapter 126.

There are generous men, as Cicero says in his *De officiis*, Book II, who pour out money in banquets, games and in the preparation of games and hunts. 'Games' are *caroles*, which are customarily danced during banquets, the gesture of actors and the playing of musical instruments. A certain kind of *carole* is religious praise, that is to say when it is danced for the worship of God as when Miriam, the sister of Moses, took up a drum and led *caroles* while crossing the Red Sea; [a *carole*] is disgusting and depraved when it is done for the sake of wantonness and abandonment. However, this may be done without mortal sin if four conditions are met: that it be not done in a forbidden time, as in Lent or Easter, or during communion; that the manner (*modus*; ?music) of the dancing be neither wanton nor an incitement to lust; that it be done without a wanton that is to say an evil intention, and that it be not done by forbidden persons, worst of all by a person in religious orders . . .

Concerning minstrels . . . Concerning string-players and others who use musical instruments. Note that according to John one may legitimately give to such people and one may hear or play such instruments to the extent that it is done in a just cause, that is to say in the praise of the Lord, as David did, and Samuel who said: 'bring me a string-player', and St Francis, in whose honour angels harped a melody. This kind of music may also be played and heard for the sake of relief when one is weak or infirm, or for any honest or customary reason, as for a wedding, or because of strife, or because there has been a victory, or because someone has come home from a long journey, or on account of any reason for which [such music] is customarily performed. Whence those who play upon musical instruments in a just cause may take communion. Those who do so in an unjust cause may not do so unless they desist.

1208–1212/13 Robert of Courson: *Summa*

Base manuscript: Cambridge, Gonville and Caius College, MS 331/722, f.24r–v.

Baldwin (*Masters, Princes and Merchants*, II, p. 14, n. 66) lists fourteen extant manuscripts of Courson's *Summa*. The following is based upon three of these manuscripts and is therefore not a full critical edition of the material. The sources are: Cambridge, Gonville and Caius College, MS 331/722 (C); London, British Library, MS Royal 9 E.xiv (L), and Bruges, Stedelijke Openbare Bibliotheek, MS 247 (B). Courson was an Englishman who studied with Peter the Chanter in Paris during the 1190s. By 1200 he was a Master of Theology in the university; the *Summa* doubtless contains much of his teaching. He was elected to the rank of cardinal in 1212. For further details see Baldwin, *Masters*, I, p. 19ff.

The first passage shows how, in the thirteenth century, discussions of the minstrel trade and its legitimacy were often conducted in a broad context that embraced many other kinds of specialised craftsmen and workers whose activities lay on the margins of respectability. Here, as so often, the theme of the discussion is money: what tradesmen may legitimately hire their services for cash? Courson is prepared to lift string-players away from other marginal trades. They are the only ones for whom Courson can find some comfort in the Bible: a string-player and singer with a wife and children to support may be allowed to pursue his trade – for King David, Miriam and many other pious persons have lent their lustre to musical instruments.

Item queritur de mimis et joculatoribus et histrionibus et adulatoribus utrum possint de jure locare operas suas. Videtur quod non quia sic emolliunt et effeminant et sepe infatuant animos auditorum et ita emungunt subdole bona eorum; ergo non licet eis aliquid accipere intuitu talium. Quid ergo dicetur
5 citharedo habenti uxorem et multos filios secum et viventi tamen ex canticis et cithara quod videtur ei licere cum David et Maria soror Moysi et multi alii timorati viri in liris in citharis et tympanis et psalteriis et organis et canticis commendentur. Eadem est questio de deciariis et compositoribus scacorum et alearum et de compositoribus toxicorum et stibii et cerusse et balistarum
10 et hastarum et novorum indumentorum ferreorum que quidam exactores adinveniunt ad inducendos quosdam quos volunt torquere quousque tanquam spongia evomant quicquid licite vel illicite adquisierunt. Eadem est de mangonibus sive cotionibus et aliis mercatoribus qui ultra iustum precium solent merces suas vendere. Similiter et de buculariis et cardatoribus vestium et de omnibus
15 illis quorum opera non sunt ad esculentem vel poculentem vel indumentum vel aliquem usum sed potius ad hominum detrimentum et libidinis incitamentum et de omnibus quibus cum nullatenus ut videtur liceat eis operas suas locare quia omnino perniciose et inutiles sunt. Utrum si sint incorrigibiles eliminandi sint per episcopum et sacerdotem ab ecclesia et sacramentis eis permissa
20 illa admonitione evangelica: 'Si peccaverit in te' etc ... [f.24v] Ideo est juditium de adulatore vel mimo sive histrione qui si infatuat adolescentes vel simplices per adulationes, et sic emungat ab eis bona eorum, tenetur ad restitutionem. Si vero adulatur eis qui sciunt sibi percavere et modo volunt, promittentes se infatuari, et dent eis aliqua quod dare possunt, non tenentur ad restitutionem.
25 Sed qui dant talibus mittendo eos in suis erroribus peccant mortaliter cum forte expediti sint ad laborandum iuxta Jeronimum qui dicit: histrionibus dare demonibus est immolare nisi forte tali intencione det aliquis ne ipsi accusent eum vel infament apud malivolos prelatos vel tirannos ...

1 joculatoribus] C adds *osculatoribus*. *3 et immo emergunt sub dolo* C. *7 liris*] *li/b's* C. *7 cantici* C. *8 decimariis* C. *19 eis*] *eius* C. *20* Matthew 18 :15.

The question now arises of whether *mimi, joculatores, histriones* and *adulatores* may legitimately hire their services for money. It will be seen that they may not, for they soften, weaken and often dupe the minds of their hearers so that they somewhat deceitfully cheat them of their gifts; therefore it is not permitted for them to accept any service in respect of such things. What, therefore, will be said to a string-player having a wife and many children with him, and living by his songs and his stringed instrument – which will be seen to be allowed to him, for David, Miriam the sister of Moses, and many other God-fearing persons have lent their lustre to *lire, cithare, tympana, psalteria, organa* and songs. The same question arises in connection with dice-makers, and makers of chessmen and board-games, and in connection with the compounders of toxic substances, stibium, white lead, crossbows, spears and the new kinds of metal garments which torturers devise to draw information out of those whom they wish to wring tight until, like a sponge, they shed whatever they have licitly or illicitly obtained. The same question arises in connection with dealers, brokers and other merchants who make a habit of selling their wares above the just price. It is the same with buckle-makers and carders of clothes, with all those whose work does not contribute to the production of food, drink and essential raiment but rather to the detriment of men and to the incitement of lust, and with all those who should under no circumstances be permitted to hire their services because they are entirely pernicious and useless. If they are incorrigible let them be rejected by a bishop and a priest from the Church and from the sacraments as this injunction from the Evangelist is cast before them: 'Moreover if thy brother shall trespass against thee [go and tell him his fault between thee and him alone: if he shall hear thee, thou hast gained thy brother'] . . .

[A little later Courson returns to minstrels:]

The same judgement is to be made with respect to an *adulator, mimus* or *joculator* who, if he dupes adolescents and simple people with his flattery, is obliged to return whatever he has taken. If, however, he flatters those who know how to look after themselves, and who want it in any way, and who willingly hold themselves out to be duped, and who may give to them what they can well spare, then the minstrel is not obliged to return what he has taken. But those who give to such minstrels sending them forth in their error commit a mortal sin, since perhaps they will be in a stronger position to work thereafter. Jerome says 'to give to *histriones* is to sacrifice to demons', unless perhaps someone gives with the intention of preventing them from accusing or defaming him in the presence of corrupt prelates and tyrants . . .

b.1249/50 Guillaume Peyraut: *Summa de vitiis et virtutibus*

Base manuscript: Cambridge, University Library, MS Ii.4.8, f.18r–v (Figure 9).

This section on *caroles* by the Dominican Guillaume Peyraut exerted a great influence on later writers. Many borrowed passages from it verbatim, or alluded to it simply as the 'chapter on *caroles* in the *Summa de vitiis*'. The *Summa* was one of the standard reference books in the libraries of the Dominican friars. For a translation of substantial sections from this passage see Chapter 5. The recurrent scriptural source is Apocalypse 9:2-II.

> f.18r Fumus ascendens de puteo abyssi est fetor et ardor luxurie qui obscuravit solem, id est cetum sacerdotum quorum est illuminare ecclesiam, et aerem, id est cetum contemplativorum pro magna parte. De hoc fumo exierunt locuste, id est cantatrices et saltatrices se non regentes ratione sed incedentes inordinate
> 5 ac si bruta animalia essent. Hee locuste *nichil omnino virens* relinquunt in terra Ecclesie, sicut de locustis Egipti legitur Exo.X. Hee locuste dicuntur exisse

de fumo putei non quia habeant ab eo quod sunt, sed quia habent inde quod locuste sunt. Alique enim, quorum corda interfecta sunt ex fumo putei, procurant coreas; alie vero, ex levitate sola in principio, eis consenciunt. Iuxta hunc
10 modum loquendi dicitur diabolus esse pater malorum, non quia ipsi habeant ab eo quod sunt, sed habent ab eo, id est ab eius imitacione, quod mali sunt. Sequitur in visione Johannis, quibusdam interpositis: *Et similitudines locustarum similes equis paratis ad prelium.* Innuitur hoc quod ornatus mulierum est quedam preparacio ad hoc quod diabolus eis insidiat, et Dominum in eis inpugnat.
15 Unde sicut dicit propheta de Domino, quod ipse imposuerat Jerusalem [sicut] equum glorie sue in prelio, similiter facit diabolus de talibus mulieribus. Sequitur: *et supra capita eorum tanquam corone similes auro.* Hoc pertinet ad ornatum quem habent mulieres in [f.18v] capitibus; insinuatur quod ornatus quos iste mulieres deferunt in capitibus, quos acquisierunt a suis amasiis, sint quasi
20 corone pro multiplici triumpho quod habuit [diabolus] per eas de filiis Dei. Sic solent strenui milites in torneamentis in capitibus equorum suorum coronas ponere de floribus. Sequitur: *et facies eorum sicut facies hominis.* Dicit 'sicut facies hominum' propter mulieres que se depingunt, quarum facies sunt quasi larve sub quibus latent facies naturales quas Dominus eis dedit, que sunt palide.
25 Ad quas facies pertinent quod dicit Jeronimus: 'Qua fiducia', inquit, 'erigit ad celos vultus quos conditor non agnoscit'. Sequitur: *Et habebant capillos sicut capillos mulierum.* 'Sicut' dicitur propter illas que deferunt crines a mortuis mulieribus abscisos, qui non sunt capilli mulierum quia nec mortuarum sunt, quia ab eis abscisi sunt, nec illarum que eos deferunt, sicut uve non sunt spi-
30 narum si eis alligentur. Et mirum est quomodo mulieres non timent deferre capillos mulierum mortuarum et habere eas de nocte ad capud suum. Sed verisimile est quod diabolus hanc audaciam procurat eis, cuius signum est hoc, quod ipse timerent deferre camisiam vel aliam vestem mulieris mortue, de capillis vero non timent, de quibus magis videtur esse timendum. Sequitur:
35 *et dentes eorum sicut dentes leonum.* Hoc pertinet ad rapacitatem talium mulierum, ad quod pertinet quod legitur Eccl. IX: Ne respicias mulierem multivolam. Tot enim volunt ab amatoribus suis rapere quod mirum est. Sequitur: *et habebant loricas ferreas.* Hic insinuatur incorigibilitas eorum. Sicut enim in lorica non potest una macula ab alia separari, sic non potest eis persuaderi ut unum de
40 ornamentis suis dimittant. *Et vox alarum illarum sicut vox curruum equorum multorum currencium ad bellum.* Et sicut exercitus magnus solo tumultu hostes fugat quandoque et devincit, et clamore aves volantes cadere facit, sic exercitus corearum diabolicus solis irrisionibus et clamoribus suis devincit bonos et illos qui habebant pennas virtutum a sublimitate vite inchoate cadere facit. Quod dicitur
45 'alarum' pertinet ad velocitatem quam habent in discurrendo; quod dicitur 'vox curruum' pertinet ad tumultum quem faciunt. Sequitur: *et habebant caudas similes scorpionibus, et aculei erant in caudis earum.* Hoc referendum est ad hoc quod mors eterna est finis voluptatis carnalium, vel ad hoc quod ad mortem culpe homines pertrahunt. Sequitur: *et potestas eorum nocere hominibus mensibus .v.*
50 Hoc potest referri ad hoc quod a pascha usque ad autumpnum precipue nocent coree ecclesie. Sicut enim reges tempore isto solent ad bella procedere, ut hostibus suis auferant quod in hieme labore adquisierunt, sic diabolus, quam cito est pascha, congregat exercitus corearum et aufert ecclesie quod in adventu et in quadragesima fecit. Sequitur: *et habebant super se angelum regem abysi.* Diabolus
55 enim eos regit *cui nomen Abadon hebraice Grece autem Apollion et Latine habens nomen*

exterminans. Interlinealis. A patria vite exterminare est exulem facere, unde merito vocabatur 'exterminans' diabolus temptans homines per mulieres, quia per eas in hoc exilio sumus (iuxta verbum Jeronimi superius positum). Memento semper quod paradisi colonum mulierum de possessione sua eiecerit et valde 60 potens est demon ille ad faciendum exulare homines a celesti patria.

2 *solem*] *celum*. Other MSS (eg. Cambridge, University Library, MS Gg.4.30) and early printed editions which I have examined all read *solem*; this accords with the text of Apocalypse 9:2 and must therefore be the correct reading. *5* Exodus 10:15. *6* Exodus 10:5–19. *16* Zechariah 10:3. *20* [*diabolus*] so Gg.4.30 and early printed editions. *17* There are many such mistakes of gender in the pronouns in this passage; they have not been corrected here. *36* Ecclesiasticus 9:3.

c. 1220 William of Auxerre: *Summa Aurea*

Source: London, British Library, MS Royal 8 G.iv. Late 13c.

William of Auxerre was active in theological circles at Paris from at least 1219 until his death in 1231. In the first extract below William discusses the pleasure given by stringed instruments. It is preceded by a passage (not given here) in which he assembles some standard Patristic authorities which warn against the pleasure derived from music; they include Augustine's famous remarks about the dangers inherent in beautiful church music (the ultimate source is *Confessions* 10:32) and Gregory's dictum that true piety is lost the moment a *blanda vox* is sought. For good measure William adds Isaiah 5:12 (for which *AV* reads 'And the harp and the viol, the tabret, and pipe, and wine, are in their feasts: but they regard not the work of the Lord'). The text given below begins as William gathers authorities which legitimise pleasure in music. In the second extract his topic is the familiar one of whether it is legitimate to give money to minstrels.

f.210v David citharabat coram domino et psallebat . . . ergo bonum est citharizare et audire sonitum cithare, ergo non est peccatum. Item, David ad vocem cithare et psalterii exc[i]tabat in se spiritum prophetie et hoc erat bonum, ergo bonum erat citharizare et inde ut prius. Item, licitum est videre pulcritudinem firma-
5 menti et ceterarum creaturarum ut per hoc admiremur et cognoscamus sapientiam creatoris, ergo licitum est audire sonum dulcem cithare ut per dulcedinem creature cognoscamus dulcedinem creatoris; ergo audire talia non est peccatum, quod concedimus si hac intencione audiantur. Duplici enim de causa licet huiusmodi instrumenta audire. Prima est ut per dulcedinem soni consideremus dulce-
10 dinem dei qui dulcedinem soni creavit. Secunda causa est ut consolacionem aliquam in huiusmodi sonis habeamus ad fugiendum tristiciam seculi, quam aliquam mortem anime operatur, et ad fugiendum inhonestas et illicitas occupaciones. [*A fourteenth-century marginal note reads:* Nota quod secunda de causa licet audire cantum, musicam et cetera genera musicorum.] Sola ergo voluntas
15 improba delectandi in creatura cum consensu rationis reprehensibilis [et] vituperabilis est in huiusmodi sicut patet in auctoritate Gregorii et Augustini. Hic etiam patet per Ysaiam dicentem: cithara et lira et tympanum in conviviis vestris et opus domini non respicitis etc. [*On giving alms*]:
f.212 Ex predictis patet quibus danda est elemosina, scilicet pauperibus in quibus
20 est ymago dei et nostra; et quod eis damus quodammodo deo damus cum

ipsi sint ymago dei et eis demus in quantum tales sunt. Sed cum in hystrionibus sit ymago dei videtur ergo quod dare ystrionibus non sit peccatum. Mentitur ergo Jeronymus dicens qui dat ystrionibus immolat demonibus. Item ystriones utuntur arte sua sine peccato, quoniam non est peccatum citharizare vel psallere
25 quod patet per Helyseum qui cum consuleretur a tribus regibus iussit sibi adduci psaltem et cum caneret psaltes facta est super eum manus domini. Ergo secundum hoc dare ystrionibus non est peccatum et ystrio non sonat in vicium. Item ille qui dat ystrioni non cogitat de diabolo ergo non ymmolat diabolo. SOLUTIO. Hystrio proprie dicitur qui gesticulacione corporis provocat ad
30 risum homines, unde hystoria rerum, gestarum narracio. Sed modo ampliatum est nomen ut dicatur ystrio quicumque joculator qui per musica instrumenta vel alio modo excitat homines ad voluptatem et ad gaudium huius mundi, et sic sonat in vicium. Et hac intencione dare hystrioni est demonibus immolare ... sed si alia intencione detur ystrioni, scilicet aut quantum indiget aut quan-
35 tum volumus habere consolacionem ad removendum tristiciam huius seculi que mortem anime operatur, huius dare non est peccatum.

8-9 licet huiusmodi instrumenta written twice. *16 sicut patet* written twice. *25 e/helyseum 25f 4* Regum 3 :15 (*AV* 2 Kings 3 :15). *27 ystrionibus]* lystrionibus

David played the *cithara* in the presence of the Lord and made music . . . therefore it is a good thing to play the *cithara* and to hear the music of the *cithara*, and therefore it is not a sin. Again, to the music of the *cithara* and *psalterium* David inspired in himself the spirit of prophecy and this was good, therefore it was good for him to the play the *cithara*, from which the same conclusion ensues as above. Again, it is legitimate to see the beauty of the firmament and of other created things so that in this we may wonder at the wisdom of the Creator and recognise it, and therefore it is legitimate to hear the sweet sound of the *cithara* so that through the sweetness of a created thing we may know the sweetness of the Creator; therefore it is not a sin to hear such things and we allow it, providing that it is done with this intention. It is legitimate to hear instruments for the following two reasons. The first is that through the sweetness of the sound we may know the sweetness of God who created the sweetness of sound. The second reason is so that we may have some comfort in sounds of this kind so as to shun the sadness of worldly life, which is mortal to the soul, and to flee immodest and illicit behaviour. [*Marginal note:* Note that according to this second argument it is legitimate to hear song, music and other kinds of musical instruments.] Therefore it is only a corrupt will to delight in a created thing with the consent of a reason which is reprehensible and blameworthy in this kind of thing, as may be seen on the *auctoritas* of Gregory and Augustine. This may also be seen from Isaiah saying: 'the *cithara*, the *lyra* and the *tympanum* are in your feasts and you do not regard the work of the Lord etc' . . .

From what has gone before it is plain to whom alms should be given, that is to say to the poor in whom is both the image of God and of ourselves. Whatever we give to them we give, in a manner, to God, since they are the image of God and we must give to them insofar as they are such. Because the image of God may be seen in minstrels it may be seen therefore that to give to minstrels is not a sin. Jerome is therefore mistaken when he says that to give to minstrels is to sacrifice to demons. Again, minstrels practice their art without sin, for it is not a sin to play upon the *cithara* or to play an instrument as may be seen in Elisha who, when he was consulted by three kings, commanded a minstrel to be brought to him, and when the minstrel sang the hand of the Lord came upon him. Therefore according to this it is not a sin to give to minstrels and 'minstrel' is not synonymous with vice. Again, he who gives to a minstrel does not think of the Devil, therefore he does not sacrifice to the Devil. The Solution. Strictly speaking a *histrio* is one who makes men laugh with gesticulations of his body [thus the word is formed from] *historia rerum*, that is to say 'the narration of deeds'. But in a broader sense a *histrio* is any minstrel who provokes in mankind delight and the joy of this life, either with musical instruments or in some other way and can thus provoke vice; to give to minstrels with this intention is to sacrifice to demons ... but if one gives to a minstrel with some other intention, perhaps to the extent that he is poor or to the extent that we wish to have some consolation for the sadness of this present life which kills the soul, this is not a sin.

Unpublished *similitudines* relating to minstrels from commentaries upon the Bible, from sermons and from notes for preachers.

The *similitudo* was a means of expressing some religious truth by means of a simile – often an extended simile – drawn from contemporary life and customs. As these examples show, the life and work of minstrels sometimes attracted the attention of preachers and commentators, with surprising results. The first extract, in particular, reveals the density of verbal texture and allusion which could result from the use of such *similitudines*. The preacher in this case has observed that minstrels are always keen for gifts of precious clothes (and especially, he seems to imply, for gowns trimmed with fur). He also distinguishes between winter and summer issue. The text he has chosen as the theme for his sermon shows that he is thinking of the lavish entertainments (followed by lavish rewards) which took place at royal and aristocratic weddings, and which are so often described in Old French romances of the thirteenth century. However, the details of contemporary practice which the preacher has observed dissolve into the passages from Scripture in such a way that an almost trivial daily reality merges with the intense and ancient authority of Holy Writ. The language of Scripture can reach back to Genesis and the beginning of Man, while the preachers and commentators are constantly pressing the significance of their own language forward to the end of the world which they believe to be close. The raw material of the *similitudo*, drawn from contemporary life, occupies a timeless space somewhere in the middle. This quality of timelessness is to be found everywhere in sermons, in treatises on the virtues and vices, and in many of the Latin sources drawn upon for this book.

I Source: Cambridge, Gonville and Caius College, MS 52/29, f.158v (Figure 13). From an anonymous sermon on the text *venite ad nupcias* (Matthew 22:4).

... invitat nos ad has nupcias esse robarum adepcio. Ystriones libenter veniunt ad nupcias ubi dantur robe preciose. Nos autem ystriones sumus. Alii propter terrena saltant et tumbant coram diabolo. Mc. 6 *Cumque introisset filia herodiadis et saltasset et placuisset herodi rex ait puelle pete a me quod vis* et cetera. Quidam
5 coram domino propter celestia. Regum 6. *David percussiebat in organis et armigatis*

id est ad armum ligatis quomodo ad eos qui in seculo sunt, et bene saltabat
coram domino quomodo ad illos qui faciunt saltum usque ad religionem. Istud
autem est totum secundum aliam translacionem ut patet in alio titulo psalmi
Benedicam. Dabit autem diabolus suis robam furratam de quam psalmus *Induantur*
10 sicut deployde *confusione sua,* id est anime et corporis dampnacione. Christus
vero suis dabit robas optimas post estivales. Apo. 6. *Date sunt illis singule stole
albe* et cetera. Deinde dupplices contra omnis hyemis intemperies. Proverbiorum
ultimo. *Non timebit domui sue a frigoribus nivis omnes enim domestici eius vestiti sunt
dupplicibus,* id est dotibus anime et corporis.

3–4 Mark 6:22. The MS reads 'Mt'. *5f* The passage cited from Regum 6 (i.e. 2
Samuel 6:5) is indeed an *alia translacio* departing from the standard Vulgate text.
This variant was widely known, however; see L.W.Daly and B.A.Daly, eds., *Summa
Britonis sive Guillelmi Britonis Expositiones Vocabulorum Biblie,* I (Padua, 1975), sv *Armigata.*
9–10 Psalms 34:26 and 131:18 (*AV* 35:26 and 132:18). *11–12* Apocalypse 6:11. The MS
reads *arbe. 13–14* Proverbs 31:21.

... he invites us to these nuptials as if to a receiving of robes. Minstrels gladly
come to nuptials where costly robes are given. We too are minstrels, moreover.
Some, for worldly things, leap and tumble before the Devil. 'And when the
daughter of the said Herodias came in and danced, and pleased Herod ...
the king said unto the damsel, Ask of me whatsoever thou wilt etc.' Some
[leap and tumble] before the Lord for heavenly things. 'David played upon
instruments tied to his arm', that is to say bound to his arms like those who
are in secular life, and he leapt well in his dancing before the Lord like those
who leap into a religious order. However this is all according to an alternative
translation as is clear in another heading for the psalm *Benedicam.* The Devil
will give a fur-trimmed robe to all his own, of which the psalm speaks, 'let
them be covered', as with a doublet, 'with their confusion', that is to say with
damnation of body and soul. Christ will afterwards give the best summer robes
to His own. Apocalypse 6: 'And white robes were given unto every one of
them etc'. Afterwards [Christ will give] robes of double thickness against the
intemperateness of the winter as it says in the last chapter of Proverbs: 'he
will not fear in his house the coldness of the snow for all his servants have
been clad in garments of double thickness', that is to say with the gifts of
body and of spirit.

II Source: Troyes, Bibliothèque Municipale MS 144, volume I, f.304v, collated
with Douai, Bibliothèque Municipale, MS 45, volume II, f.133v. Pierre de
Palude, *In Psalmos,* commentary upon Psalm 32:3 (*AV* 33:3) *Cantate ei canticum
novum.*

Cantate canticum novum ... quia canticum novum requirit hominem innova-
tum. Ecce enim mimus volens viellare exuit vestem exteriorem, parat inter-
iorem, cinctus in tunica exuit, deponit cucusam, componit capillos, superponit
feltrum ...

Sing a new song ... because a new song requires a renewed man. For see,
a minstrel wishing to play the fiddle takes off his outer clothing, adjusts his

inner garments, takes off the belt of his tunic, puts down his hood, smoothes down his hair, puts a woollen cap on top of it . . .

III Source: Oxford, Lincoln College MS Lat.113, f.105v, compared with Oxford, Jesus College, MS E.8, p. 320. Guido of Evreux, *Sermones*. Sermon on the text *Opus autem suum probet unusquisque* (Galatians 6:4) 'But let every man prove his own work'. The passage describes the way itinerant minstrels present themselves at the residence of a distinguished man who wishes to hold a feast, and are duly questioned, those with a good reputation being allowed into the feast. The words *et nititur quod bene faciat officium*, referring to a stage *before* the minstrel has been admitted to the feast, may suggest that some kind of brief auditioning process took place (which seems highly plausible).

Videmus quando aliquis homo vult tenere unum magnum festum ubi veniunt multi joculatores quilibet qui venit non admittitur ad festum sed debet prius scire de quo ministerio scit servire, et ideo quilibet qui vult admitti multum gaudet quando est famosus in ministerio suo et nititur quod bene faciat officium
5 et tunc introducitur ad festum. Alii qui nil sciunt facere non permittuntur. Sic certe in fine mundi faciet dominus unum festum maximum amicis suis, et inimici etiam vocabuntur . . . Ideo multi *menestrels* venient, id est et de bonis et de malis . . .

We may see that when any man wishes to hold a great feast to which many minstrels come, not every minstrel who presents himself is admitted; it must first be determined what minstrelsy he has to offer, and therefore whosoever wishes to be admitted rejoices greatly when he finds that he is famous for his minstrelsy and strives to perform his duties well, and then he is introduced into the feast. Others who are no good are not admitted. So, certainly, the Lord will hold a great feast at the end of the world for His friends, and even His enemies will be invited . . . Thus many minstrels will come, that is to say both good and bad . . .

IV Source: London, British Library, MS Harley 103, f.13v-14. The *Dieta salutis* of Guillaume 'de Lavicea'. This *similitudo* provides an oblique reflection of the special importance of the professional *viellator* in French courtly society, an importance that is also mentioned by the music-theorist Johannes de Grocheio.

Et notandum quod confessio in qua sunt .vij. condiciones comparatur vielle in qua sunt similiter .vij. corde. Viella confessionis que habet istam septempli-cem cordam reddit auribus dei suavissimam et dulcissimam melodiam, nec est aliquod organum musicum quod ita libenter deus audiat sicut veram confes-
5 sionem peccatorum et immo manus que sic tangit coram deo viellam confessionis reportat statim salarium scilicet veniam de omnibus peccatis. Unde dicitur Osie .xliij. *Narra siquid haberes ut iustificeris*. Et David consulit omnibus nimis scilicet peccatoribus penitentibus qui volunt in curia regis eterni introire quod tangant eo modo quo supradictam est viellam confessionis. Dicit enim psalmista
10 *Introite portas eius in confessione et cetera.*

7 Isaiah 43:26 *10* psalm 94:2 (*AV* 95:2).

It is to be noted that confession, to which there are seven conditions, is like a fiddle in which there are similarly seven strings. The fiddle of confession which has the regulation number of seven strings renders the sweetest and most delightful melody in the ear of God, nor is there any other instrument which God so willingly hears as the true confession of sinners, and so the hand which plays upon the fiddle of confession before God will quickly earn a payment, that is to say a pardon for all sins. Whence Isaiah says 'declare thou, that thou mayest be justified'. And David counsels all penitent sinners who wish to enter the court of the eternal king that they play, in the manner described above, the fiddle of confession. The psalmist says: 'Enter through his gates in confession etc'.

1230–1240/5 A thirteenth-century curriculum for students of the Arts course in Paris: the introductory section pertaining to music

Source: Barcelona, Archivo de la Corona de Aragon, MS Ripoll 109, f.135.

This curriculum, compiled between 1230 and 1240/45, contains a section on music which consists of a brief introduction to the *De institutione musica* of Boethius, followed by a list of questions (together with their solutions) such as the students might expect to be asked in the examinations in Arts. The introductory section pertaining to music in the Barcelona manuscript (Figure 10) has not hitherto been printed in an accurate form; nor, as far as I am aware, has it been translated into English.

De Musica. Auctor musice Boecius

De quantitate discreta mobili est musica; est enim de sono qui est contractus numerus in proportionem sonoritatis que est triplex. Una est instrumentalis, alia mundana, alia humana. Instrumentalis musica est que perspicitur in sono tybiarum, timpanarum et huiusmodi instrumentorum. Mundana percipitur
5 in sonoritate partium mundi et maxime corporum supracelestium. Posuerunt enim philosophi quod dulcisona est armonia in corporibus inferioribus que forte non auditur a nobis propter nimiam distanciam inter nos et illa. Humana percipitur in modulata elevacione et depressione vocis secundum diversas canta-lenas.

10 Divisio musice

Huius autem scientie Boecius est auctor et dividitur in V libros particulares. In primis duobus agitur de eis que pertinent ad scientie veritatem. In tribus sequentibus agitur de ipsis reprobando opiniones aliorum secundum quod dici-tur in principio elencorum quod sapientis opus est non mentiri de quibus novit
15 et mentientem manifestare posse. Leguntur autem duo libri huius totalis scientie quia in istis duobus, ut dictum est, manifestat auctor omnium illorum scientiam de quibus intendit, sed in primo libro exequitur de eis generaliter, in secundo vero specialiter, demonstrando proprias passiones in tonis et consonantiis. Et notandum, quod hic agit de musica instrumentali etsi de humana, hic est in
20 quantum proportionem quandam et consonantiam habet cum instrumentali.

De mundana autem nullatenus hic agitur eo quod, sicut dictum est, de ipsa apud nos non est certa cognitio.

Concerning music. The set book is by Boethius

Music is composed of distinct and mobile quantity, and it deals with sound, which is number drawn into a proportion of musical consequence. Music is threefold. One is *musica instrumentalis*, another is *musica mundana*, and another is *musica humana*. *Musica instrumentalis* is that which is perceived in the sound of pipes, drums, and of instruments of that kind. *Musica mundana* is that which is perceived in the sounds produced by parts of the world and especially by supercelestial bodies. The philosophers have declared that there is a sweet sounding harmony in the lower [heavenly] bodies which is perhaps not audible to us because of the great distance which separates us from them. *Musica humana* is perceived in the controlled rising and falling of the human voice in various kinds of songs.

The division of the [treatise] *musica* [by Boethius]

Boethius is the author of the set book and it is divided into five individual books. The first two are concerned with those things which relate to true knowledge about this subject. The following three are further concerned with this, correcting the opinions of others according to what is said at the beginning of [Aristotle's] *Elenchus* that it is the work of a wise man to speak no falsity of those things which he knows and to be able to expose the falsities of others. Two books of all this science are studied (?lectured upon), because in these two, as has been said, the author manifests the means of knowledge of all the things which are at issue; in the first book they are pursued in general terms, and in the second they are pursued in specific terms, demonstrating the author's theses in tones and in consonances. Note well, moreover, that all this pertains to *musica instrumentalis* and to *musica humana*, to the extent that the latter conforms in consonance and proportion to *musica instrumentalis*. None of this pertains to *musica mundana* because, as has been said, we have no definitive knowledge of it.

The Parisian minstrel statutes of 1321. From Faral, *Les jongleurs*, pp. 128–30.

I C'est assavoir, que d'ore en avant nuls trompeur de la ville de Paris ne puist alouer à une feste que luy et son compagnon ne autre jongleur ou jongleresse d'autrui mestier que soy mesmes; pour ce qu'il en y a aucuns qui font marchié d'amener taboureurs, villeurs, organeurs, et autres jongleurs d'autre jonglerie avecq eulx, et puis prennent lesquiex que il veulent dont il ont bon loier et bon courratage, et prennent gent qui riens ne sevent et laissent les bons ouvriers; de quoy li peuples et les bonnes genz sont aucune fois deçeüs, et ainssi le font ou préjudice du mestier et du commun proufit. Car, comment que ceus qu'il prennent sachent peu, ne leur font il pas demander mendre salaire et a leur proufit et les tesmoignent autres qu'il ne sont, en decevant les bonnes gens.

II Item que se trompeurs ou autres menestreurs ont fait marchié ou promis à aler à une feste, que il ne la puissent laissier tant comme ycelle feste durra pour autre prendre.

III Item, que il ne puissent envoier à la feste à laquelle ils seront aloués nulle autre personne pour euls, si ce n'estoit ou cas de maladie, de prison ou d'autre nécessité.

IV Item, que nuls menestreurs ou menestrelles, ne aprentiz quelque ils soient, ne voisent aval la ville de Paris pour soy presenter à feste, ne à noces pour euls, ne pour autres, et s'il fait ou font le contraire qu'il en chée en l'amende.

V Item, que nuls menestreurs aprentis qui voist aval taverne ne puisse louer autrui que lui, ne enviter ou amonester, ou faire aucune mencion de son mestier ou dit louage par fait, ne par parole, ne par signe quelque il soit, ne par inter-pointe coustume, se ne sont ses enfants à marier tant seulement ou de qui les maris seroient alé en estrange païs ou estrangé de leurs fames. Mais se l'en leur demande aucun menestrel jongleur pour louer, qu'ils respondent tant seulement à ceus qui les requerront: 'Seigneur, je ne puis alouer autrui que moy mesmes par les ordenances de nostre mestier, mais se il vous fault menes-treurs ou aprentis, alés en la rue aus jongleurs, vous en trouverés de bons'. Sanz ce que ledit apprentis qui en sera requis puisse nommer, enseingner, ne présenter aucun par especial; et se li aprentis fait le contraire, que ses maistres ou lui soient tenuz de l'amende lequel qu'il plaira miex aus maistres du mestier; et se le maistre ne veult païer l'amende, que le vallet aprentis soit bannis du mestier un an et un jour de la ville de Paris, ou au moins jusques à tant que le maistre ou aprentis aient paié l'amende.

VI Item, que se aucun vient en la rue aus jongleurs pour louer aucuns jongleurs ou jongleresse, et sus le premier qui li demanderres appelera pour louer, nuls autres ne s'embate en leurs paroles, ne ne facent fuers, ne facent faires, et ne ne l'appellent pour soy presenter ne autrui, jusques à tant que li demanderres et le premier jongleur appelé soient departis de marchié et que li demanderres s'en voit pour louer un autre.

VII Item, que ce mesmes soit fait des aprentis.

VIII Item, que tous menestreus et menestrels, jongleurs et jongleresses, tant privé comme estrange, jurront et seront tenuz de jurer à garder les dites ordenances par foy et serement.

IX Item, que se il vient en la dite ville aucun menestrel, jongleur, mestre ou aprentis, que li prevost de Saint-Julian ou ceus qui y seront establis de par le roy pour mestres du dit mestier et pour garder iceluy, li puissent deffendre l'ouvrer, et sus estre bannis un an et un jour de la ville de Paris jusques à tant qu'il auroit juré à tenir et garder les dites ordenances et sur les poines qui mises y sont.

X Item, que nulz ne se face louer par queux ne par personne aucune qui loier, ne promesse aucune, ne aucune cortoisie en prengne.

XI Item, que ou dit mestier seront ordené .II. ou .III. preudes hommes de par nous ou de par nos successeurs prevos de Paris ou nom du roy, qui corrigeront et punir puissent les mesprenans contre les dites ordenances, en telle manière que la moitié des amendes tournent par devers le roy, et l'autre moitié au proufit de la confrairie du dist mestier; et sera chascune amende tauxee à .X. sous parisis toutes les foiz que aucun mesprendra contre les ordenances dessus dites ou contre aucun d'icelles.

c. 1230 Richard of St Laurent and the minstrel as composer of courtly song

Source: Richard of St Laurent, *De laudibus beate Marie virginis* (edition of Douai, 1625), column 144.

As he makes the opening moves in his conversation with Dalfi d'Alvernhe, the minstrel in Raimon Vidal's *Abril issia* says that he became a minstrel because of his father's account of the Golden Age; in particular, he admits to Dalfi, 'I became a minstrel with your verses' (*ab vostres motz*). As suggested in Chapter 2, this presumably means that the minstrel took poems by Dalfi into his repertoire. Might it also mean that the minstrel himself supplied the *sons*?

This is only speculation of course, although it may at least be said, on the authority of the *Vidas*, that there were some troubadours who composed words but no music. It may have been considered a gracious compliment in some courtly contexts for a minstrel to learn a magnate's love-lyric and then to find a tune for it himself if the aristocratic poet had no immediate intention of doing so (or if he had no ability to do so). There is one piece of evidence to suggest that the compositional history behind some songs, at least, is not as simple as it may appear in the chansonniers where very many songs are attributed to named individuals such as Gace Brulé, the Chastelain de Couci, and many others of rank. In his meditation *De laudibus beate Marie virginis* Richard of St Laurent, deacon of Rouen from 1239–1245, says this of 'courtly minstrels':

> solent enim curiales joculatores componere cantilenas et iam compositas appropriare illis a quibus magna donatia iam acceperunt vel sperant se accepturos.

> courtly minstrels are accustomed to compose songs and, once composed, to assign them to those from whom they have received, or hope to receive, lavish reward.

Richard of St Laurent seems to be saying that some minstrels who worked in courts were accustomed to compose songs (*cantilenas*; presumably both words and music are meant, but it is impossible to be sure) and then to attribute these compositions to a patron.

It is possible that some of the variant melodic settings which appear in the trouvère repertory are connected with this or some similar practice. As is well known, the music of a significant number of trouvère songs can be found in several manuscripts where the melodies are often markedly different, but extensive and striking variations – presumably arising from oral transmission – frequently occur in versions of what are clearly the same tune (or perhaps it would be more advisable to say the same 'tune idea') that it becomes an almost impossible matter to determine whether two or more melodies for the same poem are indeed different. (However, there is an important number of cases where a single poem was undoubtedly set several times.) As far as the aesthetic character of trouvère song is concerned, it can be argued that these variations are explicable, since the most persuasive account of the relationship between words and music in this repertoire, by John Stevens, suggests that the relation between the two was not an expressive one in any modern sense of the word. To compose a new melody for a trouvère song, therefore, was not necessarily to subvert its decorum.

From the practical point of view, however, it is not easy to imagine how these variant melodies arose. Did the poems of noted trouvères sometimes travel as texts only and then occasionally encounter readers who wanted to sing them but who could not do so unless a new tune were composed? It is certainly plausible that something of this order took place now and then, and the number of poems (both in the trouvère and troubadour repertoires, but especially in the latter) preserved with blank staves suggests as much.

An alternative suggestion would be that the variant melodies for some trouvère poems were composed by minstrels as a compliment to the poet who was in a position to reward them for their labour. One compliment does not preclude another, and it would therefore be possible for one minstrel to compose the music for someone else's poem (or indeed to compose the whole piece, words and music together), and then to be followed by another who produced an alternative musical setting. The notion of artistic originality which prevailed in the twelfth and thirteenth centuries was flexible enough to allow the self-serving minstrel to remain anonymous and for the finished songs to enter the repertory under the name of his benefactor.

NOTES

Introduction

[1] See Cheyette, 'The Invention of the State'.

[2] *Ibid.*, p. 150.

[3] PL 205, column 253.

[4] Text in Rohloff, *Quellenhandschriften*.

[5] For the text see E. G. Stanley, *The Owl and the Nightingale*. In lines 1091-2 the poet refers to 'king Henri' as deceased ('Iesus his soule do merci!'), which indicates that the poem was composed at some time between the year 1189, when Henry II died, and the accession of Henry III in 1216. Further precision is impossible. For a discussion of the dating see *ibid.*, p. 19. The question of the author's identity – whether he is the Master Nicholas of Guildford mentioned in the poem – has been much discussed, most recently in Eadie, 'The authorship of *The Owl and the Nightingale*', but the evidence is inconclusive, and I do not believe that matters can be taken beyond the brief but meticulous survey of the question in Stanley's edition (*ibid.*, pp. 19ff). The poem is certainly of southern origin, and might be from Guildford. The abundant musical references in the poem have received surprisingly little attention. Greene, '*The Owl and the Nightingale*' grasps the importance of the musical issues raised by the poem but does little more than state the obvious. Brief, but much more suggestive, is the treatment which the poem receives in Medcalf, 'Literature and drama', pp. 101-4, which was published after the substance of this book was written. I agree with Medcalf that the contrast between the owl and the nightingale in the poem is, in part, 'the contrast of plainchant and polyphony' (*ibid.*, p. 102).

[6] Translated from the Middle English text in Stanley, *The Owl and the Nightingale*, lines 856-874. The medieval (and especially the monastic) theology of man's misery owes much to Gregory. See Leclercq, *Love of Learning*, pp. 25ff., especially p. 29: 'At the root of this concept of the Christian life is found a lively awareness of man's misery . . . . This awareness is basic, and it is always close to the surface in St Gregory's vocabulary, in his modes of expression and in the themes habitual with him. Man's wretchedness comes from his physical nature, from Original Sin, from the egoism which harries each one of us, which is always on the watch, and which tends to vitiate all our actions, even the good ones.' Cf. Stanley, *The Owl and the Nightingale*, note to lines 854-92.

[7] Stanley, *The Owl and the Nightingale*, lines 959-60 and 1337-8. For the potent association between the nightingale's voice and secular love-song see the sermon in London, British Library MS Royal 4 B.viii, f.134v. The nightingale is also associated with the pain and poignancy of love, as sublimely revealed in Marie de France's *lai* of *Laüstic* (text in Ewert, *Marie de France*, pp. 97-101).

[8] Stanley, *The Owl and the Nightingale*, lines 997–1024.

[9] Translated from the Middle English text in Stanley, *The Owl and the Nightingale*, 712–24.

[10] Webb, *Policraticus*, I, p. 42: *quibus philomena vel sithacus, aut si quid sonorius est, modos suos nequeunt coaequare*. All of John's material on music and entertainers from the first book of the *Policraticus* can be found in English translation in Pike, *Frivolities of Courtiers*, pp. 26ff.

[11] For the most recent description of this manuscript, with bibliography, see Fenlon, *Cambridge Music Manuscripts*, pp. 40–4, and also Stevens, *Words and Music*, p. 514 (source 8).

[12] See especially Southern, *Medieval Humanism*, and Bynum, 'Did the twelfth century discover the individual?'.

[13] See Chapter 1, *passim*.

[14] *The Formation of a Persecuting Society*, p. 140.

[15] *Ibid.*, p. 11.

[16] *Ibid.*, pp. 6ff.

Chapter 1: *Minstrels and the clergy*

[1] For example by Faral, *Les jongleurs*, pp. 26 (in translation) and 277 (in Latin). During its long history the English word 'minstrel' has been used to denote virtually every kind of professional entertainer that can possibly be imagined (OED sv *minstrel, minstrelsy*; MED sv *minstral, minstralsi(e)*; Carter, *Dictionary*, sv *Menestral, Menestralcie*). There is a powerful sense, however, that associates the term with professional musicians and especially with instrumentalists, as some modern attempts (e.g. by Greene, *The Early English Carols*, cxxxv–cxxxvii) to prove that the term *generally* meant 'an instrumentalist' readily demonstrate. While believing that Greene is mistaken in his view, I shall use the term 'minstrel' in what follows to denote all professional entertainers but with a prevailing understanding that musicians are meant unless the context indicates otherwise. The literature on minstrelsy is vast, and the following list of studies is accordingly confined to those which deal with the social and moral position of minstrels in France, both north and south, and in the Anglo-Norman realm. See Faral's study and Baldwin, *Masters, Princes and Merchants*, I, pp. 198ff; Casagrande and Vecchio, 'Clercs et jongleurs'; Geremek, *The Margins of Society*, pp. 159ff; Gushee, 'Two central places'; Kendrick, *The Game of Love*, pp. 157ff; Le Goff, *Time, Work and Culture*, pp. 64ff; Morgan, 'Old French *jogleor*'; Ogilvy, '*Mimi, Scurrae, Histriones*'; Paden, 'The role of the joglar'; Wright, 'Misconceptions' and *idem*, 'The role of musicians'. Further studies will be cited in due course.

[2] *Les jongleurs*, p. 26.

[3] Bowles, 'Liturgical service', p. 45.

[4] Geremek, *The Margins of Society*, p. 160.

[5] For the ardour of preaching (*fervens dei sicut ignis*) and the effect of Scripture, 'joyous and refreshing' (*iocundum et solaciosum*) I refer to the sermons of Evrard du Val-des-Ecoliers, signatures Iv[v] and Hi[v].

[6] For an inventory of the contents of this manuscript see Schneyer, *Repertorium*, sv Petrus de Limoges, pp. 686–94.

[7] On the minstrel-life of Paris see Baldwin, *Masters, Princes and Merchants*, I, pp. 198ff, and Gushee, 'Two central places'.

[8] Guenée, 'L'historien et la compilation'.

[9] Many sermons which mention minstrels merely repeat commonplace *exempla*. There is original material of interest in the sermons of Evrard du Val-des-Ecoliers, the *Fundamentum aureum* of Nicholas de Gorran and the sermons of Guido of Evreux. For the sermons of Guido, widely distributed, I have used Oxford, Lincoln College, MS lat.113 (see f.105v) and Oxford, Jesus College, MS E.8 (see pp. 286 and 320; the MS is paginated at this point). For material of a more commonplace and perhaps more representative kind, see the sermons in London, British Library, Additional MSS 16590 (f.167v) and 37670 (f.146v and 149r), MSS Royal 2 D.vi (f.207v) and 3 A.xiii (f.49r/v), MS Arundel 395, (f.10r and f.36r), Cambridge, Gonville and Caius College, MS 52/29 (f.158v, see Figure 13).

[10] P. Brown, *The World of Late Antiquity*, pp. 53–4.

[11] This early patristic opposition to secular music and its instruments is most illuminatingly discussed in the various publications by McKinnon listed in the bibliography. See also Jürgens, *Pompa diaboli*, and Bonaria, *Romani mimi*.

[12] For an exception see the penitential by Thomas Chobham cited below.

[13] See, for example, London, British Library MS Harley 3823, ff.372v–378v, or the extensive treatment of *choreae* in the *Summa de vitiis et virtutibus* of Guillaume Peyraut (Figure 9 and Appendix).

[14] London, British Library, MS Harley 3823, f.376r.

[15] This aphorism was almost always attributed to St Jerome in the Middle Ages but it has not been traced in his surviving writings.

[16] On the reaction of Christian theologians to the proliferating economic activity of the twelfth and thirteenth centuries, with all its complex financial and spiritual consequences, see Baldwin, *Masters, Princes and Merchants*; *idem, The Medieval Theories of the Just Price*; d'Avray, *The Preaching of the Friars*, especially pp. 204ff.; Chenu, 'Civilisation urbaine et théologie'; Le Goff, 'Apostolat mendiant et fait urbain'; *idem, Time, Work and Culture*, especially pp. 107ff. and pp. 122ff; Little, 'Pride goes before Avarice'; *idem, Religious Poverty and the Profit Economy*; Murray, *Reason and Society*; Rosenwein and Little, 'Social meaning in monastic and mendicant spiritualities', and Verger, 'Abélard et les milieux sociaux de son temps'.

[17] PL 172, col. 1148: *D. Quam spem habent mercatores? M. Parvam, nam fraudibus, perjuriis, lucris omne pene quod habent acquirunt.*

[18] The most recent review, with special reference to sermons diffused from Paris, is by d'Avray, *The Preaching of the Friars*, pp. 204ff.

[19] *Ibid.*, p. 207.

[20] Chédeville, *La ville médiévale, passim*.

[21] On the Franciscans and the Dominicans see the studies cited in note 16 above. The Chanter and his circle are treated in great (and illuminating) detail in Baldwin, *Masters, Princes and Merchants*.

[22] For the full context see the Appendix, pp. 198–200. For the recognition of minstrel poverty see also Alexander of Hales, *Summa Theologica*, IV, p. 908: *Item, cum in histrionibus, quocumque modo accipiantur, sit imago Dei, et indigeant, si datur eis in quantum huiusmodi, datur eis intuitu Dei. Ergo in hoc non immolatur idolis sive daemonibus.* The extent to which some kinds of minstrels were finding their way into the contemporary conception of urgent poverty can be gauged from the writers who oppose this development by contrasting minstrels with the 'real poor'. See, for

example, Jordan of Saxony, preaching in England in 1229 : *Item, qui dat uni panem integrum et alii micam, signum est quod plus diligat unum alio, sed plus datur histrionibus et adulatoribus quam vere pauperibus.* Text in Little and Douie, 'Three sermons of Friar Jordan of Saxony', p. 18. See also the careful discussion by Simon of Tournai of whether it is better to give alms to a minstrel or to a priest when both are in equal need. Text in Warichez, *Simon de Tournai*, p. 102. It is tempting to detect a display of fellow feeling by a minstrel to paupers in a story told in Bromyard's *Summa predicantium* (I, f.229r); a *histrio* entertaining a magnate in his hall calls for silence, and the clamour of the poor crying for alms at the door is instantly heard.

23 Mollat, *The Poor in the Middle Ages.* See also Planche, 'Omniprésence ... des pauvres'.

24 Text from Wailly, *Histoire de St Louis*, section 478. On the charitable initiatives of St Louis see Mollat, *The Poor in the Middle Ages*, p. 138. For a different kind of charitable initiative to a minstrel see the *exemplum* paraphrased from Paris, Bibliothèque Nationale, MS lat. 14799, f.174v (Jean de Baume), in Histoire littéraire de la France, 27, pp. 153–4. In this *exemplum* an old and poor minstrel named Roland continues to go the rounds of feasts and celebrations, and the women give him small gifts of money.

25 *Fundamentum aureum*, p. 189 (*In festo beatae Caeciliae, sermo* 4). See Schneyer, *Repertorium*, sv Nicolaus de Gorran, p. 309.

26 For the text see Jubinal, *Jongleurs et trouvères*, pp. 164–9. Concern about the threat posed by artists of 'inferior' talent is expressed throughout medieval literature and takes many forms. One variety of it receives very elaborate expression in the famous 'Supplication' which Guiraut Riquier de Narbonne addressed to Alfonso el Sabio. For the text see Pizzorusso, *La supplica di Guiraut Riquier.* Compare the anxiety of the Parisian minstrels in 1321 about competition from inferior practitioners of the art of minstrelsy (see below, p. 65). For other examples of the 'complaint' topos see Salter, *Fourteenth Century English Poetry*, pp. 92ff. The complaints of an author like Chrestien de Troyes about inferior narrators find a loud echo many centuries later in a letter from Dylan Thomas to Pamela Hansford Johnson, dated to mid-September, 1933 : 'There was a time when only poets were called poets. Now anyone with an insufficient knowledge of the English language, a Marie Corelli sentiment, and a couple of "bright" images to sprinkle over the lines, is called a poet'. Ferris, *Dylan Thomas: The Collected Letters*, p. 21.

27 Arras, Bibliothèque muncipale, MS 1019, f.104: *Dicitur quod quidam homo simplex, in quadam villa Franciae, vidit quendam cantantem canciones multas, et inde multa acquirentem, et rogavit istum secrete ut sibi venderet de cantilenis. Iste, volens illudere suae simplicitati, dixit quod bene venderet ei si aportaret unum saccum, et venderet ei plenum saccum de cantilenis. Et veniens ad quendam vesparium, posuit multas apes silvaticas in sacco, et cum, quadam die dominica, rustici essent in foro congregati, iste habens saccum cum vespibus, audiens eas interius murmurantes, credebat se cantilenas emisse. Et convocatis omnibus rusticis de villa, saccum excussit et vespes famelicae exiverunt, et rusticos qui ad gaudium venerant graviter pupungerunt.* This story dates back to at least the first decades of the thirteenth century, since a form of it is told by Jacques de Vitry. See Greven, *Die Exempla ... des Jacob von Vitry*, p. 50.

28 Arras, Bibliothèque municipale, MS 1019, f.93: *Dicitur quod apud Montem Pessulanum fuit cerdo quidam pauperrimus, nomine Robinus, qui morabatur sub scalis cujusdam ditissimi viri et avarissimi. Iste vero pauper habebat viellam, et, cum labore fatigatus esset, eam tangebat*

et cantabat alacriter cantilenas; et cum de suo lucro habebat v denarios vel vi, emebat carnes, faciebat salsas et sic tempus suum alacriter deducebat.

29 Dugauquier, *Pierre le Chantre Summa de sacramentis*, III, 2a, p. 176.

30 Peter the Chanter, *Verbum abbreviatum*, PL 205, col. 253.

31 For a comprehensive treatment of Peter the Chanter and his 'circle' see Baldwin, *Masters, Princes and Merchants*.

32 Dugauquier, *Pierre le Chantre Summa de sacramentis*, III, 2a, p. 177.

33 Broomfield, *Thomae de Chobham Summa Confessorum*, p. 291.

34 Full text in Little, *Franciscan Papers*, p. 108. See below, p. 24.

35 For the full text, with translation, from Cambridge, Gonville and Caius College, MS 331/722, see the Appendix.

36 Dugauquier, *Pierre le Chantre Summa de sacramentis*, III, 2a, pp. 176–7. For a relatively tolerant attitude to instrumentalists see also Alexander of Hales, *Summa Theologica*, IV, p. 909. Alexander admits that *histriones*, strictly speaking, are those who produce empty laughter and wantonness by contorting their bodies; by an extension, however (*Alio modo extenso nomine*), the term *histrio* is also applied to instrumentalists (*quicumque per quaecumque instrumenta provocat homines ad laetitiam*), and to the extent that the entertainment they offer is chaste and moderate, it is legitimate to give money to them. Compare also the tolerant spirit of Evrard du Val-des-Ecoliers as he contemplates minstrels within aristocratic households: *Homines divites habent suos ioculatores qui utuntur musicis instrumentis ad remotionem tedii et ad promovendum iocunditatem anime* (*Sermones*, rv).

37 Broomfield, *Thomae de Chobham Summa Confessorum*, p. 292. This extract has often been quoted and commented upon. For a list of the most important contributions before 1968 see Broomfield's edition, p. 291, n.1. The most recent discussions are in Stevens, *Words and Music*, p. 235, and Kendrick, *The Game of Love*, p. 222. Stevens and Kendrick both place the period of Chobham's activity in the late thirteenth century (although Stevens acknowledges that there is some uncertainty); I do not believe it is possible to oppose the arguments adduced by Broomfield for a date of *c.* 1216 for the *Summa* – arguments which were by no means new in 1968. See Little, *Franciscan Papers*, p. 108, n.3. Chobham's penitential was much copied, and in this sense at least it may be spoken of as an important and even influential work. On the question of Chobham's influence there is an outdated but still useful article by Rubel, 'Chabham's [sic] penitential and its influence'. To the cases of influence cited there may now be added (1) a discussion in the *Tractatus de quattuor virtutibus cardinalibus ad cives venetos*, 4:4:7, by the late thirteenth-century Dominican Henricus de Arimino, and (2) an example in the (? fifteenth-century) *Jardin des nobles* in Paris, Bibliothèque Nationale, MS fr.193, f.342v, where the material on minstrels is attributed to Jean de la Rochelle (d. 1245). I have been unable to find a discussion of minstrelsy in Jean's works.

38 The most recent discussion of the musical aspects of medieval narrative poetry, including the very fragmentary remains of music deriving from the *chanson de geste* tradition, is provided by Stevens, *Words and Music*, pp. 199ff.

39 Compare the remarks of the music theorist Johannes de Grocheio (text in Rohloff, *Quellenhandschriften*, p. 130; quoted, with translation and commentary in Stevens, *Words and Music*, p. 236). Grocheio also speaks of saints' lives and narratives of secular heroes in the same breath, associating both with the same, salutary effect upon the common people and the middle classes of Paris. Stevens, *Words and Music*, pp. 199ff, wisely treats the musical evidence relating to secular narratives

and to saints' lives together. The interdependence of certain kinds of secular and hagiographic narrative in the Middle Ages can be seen with particular clarity in many Middle English romances, generally cruder and more elemental than their French counterparts. See Childress, 'Between romance and legend', and the many illuminating comments in Pearsall, *Old English and Middle English Poetry*, pp. 113ff.

40 Text from Little, *Franciscan Papers*, p. 108.

41 For the full text, with translation, from Cambridge, Gonville and Caius College MS 331/722, see the Appendix.

42 *Cantare cum instrumentis* would seem to imply 'to sing *with* instruments' and therefore to sing, or to declaim, with some kind of accompaniment. The sense 'to play *upon* instruments' is generally expressed in medieval Latin with *cantare in instrumentis*, a usage which involves a transferred use of *cantare*. See Page, *Voices and Instruments*, p. 161.

43 Dugauquier, *Pierre le Chantre Summa de sacramentis*, III, 2a, p. 177, apparatus.

44 Colker, *Karolinus*, lines 9 and 12.

45 Text from Buffum, *Le Roman de la violette*, lines 1400ff. On the question of whether Gerard is saying that he finds the art of singing and playing together quite beyond his talents, see the discussion in Page, *Voices and Instruments*, pp. 188ff. For references to other texts which associate a stringed instrument – almost invariably the fiddle – with the performance of *chansons de geste*, see *Voices and Instruments*, p. 250, n. 13. To the five texts cited there may now be added another six. (1) The anonymous *Dit des taboureurs* in which fiddle players lay claim to the *chanson de geste* repertoire. Full text in Jubinal, *Jongleurs et trouvères*, pp. 164–9; the relevant section is quoted and translated above, p. 32. (2) The opening lines of the epic *Doon de Nanteuil*, a poem surviving only in fragments. See Meyer, 'La chanson de *Doon de Nanteuil*', p. 12. This refers to a minstrel playing a fiddle and performing a *laisse*. (3) The *Poème moral* quoted in Faral, *Les jongleurs*, p. 303, item 161, which mentions the fiddle in association with stories of Aiol, Roland and Fierragu (presumably Fernagu de Nazze, the saracen king killed by Roland and mentioned in various epics, including *Otinel*, *Hugues Capet* and *Les Enfances Vivien*). (4) The *Chanson des Saisnes* of Jean Bodel, composed during the last third of the twelfth century. The first two *laisses* often refer to minstrel narrators whom Bodel – with the usual snobbery and insecurity of the literate vernacular narrator faced by competition from itinerant entertainers performing the same story material – regards as his inferiors. Lines 27–9 contain a striking reference to minstrels who sing of Guiteclin, the chieftain against whom Charlemagne wages war in Jean Bodel's narrative. Bodel describes these minstrels in lines 27–9 as *Cil bastart jougleour qui vont par ces viliaus/A ces longues* [vars: *grandes/grosses*] *vïeles a depeciés forriaus*: 'wretched minstrels who go round the dilapidated villages with their long (also 'big' and 'fat') fiddles in torn bags'. Text in Menzel and Stengel, *Jean Bodels Saxenlied*, I, lines 27–9. (5) The second redaction of *Le Moniage Guillaume: Hui mais orés canchon de fiere geste,/Chil jougleour en cantent en vïele*. Text in Cloetta, *Moniage Guillaume*, lines 2071–2. (6) Finally (if the testimony of a wildly fantastic poem is worth anything in this context), the *fatrasie* printed in Jubinal, *Nouveau recueil des contes*, II, p. 217: *Et une viele/Chantoit em fessele/Dou danoy Ogier* (i.e. Ogier the Dane). It would probably be unwise to attach too much significance to a passage in the epic of *Aliscans* where the author praises minstrels, inveighs against avaricious patrons, and adds that 'I will not leave off my fiddling for them!' (*Je ne lairai por aus mon vïeler*;

text in Wienbeck, *et al, Aliscans*, p. 261). The evidence that bowed instruments were the preferred medium of accompaniment for the *chansons de geste* seems over-whelming.

[46] Rohloff, *Quellenhandschriften*, pp. 134–5: *in eis* [stringed instruments] *enim [est] subtilior et melior soni discretio propter abbreviationem et elongationem chordarum.*

[47] Dugauquier, *Pierre le Chantre Summa de sacramentis*, III, 2a, p. 176.

[48] The Chastelain de Couci, *Li nouviauz tanz*, lines 5–8. I take the text from Rosenberg and Tischler, *Chanter m'estuet*, p. 205, as it is the most recent text edition. This implies no approval of the transcription of the music on pp. 204–5.

[49] See Page, 'Secular Music', pp. 236ff. I am most grateful to Professor John Stevens, of Magdalene College, Cambridge, for discussing his work in progress on this subject with me.

[50] Dugauquier, *Pierre le Chantre Summa de sacramentis*, III, 2a, pp. 175–6 and 426–7. These passages appear within the *Liber casuum conscientiae.*

[51] After introductory remarks, Courson's *Summa* begins by quoting the words of John the Baptist in Matthew 3:2 *Poenitentiam agite: appropinquavit enim regnum celorum*, and Courson explains that his *Summa* has *questiones morales* relating to *penitencia* as its first concern. I paraphrase the text in Cambridge, Gonville and Caius College, MS 331/722, f.1r.

[52] The classic studies in this area are Chenu, *L'éveil de la conscience*; Southern, *Medieval Humanism* pp. 29ff, and Morris, *The Discovery of the Individual*, pp. 70ff. Compare Radding, 'Evolution of medieval mentalities'. All of these studies should now be read in conjunction with the stimulating article by Bynum, 'Did the twelfth century discover the individual?'. For the theological aspects of attitudes to penance, see Anciaux, *La théologie du sacrament de pénitence*, pp. 66–7 and 286–92; Blomme, *La doctrine du péché*, especially pp. 46–9, 58–61 and 85–7. The move to soften the harshness of the old penitential canons is discussed by Michaud-Quentin, 'A propos des premières *Summae confessorum*', and Longère, *Petrus Pictaviensis Summa de confessione*, pp. 64–5 with accompanying texts cited from other penitentials. On the way that this change influenced contemporary attitudes to various professions (including minstrelsy) see Le Goff, *Time, Work and Culture*, pp. 107ff.

[53] Haren, *Medieval Thought*, p. 107. See also Luscombe, 'Peter Abelard', pp. 304ff, and the introduction to Luscombe's edition of the *Ethics, passim*, but especially xvii and xxxii. Abelard's position in this development is very judiciously stated by Luscombe in his introduction to the *Ethics*, xxxiii: 'With the increasing refinement of thought in the eleventh and twelfth centuries, the theologian-canonists sought to formulate more discerning views on the dispositions required for the commission and the absolution of sins, and Abelard as a dialectical theologian may well have profited from the example of a Burchard or an Ivo when deciding to establish a notion of sin which is always and everywhere verifiable, and which emphatically recognises the role of intention. But he was no reformer of the penitential system.'

[54] Longère, *Petrus Pictaviensis Summa de confessione*, pp. 64–5.

[55] For the *voluptuosa digressio* of Cassiodorus, in a letter to Boethius, see Mommsen, *Cassiodori Senatoris Variae*, pp. 70–2, and for a striking twelfth-century example of such a 'delicious digression' see Dimock and Brewer, *Giraldi Cambrensis Opera*, V, pp. 155ff. (from the *Topographia Hibernica*; the passage occurs just after Gerald's famous reference to the musical skills of the Irish).

[56] See, for example, Waesberghe, *Aribonis De Musica*, pp. 47–8.

[57] Text in Waesberghe, *Johannis ... De Musica*, p. 109. The treatise is translated in Palisca, *Hucbald, Guido and John*, the relevant passage appearing on pp. 133ff. See also Stevens, *Words and Music*, pp. 386ff.

[58] See the remarks in Stevens, *Words and Music*, p. 391 and pp. 404ff.

[59] For the text see above, p. 24.

[60] Geremek, *The Margins of Society*, p. 160. Much the same point is made by Bowles, 'Liturgical service', p. 45.

[61] Text from Rohloff, *Quellenhandschriften*, p. 130.

[62] For an encyclopedic treatment of the presentation of human character in the epics see Combarieu de Grès, *L'idéal humain*.

[63] Text from Meyer and Longon, *Raoul de Cambrai*, lines 1481–90. The translation is adapted from Muir, *Literature and Society*, p. 24.

[64] London, British Library MS Arundel 395, f.32r: *in domibus nobilium recitari solent probitates antiquorum*.

[65] Text in Jubinal, *Jongleurs et trouvères*, pp. 164–9.

[66] *Ibid.*, p. 168–9.

[67] On this epic and its historical background see Matarasso, *Recherches historiques et littéraires sur 'Raoul de Cambrai'*. For the *Annales Flodoardi* see Lauer, *Les Annales de Flodoard*.

[68] The Latin *Vita Sancti Guillelmi* is printed in *Acta Sanctorum*, Maii, VII, pp. 801–9. The general point is well made by Stevens, *Words and Music*, p. 236: 'The "sacred" and the "secular" are not so easily distinguished in an age which saw Christianity through an heroic lens – and heroes through a Christian lens. Is not Roland designated in old Passionals as *Sanctus Rolandus comes et martyr in Roncevalla* and commemorated, wearing the saintly nimbus, in the window of Chartres Cathedral?' Keller ('La chanson de geste et son public', p. 264) goes so far as to suggest that in the early twelfth century 'la chanson de geste n'était qu'un type particulier de chanson hagiographique'. The case of St William is a particularly striking one. In the early decades of the twelfth century Orderic Vitalis relates that in the time of the Conqueror (d.1087) the household of Hugues d'Avranches, Earl of Chester, included a cleric who 'made a great collection of tales of the combats of holy knights, drawn from the old Testament and more recent records of Christian achievements, for [great lords, simple knights and noble boys] to imitate'. The lives of certain saints were also included. One of the heroes was William of Aquitaine, and the material included clearly overlapped with some of the narrative content of the *chanson de geste* known as *Le Moniage Guillaume*. Text in Chibnall, *The Ecclesiastical History of Orderic Vitalis*, III, pp. 216ff. Orderic goes on to mention a 'popular song' (*cantilena*) about William sung by minstrels (*a ioculatoribus*), but he adds that 'a reliable account written by pious scholars and reverently read aloud by learned readers for all to hear is certainly to be preferred to that'. Towards the end of the twelfth century Jean Bodel draws a similarly firm distinction between the stories told by *vilains jougleres* and his own written work for which he claims an earlier written source: *bonne chançon vaillant/Dont li livre d'estoire son tesmoing et garant*. Text in Menzel and Stengel, *Jean Bodels Saxenlied*, I, lines 2–3. There can be no simple explanation for the sense of superiority which literate authors like Orderic and Jean Bodel felt with respect to minstrel narrators. It owes much to the mystique of literate skills and to the authority of the documents – legal, liturgical and financial – on which those skills were lavished to meet the needs of the powerful. The mere fact that literate men often felt in this way does not

indicate that the narrative songs of minstrels were generally held in low esteem; the habit of drawing a firm distinction between oral tradition and written tradition in terms of reliability and authority was certainly emerging during our period, but it was by no means widely disseminated in society at large. The expressions of literate elitism by Orderic and Jean Bodel are typical of many such pronouncements; both authors wish to establish the superior quality and authority of their own material over minstrel versions whose influence may be judged from the alacrity with which both writers disparage them as they present their own.

[69] Interest in the 'historical' kernel of the Old French epics has subsided somewhat in recent years; see Limentani, 'Les nouvelles méthodes de la critique et l'étude des chansons de geste', pp. 296ff. The trend has been away from the 'positivist' works of a scholar like Gaston Paris (who wrote that 'La recherche du rapport exact des faits aux traditions épiques est un des objets principaux de la critique des épopées'), and towards the critical conundrums of a Zumthor ('Moins que reflet d'une réalité ou d'une expérience passée, la chanson [de geste] est conscience de soi'). Limentani comments that there are undoubtedly still many specialists who 'opteraient encore et sans hésiter pour la position de Gaston Paris' (*ibid.*, p. 297), but that was now more than a decade ago. The major studies on the historical background of epic are not very recent ones. See, for example, Aebischer, 'L'élément historique dans les chanson de geste'; Lejeune, *Les chansons de geste et l'histoire*, and Matarasso, *Recherches historiques et littéraires sur 'Raoul de Cambrai'*. Nichols, 'The interaction of life and literature', p. 52, lays out the issue of a historical background to the *chansons de geste* in a most satisfactory way: 'Let us admit the hypothesis that the creative process of the Old French epic was not limited to the interaction of a literary or oral tradition and an historic fact ... instead of an inexorable progression from a well-defined historical event to a pre-eminent literary work, we find in the chronicles and poems dealing with the battle of Roncevaux, for example, a number of interrelated but distinct perceptions looking not so much back to the event itself as at a continually evolving *idea* of the event, an idea as broad as the sum of the attested perceptions.' This is very helpful; the most interesting questions are not just whether the epics contain a kernel of historical truth that can now be retrieved by research, but whether contemporary audiences felt these poems to be deeply involved with their sense of the meaning of the past. For a recent review of all the respects in which the *chansons de geste* may be of interest to historians see Boyer *et al.*, *L'épopée*.

[70] I find myself here in complete agreement with the points that were so well made by Pauphilet more than half a century ago: 'ils entremêlent [les textes historiques et les poèmes épiques] sans s'enquérir de l'âge des poèmes. Cet âge, d'ailleurs, pouvaient-ils le connaître? La première fois qu'ils entendaient une chanson, étaient-ils contraints de la reconnaître pour récente? Qui pouvait les en avertir? Les incessantes allusions des auteurs eux-mêmes à d'anciennes et vénérables sources, "ço dit la geste a s. Denis, ... a s. Riquier, ... al mostier de Loon, etc." invitaient au contraire leurs auditeurs à croire qu'ils entendaient là des récits aussi anciens que les événements, et que la voix du poète était la voix même du passé. Vrai ou faux, un arrière-plan de tradition sans âge se laissait toujours entrevoir derrière les contes épiques' ('Sur la *Chanson de Roland*', pp. 172–3).

[71] Paris, Bibliothèque Nationale, MS lat.16481, f.17v.

[72] Text in Rohloff, *Quellenhandschriften*, p. 130. See also below, p. 219, n. 10.

[73] *Magistri Petri Lombardi ... Sententiae*, IV:xvi:2. The same passage appears a

little earlier in Gratian's *Decretals* (PL 187, col. 1634). The ultimate source is Augustine, *Liber de vera et falsa poenitentia* (PL 40, col. 1126). Medieval commentaries upon the *Sentences* are catalogued in Stegmüller's invaluable *Repertorium commentariorum in Sententias P. Lombardi*. There is a supplement by Doucet, 'Commentaires sur les *Sentences*'.

74 For the passage from Augustine that is perhaps intended see PL 36, col. 439, and compare Borgnet, *Beati Alberti Magni . . . Opera Omnia*, 29, p.632.

75 Cambridge, Gonville and Caius College, MS 322/523, ff.95v-6.

76 *Ibid., spectacula omnia ad aliquam utilitatem instituta sunt.*

77 For the chronology of the Aristotelian translations see Haren, *Medieval Thought*, pp. 132ff., and most recently the essays by various authors in Dronke, *A History of Twelfth Century Western Philosophy*, pp. 407ff. ('The "new" Aristotle').

78 For a review of recent scholarship on this question see Holton, *Cities, Capitalism and Civilisation*, p. 28, and Krupat, *People in Cities*, pp. 67ff. Holton's book shows that many recent assessments of the influence of urbanism upon patterns of civilisation and culture share little with Sjoberg's famous treatment in *The Preindustrial City*, first published in 1960. Sjoberg's confident belief that it is possible to generalise extensively about the social life and cultural contexts imposed by *the* preindustrial city – be it Akkadian, Roman, medieval or early modern – has not lasted well.

79 See Chédeville, *La ville médiévale*, pp. 59ff.

80 On the contemporary debate concerning the legitimacy of the income which *magistri* earned for their teaching, and the careerist ambitions of many of their pupils, see Baldwin, *Masters, Princes and Merchants*, I, pp. 125ff. and *idem*, 'Masters at Paris from 1179-1215', with bibliography there cited; Murray, *Reason and Society*, pp. 218ff.; Post, 'Masters' salaries', supplemented by Le Goff, *Time, Work and Culture*, pp. 101ff., with valuable further discussions and commentary in the accompanying notes, pp. 312ff. For an illuminating discussion of the common dictum *scientia donum dei est, unde vendi non potest* ('learning is a gift of God, whence it cannot be sold'), see Post, *et al.*, 'The medieval heritage of a humanistic ideal'.

81 Rainerus of Pisa, *Pantheologia*, sv *Ludi*.

82 Webb, *Policraticus*, I, p. 48: *Iocundum quidem est et ab honesto non recedit uirum probum quandoque modesta hilaritate mulceri, sed ignominiosum est grauitatem huiuscemodi lasciuia frequenter resolui.*

83 Gauthier, *Ethica Nicomachea Translatio Roberti Grosseteste Lincolniensis*, 3, pp. 170 and 174.

84 Durandus de Sancto Porciano, *In Sententias Theologicas Petri Lombardi*, f.337v. See also the following curious remark, from f.338r, which seems to classify the use of liturgical polyphony as a kind of *ludus : Alli sunt ludi qui procedunt ex gaudio devocionis, sicut contingit quod cum organis dicitur unus versus sequentiae et a choro alius . . . .*

85 Richard of Middleton, *Super IV Libros Sententiarum*, on *Sentences* IV :16. For other discussions of *ludi* in the *Sentences* commentaries see Humbert de Prully's commentary in London, British Library, Additional MS 18322, f.17v. The commentary by Richard of Fishacre (Oxford, Oriel College, MS 43, f.395v) is a strange one which seems to be devoted to a discussion of the theatre of the ancients. The commentary by Pierre de Palude (*In quartum Sententiarum*, f.75v-6) is strange in a different way, avoiding the usual subject matter but containing instead the following reference to minstrels' schools held during Lent in Paris: *Cum et nobiles abstineant quia in quadragesima quando est tempus penitencie ioculatores licentiant quod tunc veniunt parisius addiscere ea quod postea possunt ludere.*

[86] Kübel, *Alberti Magni . . . Super Ethica*, p. 298. See also Borgnet, *Beati Alberti Magni . . . Opera Omnia*, 7, pp. 323ff. (*De eutrapelia, circa quid sit?*).

[87] See, for example, the views of Konrad of Megenburg; text and translation in Page, 'German musicians and their instruments'.

[88] John of Freiburg, *Summa confessorum*, f.213v. For John of Freiburg's 'popularisation' of certain elements of scholastic teaching see Boyle, 'The *Summa confessorum* of John of Freiburg'.

[89] The Darmstadt manuscript of Grocheio's treatise, reproduced in facsimile in Rohloff, *Quellenhandschriften*, ends thus: *explicit theoria magistri iohannis de grocheio regens parisius*. The words *regens parisius* are fainter and may be a slightly later addition.

[90] Rohloff, *Quellenhandschriften*, p. 124: *Si tamen eam* [sc. *musica*] *diviserimus, secundum quod homines Parisiis ea utuntur et prout ad usum vel convictum civium est necessaria.*

[91] *Ibid.*, pp. 130ff.

[92] On the *sermones ad status* see d'Avray, *The Preaching of the Friars*. A particularly striking example is provided by the sermons of the celebrated Dominican Humbert of Romans who remained in Paris in the convent of St Jacques during his novitiate. Text in *Sermones beati Umberti Burgundi*. For an account of these sermons and their contents see Brett, *Humbert of Romans*, pp. 160ff., and for an attempt to use a passage from one to elucidate a reference in Grocheio's treatise, see Page, 'The performance of Ars Antiqua motets', pp. 147–9 and n.3.

[93] Rohloff, *Quellenhandschriften*, pp. 130ff.

[94] *Ibid.*, p. 136: *coram divitibus in festis et ludis.*

[95] *Ibid.*

[96] *Ibid.*

[97] *Ibid.*

Chapter 2: Minstrels and the knightly class

[1] Meyer, *Guillaume le Maréchal*, lines 18481–8 and 18495–6:

> Li clerc sunt vers nos trop engrès:
> Trop nos vunt barbïant de près.
> Car j'ai pris .v. cenz chevaliers
> Dont j'ai et armes et destriers
> E tot lor herneis retenu:
> Se por ço m'est contretenu
> Li reignes Dé, n'i a que prendre,
> Car je nel porreie pas rendre . . .
> Ou lor arg[u]ment est ci fals,
> Ou nuls hom ne puet estre sals.

The fundamental treatment of the historical aspects of this poem, including the poet's relation to the events that he describes, is Painter, *William Marshall*, to which may now be added the brief but stimulating book by Duby, *William Marshall*. The musical references in this poem do not appear to have received the attention that they deserve.

[2] *Ibid.*, lines 3471ff. (the *carole* episode) and lines 18529ff. (the *rotruenge* passage).

[3] 'Clercs et jongleurs', p. 914.

[4] Evrard du Val-des-Ecoliers, *Sermones* rviij. Here Evrard lists three forms of Luxuria: *preciositas vestimentorum, delicie ciborum* and *distributio munerum*.

[5] Text in Strange, *Dialogus miraculorum*, I, pp. 78–9

[6] Text in Hinnebusch, *Historia occidentalis*, p. 81: *Et plerumque ad carceres et uincula trahebantur insontes, et cruciabantur innocentes, nulla alia causa, nisi quod aliquid habere credebantur, et maxime cum domini prodigalitate uacantes et luxui, pro torneamentis et pomposa seculi uanitate, expensis superfluis et debitis astringebantur et usuris. Sed et mimi et ioculatores, scurre, uagi et hystriones, canes aulici et adulatores, spoliatorum patrimonia consumebant.*

[7] Evrard du Val-des-Ecoliers, *Sermones*, Zviij: *histrionibus vel hiraldis qui in torneamentis milites ad strenue pugnandum incitant.* Cf. Paris, Bibliothèque Nationale, MS lat. 16481, f. 249r (a sermon by the 'cancellarius parisiensis' preached at Notre-Dame-des-Champs, 1271): *Isti hayraudi quando sunt in istis torneamentis et ipsi vident quod unus miles pugnat cum altero tunc animant ipsum dicentes: 'Ha! vade illi fili valentis patris qui fuit ita valens et ita strenuus'.* For the association of minstrels and heralds see also Bromyard, *Summa predicantium*, I, f.454v: *in ludis armorum, maximis dico expensis equorum, et donorum, quae heraldis, et menestrallis copiosius dantur pro laude humana.*

[8] Evrard du Val-des-Ecoliers, *Sermones*, qviij^v.

[9] Oxford, Jesus College, MS E.8, p. 166.

[10] For texts in which the heroes of *chansons de geste* express their determination that nobody will be able to make a 'bad song' of their enterprise see Whitehead, *La Chanson de Roland*, lines 1014 and 1465–6, where the speaker is Roland: *Tantes batailles en avum afinees!/Male chançun n'en deit estre cantee*; Wienbeck *et al.*, *Aliscans*, line 450 d–h. There is no specific reference to minstrel narrators in the lines from the *Song of Roland*, but the parallel passage in *Aliscans*, and the fact that narrative material about military exploits seems to have formed an exclusively professional repertoire, strongly suggest that minstrel narratives are meant. It is striking that some epics seem to blur the distinction between the warrior aristocracy and the minstrel-narrator, by referring to minstrels who are of respectable lineage, or who are even members of the fighting band in the manner of the famous Taillefer, the Norman *histrio* who taunted the English at Hastings according to the *Carmen de Hastingae Proelio*. These epics may preserve an echo of a rather more complex relationship between the performers of epic stories and the warrior class whom they served than most other texts reveal. For a study of this fascinating and neglected aspect of minstrelsy see Györy, 'Réflexions sur le jongleur guerrier', and Gitton, 'De l'emploi des chansons de geste pour entraîner les guerriers au combat'. The evidence pertaining to Taillefer is detailed, mildly contradictory, and of great interest. William of Malmesbury, writing two generations after the battle of Hastings, believed that a narrative song about Roland (*cantilena Rollandi*) had been used to hearten the Norman troops, while Wace, writing a generation or so later still, believed that Taillefer had sung this song as he rode before the Norman army *'chantant/De Karlemagne e de Rollant'*. (The relevant texts are quoted and discussed in Morton and Muntz, *The Carmen de Hastingae Proelio*, pp. 81ff.; it is less fashionable now than it once was to associate this *cantilena Rollandi* with the surviving *Song of Roland*.) All the sources are agreed that Taillefer took part in armed combat during the opening moves of the battle. Compare the illustration of a minstrel, complete with fiddle (which he is playing), unarmed but apparently mounted, and riding with crusading knights setting off to do battle in Syria, reproduced in the article by Gitton cited above (Fig. 2). Chronicle sources describing comparable events are discussed in Page, *Anglo-Saxon Hearpan*, pp. 67–8. Com-

pare also the description of Count William of Aquitaine's warrior-jongleur in the *Chanson de Guillaume*, probably of *c.* 1140 (text in Wathelet-Willem, *Recherches sur la Chanson de Guillaume*, lines 1258ff.); William's *jugleür* knows the *gestes* of all the great figures of *duce France*, including Clovis, Flovent, Pepin, Charlemagne, Roland, Oliver and more besides, but he is not only a *bons chanteür*, he is also *en bataille vassals conquereür*. The conclusion seems inescapable that the minstrels of the later twelfth and thirteenth centuries who performed epic narratives were making a living from material which, in the eleventh century (and perhaps still in their own day), was sometimes associated with warrior-narrators who were minstrels but were also valued members of the military retinue.

[11] Vale, *Edward III and Chivalry, passim,* using both French and English evidence, and relying very heavily (as is necessary) upon the French material.

[12] The phrase is from Caesarius of Heisterbach (Strange, *Dialogus miraculorum,* I, pp. 78–9).

[13] For full text and translation see above, p. 12.

[14] *Sermones,* Cvj[v].

[15] Broomfield, *Thomas de Chobham Summa Confessorum,* p. 291: *circueunt curias magnatum et loquuntur obprobia et ignominias de absentibus.* This was a constant complaint, and the number of texts which voice it in various forms is enormous. Compare Robert of Courson: *De mimis et detractoribus et adulatoribus . . . per detractiones et adulationes et scurilia et effeminata verba alliciunt favorem magnatum et adolescentes nobiles infatuant et sic pecunias emungunt* (Cambridge, Gonville and Caius College, MS 331/722, f.6v).

[16] The importance which music could assume in the competitive and careerist environment of the court is shown by the remarks of John of Salisbury in his treatise concerning the 'trifles of courtiers', the *Policraticus,* of 1159: *Non tamen curialium nugis musicam calumpnietur aliquis sociatam, licet se beneficio eius conentur nugatorum plurimi commendare* (Webb, *Policraticus,* I, p. 39, which is rendered by Pike, *Frivolities of Courtiers,* p. 30, as 'One should not slander music by charging it with being an ally of the frivolities of courtiers, although many frivolous individuals endeavour by its help to advance their own interests'). The best descriptions of court-experience have been provided by historians such as Norbert Elias, whose book *The Court Society,* though devoted to the court-culture of Versailles under the *ancien régime,* provides a stimulating discussion of court behaviour and will be referred to several times in what follows. See also Ferrante, 'The court in medieval literature'.

[17] Evrard du Val-des-Ecoliers, *Sermones,* Iij[v].

[18] Peter the Chanter, *Verbum abbreviatum,* PL 205, col. 266, attacking the vices of the clergy: *sed clerici habitu milites, sermone histriones, opere et gestu meretrices, occupatione curarum temporalium saeculares, in qua harum facierum Deum sequuntur, vel in quo habitu resurgent, qui in nullo vivunt?* Compare a passage by Evrard du Val-des-Ecoliers which encapsulates what was perhaps the clerics' principal objection to minstrelsy: *multi enim sunt qui libencius audirent unum ioculatorem quam unum bonum predicatorem* (*Sermones,* Ei[v]).

[19] Troyes, Bibliothèque Municipale, MS 144, volume II, f.107r: *illos qui in choro cantant . . . habent canticum non cytharam sicut sunt mimi solo ore nescientes instrumentum musicum manibus tractare.*

[20] Alexander of Hales, *Summa Theologica,* III, p. 424.

[21] London, British Library, MS Royal 3 A.xiii, f.49r–v.

[22] This aspect of courtliness is discussed at length in Elias, *The Court Society,* especially pp. 106ff.

[23] See p. 56.

[24] The text is edited and (often somewhat adventurously or loosely) translated, with copious notes but without an introduction, in Field, *Raimon Vidal*. The poem has attracted relatively little attention. The principal studies and relevant articles are Limentani, 'Il guillare nelle novas di Ramon Vidal'; Paden, 'The role of the joglar'; Page, *Voices and Instruments*, p. 25ff.; and Poe, 'The meaning of *saber* in Raimon Vidal's *Abril issia*'. A valuable study might be made of the relationship between Vidal's poem and the rich tradition of the Latin 'courtesy' books which developed particularly in the twelfth century. It seems very likely that Raimon Vidal is drawing upon this tradition in order to dignify a certain kind of minstrel profession with a manual. For the courtesy books see Nicholls, *The Matter of Courtesy*.

[25] Field, *Raimon Vidal*, lines 10–11 and 19–25; translation from p. 61. The English version here, as throughout this chapter, is taken from Field's edition with a few minor modifications.

[26] *Ibid.*, lines 755–61; translation from p. 72.

[27] Boutière and Schutz, *Biographies des troubadours*, p. 39: *tota la estat anava per cortz*.

[28] *Ibid.*, p. 167: *E si tolc moiller una soldadera qu'el menet lonc temps ab si per cortz*.

[29] Field, *Raimon Vidal*, lines 142–51, 154–63 and 168–71; translation from p. 63.

[30] For an edition of the poems of Dalfi, with documentation concerning his life and many literary contacts, see Brackney, *A Critical Edition of the Poems of Dalfin d'Alvernhe*. Although this is an unpublished dissertation, it is preferable for scholarly purposes to the recent edition (with a French translation of the poems) by de Labareyre.

[31] Brackney, *A Critical Edition . . .*, xxiiiff.

[32] The *Vida* of the troubadour Peire d'Alvernhe reports that Peire lived in good society, 'according to what Dalfi d'Alvernhe has to say on the matter' (*segon qu'en dis lo Dalfins d'Alvernhe*; Boutière and Schutz, *Biographies des troubadours*, p. 264). The *razos* associated with Dalfi's own poems contain a good deal of information, both of a historical and of a gossipy sort, which may derive from Dalfi himself or from his circle.

[33] For full bibliography on this and all the other drawings by Revel, together with a discussion and bibliography pertaining to Dalfi's castle (and indeed to his life) see Fournier, *Châteaux, villages et villes d'Auvergne*, especially pp. 78–85.

[34] *Ibid.*, pp. 78ff.

[35] *Ibid.*

[36] This account is based upon Fournier, *Châteaux, villages et villes d'Auvergne*; idem, *Le château dans la France médiévale*, especially pp. 82 and 290–1, and Gardelles, 'Les palais dans l'Europe occidentale chrétienne du Xe au XIIe siècle'.

[37] Guillaume 'de Lavicea', *Dieta salutis*, p. 334.

[38] On the *estage* see Fournier, *Le château dans la France médiévale*, pp. 114ff., and Poly and Bournazel, *La mutation féodale*, p. 86.

[39] Field, *Raimon Vidal*, line 170.

[40] *Ibid.*, lines 619–22; translation p. 70.

[41] Boutière and Schutz, *Biographies des troubadours*, pp. 229–30 (the *vida* of Gausbert de Poicibot). Such equipment was vital for travelling between households; as Gausbert's *vida* says, the moment he received his, *el poi anet per cortz*: 'he went afterwards around the courts'.

[42] Field, *Raimon Vidal*, lines 625–6; translation p. 70.

[43] *Ibid.*, lines 627-32; translation p. 70.

[44] *Ibid.*, lines 634-5; translation p. 70.

[45] *Ibid.*, lines 643-4; translation p. 70.

[46] On restrictions during Lent see p. 217, n. 85.

[47] For the first-hand account of these travels see Hughes, *An Itinerary of Provence and the Rhone*.

[48] Oxford, Jesus College, MS E.8, f.13v.

[49] See Chapter 4.

[50] Elias, *The Court Society*, pp. 106ff.

[51] Field, *Raimon Vidal*, lines 1081-5; translation p. 77.

[52] *Ibid.*, lines 1195-1200; translation, p. 79.

[53] *Ibid.*, lines 782-91; translation, p. 73.

[54] *Ibid.*, lines 1694-7; translation, p. 87.

[55] Elias, *The Court Society*, p. 108.

[56] *Ibid.*

[57] Field, *Raimon Vidal*, lines 176-7; translation, p. 63.

[58] *Ibid.*, line 201.

[59] *Ibid.*, lines 218-21; translation, p. 64.

[60] *Ibid.*, lines 226-7; translation, p. 64.

[61] Towards the end of his discourse to the minstrel (that is to say, after a suitably discreet interval) the narrator tries to give the minstrel an objective view of his blunder at Dalfi's court: 'Some jongleurs are obstinate and sing their own praise [which is exactly what the minstrel did before Dalfi] and because they are stupid they want to sit down beside you even if you were before the king, almost as if they were more knightly and of higher rank' (*ibid.*, p. 86). The narrator's message to the minstrel could scarcely be more discreet and yet more plain.

[62] *Ibid.*, lines 531ff; translation, p. 69.

[63] *Ibid.*, line 1152. I cannot tell what reason Field has (*ibid.*, p. 78) for translating *nostres* here as 'your' (i.e. as if the reading were *vostres*).

[64] *Ibid.*, line 660; translation, p. 71.

[65] *Ibid.*, lines 1038-41; translation, p. 76.

[66] *Ibid.*, lines 38ff.; translation, p. 61.

[67] *Ibid.*, lines 1445-60; translation, p. 83.

[68] *Ibid.*, lines 1690-1; translation, p. 87.

[69] *Ibid.*, lines 1574-9; translation, p. 85.

Chapter 3: Minstrels in Paris c. 1300: rules and repertoire

[1] For the original text of the statutes see the Appendix.

[2] Principally by Bernhard, 'Recherches sur l'histoire de la corporation des ménétriers', where the text of the statutes is given, by Faral, *Les jongleurs*, pp. 128ff., which also prints the statutes, and by Gushee, 'Two central places'.

[3] On this street, and on the general integration of minstrels into the topography of Paris *c.* 1300, see the excellent study by Gushee, 'Two central places', and Geremek, *The Margins of Society*, p. 74 and *passim*.

[4] Appendix, p. 205, Statute VIII.

[5] For a summary of the conventional aims and purposes of confraternities see Mollat,

The Poor in the Middle Ages, pp. 142ff., and with special reference to Paris, Geremek, *The Margins of Society, passim.*

6 Statute XI.
7 In practice the duration of apprenticeships in guilds of the later thirteenth and fourteenth centuries appears to have been variable.
8 Statute XI.
9 These synopses omit little of substance, although their principal purpose is to indicate the contents of the statutes which bear directly upon the arguments that will be adduced in this chapter.
10 Roques, *Erec et Enide*, lines 1978ff.
11 For the terms *li peuples* and *les bonnes genz* see Statute I, and for the meaning of the latter, Matoré, *Le vocabulaire et la société médiévale*, p. 115.
12 Statute I. On the term *ouvrier* see Matoré, *Le vocabulaire* ... p. 174; it denotes manual, non-agricultural labour.
13 Ruelle, *Huon de Bordeaux*, lines 7256–60.
14 Field, *Raimon Vidal*, lines 38–46; translation p. 61.
15 Statute I.
16 Statute V.
17 *Ibid.*
18 *Ibid.*
19 For the power of the trumpeters, which the statutes seek to limit, see Statute I.
20 For the names, and for what is known of the individuals concerned, see Gushee, 'Two central places', pp. 140ff.
21 With his usual insight into the habitual difficulties of the minstrel life, the narrator in Raimon Vidal's *Abril issia* reflects that in courtly society there are always some 'among the barons ... who think that you are sufficiently rewarded if they listen to you and condescend merely to address you' (Field, *Raimon Vidal*, p. 83).
22 Gerbert's continuation of *Perceval le Gallois* (*c.* 1220) refers in biting terms to the failure of magnates to meet the standards of the Arthurian period when the young men and knights at a feast would unrobe themselves, taking off their *cotes, sorcos et roubes vaires* to present them to minstrels. Their modern counterparts, Gerbert complains, promise their robes, and set a time to give them over, but then fail to honour their obligations. The relevant passage is readily accessible in Faral, *Les jongleurs*, pp. 306–7.
23 Mollat, *The Poor in the Middle Ages*, p. 107.
24 Geremek, *The Margins of Society*, p. 254. While the minstrels were proverbial for having itchy feet (see extract II from Paris, Bibliothèque Nationale, MS lat. 16481 above, p. 11), it should be emphasised that the essentially itinerant life which was led by many (perhaps most) minstrels was not regarded as disreputable *per se*. As Geremek comments (*ibid.*, p. 262), referring to the tendency of many medieval social groups to be mobile, it would be 'unwise to see travel in itself as a factor in social downgrading .... We can see in these travels the need to perfect technical education and the need to see the world. These motives were, in fact, complementary. The same desire to improve skills and see the country were found in worlds as far apart as the art of war and intellectual endeavour. For knights, for students and for clergy, as for journeymen, the discovery of the world, of feudal courts, of tournaments, or of famous schools and universities constituted an indispensable element in professional and social initiation.' This aspect of

medieval life is succinctly summarised in one line of *The Owl and the Nightingale*; referring to the nightingale's resourcefulness and cunning, the poet comments: 'she had thoroughly gained her knowledge *everywhere*' (Stanley, *The Owl and the Nightingale*, line 216).

[25] Statute V.

[26] The names are listed in Gushee, 'Two central places', p. 141.

[27] The phrase comes from a section of the statutes not reproduced here. See Bernhard, 'Recherches sur l'histoire de la corporation des ménétriers', I, p. 400.

[28] Page, 'German musicians', gives text and translation of some fourteenth-century comments upon this subject by Konrad of Megenburg, who studied in Paris.

[29] Paris, Bibliothèque Nationale, MS lat. 16481, f.64v.

[30] *Multi enim sunt qui libentius audirent unum ioculatorem quam unum bonum predicatorem* (*Sermones*, Ei^v).

[31] Rohloff, *Quellenhandschriften*, p. 136.

[32] For further discussion of this issue, with citation of sources, see Chapter 8.

[33] Statute I. For the popular audience for *chansons de geste* in Paris, exploited by minstrels, see further Chapter 8.

[34] Page, *Voices and Instruments, passim.*

[35] Broomfield, *Thomae de Chobham Summa Confessorum*, p. 292: some minstrels with musical instruments *frequentant publicas potationes et lascivas congregationes ut cantent ibi lascivas cantilenas, ut moveant homines ad lasciviam, et tales sunt damnabiles* .... The words *publicas potationes* undoubtedly refer to the communal alehouses which England seems always to have possessed, back to the festive drinking gatherings (*gebeorscipe*) of the Anglo-Saxons.

[36] Rohloff, *Quellenhandschriften*, p. 130.

[37] *Ibid.*, p. 132. It should not go unnoticed that this, the prevailing interpretation of what Grocheio is saying about the musical style of the *chansons de geste*, incorporates several significant emendations of the text as transmitted by both manuscripts. Having established a terminology whereby *versus* means a laisse and *versiculus* a line (i.e. the constituents of a laisse), Grocheio's text, as witnessed by both manuscripts, proceeds to use the term *versus* to mean both laisse and line. I do not doubt that the text as emended by Rohloff, and as interpreted here, embodies Grocheio's intended meaning, but strictly speaking this can only rank as a supposition about what he intends, since the meaning of the text as transmitted seems unaccountably confused.

[38] *Ibid.*, p. 130.

[39] See Chapter 8.

[40] *Sermones*, q8^v.

[41] For a discussion of the melodic traditions of the *chansons de geste*, and of the few musical remains of them, see Stevens, *Words and Music*, pp. 199ff.

[42] This subject touches upon the enormous scholarly literature relating to oral composition and formulaism in medieval narrative. For the strain in modern literary criticism which associates 'leisured' or 'written' composition with sophistication and 'oral' or 'minstrel' composition with untidiness, repetitiveness and thinness of texture, see Mehl, *The Middle English Metrical Romances*. In relation to the Old French *chansons de geste* the principal axes of the debate are still Rychner's seminal book *La chanson de geste: Essai sur l'art épique des Jongleurs* of 1955, and the papers of the colloquium organised in response to it, *La technique littéraire des chansons de geste* of 1957. See especially the articles by Riquer ('Epopée jongleresque') and

Delbouille ('Les chansons de geste et le livre'). For recent comment upon the question of the minstrels as authors of the *chansons de geste* see Siciliano, *Les chansons de geste*, pp. 106ff., and Delbouille, 'Le mythe du jongleur poète'.

43 For a summary, with bibliography, see Boyer *et al.*, *L'épopée*.
44 Lord, *Singer of Tales*, and Hymes, *A Bibliography of Studies relating to Parry's and Lord's Oral Theory*.
45 This claim is in fact an old one, being deeply ingrained into the traditional notion of a 'Heroic Age'. See Chadwick, *The Heroic Age*, pp. 220ff.
46 See Rychner, *La chanson de geste*, and for a recent detailed examination of one group of formulas in the best known of the epics, *The Song of Roland*, Ashby-Beach, *The Song of Roland*.
47 Whitehead, *La Chanson de Roland*, lines 1644–6.
48 On this formula see Ashby-Beach, *The Song of Roland*, p. 108.
49 Seay, *Johannes de Grocheo* [sic], p. 18.
50 Yeandle, *Girart de Vienne*, lines 6598–6605.
51 Gushee, 'Two central places', p. 143.
52 Boutière and Schutz, *Biographies des troubadours*, numbers 9 (Arnaut Daniel, who abandoned his studies to become a minstrel), 29 (Gausbert de Poicibot, who left his order for a woman and became a minstrel), 33 (Uc de St Circ, sent to study at Montpellier, but learned songs and became a minstrel), 40 (Peire Rogier, who, being of nobler background, abandoned his canonry and became a minstrel).
53 *Liber Sextus Decretalium*, cols. 423–4.
54 Geremek, *Margins of Society*, p. 136.
55 *Ibid.*, pp. 136ff.
56 Murray, *Reason and Society*, p. 307.
57 Greven, *Die Exempla . . . des Jakob von Vitry* p. 51: *Memini, cum essem Parisius, quod tres adolescentes de partibus Flandrie, cum causa studendi venirent Parisius, ceperunt in via mutuo se querere, quale propositum haberent et ad quid tenderet vnusquisque eorum. Vno autem respondente: 'Volo laborare et studere, vt sim magister Parisiensis'; alio vero dicente: 'Et ego volo litteris imbui, ut postmodum sim monachus Cysterciensis ordinis'; tercio dicente: 'Durum est tantos labores sustinere, volo esse organizator, hystrio et ioculator'.*
58 Rohloff, *Quellenhandschriften*, p. 136. On the instrumental *stantipes* and *estampie* (the form could be provided with words, as Grocheio acknowledges and as surviving examples in Old French, Old Provençal and Catalan prove) see Aubry, *Estampies et danses royales*; Handschin, 'Über Estampie und Sequenz'; Hibberd, '*Estampie and Stantipes*'; Jammers, 'Studien zur Tanzmusik des Mittelalters'; Levarie, '*Ductia and stantipes*'; Wagenaar-Nolthenius, 'Estampie/Stantipes/Stampita', and Vellekoop, 'Die Estampie'. Using literary references, Vellekoop demonstrates that the estampie was primarily a free-standing kind of instrumental music, and not a dance-form.
59 Rohloff, *Quellenhandschriften*, p. 34.
60 For the music see Tischler, *The Montpellier Codex*, tenor parts of numbers 270, 292 and 294 (this last being one of the texts beginning with the *Entre . . .* topos and almost certainly reflecting a Parisian milieu of students). It should be noted that in Wolf's transcription of the *chose* corresponding to Tischler's number 270 ('Die Tänze des Mittelalters', p. 22), the second *punctum* is spurious, being the tenor part of the next motet in the manuscript (Tischler's number 271). For a comparable snatch of music, probably another detached *punctum* from an estampie, see Tischler's number 297 (*Chose Loyset*).

[61] Holton, *Cities, Capitalism and Civilisation*, pp. 27ff., and Krupat, *People in Cities*, p. 67. It is tempting to interpret the extraordinary fascination which medieval Paris exerted in terms of what some historians of urban civilisation would call its pronounced *imageability*: the ease with which its shape and topography could print a coherent image on the individual's mind, leaving him with a clear sense of its socio-physical structure. The Ile de la Cité, bearing the Cathedral of Notre Dame and set in the waters of the Seine, joined to the left and right banks by two famous bridges, constituted one of the most 'imageable' urban configurations that any medieval city produced.

[62] Denifle and Chatelain, *Chartularium*, I, p. 55.

[63] Quoted in d'Avray, *The Preaching of the Friars*, p. 31.

Chapter 4: Jeunesse *and the courtly song repertory*

[1] Such, at least, is the impression we receive from later (i.e. fifteenth century) narrative sources, where the excellence of young amateurs at court in singing and dancing *caroles* brings a grant of money or some other form of reward (an allowance of cloth, for example). The outstanding text here is the prose tale of *Jehan de Saintré*, composed during the first half of the fifteenth century by Antoine de la Sale, but set in the time of King John II of France (ruled 1350-64). The story tells of Jehan's experiences at the French court as a *valeton*, the son of the seigneur de Saintré placed in the *hostel* of the king to receive his education in matters chivalric, political and courtly. See Misrahi and Knudson, *Jehan de Saintré*. Saintré's preferment at court, and the presents he receives, all spring from his gracious and festive demeanour, singing and dancing being amongst the principal manifestations of those qualities – and ones, furthermore, which are made in the public arena of the royal hall. For a general and wide-ranging discussion of chivalric education, primarily based upon English sources, see Orme, *From Childhood to Chivalry*.

[2] Foster, *The Iconology of Musical Instruments and Musical Performance in Thirteenth Century French Manuscript Illuminations*.

[3] Page, 'Music and chivalric fiction'.

[4] Here I gladly acknowledge my debt to the magisterial chapter entitled 'From epic to romance' in Southern, *The Making of the Middle Ages*.

[5] For the usual constituents of this motif see Page, 'Music and chivalric fiction', pp. 25-6.

[6] Castets, *La chanson des quatre fils Aymon*, lines 6595-6602.

[7] *Silas Marner*, Chapter 1.

[8] *The Making of the Middle Ages*, pp. 209ff.

[9] *Medieval Humanism*, p. 35: 'In the early Middle Ages God had not appeared as a friend. By great labour and exertion, by crippling penances and gifts to the Church, by turning from the world to the monastic life, men might avert God's anger: but of God as a friend they knew little or nothing.'

[10] For the probable date of this romance, not published in modern times, together with a full discussion of its literary affiliations, see Lathuillère, *Guiron le courtois*.

[11] I quote the text in London, British Library, Additional MS 12228, ff.55v-6. This manuscript, of fourteenth-century date and Italian provenance, is of exceptional

interest for the illustrations which accompany the text. For an example see *Grove 6*, sv. 'Performing practice'.

[12] Webb, *Policraticus*, I, p. 41: translation in Pike, *Frivolities of Courtiers*, p. 32.

[13] See Page, 'Music and chivalric fiction'. In romances musical activity is closely connected with what Matoré has called 'focalising centres' (*Le vocabulaire et la société médiévale*, p. 98): 'l'aspect statique [of the perception of space in the twelfth and thirteenth centuries] est le plus apparent: il se concrétise en premier lieu par l'existence d'un certain nombre de ''centres focalisants'' où la vie d'un groupe est concentrée: *eglise, hostel, mesnie, tournois, festes*, etc., où les rapports entre individus sont soumis à des règles fixes, à des *coutumes*, à des rites, dont l'observance exclut autant que possible les décisions individuelles qui n'appartiennent qu'au chef'.

[14] Page, 'Music and chivalric fiction', p. 23.

[15] *Ibid.*

[16] Flori, 'La notion de chevalerie', and Paterson, 'Knights and the concept of knighthood'.

[17] Michelant, *Escanor*, lines 6136–40. This romance, written for Eleanor, wife of King Edward I of England, towards 1280, is a rich source of information about the festive decorum of music in a royal court during the late thirteenth century.

[18] Roques, *Erec et Enide*, line 1993.

[19] A valuable study could be made of the way in which courtly *caroles*, performed in the body of the hall, could assume the character of an entertainment, watched by those who, for whatever reason, did not choose to participate. In fifteenth-century narrative sources, where descriptions of courtly festivities abound, there is often an acknowledgement that when a dance was going forward *le roy* watched it with pleasure, or that when a song was performed to general acclaim, that *le roy meesmes* was impressed. See particularly the romance of *Jehan de Saintré*, mentioned in note 1 above.

[20] I quote the text in Foerster, *Yvain*, lines 2354–5; for *bacheler* the text in Roques, *Yvain*, line 2357, reads *sailleor*.

[21] Lecoy, *Le conte du graal*, lines 8716ff. Other texts in this genealogy of women's celebratory songs would include (1) the references to dance-songs of women about the Anglo-Saxon warrior Hereward the Wake soon before 1066 (Page, 'Secular Music', p. 235; the source is the early twelfth Century *Gesta Herwardi*); (2) the reference by Hildegaire of Meaux (*c.* 869) to a popular song (*carmen publicum*) concerning Clothar, King of the Franks, and sung by women as they danced (Van der Veen, 'Les aspects musicaux des chansons de geste', p. 83).

[22] On the term *bacheler*, and the epithets used to qualify it in Old French (*legier* being by far the most common), see Flori, 'Qu'est-ce qu'un *bacheler*?'.

[23] Noiriel, 'La chevalerie dans la geste des Lorrains'.

[24] Stengel, *Hervis von Metz*, lines 4862–3.

[25] *Ibid.*, lines 5504–5.

[26] On this tournament see Painter, *William Marshall*, pp. 41 and 58–9, and Duby, *William Marshall*, pp. 41ff.

[27] Meyer, *L'Histoire de Guillaume le Maréchal*, I, lines 3471–82.

[28] Duby, *William Marshall*, p. 41, and Benson, 'The tournament'.

[29] Fréville, *Les quatre âges de l'homme*, p. 23: *Il est ecrit ou livre Lancelot, ou il a mout de biaus diz et de soutis* . . . .

[30] Kennedy, *Lancelot*, p. 40. Cf. p. 230, where a queen and her ladies watch a tournament.

[31] *Ibid.*, p. 135.

[32] See, for example, the essays in Benson and Leyerle, *Chivalric Literature*; Vale, *War and Chivalry* (especially pp. 14ff); Vale, *Edward III and Chivalry*; and Green, *Poets and Princepleasers*.

[33] Quoted in Benson and Leyerle, *Chivalric Literature*, xiii.

[34] For an edition of Jean Bretel's poem which celebrates this tournament, see Delbouille, *Le Tournoi de Chauvency*.

[35] Henry, *Le Roman du Hem*, lines 3336–41. Vale, *Edward III and Chivalry*, provides an indispensable point of reference for the study of the depiction of reality in this poem and in Jean Bretel's *Le Tournoi de Chauvency*.

[36] Nicholas de Braia, *Gesta*, pp. 88ff. :

> . . . circum pagos et compita lata choreas
> Reducunt festi juvenes trepidaeque puellae ;
> Occurrunt lyrici modulantes carminis odas,
> Occurrunt mimi dulci resonante viella,
> Instrumenta sonant, non sistrum defuit illic,
> Tympanum, psalterium, citharae, symphonia dulcis,
> Dulce melos Regi concordi voce canentes.

[37] Terracher, *La Chevalerie Vivien*, line 1016.

[38] Friedwagner, *Meraugis von Portlesguez*, lines 2880–91.

[39] Lécuyer, *Jehan et Blonde*, lines 5837–52.

[40] Williams, *Floriant et Florete*, lines 6051–8.

[41] Hippeau, *Godefroid de Bouillon*, II, lines 3471–5. Like *La Chevalerie Vivien*, this text associates carolling with the town squares (*places*), a clear link with the *coreae* described in the treatises on the Seven Deadly Sins where the location of the dances is often a *platea*. See Chapter 5. Another striking passage in this connection is *Godefroid de Bouillon*, II, lines 3543ff., where Godefroid and his men have just completed a ceremonial banquet in the city of Bouillon. After the meal some rise to play chess and other board games, some go off to fence, and others go down into the city (*aval le borc*) for carolling. Details such as those contained in the epics and romances just cited are easily matched in chronicles of the thirteenth century: 'Les bourgois de Paris firent feste grant et solempnel, et encourtinerent la ville de riches dras de diverses couleurs et de pailes et de cendaulx. Lez dames et les pucelles sesbaudissoient en chantant diverses chançons et diverses motès' (Guillaume de Nangis, *Vie de Philippe III*, p. 497, recounting events of 1275).

[42] Duby, 'Les "Jeunes"'.

[43] Cloetta, *Moniage Guillaume*, second redaction, lines 951–2 and 954–8.

[44] *Ibid.*, line 1202 (*d'un viel estoire*). In the first redaction (*ibid.*, lines 446ff.), the *vallet* sings a *chanson de geste*.

[45] *Ibid.*, second redaction, lines 1248ff. For further discussion of this passage see Chapter 8.

[46] Tobler-Lommatzsch, *Altfranzösisches Wörterbuch*, sv *famle*; Godefroy, *Dictionnaire*, sv *famle*.

[47] *Monumenta Germaniae Historica, Scriptorum*, IV, p. 760: *Ingeniosos namque pueros et eximiae indolis secum vel ad curtem ducebat vel quocumque longius commeabat, quos, quicquid dignius in ulla arte occurrebat, ad exercitium impellebat.* For the preferment of talented

young men at court through episcopal patronage in the tenth and eleventh centuries see Jaeger, *The Origins of Courtliness*.

48 Auctor B (*c.* 1000), in Stubbs, *Memorials of St Dunstan*, p. 21. Auctor B's *Vita* provides several illuminating glimpses of aristocratic and domestic amateur string-playing in tenth-century England. For texts, translations and discussion see Page, *Anglo-Saxon Hearpan*, pp. 211ff.

49 Stubbs, *Memorials of St Dunstan*, p. 80. It is the nature of saints' legends to grow in richness of details each time the story is retold by a new writer. The claim of each new hagiographer upon his readers' attention is usually that he has discovered new information (usually a bogus claim), or that he has elaborated the content and style of his predecessors. It is best to keep an open mind about Dunstan's court minstrelsy; as Stubbs points out (*ibid.*, lxv), it is often impossible to tell with Osbern's account what is derived from tradition and what is 'the product of an imagination intent upon the contemplation of what ought to have happened'.

50 *Monumenta Germaniae Historica, Scriptorum*, II, p. 94. See Page, 'Instruments and Instrumental music to 1300'.

51 For an account of the French *familia regis* in the twelfth century, and of the importance of the *juvenes* within it, the 'jeunes nobles en apprentissage', see Poly and Bournazel, *La mutation féodale*, pp. 189ff, and especially pp. 277ff.

52 *Ibid.*, pp. 277ff.

53 *Ibid.*, p. 278: 'Qui sont ces gens de la *familia*? Beaucoup sont des "jeunes" qui font partie très tôt de la mesnie, et qui ont dû être élevés avec le jeune prince'.

54 It is profitable to compare the texts about to be cited in tandem with a key document in the history of the *familia regis* in the twelfth century, the *Historia Karoli Magni*, also known as the chronicle of pseudo-Turpin. This Latin prose work of the mid-twelfth century, which poses as a chronicle by Charlemagne's archbishop Turpin, is preserved in the celebrated codex Calixtinus, well-known to musicologists for its leaves containing items of liturgical polyphony, also from the mid-twelfth century. For the significance of the *Historia* see Poly and Bournazel, *La mutation féodale*, p. 277 (it should be noted, however, that Poly and Bournazel interpret the text as stating that Charlemagne had 1200 in his *familia*, whereas the correct sum is 120, in three shifts of forty). The vernacular texts now to be used clearly reflect the same interest in the details of Charlemagne's *familia*, and like the *Historia Karoli Magni* which is approximately contemporary with them, it may be assumed that they present a hyperbolised version of mid-twelfth-century reality. For the text see Meredith-Jones, *Historia Karoli Magni*.

55 Borg, *Aye d'Avignon*, lines 1ff.

56 *Ibid.*, lines 10–12.

57 *Ibid.*, lines 13ff.

58 Brandin, *La Chanson d'Aspremont*, lines 9483–9.

59 Tobler-Lommatzsch, *Altfranzösisches Wörterbuch*, sv *deduitor*, refers the reader to Godefroy, *Dictionnaire*, sv *deduitor*, where there is one example, from *Meraugis de Portlesguez*.

60 For epics and romances which refer to the education of *vallets* see Cremonesi, *Enfances Renier*, lines 1563ff.; Raynaud de Lage, *Eracle*, lines 3382ff.; Foerster, *Richars li biaus*, lines 683ff.; Goldschmidt, *Sone von Nausay* lines 79ff. (I cite this romance using the French form of its title); Hippeau, *Godefroid de Bouillon*, II, lines 750ff.; Holden, *Ipomedon*, lines 185ff; Meunier, *La Chanson de Godin*, lines

12138ff; Todd, *La naissance du chevalier au cygne*, line 3028; Vernay, *Maugis d'Aigremont*, lines 630ff.; Williams, *Floriant et Florete*, lines 733ff. In these accounts the education of the young men is dominated by martial and sportive pursuits such as fencing and hunting with dogs and birds. A degree of literacy is sometimes involved; *letres*, for example, are mentioned in *Godefroid de Bouillon*, *Sone de Nansay* and *Ipomedon*; in *Floriant et Forete* there is mention of the seven Liberal Arts, exceptional in texts of this kind. Advanced literacy, including the ability to read musical notation, is regarded with suspicion to the extent that it is often imparted to humans by members of the otherworld. In *Floriant et Florete*, for example, the hero is taught the seven arts by members of the otherworld (*fees*), while in *Maugis d'Aigremont* we find a hero who can sing from musical notation (line 637: *Et par ordre de game sot trestoz chanz chanter*), but who is taught to do so by a *fee*, and there is talk also of Maugis studying the seven arts at Toledo; the exotic, 'pagan' associations seem very strong. A conspicuous ability to sing well is only mentioned in one of these texts (*Sone de Nansay*), no doubt because it was, at best, a minor star in the constellation of chivalric virtues. It is quite clear, however, that the absence of references to musical skills in many descriptions of education and accomplishments cannot be used as the basis for an argument from silence to the effect that musical skills were rare. See Reinhard, *Amadas et Ydoine*, lines 53ff., describing the hero's education but making no reference to music; later in the text Amadas sings *un sonnet poitevin*, i.e. a song in some form of Occitan and possibly to be understood as a troubadour song.

The question of string-playing skills proves more complex. *Eracle*, lines 3382ff., includes a remark which clearly indicates that the author, Gautier d'Arras, regarded it as having been the custom in antiquity that *li baron et li haut per* would have their children instructed in the art of playing upon instruments (the harp is mentioned); for other references to *vallets* playing the harp and other instruments see lines 3430ff. and 3450ff. The implication in this text seems to be that this custom has now died out. What seems clear is that most of the references to such a practice in texts of the twelfth and thirteenth centuries are in works produced in the Anglo-Norman realm (e.g. the *Roman de Horn*, the Tristan romances – including Marie de France's *Chevrefoil* – all of *c.* 1170), and it is very likely that those romances are reflecting a particularly British practice that can be traced, in England, back through texts like the *Gesta Herwardi* (Ely, *c.* 1109–31), the 'harper-hero' stories recounted by Wace and William of Malmesbury, the 'Lives' of St Dunstan (beginning *c.* 1000), and beyond to Old English poems such as *The Fortunes of Men*. For these texts see Pope, *The Romance of Horn*; Payen, *Les Tristan en vers*; Miller and Sweeting, *De gestis Herwardi Saxonis*, pp. 17ff.; Arnold, *Le Roman de Brut*, lines 3694ff. and lines 9101ff. (following Geoffrey of Monmouth, *Historia Regum Britannie*, III:19 and IX:1); Stubbs, *Willelmi Malmesbiriensis monachi De Gestis Regum Anglorum*, II, pp. 126 and 143; *idem.*, *Memorials of St Dunstan*; Page, *Anglo-Saxon Hearpan*.

61 There is still no more succinct and accurate an assessment of Marie's sources and achievement than Ewert's introductory notes to his edition (Ewert, *Marie de France*, v–xviii).

62 And Brittany, of course, which Marie variously calls *Bretaigne*, *Bretaigne la menur*, or *Brutaine*.

63 Ewert, *Marie de France*, v–xviii, summarises the information.

64 A late example is the fifteenth-century prose romance of *Cleriadus et Meliadice*,

whose hero, a young squire (later a knight) of aristocratic birth, is a gifted harpist and composer. Much of the story is set in ancient Britain shortly after the time of King Arthur, and some of the narrative motifs connected with music (the hero asking for a harp at his lodgings, for example) can be found in thirteenth-century romances set in ancient Britain, including *Guiron le courtois*. See Page, 'The performance of songs'.

65 The name Graelens has certainly been borrowed by the author of *La chanson d'Aspremont* from a *lai* by an imitator of Marie. This is the *lai* which, in Paris, Bibliothèque Nationale, MS fr.2168, f.65r, begins with blank staves. This detail has often been mentioned as if it were of some significance for the vexed question of Breton *lais*, including Marie's, and their performance (e.g. in *Grove 6* sv 'Lai'). It is important to remember, however, that (1) the blank stave is almost certainly a scribal mistake, for a text of *Aucassin et Nicolette* immediately follows in the manuscript (f.70r) complete with head stave, (2) the *lai* of *Graelens* is almost certainly not by Marie, and (3) Marie's poems are not themselves Breton *lais*, but versified accounts of the events which inspired the ancients of Bretaigne to compose commemorative songs/instrumental pieces. It is these commemorative compositions that were the *lais* whose manner of performance can never be known. Compare Alton, *Anseïs von Karthago*, lines 4975–7.

66 Ewert, *Marie de France, Chevrefoil* lines 112–13.

67 *Vie de St Louis*, p. 66: 'Ni il ne chantoit pas les chançons du monde, ne ne soufroit pas que cil qui estoient de sa mesniee les chantassent, por qu'il le seust; ainz commanda a un sien escuier qui bien chantoit teles choses el tens de sa joenece, que il se tenit de teles chançons chanter, et li fist aprendre aucunes antienes de Nostre-Dame et cest hympne *Ave maris stella*, comment que ce fust fort chose a aprendre'.

68 *Ibid.*, 'et cil escuies et il meesmes li benoiez rois chantoit aucune foiz ces choses meemes desus dites avec cel escuier'.

69 For studies of Old French *vallet* see Guilhiermoz, *Essai sur l'origine de la noblesse*, pp. 483ff.; Laugesen, 'Un cas de synonymie'; Matoré, *Le vocabulaire et la société médiévale*, p. 142; Stefenelli, *Der Synonymenreichtum*, pp. 59ff.

70 Place, *Gille de Chyn*, 3592ff.

71 Mauclère, *Doon de Mayence*, line 1273.

72 Fossier, *Enfance de l'Europe*, pp. 341ff.; Poly and Bournazel, *La mutation féodale*, pp. 189ff. In the vernacular narratives, perhaps the most ringing endorsement of the *vallets* is provided by these lines from *La naissance du chevalier au cygne*:

> Li vallet sont a cort a molt grant segnorage,
> Molt i a bels vallés, tot sanblent d'un eage;
> Il porsivent le roi quel part qu'il onques aille,
> Il se pruevent molt bien cascuns en vasselage.
> S'il parolent a gent, bien sanblent estre sage,
> Et s'il vont behordant, il ne sont pas ombrage
> De ferir en quintaine ne de porter leur targe . . .

Todd, *La naissance du chevalier au cygne*, lines 3028ff.; the description continues in these terms.

73 Goldschmidt, *Sone von Nansay*, lines 81ff.

[74] This valuable description of Sone's accomplishments seems worth citing here in its full context:

> Ki bien l'esgarde, a voir conter,
> De biauté nus ne set son per . . .
> Mais Sones qui est li mainsnés,
> Adiés est crus et amendés.
> Quant crus fu, as letres ala,
> D'aprendre nus ne le passa.
> D'eschiés, des tables tant savoit
> Que nus a lui ne s'en tenoit.
> Des chiens savoit et des oysiaus,
> Escremissieres iert mout byaus;
> De tout aprendre estoit en grant
> Que on sëust, de jone enfant.
> Quatre diviers mestres avoit,
> D'aprendre tous les anuioit.
> Mout en a grant joie Henris,
> Ses freres qui tant iert petis.
> Sonez avoit .xii. ans passés,
> Plus biaus enfes n'estoit trouvés
> Ne nus enfes mieus ne cantoit.
> De tous biaus jus juër savoit,
> S'ot tel grasce que mout l'amoient
> Chil et chelles qui le vëoient.

Goldschmidt, *Sone von Nansay*, lines 81-2 and 85-104. For a fifteenth-century source in which the term *enfant* is used to describe a young page in an aristocratic retinue who takes part in impromptu performances of polyphonic secular chansons, see Page, 'The performance of songs', p. 448.

[75] Michelant, *Guillaume de Palerne*, lines 2928-9.

[76] Lécuyer, *Jehan et Blonde*, line 5852.

[77] Castets, *La chanson des quatre fils Aymon*, lines 1765-6. Cf. also the following three texts: Hilka, *Athis et Prophilias*, lines 2557-60:

> La vëissiez ces jeus noviaus
> Et oïssiez mil chalemiaus,
> Gigues, harpes rotes, vieles,
> Vaslez juer, chanter puceles.

Michelant, *Escanor*, lines 8087-93:

> Et cil qui esoient joli
> et baceler net et poli
> venoient trop mingnotement
> et se penoient doucement
> de plaire a teles y avoit;
> et cil qui mix chanter savoit
> n'en faisoit mie grant dangier.

Stengel, *Durmart le Galois*, lines 993–8:

> Jone bacheler et legier
> o les puceles vont servir.
> Et si vos di sens escharnir,
> Que a chascun mes aporter
> Les oissies en halt chanter
> Chanson d'amor(s) bien envoisie.

78 See note 60.

79 Lecoy, *Guillaume de Dole*, line 2387. Jean Renart's romance is replete with interest-ing and useful references to the qualities and duties of *vallets*; see lines 343, 397, 468, 509 (*les puceles et li vallet* dance in caroles), 520 (a song is performed by *uns vallez au prevost d'Espire*), 639, 643, 880–1180, 1220, 1260, 1296ff., 1316 (a vallet who *ot de grant beauté le los*), 1808ff., 2000ff. (Guillaume de Dole's *vallets* include *des pluz sachanz/que chevaliers peüst avoir*), 2386ff., 2437, 3258, 3798, 3914, 3998, 4120, 4233ff., 4275ff. (a *vallet* entrusted with a message is *bel et gent*), 4483.

80 For the importance of *sagesse*, a counterbalance to martial and sportive excellence, see the lines from *La naissance du chevalier au cygne* quoted in note 72, and Page, *Voices and Instruments*, pp. 3ff.

81 *Ibid.*, p. 8.

82 Mauclère, *Doon de Mayence*, lines 8128–9: '. . . *un vallet qui bien fu emparlés,/Ses letres li bailla et ses briés séélés*'.

83 Lecoy, *Guillaume de Dole*, lines 4275ff.

84 Holden, *Waldef*, lines 6651 and 6613.

85 Lecoy, *Guillaume de Dole*, lines 520 and 2387.

86 *Ibid.*, lines 4120ff.

87 Page, *Voices and Instruments*, p. 9.

88 Lecoy, *Guillaume de Dole*, lines 343ff., 639ff and 1260 (*vallets* bring water).

89 *Ibid.*, line 2438.

90 For the few surviving Old French treatises on polyphony see *Grove 6*, 'Anonymous theoretical writings'.

91 Scheler, *Dits et contes*, 2, p. 305; this text is discussed by Fuller, 'Theory of fifthing'.

92 *Ibid.*, lines 65ff.

93 *Ibid.*, lines 82–5.

94 Fuller, 'Theory of fifthing'.

95 On *doubler* see Page, 'Machaut's "pupil" Deschamps', p. 491, note 35.

96 For Jacques' comments on this piece and facsimiles of the original, see Bragard, *Jacobi Leodiensis Speculum Musicae*, 7, pp. 68–9; there is a transcription in Husmann, 'Der Hoketus *A l'entrade d'avril*'. The transcription offered here differs from that of Husmann in certain respects.

97 Foulet, *Galeran de Bretagne*, lines 3878–87. There is much material of interest in this romance. For other references to the education and accomplishments of young girls see Alton, *Claris et Laris*, lines 15329–31; Boer, *Philomena*, lines 172ff. (based on Ovid – a particularly impressive passage); Goldschmidt, *Sone von Nansay*, lines 12569 (a *puchielle . . . /Qui de harper avoit le pris*), 16332ff. and 17624ff.; Guessard and Chabaille, *Gaufrey*, lines 1777ff. (a pagan girl); Hilka, *Athis et Prophilias*, lines 19709ff.; Michelant, *Escanor* (a romance whose author has a highly developed sense of the way in which courtly women could enliven court festivities and even be summoned to do so), lines 6163ff., 6324ff., 8596ff. and *passim*; Stengel, *Durmart*

le Galois, lines 3217ff. (a *pucele* harping, so too lines 6344ff. and 11327ff.); Wallensköld, *Florence de Rome*, I, p. 135. For the extent to which women and young girls could be regarded as a means to provide entertainment, and transported from place to place for the purpose – like a chess set – see Régnier, *Prise d'Orange*, lines 58 and 1089.

[98] Lecoy, *Guillaume de Dole*, lines 1148-51.

[99] Doutrepont, *La clef d'amors*, lines 2589ff.

[100] Compare *Ars amatoria*, III, 315ff.

[101] Ulrich, *Robert von Blois*, III, lines 453-69.

[102] Michelant, *Escanor*, lines 8322-3.

[103] *Ibid.*, lines 6090ff.

[104] *Ibid.*, lines 6324ff.

[105] *Ibid.*, lines 6165-6.

[106] See note 10 above.

[107] London, British Library, Additional MS 12228, f.221r.

[108] *Ibid.*

[109] *Ibid.*, f.221v.

[110] See Painter, *William Marshall*, and Duby, *William Marshall*.

[111] Meyer, *Guillaume de Maréchal*, lines 18528ff.

[112] *Ibid.*, lines 18547ff.

[113] *Ibid.*, lines 18559-60.

[114] *Ibid.*, lines 18562-72.

[115] See *Grove 6*, sv 'Rotrouenge'.

[116] *Ibid.* In addition to the material cited there by Van der Werf, see London, British Library, MS Royal 19 C.v, f.207r, an Anglo-Norman commentary upon the psalms where the words *canticum vetus* (i.e. 'the old song') are interpreted as *une vielz chancun . une vielz rotruenge.*

[117] See Räkel, *Die musikalische Erscheinungsform der Trouvère Poesie.*

[118] Lecoy, *Guillaume de Dole*, lines 1ff.

[119] For discussion and a facsimile see Coldwell, *'Guillaume de Dole'.*

[120] Lecoy, *Guillaume de Dole*, line 2.

[121] Bell, *L'estoire des Engleis*, lines 6477ff.

[122] *Ibid.*

[123] *Ibid.*, line 6486.

[124] Rohloff, *Quellenhandschriften*, p. 132.

[125] Bell, *L'estoire des Engleis*, p. 278.

[126] Foulet, *Galeran de Bretagne*. For the abundant and detailed musical references in this romance see lines 918ff., 1157ff., 2276ff., 3878ff., 4188ff., 4315ff., 4810ff., 5420ff., 6668ff., 6899ff., 7054ff., 7103ff. and 7204ff.

[127] *Ibid.*, lines 918-19 and 924-7.

[128] Page, *Voices and Instruments*. pp. 57-9.

Chapter 5 : The carole, *the pulpit and the schools*

[1] Page, *Voices and Instruments*, pp. 77ff.

[2] For some account of these texts, with bibliography, see the section entitled 'Treatises on the virtues and vices' in the brief conspectus of some major types of sources in the Appendix.

3 *Ibid.*, sv 'Exempla'.

4 *Thomae Cantipratani . . . miraculorum . . . libri duo*, p. 418. For other pertinent references in this collection see pp. 450–2, 455 (a curious passage) and 570–1.

5 Rivière, *Pastourelles*, 2, LX.

6 In reading this and other *exempla* it is always necessary to bear in mind the remarkably international character of these stories, virtually none of which can be precisely
localised or accurately dated.

7 Bromyard, *Summa predicantium*, I, f.153v.

8 Reproduced and discussed, *inter alia*, in Brown's illuminating article, 'Fantasia
on a theme by Boccaccio', p. 330.

9 Hubert, 'Evolution de la topographie et de l'aspect des villes de Gaule'.

10 For comparative maps see Ganshof, *Etude sur le développement des villes*.

11 Brown, *Society and the Holy in Late Antiquity*, p. 223; see also Ward-Perkins, *From
Classical Antiquity to the Middle Ages*, p. 55.

12 Ganshof, *Etude sur le développement des villes*, pp. 60–1.

13 London, British Library, MS Harley 3823, f.375r.

14 See the Appendix for the full text.

15 *circa corpora mortuorum.* Oxford, Bodleian Library, MS Bodley 801, f.190r.

16 For a minstrel (*tibicen*) convening a *carole* with a wind instrument see Bromyard,
Summa predicantium, I, f.152v, and for a *garcia* beating a drum, Nicolas de Bayard
in London, British Library, Additional MS 37670, f.14v. The extent to which
minstrels were involved in *caroles* is difficult to establish from the evidence that
survives. Bromyard, *Summa predicantium*, I, f.153v, refers to a minstrel (*mimus*)
in Germany who cannot fulfil his function (*exercere . . . opus*) in a *carole* because
of illness; the Devil takes his place and begins to *musare* (? 'play the bagpipe').

17 Guido d'Evreux in Paris, Bibliothèque Nationale, MS lat.15966, f.207: *Multi sunt
promptiores vocationi diabolice quam Dei. Si diabolus vocat 'a la touche de karoles', statim
currunt ad locutiones, ad cantatores 'de geste'.*

18 *Summa predicantium*, I, f.153v.

19 Birmingham, University Library, MS 6/iii/19, f.103r.

20 London, British Library, MS Harley 3823, f.375v.

21 f.271v.

22 Cambridge, University Library, MS Ii.4.8, f.18r.

23 f.375v.

24 For the town square (*platea*) as a place for carolling, compare the Old French narrative
sources cited in Chapter 4, where the location of the *carole* is sometimes the *place*.

25 The phrase is from the Mainz print of 1618 (II, p. 30); the Cambridge manuscript
I am following reads *motu . . . seculari* (f.18v), but the context proves that this
is a corruption of Peyraut's words.

26 Cambridge, University Library, MS Ii.4.8, f.19.

27 Birmingham, University Library, MS 6/iii/19, f.103r.

28 Cambridge, University Library, MS Ii.4.8, f.18r.

29 London, British Library, MS Harley 3823, f.375v.

30 Cambridge, University Library, MS Ii.4.8, f.18v.

31 As remarked by Peyraut; see the Latin text in the Appendix, lines 26ff.

32 *Ibid.*, lines 22ff.

33 *Ibid.*, line 19.

34 Hinnebusch, *Historia occidentalis*, p. 82: '*mulieres non solum in ornatu meretricio et
superfluitate uestium, in tortis crinibus, in auro et margaritis et ueste pretiosa, in plausu*

illicito et choreis . . .'. For the blushes of those who did not have such adornments see Cambridge, University Library, MS Ii.4.8, f.19r–v.

35 Cf. Strange, *Dialogus miraculorum*, I, p. 183.

36 Bromyard, *Summa predicantium*, II, f.161v.

37 Cf. Stevens, *Words and Music*, pp. 163ff.

38 *Sermones beati Umberti Burgundi*, II, pp. 96–7.

39 f.58v: *quando plures sunt in chorea vel quando plures spectant tanto est letior.*

40 London, British Library, Additional MS 37670, f.14v.

41 See, for example, Wright, *British Calendar Customs: England* (London, 1936).

42 Lecoy, *Guillaume de Dole*, lines 522–7.

43 Paris, Bibliothèque Nationale, MS lat.16481, f.52v. The full text runs: *hodie angeli . . . cantabant pro gaudio dicentes gloria in altissimis domino et in terra pax hominibus bone voluntatis. Tu dices mihi certe domine ego feci in isto festo sicut angeli fecerunt quia optime cantavi in isto festo quia per totam istam noctem ego fui et cantavi ad coream. Certe karissime, tu non cantasti sicut angeli; non eis ibant ad coream propter cantandum de marion ne de robecon, sed cantillena eorum vult dicere in gallico: gloria sit sursum in celo domino et pax in terra hominibus qui sunt bone voluntatis.*

44 Koenig, *Les Miracles de Nostre Dame*, III, p. 277, lines 324–5.

45 W2, f.230 r–v. A note in a manuscript of thirteenth-century Latin sermons from France casts a sidelight on the vogue for *pastourelles*: *Amenum est multis cantilenas pastorales vitiorum incendiis plenas audire sed cantilenas Ihesu Christi id est verba salutifera fastidiunt* (Cambridge, Gonville and Caius College, MS 233/119, f.122r).

46 The point of departure here is still Gennrich's monumental *Rondeaux, Virelais und Balladen*, although it is becoming increasingly obvious, thanks to the work of Ardis Butterfield and Mark Everist (still in progress), among others, that a fresh survey of the material covered by Gennrich would produce a much more complex and variable picture than he left.

47 Oxford, Bodleian Library, MS Bodley 801, f.203v: *De Superbia . . . . Si coreas celebraverit et hoc multipharie fuerit in contrahendo, in vestes comodando, in inquietando puellas et huiusmodi.*

48 *Ibid.*, f.205r–v: *De Luxuria . . . . Si cum meretrice se polluerit vel virginem defloraverit vel viduam frequentaverit . . . . Si choreas vel huiusmodi spectacula secutus fuerit plurimum et in aliis delectatus.*

49 Birmingham, University Library, MS 6/iii/19, f.103.

50 London, British Library, MS Harley 3823, f.374v.

51 Kühne and Stengel, *Maître Elie's Uberarbeitung*, lines 101–7 and 133–8.

52 London, British Library, MS Harley 3823, f.375v.

53 Strange, *Dialogus miraculorum*, I, p. 279,

54 As usual, I follow Cambridge, University Library, MS Ii.4.8., but the text at this point (f.19) is slightly incomplete and lacks the Old French line, supplied here from London, British Library, MS Cotton Appendix xxiv, f.33v. Compare Boogaard, *Rondeaux et refrains*, 1019. The manuscripts of Peyraut's treatise do not agree on what the reading for the Old French words should be. Among other sources in the British Library, Additional MS 14081, f.20v, has 'Pour mon mari .fi. et cetera', while Additional MS 22571, f.191v, has 'portum (?) mari .fi. et cetera'. Cf. Wenzel, *Preachers, Poets and the Early English Lyric*, pp. 216ff.

55 Wilkins, *Adam de la Hale*, rondeau 6 (*Fi, maris, de vostre amour*).

56 Cambridge, University Library, MS Ii.4.8, f.19: *Unde in nullo festo timeant coreas ducere, nulli sancto timent contumelia inferre.*

57 In his *Summa de poenitentia* (b.1302), John of Erfurt seems to allow that some *caroles* are a form of devotion. See the text and translation in the Appendix. For the tendency for dancers on religious festivals to join religious processions on feast-days but to turn aside when the church is reached and to go carolling, see the vivid passage from a thirteenth-century sermon quoted in Hauréau, *Notices et extraits*, IV, p. 176.

58 As pointed out by Peyraut.

59 This is the *Vitae fratrum* composed 1259–60 by the Dominican Gerardus de Fracheto: *Frater quidam de provincia Romana, qui in seculo multum in audiendis et cantandis secularibus cantilenis fuerat delectatus, nec adverterat quod confiteretur huiusmodi vanitatem, in infirmitate gravi positus, dictos cantus quasi continue in aure et cerebro habebat, et inde non delectacionem ut prius, sed vexacionem et penam non modicam sustinebat* (Reichert, *Vitae Fratrum*, pp. 100–1).

60 Dimock and Brewer, *Giraldi Cambrensis Opera*, 2, p. 120.

61 See the *distinctiones* of Nicholas de Bayard in London, British Library, Additional MS 37670, f.14v, and the collection of *exempla* in the same MS, f.149 (where a nun who hears a *cantilena* but without confessing it endures 18 days in purgatory). In the story cited in n. 59 above, the friar is afflicted with a jangling memory of the secular songs he has heard because he does not confess to having heard them.

62 The substance of Peyraut's attack on the *carole* is given in the Appendix. It was so frequently copied, and became so well-known, that thirteenth-century writers could refer to it as 'the treatise on vices', knowing that the allusion would be understood. See, for example, the *De instructione puerorum* by William of Tournai, a book commended at the General Chapter of the Dominicans in 1264 at Paris: *De choreis require in Summa de viciis* (Corbett, *The De instructione puerorum*, p. 24).

63 Leclercq, *The Love of Learning*, p. 116.

64 Borgnet, *Beati Alberti Magni . . . Opera Omnia*, 29, pp. 632ff., from which all the quotations used in what follows are taken.

65 This point about the dances of Miriam is made, with characteristic firmness, by Pierre de Palude in his commentary upon the *Sentences*: *coree . . . damnabiles sunt quia non sunt quales olim soror Moysi ducebat* (f.75v).

66 See, for example, the usage of Guillaume 'de Lavicea': *chorus vel chorea vel ballata* (*Dieta salutis*, p. 346).

67 *Summa Theologica*, III, p. 472.

68 *Summa confessorum*, III, questio cclxxviii.

69 Rohloff, *Quellenhandschriften*, p. 132.

Chapter 6: The Masters of organum: the study and performance of Parisian polyphony during the early thirteenth century

1 For an elaborate set of stipulations about conduct in the monastic choir and concerning the decorum of chant-performance see pseudo-Bonaventura, *De institutione novitiorum*, pp. 301ff.

2 Stanley, *The Owl and the Nightingale*, line 313.

3 For an anthology of twelfth- and thirteenth-century texts pertaining to this debate see Oxford, Bodleian Library, MS Bodley 240, pp. 894–8, compiled after 1377

at Bury St Edmunds. Also see pseudo-Bonaventura, *De institutione novitiorum*, pp. 301ff.

4 Webb, *Policraticus*, I, p. 42.

5 PL 176, col. 1081.

6 For a modern edition of some of the key documents in the Cistercians' various programmes of chant reform, with bibliographical references to others, see Guentner, *Epistola S. Bernardi* ..., and for studies of the reforms see Waddell, 'The early Cistercian experience of liturgy' and *idem*, 'The original and early evolution of the Cistercian antiphonary'.

7 Leclercq, *Love of Learning*, p. 143 and *passim*.

8 Strange, *Dialogus miraculorum*, I, p. 83.

9 *Ibid.*, p. 181.

10 For hostile references to the secular clergy in writings by Parisian masters who were contemporaries of Caesarius of Heisterbach see Gilbert of Tournai, *Collectio de scandalis ecclesiae*, pp. 44ff. (their superfluity of benefices, indiscipline and carelessness in divine services; their careerist ambitions and sojourns in the university where they neglect theology in favour of the lucrative sciences); *idem, Sermones ad omnes status*, lxxix *ad canonicos seculares* (they gather benefices; they sing for money rather than for God, and 'they are wakeful in entertainments, in songs and in banquets, but they sleep in their spiritual duties'); Jacques de Vitry, *Historia occidentalis*, pp. 152ff. (the minstrels who sing at their feasts); J. Halgrin d'Abbeville, *Expositio in psalmos*, col. 891 (the minstrels who sing at their feasts with secular songs and with musical instruments; this passage also contains a reference to organum, discussed below, n. 35).

11 The institution of this custom is associated with the name of Ivo of Chartres; see Le Bras, *Institutions ecclésiastiques de la chrétienté médiévale*, II, p.384, n. 58.

12 For a Cistercian view of the personal wealth that could be accumulated by a canon of Notre Dame at Paris, see Strange, *Dialogus miraculorum*, I, p. 83: *multa habens stipendia delicatissime vixerat*.

13 On the welcome which minstrels could find in the houses and refectories of the secular canons see n. 10 above.

14 Roze, *Nécrologie de l'église d'Amiens*, p. 463.

15 PL 205, col. 98.

16 *Music in the Medieval and Renaissance Universities*, p. 48.

17 *Grove 6*, sv 'Paris', p. 186.

18 Mathiassen, *The Style of the Early Motet*, p. 35. Mathiassen reaches this conclusion in translating the words *quinque positiones solemnes* ('renowned treatments') which are used by Jerome of Moravia to describe the polyphonic treatises inserted into the twenty-sixth chapter of his *Tractatus de musica*. I have been unable to find evidence to support Mathiassen's translation of *positiones solemnes* as 'university lectures'. It was on the basis of Jerome's usage that Coussemaker gave the name *Discantus positio vulgaris* to the first polyphonic treatise in Jerome's compendium, and Jerome himself says that the work in question is *vulgaris*, meaning 'commonplace' or 'widespread'. This was presumably because part of it is concerned with the rudimentary and quasi-improvisatory technique of fifthing. It is in this context, I believe, that we should understand Jerome's later reference to the treatise as being used 'commonly by all nations' (Cserba, *Hieronymus de Moravia*, p. 97); there seems no good reason here to interpret *nationes* as a reference to the four academic 'nations' of the University of Paris (cf. Reimer, *Johannes de Garlandia*,

I, pp. 13–14). Even if we do interpret Jerome's use of the term *natio* in that way, it does not necessarily follow that polyphony was a subject of formal study.

19 For a published example of one of the 'musical' quodlibets see *Quo[d]libeta . . . Ricardi de Mediavilla*, pp. 97–8, which gives the text of Richard of Middleton's discussion of the question 'of whether herbs or harmonies can hinder a demon from vexing a man'. This is one section of a quodlibet pronounced at Paris in 1287. See Glorieux, *La littérature quodlibétique*, p. 270. I find no relevant material in the two disputations by Petrus de Alvernia, pronounced in Paris at Christmas, 1301, and contained in Paris, Bibliothèque Nationale, MS lat.14562 (Glorieux, *La littérature quodlibétique*, p. 263, Quodlibet VI, items 15 and 16). I am most grateful to Dr Mark Everist for the loan of a microfilm of this manuscript.

20 Denifle and Chatelain, *Chartularium*, I, pp. 78–9; see also Ferruolo, 'The Paris statutes of 1215 reconsidered', p. 5: 'Together the legate and the Masters set out to draw up a set of statutes which would secure the corporate achievements and complete the programme of educational reform begun years before when Courson himself had been teaching in Paris'.

21 Haskins, 'A list of text-books', p. 374.

22 See Appendix. There is a poor edition of the text, and of the questions and answers, in Haas, 'Studien zur Mittelalterlichen Musiklehre . . . I', pp. 354ff.

23 See Appendix.

24 The author's only comment on the contents of Books III–V of the *De musica* is that they set out to 'correct the opinions of others'.

25 Haas, 'Studien', pp. 358–9.

26 *Sermones beati Umberti Burgundi*, I, pp. 63ff.

27 Bridges, *Opus maius*, I, pp. 236–7, and compare Brewer, *Opus tertium*, pp. 228ff.

28 Text in Pitra, *Analecta novissima*, p. 368.

29 For examples in the works of Paris-trained theologians from the first half of the thirteenth century see Ranulph Ardens, *Homiliae*, in PL, 155, col. 1327 (a reference, partially disguised by allegory, to the position of *organistae*, newly appointed); William of Auvergne, *Opera*, p. 996 (*De universo*), where the reference to the *ars inveniendi componendique cantus, maxime harmonicos, qui omnium sunt suavissimi* presumably relates to polyphonic music; Evrard du Val-des-Ecoliers, *Sermones*, Avj^v: *Sequitur per vicos eius cantabitur Alleluia. Alleluia est verbum grecum ineffabilem exprimens jocunditatis affectum. Vero angelici spiritus ad exhilarationem illius superne curie maxime in hac sacra solemnitate non cessant alleluia organice modulationis jubilo decantare.*

30 *Opera*, p. 293 (*De tentationibus et resistentiis*). William is describing what seems to be a bagpipe with three pipes (*tribus calamis uno flatu*) performing *cantum, discantum et triplum* and with the player's voice adding a *quadruplum*. In reality, of course, the melodic material provided by the chanters cannot have possessed a high degree of mutual independence, although it is possible to imagine how a double-chanter bagpipe, equipped with a drone and further adorned by the singing voice of the player, could have produced something akin to certain effects in the melismatic sections of four-part organa by Perotin.

31 *Opera*, pp. 364ff. (*De rhetorica divina*), a long *cithara* allegory.

32 *Opera*, p. 293 (*De tentationibus et resistentiis*). For full text and translation of this passage see Page, *Voices and Instruments*, p. 204.

33 *Opera*, p. 627 (*De universo*).

34 *Opera*, p. 704 (*De universo*). For the references to music and aspects of musical life in the works of William of Auvergne which have formed the basis of our

discussion, see *Opera*, pp. 193, 226, 231, 238, 364ff., 555, 620, 627, 703–4, 757, 971 and 995ff.

35 Molinier, *Obituaires de la province de Sens*, I, pp. 95, 150, 152 and 161. On the relatively light liturgical duties of the secular canons, and the easy life-style which many clerics of other kinds associated with it, see in particular J. Halgrin d'Abbeville, *Expositio in psalmos*, p. 891, an interesting passage for an implied reference to organum: *Putant enim ipsi pingues canonici se satisfecisse, si in choro unum Alleluia, vel unum Responsorium bene cantant, et alte; et in domibus suis postea vadunt lascivire, habentes plausores, histriones, joculatores in coenis. Unde Hieronymus: Non sufficit pleni gutturis libido, nisi tibiarum, et psalterii, et lyrae canticis aures mulceantur; ut quod fecit David in cultum Domini, Levitarum ordines, et organorum reperiens varietates, vos in luxuriam convertatis.* 'These fat canons think that they have done enough if they sing in choir one Alleluia, or one Response in a loud fashion; afterwards they return to their houses to carouse, having there sycophants, minstrels and jongleurs at their dinners. Whence St Jerome [in his commentary upon Amos 6:4–6; see PL 25, col. 1059]: ''The lust of a full glutton is not sated unless his ears are soothed by the melodies of pipes, psaltery and lyre; and what David did for the cult of the Lord, instituting the order of Levites and varieties of *organa*, you have turned into lustfulness.''' When St Jerome speaks of *organa*, a general term for musical instruments, he is merely paraphrasing the biblical text upon which he is commenting: *Sicut David putaverunt se habere vasa cantici*, 'they thought themselves to have musical instruments like those of David'. J. Halgrin d'Abbeville, however, is clearly punning on the word *organum* and is referring to liturgical polyphony. The canons are therefore attacked not merely for their laziness, but for the way in which they institute elaborate liturgical polyphony in their services.

36 Wright, *Music and Ceremony*, p. 25.

37 *Ibid.*, pp. 24ff.

38 *Ibid.*, p. 25.

39 See above, p. 74.

40 PL 155, col. 1327: *Per quatuor animalia* [of Apocalypse 4:6] *quatuor evangelistas, et per viginti quatuor seniores, Veteris et Novi Testamenti Patres, id est, duodecim patriarchas et duodecim apostolos intelligimus. Ante igitur sedem et quattuor animalia et seniores canticum novum virgines cantant, qui Deum et sanctos eius, et magistratus, senatoresque coelestis curiae, novitate virtutis et laudis suae delectant. O quam beati sunt virgines, qui in coelesti curia novi organistae statuuntur, et quodammodo angelorum cantico veterascente, nova melodia, Deum totamque Dei curiam merentur praedelectare!*

41 As suggested by Baldwin, *Masters, Princes and Merchants*, II, p. 142, n. 218.

42 Waesberghe, *Johannis ... De musica*, p. 134. Johannes depicts a group of singers who, beset by the ambiguities of the chant notation prevailing in their day, have learned their chants from different teachers and now find that their versions conflict with one another: *Dicit namque unus: Hoc modo magister Trudo me docuit; subiungit alius: Ego autem sic a magistro Albino didici; ad hoc tertius: Certe magister Salomon longe aliter cantat.*

43 *Henrici cardinalis hostiensis Summa Aurea*, 392v: *Quis dicitur magister? Is qui alicuius rei, sive negotii prae ceteris curam gerit ... praeceptor cuiuslibet discipline magister vocari potest.*

44 For an early example of this Antique 'theatrical' vocabulary being used to stigmatise performances of chant see the pronouncement of the Council of Cloveshoh (?Brixworth) held in 747, quoted in Faral, *Les jongleurs*, p. 31, n. 4: ' *ut presbyteri*

*saecularium poetarum modo in ecclesia non garriant, in tragico sono sacrorum verborum com-
positionem et distinctionem corrumpant vel confundant.*

45 Roesner, 'The performance of Parisian organum', where many of these ornaments
are discussed in a most enlightening way and with full references to the original
sources.

46 The word *notula* is formed from *nota*, 'a note', with the conventional diminutive
suffix *-ula*; the literal meaning of *notule* is therefore 'little notes', and is surely
to be translated as such despite the greatly weakened force of this diminutive
suffix in a great deal of medieval Latin vocabulary.

47 For Courson's use of the verb *effemino* ('to render effeminate') in a sense denoting
the effect of secular music performed by minstrels, see the extract from his *Summa*
in the Appendix, line 3.

48 Rohloff, *Quellenhandschriften*, p. 144.

49 The most convenient exposition of the development of the thirteenth-century motet
is by Sanders in *Grove 6*, sv 'Motet', with an accompanying bibliography listing
the principal contributions to the debate about chronology between Sanders,
Tischler and others.

50 Almost a quarter of the French two-part motets in the tenth fascicle of W2 can
be classified as poems using major features of the *pastourelle* manner. In this sense
the early motet repertoire is distinct from the generally more solemn productions
of the contemporary trouvères. As pointed out by Rivière, *Les pastourelles*, I, p.
43, the *grand chant courtois* was the dominant trouvère genre during the 'classic'
period (from the end of the twelfth century to *c.* 1240), and the *pastourelle* was
considered a very minor form which few named trouvères chose to cultivate.
(This observation must be glossed with the comment that there are many unattri-
buted *pastourelles* whose dates cannot be established, and some of these may be
the work of major trouvères active before *c.* 1240.) Attributed *pastourelles* before
this approximate date are generally the work of somewhat minor or idiosyncratic
poets. These include, for example, the rather unusual poet Richart de Semilli,
whose period of activity is usually placed (on what secure evidence I do not know)
c. 1200, and who, in contrast to virtually all the major trouvères, had close contacts
with Paris. See Steffens, 'Richart de Semilli', poems II, VI, VII, and VIII. When
compared with the work of 'classic' trouvères such as Gace Brulé, or with Conon
de Béthune, Semilli's work shows a marked preference for the lighter courtly
styles of *pastourelle*, *chanson de rencontre*, and *chanson avec des refrains*. Another somewhat
anomalous trouvère who produced *pastourelles* in this early period is Jean Bodel
(d.1209/10), an anomaly amongst the northern songwriters because he produced
a substantial range of work in non-lyric genres. At first sight the exception to
all this would appear to be Thibaut de Blason (d.1229), of noble family. The
pastourelle beginning *Hui main par un ajournant* is preserved in eight manuscripts
and attributed to him in all save one. Compare, however, the important comment
in Rosenberg and Tischler, *Chanter m'estuet* (which gives a text, pp. 273–4 and
a modal transcription, p. 273), p. 275: 'This is a most unusual *pastourelle*, substitut-
ing shepherd for shepherdess and a discussion of love for the poet-knight's quest
of love.' Another *pastourelle*, *Quant se resjouissent oisel*, is also attributed to Thibaut
de Blason, and so too *En avril au tens novel* (but Rivière, *Les pastourelles*, I, p.
13, appears to reject the attribution).

51 Wright, *Music and Ceremony*, pp. 235ff.

52 *Ibid.*

53 *Ibid.*

54 *Ibid.*, p. 267.

55 *Ibid.*, p. 270.

56 If the generally accepted dating of Franco's *Ars cantus mensurabilis* (*c.* 1280) is correct, then Anonymous IV, who mentions Franco, can scarcely have been writing very much before *c.* 1285. For the text see Reckow, *Der Musiktraktat*; there is a full English translation by Yudkin. Anonymous IV is deeply interested in the history of the Parisian repertoire. Indeed, he is the first writer on *musica mensurabilis* to register such an awareness as scholars in other fields like theology or *dictamen* had long possessed – namely that measured music had not only present but also past masters: its *antiqui* and *moderni*. A brief comparison with theology helps to place his interest in the succession of Parisian *organiste* in context. Around 1200 theologians were increasingly aware of the need to distinguish the scriptures and the works of the Church Fathers, the *authentica*, from the writings of more recent date produced by theologians and possessing less authority, the *magistralia*. Since the writings of the Masters were not guided by divine inspiration in the same way as the Scriptures or the books of the Fathers, it followed that their contents could only be fully understood in terms of the contingencies which had influenced them. Chief among these was the order in which the Masters had appeared, for it was necessary to know who had followed whom and to which school of thought each Master owed allegiance. Peter the Chanter, for example, describes the precedence of theological Masters as it appeared at the end of the twelfth century, and it seems to him that the great tradition of the Masters had begun about three generations before with the first *antiqui* such as Anselm of Laon (d.1117). Great things had happened, in other words, almost within living memory. Anonymous IV is moved by exactly this sense of significant change and development within a period of about eighty years, for the earliest Master whom he names is Leonin, whose activities at Notre Dame may be tentatively placed towards 1200. There can be little doubt, indeed, that the precedence of musical Masters sketched by Anonymous IV owes something to theology and the *ars dictaminis* where such a sense of tradition was already to be found. There is no reason to regard Anonymous IV's list of *magistri* with the exaggerated scepticism that it has sometimes aroused; it was not unusual for scholars in the thirteenth century to speak in such terms and there is abundant evidence that pupils' memories of their teachers, and the international grapevine that served all learned men, were often enough to ensure a generally accurate record of names, of precedence, and of individual achievements.

57 As suggested by Reckow, *Der Musiktraktat*, I, p. 97.

58 Text from Reckow, *Der Musiktraktat*, I, p. 50; translation from Yudkin, *The Music Treatise of Anonymous IV*, save that I have changed the rendering of Anonymous IV's words about Master Petrus – that his fame is attested *ex documento suo* – to 'as may be seen from the material which he has left', which seems to me to give better sense than Yudkin's 'as appears from his own testimony'.

59 Reckow, *Der Musiktraktat*, I, p. 33; Yudkin, *The Music Treatise of Anonymous IV*, p. 25. Anonymous IV refers to Garlandia as *quidem* and *ipse idem*.

60 Reckow, *Der Musiktraktat*, I, p. 50; Yudkin, *The Music Treatise of Anonymous IV*, p. 44.

61 On the custom at Notre Dame of performing the services without liturgical books see Wright, *Music and Ceremony, passim.*

[62] There is a thin but continuous tradition in the Latin music-theorists of commenting upon the musical characteristics of songs for the *carole*. Around 1100 Johannes comments on the agreeable singing of those who lead the dances (*chorearum praecentores*) which he says is granted to them 'not by art but by nature' (Waesberghe, *Johannis ... De musica*, p. 77). Grocheio, writing *c.* 1300, mentions *carole* music under the heading *ductia*, reflecting the ubiquitous Latin idiom established since Late Antiquity, *ducere choreas*, and describes it as 'light and brisk' (Rohloff, *Quellenhandschriften*, p. 132). Around 1350 Johannes Boen describes the music of *coreae* as being strictly measured in either duple or triple time in these interesting terms: *Per has duas species numerorum, scilicet aut per ternarium aut per binarium, natura incitat ut procedat omnis cantus, ut in tripudiis experimur et choreis, quasi mensuram cuiusvis alterius numeri qui non sit reducibilis ad has natura penitus abhorreret* (Gallo, *Johannis Boen Ars Musicae*, p. 19). In the 1330s Jacques de Liège paraphrases and elaborates the remarks of Johannes from *c.* 1100 (Bragard, *Jacobi Leodiensis Speculum Musicae*, 6, p. 216). Finally, an anonymous and undoubtedly British treatise, perhaps of the early fifteenth century but probably a compilation of pre-existing material and therefore earlier in date, refers to *carollis*; it mentions their use of open and closed endings, and then dismisses them as frivolous and fantastic songs to which no serious composer has ever paid any attention (Reaney, *De origine et effectu musicae*, pp. 117–18).

Chapter 7: Plainchant and the Beyond

[1] London, British Library, Additional MS 15722, f.36. A note in the manuscript (f.43v) records that the sermon was preached at Paris *in presentia circiter mille scolarium et magistrorum multorum*. According to Schneyer, *Repertorium*, sv Humbertus de Balesma, this is the only known manuscript of this, the only known work by Humbertus.

[2] See Post *et al.*, 'the medieval heritage of a humanistic ideal'.

[3] *Catalogue of Additions to the Manuscripts in the British Museum in the years 1856–7*, p. 16.

[4] See above, p. 136.

[5] Martène and Durand, *Thesaurus*, V, p. 1586.

[6] Canivez, *Statuta*, I, p. 30.

[7] PL 185, cols. 1273–1384.

[8] Pez, *Thesaurus*, I:2, cols. 375–472.

[9] Strange, *Dialogus miraculorum*. There is a complete English translation of the *Dialogus* (not consulted for this book) by Scott and Bland, *The Dialogue on Miracles*. There is also material of interest and importance in Caesarius's *Libri VIII Miraculorum*, only three books of which survive. These are printed in Hilka, *Die Wundergeschichten*, 3, pp. 15–222. The newly-discovered miracle stories by Caesarius, printed in Vennebusch, 'Unbekannte miracula', contain nothing of relevance here. There is a large literature on Caesarius, the major studies for the present purpose being McGuire, 'Friends and tales in the cloister', and *idem*, 'Written sources and Cistercian inspiration'; Schmidt, *Der Teufels und Daemonenglaube*, and Wagner, 'Studien zu Caesarius von Heisterbach'. Since many of Caesarius's stories of the supernatural involve the lay brothers, or *conversi*, see Leclercq, 'Comment vivaient

les frères convers', and Van Dijk, 'L'instruction et la culture des frères convers'. There is material of interest in Cohn, *Europe's Inner Demons*, pp. 69ff., and Ward, *Miracles*, pp. 192ff.

[10] Constable, 'Renewal and reform in religious life', p. 50.

[11] *Ibid.*

[12] *Ibid.*

[13] See Chapter 6, *passim*, and from the multitude of original sources which might be cited in this connection, pseudo-Bonaventura, *De institutione novitiorum*, pp. 301ff. Anecdotes about the dire consequences which could ensue if a singer pitched a chant too high to show off his voice are common in medieval works of religious instruction. See the examples in Caesarius of Heisterbach (Strange, *Dialogus miraculorum*, I, pp. 181 and 283–4, the latter a particularly striking example of a young novice in a monastery who does not wish to sing the psalm at the low pitch preferred by the older monks and who therefore begins 'almost five tones higher'). A complex and ambivalent conception of high-pitched singing prevailed in the religious communities of the Middle Ages; on one hand it was clearly vain, and yet on the other it was *sublime* in both the literal sense ('high') and in the transferred sense ('delightful') of the word. Compare the influential Cistercian text by Herbertus, *De miraculis* (PL, 185, col. 1320), where the voices of angels are heard singing so high 'that no straining of human voices could possibly equal them'. In the choral institutions of the Middle Ages, where chant was often performed without any reference to a fixed pitch-standard, it must have been a common accident for singers to begin to chant too high in their voices and so find themselves unable to follow the melody into its higher reaches, leading to a breakdown of the liturgy and (no doubt) to recriminations. This phenomenon is often described, as for example by Pierre de Palude: *Sed quidam cantores multum alte intonando et cantando incipiunt, qui cito post aut raucedine totum dimittunt aut remissione cantum demittunt et voce subprimunt* (Troyes, Bibliothèque Municipale, MS 144, volume I, f.304v).

[14] Pseudo-Bonaventura, *De institutione novitiorum*, p. 461, where the surrender of will in conventual chanting and reading is made very plain indeed: *Debitus legendi et cantandi modus est, ut nec nimium festinetur, nec nimia fiat, aut inaequalis protractio: sed cum pausantibus statim pausetur, ut vox unius vix inter alios discerni possit.*

[15] For a systematic exposition of this and a wealth of other conventional teaching about the decorum of liturgical chant it would be hard to improve upon the fifteenth-century Middle English compendium *The Myroure of Oure Ladye* (ed. Blunt), *passim*, but especially pp. 22ff. The author (once thought to be Thomas Gascoign) borrows material from St Bernard and from Caesarius of Heisterbach with some frequency.

[16] According to Thomas of Cantimpré, theologians had given much attention to the question of whether heavenly praise would be genuinely vocal (*Thomae Cantipratani ... miraculorum ... libri duo*, pp. 404–5). For examples of the kind of theological discussion to which Thomas refers we can turn to William of Auvergne, who discusses this and similar questions several times in his voluminous treatise *De universo* (*Opera*, pp. 697ff. and 703–4). Compare the story told by Caesarius of Heisterbach (Strange, *Dialogus miraculorum*, II, pp. 120–1).

[17] *Summa de exemplis*, f.212r.

[18] Pez, *Thesaurus*, I:2. cols. 352–3.

[19] These concepts are eloquently and persuasively discussed in Leclercq, *Love of Learning, passim.*

[20] Genesis 3:1. It may be doubted whether a simple particle word has ever borne a greater weight of significance than *Sed* in this passage. In modern editions of the Bible the effect of these words is heightened by the fact that they begin a new chapter. In medieval Bibles this naturally does not occur, but the word *Sed* is often marked as the beginning of a major new section by a touch of rubrication, use of lineation, or by some other device.

[21] An oft-repeated story, told by Boethius among others (*De institutione musica* I:I).

[22] I Samuel 16:22. This story is recounted, or alluded to, in an infinite number of medieval writings which mention music, both of a technical and a non-technical nature.

[23] Printed in *Quo[d]libeta . . . Ricardi de Mediavilla*, pp. 97–8.

[24] *Ibid.*

[25] *Ibid.*

[26] Pez, *Thesaurus*, I:2, col. 417.

[27] *Ibid.*, col. 423.

[28] *Ibid.*, col. 393.

[29] *Ibid.*, col. 423.

[30] *Ibid.*, col. 379.

[31] *Ibid.*, col. 397.

[32] *Ibid.*, col. 378.

[33] *Ibid.*, col. 381.

[34] *Ibid.*, col. 380.

[35] *Ibid.*, col. 382.

[36] *Ibid.*, col. 377.

[37] *Ibid.*, col. 385.

[38] Strange, *Dialogus miraculorum*, I, pp. 281–2.

[39] *Ibid.*, p. 283.

[40] *Ibid.*, pp. 333–4.

[41] *Ibid.*, p. 334.

[42] *Ibid.*, p. 283

[43] *Ibid.*

[44] Of the many references to this 'abuse' which might be cited, one of the most elaborate is found in the statutes of St Paul's, London. See Simpson, *Registrum Statutorum*, pp. 65–6.

[45] *Thomae Cantipratani . . . miraculorum . . . libri duo*, p. 309: *In ordine Cisterciensi gloriosae virgini specialiter dedito, multa valde facta miracula referuntur.*

[46] Forshaw, *Speculum religiosorum*, p. 74: *in verbis rithmicis aut curioso dictamine compositis.*

[47] Thomas of Cantimpré tells a story of how Adam of 'St Victor' was visited by the Virgin as he was in the process of composing the sequence *Salve mater salvatoris* (*Thomae Cantipratani . . . miraculorum . . . libri duo*, p. 279), showing that the recent origin of the sequence was well known. For a story of similar import, this time connected with the Marian compositions of Philippe the Chancellor, see Page, *'Angelus ad virginem'*. It is common for sermons in manuscripts of the twelfth and thirteenth century to incorporate short snatches of Latin devotional poetry and to ascribe them to 'a certain doctor of theology', or something similar, reflecting a clear awareness that the great theological enterprise of the twelfth and thirteenth centuries, and the rise of the *magistri*, had produced a wealth of new Latin devotional verse. See, for example, Cambridge, Gonville and Caius College, MS 358/585, f.103v; on f.138v the sequence *Sanctus spiritus assit* is attributed (as it is in many

other non-musical sources) to *Robertus rex francie*.

[48] Strange, *Dialogus miraculorum*, I, pp. 10–11.

[49] See above especially pp. 92ff.

[50] Leclercq, *Love of Learning*, pp. 72ff.

[51] Strange, *Dialogus miraculorum*, II, pp. 39–40.

[52] *Ibid.*, 2, p. 68.

[53] *Ibid.*, pp. 38–9.

[54] *Ibid.*

[55] *Thomae Cantipratani . . . miraculorum . . . libri duo*, pp. 309–10.

[56] See Leclercq, 'Comment vivaient les frères convers'.

[57] Caesarius of Heisterbach sometimes notes that a monk saw a certain vision in a dream, or that he saw it between waking and sleeping, but he does not seem to regard such experiences as a path to a rational or physiological explanation of dreams. See, for example, Strange, *Dialogus miraculorum*, 1, p. 204.

[58] On such passages in the *Dialogus miraculorum*, see McGuire, 'Friends and tales in the cloister', pp. 179ff.

[59] On the whole these stories leave the impression that the monks were much more vulnerable for their laziness, inattentiveness and boredom with the monastic life than for their sexual desire, although it is possible that the Cistercian sources deliberately conceal the true extent of the sexual tensions and problems created by monastic celibacy.

[60] Lawrence, *Medieval Monasticism*, p. 151.

[61] Strange, *Dialogus miraculorum*, I, pp. 281–2.

Chapter 8: Inventing the State

[1] Rohloff, *Quellenhandschriften*, p. 144.

[2] In this respect northern France must be distinguished from the south, including Catalonia, where a tradition of writing about the metrical and (by Grocheio's lifetime) the musical characteristics of vernacular songs had become established. A striking example is provided by the *Doctrina de compondre dictats* (*c.* 1300), probably by Jofre de Foixà; for excerpts see Page, *Voices and Instruments*, pp. 40ff. Grocheio is quite alone, however, in his decision to write about the literary and musical aspects of the *chansons de geste*.

[3] Text from Rohloff, *Quellenhandschriften*, p. 130, with the crucial difference that the word *exequiarium*, printed by Rohloff in his text (as in his edition of 1943, p. 50), has been replaced here by *exaquiensem*, surely implied by the mildly contracted form of the relevant word in both of the surviving manuscripts of the treatise, presented in facsimile in Rohloff's 1972 edition. Wolf ('Die Musiklehre', p. 90) printed *exaquiansem* but could offer no interpretation of the word. However, in the phrase *ad Clementem exaquiensem monachum*, *exaquiensem* surely denotes Clement's abbey, and *Orbis Latinus* interprets this as Lessay, about 40 miles due west of Bayeux in western Normandy, where there was a Benedictine Abbey founded in the eleventh century. It is striking that the only area of France to which Grocheio refers, apart from Paris, is Normandy (*puta in Normannia*); he is referring to the dance-songs of young people (Rohloff, *Quellendhandschriften*, p. 132).

4 There seems no reason to question the identification which *Orbis Latinus* offers for *Groceium*, associating it with Gruchy in western Normandy.

5 Rohloff, *Quellendhandschriften*, p. 130.

6 Instances of the term *civitas* are scattered throughout the earlier pages of the treatise.

7 I concur with Moore (*The Formation of a Persecuting Society*, p. 128, n. 8) that 'the *literati* of the twelfth century should be viewed pre-eminently as a single class, ultimately serving the same interests and causes (for better or worse) whether they happened to find themselves agents at any particular moment of "church" or "state"'.

8 Murray, *Reason and Society*, p. 290.

9 Borgnet, *Beati Alberti Magni . . . Opera Omnia*, 7, p. 30. I translate *comoedia* as 'the recitation of epics' on the basis of Albertus's use of the term *comoedi* to denote minstrels with fiddles who perform the 'deeds of heroes' (*Opera*, 8, p. 748).

10 Durandus de Sancto Porciano, *In Sententias Theologicas Petri Lombardi*, 337v: *Item illa sine quibus respublica non potest conservari non sint impedimenta operum penitentie et cuiuscunque virtutis.* Compare Pierre de Tarentaise: *Item videtur quod negociatio et milicia penitentiam non impediant quia sine quibus respublica non bene regitur* (Cambridge, Gonville and Caius College, MS 322/523, f.96).

11 Borgnet, *Beati Alberti Magni . . . Opera Omnia*, 8, p. 150.

12 Cheyette, 'The Invention of the State', p. 150.

13 Post, 'The naturalness of society and the State'.

14 Bartholomaeus de Pisa, *Summa Pisana* (completed in 1338), M3.

15 *The Formation of a Persecuting Society*, p. 140.

16 Murray, 'Confession as a historical source', pp. 279ff.

17 Moore, *The Formation of a Persecuting Society*, p. 7. For the original text see Mansi, *Sacrorum conciliorum nova et amplissima collectio*, 22, cols. 978–1058.

18 For material relating to minstrels, for example, in legal works and commentaries upon the standard legal texts see Baldwin, *Masters, Princes and Merchants*, I, pp. 198ff., with useful quotations from original sources in the accompanying volume of notes.

19 Moore, *The Formation of a Persecuting Society*, p. 102.

20 *Ibid.*, p. 132, and Peters, *Torture*, pp. 30–31, 44–5.

21 Broomfield, *Thomae de Chobham Summa Confessorum*, p. 291: *Cum igitur meretrices vel histriones veniunt ad confessionem, non est eis danda penitentia nisi ex toto relinquant talia officia, quia aliter salvari non possunt.*

22 Post, 'The naturalness of society and the state', explains this concept admirably.

23 *Ibid.*, p. 553, with the relevant passage from Nicholas de Lyra.

24 John of Freiburg, *Summa confessorum*, III, *questio* cclxxviii.

25 For the ready use which thirteenth-century theologians often make of the phrase *tristicia huius seculi* see the excerpts from William of Auxerre's *Summa Aurea* in the Appendix.

26 *Histriones et bedelli communes vestes sibi datas induunt per paucos dies ad ostentationem, nec consumunt eas in servitio domini; immo vendunt eas alteri. Videbitis hodie histrionem indutum ita pulchre ac si esset filius unius comitis; cras apparebit in una veste misera.* From a sermon by Guillaume de Saccovilla, quoted in Faral, *Les jongleurs*, p. 291.

27 Spufford, *Money and its Use in Medieval Europe*, p. 383.

28 Text in Jubinal, *Jongleurs et trouvères*, pp. 164–9.

29 Cloetta, *Moniage Guillaume*, lines 1248–50.

30 Paris, Bibliothèque Nationale, MS lat.14925, f.132, and MS lat.3495, f.192.

[31] The phrase is from a version of *Beuve de Hantonne*, quoted in Faral, *Les jongleurs*, p. 292.

[32] For the prevailing attitudes to the clergy and to mercantile success in the *chansons de geste* see Rossi, *Huon de Bordeaux*, pp. 555ff., and Combarieu du Grès, *L'idéal humain*, pp. 1ff.

[33] Rohloff, *Quellenhandschriften*, p. 130.

[34] Moore, *The Formation of a Persecuting Society*, p. 103.

[35] Paris, Bibliothèque Nationale, MS lat.16481, f.104v (Arnulphus de Albumeria on the Virgin's marriage to Joseph): *uni pauperi homini fuit desponsata, scilicet uni fabro vel carpentario. Bene scitis quod tales homines qui manibus suis panem suum lucrantur non sunt consueti esse multum divites in hoc mundo. Non fuit uxorata uni diviti magno vel potenti militi nec uni burgensi [nec] magno usuario sed carpentatori modico.*

[36] Broomfield, *Thomae de Chobham Summa Confessorum*, p. 290. There is an illuminating discussion of *officium* and similar crucial concepts of twelfth-century thought in Bynum, 'Did the twelfth century discover the individual?'. The importance which the concept of *officium* was believed to possess in relation to minstrelsy may be judged from the appearance of this issue in a widely disseminated manual for confessors arranged alphabetically by topics, the *Summa Pisana* of Bartholomaeus de Pisa, completed in 1338, sv *Histrio*. Bartholomaeus accepts, following Aquinas, that any *officium* ordained *ad solatium hominibus exhibendum* is not evil *secundum se*, and that therefore some minstrel earnings are legitimate: *unde et illi qui moderate eis subveniunt non peccant.*

[37] Le Goff, *Time, Work and Culture*, pp. 58ff.; compare Bynum, p. 15.

[38] 'The Invention of the State', p. 169.

[39] Tobler-Lommatzsch, *Altfranzösischer Wörterbuch*, sv. 'menestrel', columns 1422–3. See also Wright, 'Misconceptions', p. 36.

[40] See the *Capitulare de villis* of *c.* 800, or possibly later, in Boretius, *Capitularia regum francorum*, p. 87 (clause 45).

[41] For examples see Depping, *Réglemens sur les arts et métiers*, pp. 43, 44, 124, 219 and 221. In the French version of the Latin surgical treatise by the royal surgeon Henri de Mondeville, the Latin word *artifex* ('craftsman') is rendered *menestrel*. See Bos, *La chirurgie de Maître Henri de Mondeville*, p. 22.

[42] See, for example, Molenaer, *Li livres du gouvernement des rois*, p. 245.

[43] The distinction between *menestrel* and *jongleur* is discussed in Wright, 'Misconceptions', pp. 36–7.

[44] Ruelle, *Huon de Bordeaux*, lines 7255 and 7257.

[45] *Society and the Holy in Late Antiquity*, pp. 302ff.

[46] Ferruolo, 'The Paris statutes of 1215 reconsidered', p. 5.

[47] Moore's stimulating book, *The Formation of a Persecuting Society*, is devoted to this phenomenon.

[48] PL 88, cols. 813–14.

[49] Koenig, *Miracles*, 2, p. 103, lines 52–3.

[50] Fita, 'Cincuenta leyendas', p. 95.

[51] Moore, *The Formation of a Persecuting Society*, pp. 64–5.

[52] *Ibid.*, p. 133.

[53] Brett, *Humbert of Romans*, p. 144.

[54] Quoted in d'Avray, *The Preaching of the Friars*, p. 31.

[55] Moore, *The Formation of a Persecuting Society, passim.*

[56] Text in Prou, *Raoul Glaber*, p. 94. On Glaber's demonic visions see Colliot,

'Rencontres du moine Raoul Glaber avec le diable', and on Glaber's references to heretics, Moore, *The Formation of a Persecuting Society*, pp. 13ff.
57 Text in Prou, *Raoul Glaber*, pp. 115–16.
58 Radding, 'Superstition to science', p. 966.

Appendix: Documents

1 d'Avray, *The Preaching of the Friars*, p.1.
2 The indispensible guide to sermon literature, both published and unpublished, is Schneyer, *Repertorium*. A most useful guide to the social and intellectual background of thirteenth-century Latin sermons in northern France (home of very many of those that will be cited here) is d'Avray, *The Preaching of the Friars*. As d'Avray points out (*ibid.*, p. 206), the business of 'studying sermons to find nuggets of evidence for social history ... is by no means a new approach'. I do not believe, however, that this field of material, most of it unpublished, has been much exploited hitherto for the evidence it can provide about musical life in the Middle Ages. For the use of sermon evidence in the context of general social history see Lecoy de la Marche, *La chaire française au moyen âge* (the section entitled 'La société d'après les sermons'), and Bourgain, *La chaire française au XIIᵉ siècle*, pp. 271-369 ('La société d'après les sermons'). See also Longère, *La prédication médiévale* and *idem, Oeuvres oratoires des maîtres parisiens*.
3 The standard guide to these sources is Bloomfield, *Incipits of Latin Works on the Virtues and Vices*. Most of the solid information in these treatises relates to the *carole*. Although the number of surviving sources is very large, it may be said with some confidence that a more systematic investigation than it has been possible to mount here would confirm the finding that the greater part of the material about the *carole* is stereotyped and derivative, the principal source being Guillaume Peyraut's highly influential *Summa de vitiis et virtutibus*. Apart from Peyraut's *Summa*, the main sources of this kind used for this book have been the anonymous *collationes* in Birmingham, University Library, MS 6/iii/19, the chapter *De choreis* in London, British Library, MS Harley 3823 (ff.372v-8v), and the material in MS Royal 11 B.iii, ff.271v-2r.
4 Schneyer's catalogue of sermons, the *Repertorium der Lateinischen Sermones des Mittelalters*, runs to nine volumes and contains over 7,300 pages in all. On the device of the *similitudo* see d'Avray, pp. 228ff.
     The presence of a relatively high proportion of vernacular words or phrases in a sermon is often some indication that the text will accommodate references to contemporary life. A striking example is provided by the Parisian Latin sermons of 1272-3 in Paris, Bibliothèque Nationale, MS lat. 16481 (for extracts from this manuscript pertaining to minstrels see Chapter 1). For French words see extracts II (*jugleor ou a menestrere*) and IV (*soper*). Other important examples include the anonymous sermons in Cambridge, Sidney Sussex MS 34 (for a reference to minstrels in this manuscript see figure 4), and the sermons of Guido of Evreux (as preserved, for example, in Oxford, Jesus College, MS E.8, or in Oxford, Lincoln College, MS lat.113). On the spread of a vernacular or vernacular-based vocabulary in Latin theological writing see Page, *Voices and Instruments*, pp. 53-4.
5 *Thomae Cantipratani ... miraculorum ... libri duo*, pp. 451-2. The best introduction

to the *exemplum* literature is provided by the systematic collections of *exempla* which were compiled in the twelfth and thirteenth centuries for the use of preachers. Printed collections, in addition to the one of Thomas of Cantimpré, include Little, *Liber exemplorum ad usum praedicantium*; Greven, *Die Exempla ... des Jakob von Vitry*; Welter, *Speculum laicorum*, and *idem, La Tabula exemplorum*. Other collections are usefully calendared in various volumes of the Histoire Littéraire de la France, and some are cited from manuscript sources in Hauréau, *Notices et extraits, passim*. Many *exempla* can be found scattered through the theological miscellanies of the twelfth and thirteenth centuries. See, for example, London, British Library Additional MS 37670, ff.125ff., and Paris, Bibliothèque Nationale, MSS lat.16481 and 16482 *passim*. An index of *exempla*, covering most of the standard printed collections, is available in Tubach, *Index exemplorum*. For discussions of the *exemplum* genre see Bremond, *et al., L'exemplum*; McGuire, 'The Cistercians and the rise of the exemplum', and Welter, *L'exemplum*.

6 *Thomae Cantipratani ... miraculorum ... libri duo*, pp. 570–1.

7 *Ibid.*, p. 451: *Excusantur tamen in parte, sed non in toto, choreae quae in nuptiis fidelium fiunt, in quibus solatium modesti gaudii habere decet illos qui ad vitam laboriosi matrimonii convenerunt. Unde vulgariter dicitur: Virum dignum habere parvam nolam cum aurea cathena suspensam, qui infra annum de suscepta uxore non doluerit.* This is a pleasing variation upon the theme of misogyny so common in theological writings about the *chorea*. For a further reference to *caroles* at wedding celebrations see the *Summa de poenitentia* of John of Erfurt (Appendix, p. 193). References to carolling at court during royal and aristocratic marriage celebrations appear in the earliest layers of Old French romance. See, for example, the description of the marriage celebrations of Erec and Enide in Chrestien's *Erec* (text in Roques, *Erec et Enide*, lines 1993–4).

8 See particularly Longère, 'Quelques *Summae de poenitentia*'; Michaud-Quentin, 'A propos des premières *Summae confessorum*', and Murray, 'Confession as a historical source'. Longère's edition of the *Summa de confessione* of Peter of Poitiers (as surviving in a redaction made by Jacques de St Victor *c.* 1200) provides an excellent entry into this literature with its footnotes giving parallel passages from other manuals of confession.

9 The text includes the following passages:
CHOREE ... sicut deus habet ecclesiam sanctam in qua salvandis dantur sacramenta salutis, ita diabolus suo modo habet ecclesias suas sicut tabernas et cetera mala loca in quibus conveniunt homines loco sancte ecclesie. Et inter ceteras ecclesias taliter vel ita factas habet unam ecclesiam, scilicet choreas, in quibus diabolus nititur suprimiare sanctam ecclesiam. In ecclesia, inter cetera, ceremonia solent fieri; ibi deus habet ministerios suos qui sollempnitates in ecclesia faciunt et processiones; ibi ostenduntur reliquie sanctorum, et ipse, sanctissimus sanctorum, et ibi dantur indulgentie. Ista ceremonia diabolus nititur in choreis tanquam in ecclesia sua suprimiare. . . .

Inspiciatis illa processio totum e contrario vadit respectum processionis ecclesie; vadit enim ad sinistram at alia ad dexteram; ibi et ostenduntur reliquie diaboli a domino relicte, scilicet corpora fatuorum virorum et mulierum, et fiunt indulgentie totaliter contrarie eis que fiunt in ecclesia, quia in ecclesia domini fiunt indulgencie propter remissionem peccatorum, ibi vero propter relaxationem omnium bonorum, quia ibi sepe omnia bona que unus bonus iuvenis vel bona iuvencula vel puella vel coniugata vel alia congregaverat ibi amittit per unum vanum aspectum. . . .

Irreligiosa consuetudo est quam vulgus per sanctorum sollempnitates agere consuevit: populi quondam deberent divina officia attendere saltationibus invigilant,
cantica non solum mala canentes sed etiam religiosorum officiis perstrepunt; hoc
etenim ut ab omnibus provinciis propellatur vel depellatur sacerdotum et iudicum
a concilio sancto cure committitur. . . .

CAROLES . . . just as God has Holy Church in which the sacrament of salvation
is given to those who must be saved, so the Devil, in his own fashion, has his
churches such as taverns and other evil places in which men gather instead of
in Holy Church. Among other churches set up in this way he has one church,
that is to say the *caroles*, in which the Devil attempts to overturn Holy Church.
In [Holy] Church, amongst other things, it is the custom to have ceremonies;
there God has his ministers who perform the ceremonies in the Church and processions; there the relics of the saints are displayed, and He, the most Holy
of Holies, and there indulgences are given. The Devil attempts to ruin these
ceremonies in his own church through *caroles*. . . .

The procession [of a *carole*] is utterly contrary to a procession of [Holy] Church,
for [the *carole*] goes to the left, and the other [the procession of Holy Church]
goes to the right. There also [in the *carole*] are shown the relics of the Devil,
forsaken from God, that is to say the bodies of foolish men and women, and
indulgences are made there which are entirely contrary to those which are made
in [Holy] Church, because in the Church of God indulgences are given for the
remission of sins, but there [in the church of the Devil] they are given for the
remission of all good things, because there all the good things that a good young
man or a good young girl or a young woman or a wife or another possess are
let slip in a show of vanity. . . .

It is an irreligious custom amongst the people that, on the feast-days of saints,
they go to watch dances when they should be present at divine services, not
only singing evil songs but also drowning out the liturgical offices of those
in religious orders; wherefore it has been committed by holy counsel to the
charge of priests and judges that the *carole* be driven out and expelled from all
provinces. . . .

[10] See note 3.

[11] For a recent collection of essays bearing upon this topic see Aers, *Medieval Literature*.

[12] I quote from a review of an epic poem, *The Siege of Acre*, in *The Gentleman's Magazine*
for 1801, p. 817.

[13] On this question see particularly Nichols, 'The interaction of life and literature',
and Beer, 'Epic imitation'.

[14] See Page, 'Music and chivalric fiction', *passim*.

BIBLIOGRAPHY

Primary sources

I   Treatises on the Vices and Virtues

London, British Library
  MS Arundel 198 (Servasanctus of Faenza)
  MS Arundel 376
  MS Arundel 379
  MS Arundel 491
  MS Arundel 691 (Franciscus of Perugia)

  MS Cotton Galba E.iv
  MS Cotton Vitellius C.iv
  MS Cotton Titus A.xi
  MS Cotton Appendix xxiv (Guillaume Peyraut)

  MS Egerton 746 (Gulielmus de Pagula)

  MS Harley 2
  MS Harley 1298
  MS Harley 3244
  MS Harley 3823

  MS Royal 4 D.iv
  MS Royal 8 A.x
  MS Royal 8 B.xvii
  MS Royal 8 C.ii
  MS Royal 9 E.iii
  MS Royal 10 B.xvi
  MS Royal 11 A.xiii
  MS Royal 11 B.iii

  Additional MS 14070
  Additional MS 14081 (Guillaume Peyraut)
  Additional MS 22571 (Guillaume Peyraut)

Cambridge, University Library
    MS Gg.4.30 (Guillaume Peyraut)
    MS Ii.4.8 (Guillaume Peyraut)

Oxford, Bodleian Library
    MS Bodley 57
    MS Bodley 440
    MS Bodley 457 (Guillaume Peyraut)
    MS Lyell 12 (Guillaume Peyraut)

Oxford, Magdalen College
    MS III (Guillaume Peyraut)

Oxford, University College
    MS 91 (Guillaume Peyraut)

II   Sermons

London, British Library

    MS Arundel 395
    MS Royal 2 D.vi
    MS Royal 3 A.xiii
    MS Royal 4 B.viii

    Additional MS 16590
    Additional MS 37670 (*Distinctiones* of Nicholas de Bayard; *exempla*)

Cambridge, Gonville and Caius College
    MS 52/29
    MS 233/119
    MS 358/585

Cambridge, Sidney Sussex College
    MS 34

Oxford, Jesus College
    MS E.8 (Guido of Evreux)

Oxford, Lincoln College
    MS lat.113 (Guido of Evreux)

Oxford, New College
    MS 92

Paris, Bibliothèque Nationale,
    MS lat.14589
    MS lat.15971
    MS lat.16481
    MS lat.16482

III   Commentaries upon the *Sentences* of Peter the Lombard

London, British Library
  MS Royal 8 G.iv (The *Summa Aurea* of William of Auxerre)

  Additional MS 18322 (Humbert of Prully)

Cambridge, Gonville and Caius College
  MS 322/523 (Pierre de Tarentaise)

Oxford, Oriel College
  MS 43 (Richard of Fishacre)

IV   Manuals of confession and notes for confessors

London, British Library
  Additional MS 18325 (Paulus of Hungary)

Oxford, Bodleian Library
  MS Bodley 801
  MS Bodley 828
  MS Laud misc. 278 (John of Freiburg)

V   Psalm commentaries

London, British Library
  MS Royal 19 C.v (in French)

Douai, Bibliothèque Municipale
  MS 45 (Petrus de Palude)

Troyes, Bibliothèque Municipale
  MS 144 (Petrus de Palude)

VI   Other theological writings

London, British Library
  MS Harley 103 (Guillaume 'de Lavicea')

  MS Royal 9 E.xiv (the *Summa* of Robert of Courson)

  Additional MS 15722 (Miscellany from the library of Cîteaux)

Cambridge, Gonville and Caius College
  MS 331/722 (the *Summa* of Robert of Courson)

Cambridge, Sidney Sussex College
  MS 97 (the *Verbum Abbreviatum* of Peter the Chanter)

Bruges, Stedelijke Openbare Bibliotheek
  MS 247 (the *Summa* of Robert of Courson)

Books and Articles

Adank, T. 'Roger Bacons Auffassung der Musica', *Archiv für Musikwissenschaft*, 35 (1978), pp. 33–56.

Aebischer, P. 'L'élément historique dans les chansons de geste ayant la Guerre de Saxe pour thème', in Bambeck, M. and Christmann, H. H. (eds.), *Philologica Romanica Erhard Lommatzsch gewidmet* (Munich, 1975), pp. 9–22.

Aers, D. (ed.), *Medieval Literature: Criticism, Ideology and History* (Brighton, 1986).

Albe, E. (ed.), *Les miracles de Notre-Dame de Roc-Amadour au XII* siècle* (Paris, 1907).

Alexander of Hales, *Summa Theologica . . . studio et cura PP. Collegii S. Bonaventurae ad fidem codicum edita* (Ad Claras Aquas, 1924-).

Alton, J. (ed.), *Anseïs von Karthago* (Stuttgart, 1892).

—— (ed.), *Li romans de Claris et Laris* (Tübingen, 1884).

Anciaux, P. *La théologie du sacrament de pénitence au XII* siècle* (Louvain and Gembloux, 1949).

Anglès, H. 'La danza sacra y su música en el templo durante el Medioevo', *Medium Aevum Romanicum: Festschrift für Hans Rheinfelder* (Munich, 1963), pp. 1–20.

Armand de Belvézer, *Sermones plane divini assumptis ex solo Psalterio Davidico thematis* (Lyon, 1525).

Arnold, I. (ed.), *Le Roman de Brut de Wace*, 2 vols., Société des Anciens Textes Français (Paris, 1938 and 1940).

Ashby-Beach, G. *The Song of Roland: A Generative Study of the Formulaic Language in the Single Combat* (Amsterdam, 1985).

Aubry, P. *Estampies et danses royales* (Paris, 1907).

—— *La musique et les musiciens d'église en Normandie au XIII* siècle* (Paris, 1906).

Bachmann, W. *The Origins of Bowing*, trans. Deane, N. (Oxford, 1969).

Baldwin, J. 'Masters at Paris from 1179–1215: a social perspective', in Benson, R. L. and Constable, G. (eds.), *Renaissance and Renewal in the Twelfth Century* (Oxford, 1982), pp. 138–172.

—— *Masters, Princes and Merchants: The Social Views of Peter the Chanter and his Circle*, 2 vols (Princeton, 1970).

—— *The Medieval Theories of the Just Price* (Philadelphia, 1959).

Bartholomaeus de Pisa, *Summa Pisana* (Venice, 1481).

Bec. P. *La lyrique française au Moyen Age* 2 vols (Paris, 1977).

Beer, J. M. A. 'Epic imitation: its serious and comic potential in two medieval histories', *Charlemagne et l'épopée romane: Actes du VII* Congrès international de la Société Rencesvals*, 2 vols (Paris, 1978), pp. 415–21.

—— 'Villehardouin and the Oral Narrative', *Studies in Philology*, 63 (1970), pp. 267–77.

Bell, A. (ed.), *L'estoire des Engleis* (Oxford, 1960).

Benson, L. D. 'The tournament in the romances of Chrétien de Troyes and *L'Histoire de Guillaume le Maréchal*', in Benson and Leyerle. See next item.

——, and Leyerle, J. (eds.), *Chivalric Literature* (Michigan, 1980).

Bernhard, B. 'Recherches sur l'histoire de la corporation des ménétriers ou joueurs d'instruments de la Ville de Paris', *Bibliothèque de l'Ecole des Chartes*, 3 (1841–42), pp. 377–404; 4 (1842–3), pp. 525–548; 5 (1843–44), pp. 254–284 and 339–372.

Blomme, R. *La doctrine du péché dans les écoles théologiques de la première moitié du XIIᵉ siècle* (Louvain and Gembloux, 1958).

Bloomfield, M. W. *et al.* (eds.), *Incipits of Latin Works on the Virtues and Vices, 1100-1500 AD* (Cambridge, Mass., 1979).

Blunt, J. H. (ed.), *The Myroure of Oure ladye*, Early English Text Society Extra Series 19 (London, 1873).

Boase, R. *The Origin and Meaning of Courtly Love* (Manchester, 1977).

Boer, C. de (ed.), *Philomena* (Paris, 1909).

Bonaria, M. *Romani mimi* (Rome, 1965).

Boogaard, N. Van den, *Rondeaux et refrains du XIIᵉ siècle au début du XIVᵉ* (Paris, 1969).

Boretius, A. (ed.), *Capitularia regum francorum*, Monumenta Germaniae Historica, Legum Sectio II, Capitularia regum francorum I (Hanover, 1883).

Borg, S. J. (ed.), *Aye d'Avignon* (Geneva, 1967).

Borgnet, A. (ed.), *Beati Alberti Magni . . . Opera Omnia*, 38 vols (Paris, 1890–99).

Bos, A. (ed.), *La chirurgie de Maître Henri de Mondeville*, Société des Anciens Textes Français (Paris, 1897).

Bourgain, L. *La chaire française au XIIᵉ siècle d'après les manuscrits* (Paris, 1879).

Boutière, J. and Schutz, A. H. (eds.), *Biographies des troubadours*, 2nd ed. (Paris, 1973).

Bowles, E. A. 'Were musical instruments used in the liturgical service during the middle ages?', *Galpin Society Journal*, 10 (1957), pp. 40–56.

Boyer, Buschinger *et al.* (eds.), *L'épopée*, Typologie des sources du moyen âge occidental, Fasc. 49 (Tunhout, 1988).

Boyle, L. 'The *Summa confessorum* of John of Freiburg and the popularization of the moral teaching of St Thomas and of some of his contemporaries', in Maurer, A. A. *et al.* (eds.), *St Thomas Aquinas, 1274-1974, Commemorative Studies*, II (Toronto, 1974), pp. 245–68.

Brackney, E. M. *A Critical Edition of the Poems of Dalfin d'Alvernhe* (Diss., University of Minnesota, 1936).

Bragard, R. (ed.), *Jacobi Leodiensis Speculum Musicae*, 7 vols., Corpus Scriptorum de Musica 3 (American Institute of Musicology, 1955–73).

Brandin, L. (ed.), *La Chanson d'Aspremont*, 2 vols (Paris, 1919 and 1921).

Bremond, C., Le Goff, J. and Schmitt, J.-C. *L'exemplum*, Typologie des sources du moyen âge occidental, Fasc. 40 (Brepols, 1982).

Brett, E. T. *Humbert of Romans* (Toronto, 1984).

Brewer, J. S. (ed.), *Fr. Rogeri Bacon opera . . . inedita*, Rolls Series 15 (London, 1859). Includes *Opus tertium*.

Bridges, J. H. (ed.), *The Opus majus of Roger Bacon*, 3 vols (Oxford, 1897–1900).

Bromyard, J. *Summa predicantium* (Venice, 1636).

Broomfield, F. (ed.), *Thomae de Chobham Summa Confessorum* (Paris and Louvain, 1968).

Brown, H. M. 'Fantasia on a theme by Boccaccio', *Early Music*, 5 (1977), pp. 324–39.

Brown, P. *Society and the Holy in Late Antiquity* (London, 1982).

—— *The World of Late Antiquity* (London, 1971).

Buffum, D. L. (ed.), *Le Roman de la violette*, Société des Anciens Textes Français (Paris, 1928).

Burnley, J. D. 'The "Roman de Horn" and its ethos', *French Studies*, 32 (1978), pp. 385–97.

Buschinger, D. and Crépin, A. (eds.), *Musique, Littérature et Société au Moyen Age* (Paris, 1980).

Bynum, C. W. 'Did the twelfth century discover the individual?', *The Journal of Ecclesiastical History*, 31 (1980), pp. 1–17.

Calin, W. C. *The Old French Epic of Revolt* (Geneva and Paris, 1962).

Canivez, J. M. (ed.), *Statuta capitulorum generalium ordinis Cisterciensis ab anno 1116 ad annum 1786*, 8 vols (Louvain, 1933–41).

Carpenter, N. C. *Music in the Medieval and Renaissance Universities* (Oklahoma University Press, 1958).

Carter, H. H. *A Dictionary of Middle English Musical Terms* (Indiana University Press, 1961).

Casagrande, C. and Vecchio, S. 'Clercs et jongleurs dans la société médiévale (XIIᵉ et XIIIᵉ siècles)', *Annales: économies, sociétés, civilisations*, 34 (1979), pp. 913–28.

Castets, F. (ed.), *La Chanson des quatre fils Aymon* (Montpellier, 1909).

Chadwick, H. M. *The Heroic Age* (Cambridge, 1912; *R* 1967).

Chédeville, A. *et al.*, *La ville médiévale*, Histoire de la France urbaine, 2 (Editions du Seuil, 1980).

Chenu, M.-D. 'Civilisation urbaine et théologie', *Annales: économies, sociétés, civilisations* 29:5 (1974), pp. 1253–63.

—— *L'éveil de la conscience dans la civilisation médiévale* (Montreal and Paris, 1969).

—— *Nature, Man and Society in the Twelfth Century* (Chicago, 1968).

Cheyette, F. L. 'The Invention of the State', in Lackner, B. K. and Philp, K. R. (eds.), *Essays on Medieval Civilisation* (Austin and London, 1978), pp. 143–78.

Chibnall, M. (ed.), *The Ecclesiastical History of Orderic Vitalis*, 6 vols (Oxford, 1969–80).

Childress, D. J. 'Between romance and legend: "secular hagiography" in Middle English literature', *Philological Quarterly*, 57 (1978), pp. 311–322.

Cloetta, W. (ed.), *Les deux rédactions en vers du Moniage Guillaume*, 2 vols., Société des Anciens Textes Français (Paris, 1906).

Cohn, N. *Europe's Inner Demons* (Sussex University Press, 1975).

Coldwell, M. V. '*Guillaume de Dole* and medieval romances with musical interpolations', *Musica Disciplina*, 35 (1981), pp. 55–86.

Colker, M. L. 'The "Karolinus" of Egidius Parisiensis', *Traditio*, 29 (1973), pp. 199–325.

Colliot, R. 'Rencontres du moine Raoul Glaber avec le diable d'après ses *Histoires*', *Senefiance*, 6 (1979), pp. 119–132.

Combarieu du Grés, M. de, *L'idéal humain et l'expérience morale chez les héros des chansons de geste des origines à 1250*, 2 vols (Aix-en-Provence, 1979).

Constable, G. 'Renewal and reform in religious life: concepts and realities', in Benson, R. L. and Constable, G. (eds.), *Renaissance and Renewal in the Twelfth Century* (Oxford, 1982) pp. 37–67.

Corbett, J. A. (ed.), *The De instructione puerorum of William of Tournai* (Notre Dame, 1955).

Coussemaker, E. de (ed.), *Scriptorum de Musica Medii Aevi Nova Series*, 4 vols (Paris, 1864–76; *R* 1963).

Cremonesi, C. (ed.), *Enfances Renier* (Milan, 1957).

Cserba, S. (ed.), *Hieronymus de Moravia O.P. Tractatus de Musica* (Regensburg, 1935).

d'Avray, D. L. *The Preaching of the Friars: Sermons Diffused from Paris before 1300* (Oxford, 1985).

Davy, M. M. *Les sermons universitaires parisiens de 1230-31* (Paris, 1931).

De la Cuesta, F. I. (ed.), *Las Cançons dels Trobadors* (Toulouse, 1979).

Delbouille, M. 'Les chansons de geste et le livre', in *La technique littéraire des chansons de geste*, pp. 295-407.

—— 'Le mythe du jongleur poète', in *Studi in onore di I. Siciliano* (Florence, 1966), I, pp. 17-28.

—— (ed.), *Le Tournoi de Chauvency* (Liège, 1932).

Denifle, H. and Chatelain, A. (eds.), *Chartularium Universitatis Parisiensis* (Paris, 1889-97).

Depping, G.-B. (ed.), *Réglemens sur les arts et métiers de Paris, rediges au XIIIe siècle* (Paris, 1837).

DeWitt, P. A. M. *A New Perspective on Johannes de Grocheio's Ars Musicae* (Diss., Michigan 1973).

Dimock, J. F. and J. S. Brewer (eds.), *Giraldi Cambrensis Opera*, Rolls Series 21 (London, 1861-81).

Doucet, P. V. 'Commentaires sur les *Sentences*', *Archivum Franciscanum Historicum*, 47 (1954), pp. 88-170.

Doutrepont, A. (ed.), *La clef d'amors* (Halle, 1890).

Dronke, P. (ed.), *A History of Twelfth Century Philosophy* (Cambridge, 1988).

Duby, G. 'Dans la France du Nord-Ouest au XIIe siècle: les "Jeunes" dans la société aristocratique', *Annales: économies, sociétés, civilisations*, 19 (1964), pp. 835-46.

—— *William Marshall: The Flower of Chivalry* trans. Howard, R. (London, 1986).

Dugauquier, J.-A. (ed.), *Pierre le Chantre: Summa de sacramentis et animae consiliis*, 3 vols in 5 (Louvain, 1954-67).

Durandus de Sancto Porciano, *In Sententias Theologicas Petri Lombardi* (Antwerp, 1617).

Eadie, J. 'The authorship of *The Owl and the Nightingale*: a reappraisal', *English Studies*, 67 (1986), pp. 471-7.

Elias, N. *The Court Society* (Basil Blackwell, 1983).

Ellinwood, L. 'Ars Musica', *Speculum*, 20 (1945), pp. 290-299.

Evrard du Val-des-Ecoliers, *Sermones*, quoted from the printed edition of Heidelberg, 1485 (published under the name of Hugo de Prato Florido).

Ewert, A. (ed.), *Marie de France: Lais* (Basil Blackwell, 1969).

Faral, E. *Les jongleurs en France au moyen âge*, 2nd ed. (Paris, 1971).

Fenlon, I. (ed.), *Cambridge Music Manuscripts 900-1700* Cambridge, 1982).

Ferrante, J. 'The court in medieval literature - the centre of the problem', in Haymes, E. R. (ed.), *The Medieval Court in Europe* (Munich, 1986).

Ferris, P. (ed.), *Dylan Thomas: the Collected Letters* (London, 1985).

Ferruolo, S. C. *The Origins of the University: the Schools of Paris and their Critics 1100-1215* (Stanford University Press, 1985).

—— 'The Paris statutes of 1215 reconsidered', *History of Universities*, 5 (1985), pp. 1-14.

Field, W. H. W. (ed.), *Raimon Vidal: Poetry and Prose. 2*, Abril Issia (Chapel Hill, 1971).

Fita, F. 'Cincuenta leyendas por Gil de Zamora', *Boletín de la Real Academia de la Historia*, 7 (1885), pp. 54-143.

Flori, J. 'La notion de chevalerie dans les chansons de geste du XIIIe siècle: Etude historique de vocabulaire', *Moyen Age*, 81 (1975), pp. 211-44 and 407-45.

—— 'Qu'est-ce qu'un *bacheler*?', *Romania*, 96 (1975), pp. 289-314.

Foerster, W. (ed.), *Richars li biaus* (Vienna, 1874).

—— (ed.), *Yvain* (Halle, 1902).

Forshaw, H. P. (ed.), *Edmund Rich: Speculum religiosorum and Speculum ecclesiae* (London, 1973).

Fossier, R. *Enfance de l'Europe*, 2 vols (Paris, 1980).

Foster, G. *The Iconology of Musical Instruments and Musical Performance in Thirteenth Century French Manuscript Illuminations* (Diss., City University of New York, 1977).

Foulet, L. (ed.), *Galeran de Bretagne* (Paris, 1925).

Fournier, G. *Châteaux, villages et villes d'Auvergne au XVe siècle, d'après l'Armorial de G. Revel* (Geneva, 1973).

—— *Le château dans la France médiévale: essai de sociologie monumentale* (Paris, 1978).

Fréville, M. de (ed.), *Les quatre âges de l'homme*, Société des Anciens Textes Français (Paris, 1888).

Friedlein, G. (ed.), *Anicii Manlii Torquati Severini Boetii . . . De Institutione Musica Libri Quinque* (Leipzig, 1867; R 1966).

Friedwagner, M. (ed.), *Meraugis von Portlesguez* (Halle, 1897).

Fuller, S., 'Discant and the theory of fifthing', *Acta Musicologica*, 50 (1978), pp. 241-75.

Fundamentum aureum. See Nicholas de Gorran.

Gallo, F. A. (ed.), *Johannis Boen Ars Musicae*, Corpus Scriptorum de Musica 19 (American Institute of Musicology, 1972).

Ganshof, F. L. *Etude sur le developpement des villes entre Loire et Rhin au moyen âge* (Paris and Brussels, 1943).

Gardelles, J. 'Les palais dans l'Europe occidentale chrétienne du Xe au XIIe siècle', *Cahiers de Civilisation Médiévale*, 19 (1976), pp. 115-34.

Gauthier, R. A. (ed.), *Ethica Nicomachea Translatio Roberti Grosseteste Lincolniensis sive 'Liber Ethicorum'*, 5 vols (Leiden and Brussels, 1972-4).

Gennrich, F. (ed.), *Rondeaux, Virelais und Balladen*, 2 vols, Gesellschaft für Romanische Literatur, 43 (Dresden, 1921 and Göttingen, 1927).

Gerbert, M. (ed.), *Scriptores Ecclesiastici de Musica*, 3 vols (St Blaise, 1784).

Geremek, B. *The Margins of Society in Late Medieval Paris* (Cambridge, 1987).

Gérold, T. *Les Pères de l'Eglise et la musique* (Paris, 1931).

—— *La musique au moyen âge* (Paris, 1932).

Gilbert of Tournai, *Collectio de scandalis ecclesiae*. See Stroick.

—— *Sermones ad omnes status* (Lyons, ?1510).

Gitton, B. 'De l'emploi des chansons de geste pour entraîner les guerriers au combat', in *La chanson de geste et le mythe Carolingien: Mélanges René Louis*, 2 vols (Saint-Père-Sous-Vézelay, 1982), I, pp. 3-19.

Glorieux, P. *La littérature quodlibétique de 1260 à 1320*, 2 vols (Kain, 1925-35).

Godefroy, F. *Dictionnaire de l'ancienne langue française* (Paris, 1880-1902).

Goldine, N. 'Henri Bate, chanoine et chantre de la cathédrale Saint Lambert à Liège et théoricien de la musique (1246-après 1310)', *Revue Belge de Musicologie*, 18 (1964), pp. 10-27.

Goldschmidt, M. (ed.), *Sone von Nansay* (Tubingen, 1899).

Green, R. F. *Poets and Princepleasers* (Toronto, 1980).

Greene, G. 'The schools of minstrelsy', *Studies in Music*, 2 (1977), pp. 31-40.

Greene, R. L. *The Early English Carols*, 2nd edition (Oxford, 1977).

—— '*The Owl and the Nightingale* and the good man from Rome', *English Language Notes*, 4 (1966), pp. 1-6.

Greven, J. (ed.), *Die Exempla aus den Sermones feriales et communes des Jakob von Vitry* (Heidelberg, 1914).

Guenée, B. 'L'historien et la compilation au XIIIe siècle', *Journal des Savants*, Jan.-Sep. (1985), pp. 119-135.

Guentner, F. J. (ed.), *Epistola S. Bernardi de revisione cantus cisterciensis et tractatus scriptus ab auctore incerto cisterciense Cantum quem Cisterciensis ordinis ecclesiae cantare*, Corpus Scriptorum de Musica 24 (American Institute of Musicology, 1974).

Guessard, F. and Chabaille, P. (eds.), *Gaufrey* (Paris, 1859).

Guilhiermoz, P. *Essai sur l'origine de la noblesse en France au moyen âge* (Paris, 1902).

Guillaume 'de Lavicea', *Dieta salutis*. Printed in *Bonaventurae Opera Omnia*, 8 (Paris, 1866). See also list of MS sources.

Guillaume de Nangis, *Vie de Philippe III*, Recueil des Historiens des Gaules et de la France, 20 (Paris, 1840).

Gushee, L. 'Two central places: Paris and the French court in the early fourteenth century', in Kühn, H. and Nitsche, P. (eds.), *Bericht über den Internationalen Musikwissenschaftlichen Kongress Berlin 1974* (Kassel, 1980), pp. 135-57.

Györy, J. 'Reflexions sur le jongleur guerrier', *Annales Universitatis Scientiarum Budapestinensis, Sectio Philologica*, 3 (1961), pp. 47-60.

Haas, M. 'Studien zur Mittelalterlichen Musiklehre . . . I', *Forum Musicologicum* 3 (1982), pp. 323-456.

Halgrin d'Abbeville, J. *Expositio in psalmos*, in *S. Antonii Paduani Opera Omnia*, Bibliotheca Patristica, Series Prima, 6 (Paris, 1880).

Handschin, J. 'Über Estampie und Sequenz', *Zeitschrift für Musikwissenschaft*, 12 (1929-30), pp. 1-20 and 13 (1930-1), pp. 113-32.

Haren, M. *Medieval Thought: The Western Intellectual Tradition from Antiquity to the 13th century* (London, 1985).

Haskins, C. H. 'A list of text-books from the close of the twelfth century', in *Studies in the History of Medieval Science* (Cambridge, Mass., 1924), pp. 356-76.

Hauréau, B. *Notices et extraits de quelques manuscrits latins de la Bibliothèque Nationale*, 6 vols (Paris, 1890-3; R 1967).

Henrici cardinalis hostiensis Summa Aurea (Venice, 1620).

Henricus de Arimino, *Tractatus de quattuor virtutibus cardinalibus* (Argentine, 1472).

Henry, A. (ed.), *Le Roman du Hem* (Brussels, 1939).

—— (ed.), *Les oeuvres d'Adenet le Roi*, 4 vols (Bruges, 1951-63).

Hentsch, A. A. *De la littérature didactique du moyen âge s'adressant spécialement aux femmes* (Cahors, 1903).

Hibberd, L. '*Estampie* and *Stantipes*', *Speculum* 19 (1944), pp. 222-49.

Hilka, A. (ed.), *Li Romanz d'Athis et Prophilias*, 2 vols (Dresden, 1912 and 1916).

—— (ed.), *Die Wundergeschichten des Caesarius von Heisterbach*, vols 1 and 3 only published (Bonn, 1933 and 1937).

Hinnebusch, J. H. (ed.), *The Historia occidentalis of Jacques de Vitry: A Critical Edition* (Fribourg, 1972).

Hippeau, C. (ed.), *La Chanson du chevalier au cygne et de Godefroid de Bouillon*, 2 vols (Paris, 1874 and 1877).

Histoire littéraire de la France (Paris, 1733-).

Holden, A. J. (ed.), *Ipomedon* (Paris, 1979).

—— (ed.), *Le Roman de Waldef* (Geneva, 1984).

Holton, R. J. *Cities, Capitalism and Civilisation* (London, 1986).

Hubert, J. 'Evolution de la topographie et de l'aspect des villes de Gaule du Ve au Xe siècle', in *La città nell'alto medioevo, Settimane di studio del centro italiano di studi sull'alto medioevo* (Spoleto, 1959), pp. 529-58.

Hüschen, H. 'Albertus Magnus und seine Musikanshauung', in *Speculum Musicae Artis: Festgabe für Heinrich Hussman* (Munich, 1970), pp. 205-18.

—— (ed.), *Das Cantuagium des Heinrich Eger von Kalkar 1328-1408* (Cologne, 1952).

Hughes, J. *An Itinerary of Provence and the Rhone made during the year 1819* (London, 1822).

Hunt, R. E. (ed. and revised Gibson, M.), *The Schools and the Cloister: The Life and Writings of Alexander Nequam (1157-1217)* (Oxford, 1984).

Hunt, T. 'The emergence of the knight in France and England, 1000-1200', in Jackson, W. H. (ed.), *Knighthood in Medieval Literature* (Woodbridge, 1981), pp. 1-22.

Husmann, H. 'Der Hoketus *A l'entrade d'avril*', *Archiv für Musikwissenschaft*, 11 (1954), pp. 296-9.

Hymes, E. R. *A Bibliography of Studies Relating to Parry's and Lord's Oral Theory* (Cambridge, Mass., 1973).

Jacques de Vitry, *Historia occidentalis*. See Hinnebusch.

Jaeger, C. S. *The Origins of Courtliness* (Philadelphia, 1985).

Jammers, E. 'Studien zur Tanzmusik des Mittelalters', *Archiv für Musikwissenschaft*, 30 (1973), pp. 81-95.

Johannes de Sancto Geminiano, *Summa de exemplis* (Antwerp, 1615).

John of Freiburg, *Summa confessorum* (Lyon, 1518).

Jubinal, A. (ed.), *Jongleurs et trouvères* (Paris, 1835).

—— (ed.), *Nouveau recueil de contes, dits, fabliaux et autres pièces inédites des XIIIe, XIVe et XVe siècles*, 2 vols (Paris, 1839-42).

Jung, M-R. 'L'empereur Conrad chanteur de poésie lyrique: fiction et vérité dans le *Roman de la Rose* de Jean Renart', *Romania*, 101 (1980), pp. 35-50.

Jürgens, H. *Pompa diaboli* (Stuttgart, 1972).

Kaeppeli, T. *Scriptores Ordinis Praedicatorum Medii Aevi* (Rome, 1970-).

Keller, H.-E. 'La chanson de geste et son public', *Marche Romane: Mélanges de philologie et de littératures romanes offerts à Jeanne Wathelet-Willem* (Liège, 1978), pp. 257-85.

Kendrick, L. *The Game of Love* (London, 1988).

Kennedy, E. (ed.), *Lancelot do Lac*, 2 vols (Oxford, 1980).

Koenig, V. F. (ed.), *Les Miracles de Nostre Dame de Gautier de Coinci*, 4 vols (Geneva and Lille, 1955-70).

Kohler, E. 'Le *Tristan* de Thomas et son époque', in Buschinger, D. (ed.), *Littérature et société au moyen âge* (Paris, 1978), pp. 7-26.

Krupat, E. *People in Cities: The Urban Environment and its Effects* (Cambridge, 1985).

Kübel, W. (ed.), *Alberti Magni Ordinis Fratrum Praedicatorum Super Ethica Commentum et Quaestiones* (Monasterii Westfalorum in Aedibus Aschendorf, 1968 and 1972).

Kühne, H. and Stengel, E. (eds.), *Maître Elie's Überarbeitung der ältesten französischen Übertragung von Ovid's Ars Amatoria*, Ausgaben und Abhandlungen aus dem Gebiete der Romanischen Philologie, 47 (1882).

La technique littéraire des chansons de geste. Actes du colloque de Liège, Septembre, 1957 (Paris, 1959).

Labareyre, F. de, *La cour littéraire de Dauphin d'Auvergne* (Clermont-Ferrand, 1976).

Lathuillère, R. *Guiron le courtois* (Geneva, 1966).

Lauer, P. (ed.), *Les Annales de Flodoard* (Paris, 1905).

Laugesen, A. T. 'Un cas de synonymie en ancien français', *Revue Romane*, special number, 1 (1967), pp. 85-93.

Lawrence, C. H. *Medieval Monasticism* (London, 1984).

Le Bras, G. *Institutions ecclésiastiques de la chrétienté médiévale*, 2 vols (Paris, 1959-64).

Le diable au moyen âge (collected essays), *Senefiance* 6 (1979).

Le Gentil, P. 'A propos du *Guillaume de Dole*', in *Mélanges . . . Delbouille*, 2 vols (Gembloux, 1964), 2, pp. 381-397.

Le Goff, J. 'Apostolat mendiant et fait urbain dans la France médiévale : L'implantation des ordres mendiants. Programme-questionnaire pour une enquête', *Annales : économies, sociétés, civilisations*, 23 (1968), pp. 335-52.

—— *Time, Work and Culture in the Middle Ages* (Chicago and London, 1980).

Leclercq, J. 'Comment vivaient les frères convers', *Analecta Cisterciensia*, 21 (1965), pp. 239-58.

—— 'Textes et manuscrits Cisterciens dans diverses bibliothèques', *Analecta Sacri Ordinis Cisterciensis*, 12 (1956), pp. 289-310.

—— *The Love of Learning and the Desire for God* (New York, 1974).

Lecoy, F. (ed.), *Le Roman de la Rose ou de Guillaume de Dole* (Paris, 1962).

—— (ed.), *Le Conte du graal (Perceval)*, 2 vols (Paris, 1972 and 1975).

Lecoy de la Marche, A. *La chaire française au moyen âge*, 2nd ed. (Paris, 1886).

—— *L'Esprit de nos aïeux* (Paris, 1888).

Lécuyer, S. (ed.), *Jehan et Blonde* (Paris, 1984).

Lejeune, R. *Recherches sur le thème : Les chansons de geste et l'histoire* (Liège, 1948).

Levarie, S. Letter concerning *ductia* and *stantipes*, in *Journal of the American Musicological Society*, 27 (1974), pp. 367-9.

Leyser, H. *Hermits and the New Monasticism : A Study of Religious Communities in Western Europe 1000-1150* (London, 1984).

Liber Sextus Decretalium (Turin, 1620).

Limentani, A. 'Les nouvelles méthodes de la critique et l'étude des chansons de geste', in *Charlemagne et l'épopée romane*, Actes du VIIe congrès international de la Société Rencesvals (Paris, 1978), pp. 293-334.

—— 'L' 'io', la memoria e il giullare nelle novas di Ramon Vidal', *Mélanges Rita Lejeune*, 2 vols (Gembloux, 1969), 1, pp. 197-212.

Little, A. G. *Franciscan Papers, Lists and Documents* (Manchester, 1943).

—— *Liber exemplorum ad usum praedicantium* (Aberdeen, 1908 ; R 1966).

—— and Douie, D. 'Three sermons of Friar Jordan of Saxony, the successor of St Dominic, preached in England in AD 1229', *English Historical Review*, 54 (1939), pp. 1-19.

Little, L. K. 'L'utilité sociale de la pauvreté volontaire', in M. Mollat, ed., *Etudes sur l'histoire de la pauvreté*, 2 vols (Paris, 1974), pp. 447-59.

—— 'Pride goes before Avarice : social change and the vices in Latin Christendom', *American Historical Review*, 76 (1971), pp. 16-49.

—— *Religious Poverty and the Profit Economy in Medieval Europe* (London, 1978).

Longère, J. *La predication médiévale* (Paris, 1983).

—— *Oeuvres oratoires des maîtres parisiens au XIIe siècle*, 2 vols (Paris, 1975).

—— (ed.), *Petrus Pictaviensis Summa de confessione compilatio praesens* (Turnhout, 1980).

—— 'Quelques *Summae de poenitentia* à la fin du XIIe et au début du XIIIe siècle', *Actes du 99e congrès national des sociétés savantes, Besançon, 1974, Philosophie et Histoire*, 1 (Paris, 1977), pp. 45-58.

Lord, A. B. *The Singer of Tales* (Harvard, 1960).

Luscombe, D. E. 'Peter Abelard'. See Dronke.

—— (ed. and trans.), *Peter Abelard's Ethics* (Oxford, 1971).

Magistri Petri Lombardi . . . Sententiae in IV Libris Distinctae, 2 vols (Rome, 1971 and 1981).

Mansi, G. D. *Sacrorum conciliorum nova et amplissima collectio* (Florence, 1759–67, and Venice 1769–98).

Marshall, J. H. *The Transmission of Troubadour Poetry* (London, 1975).

Martène, E. and Durand, U. (eds.), *Thesaurus novus anecdotorum*, 5 vols (Paris, 1717).

Matarasso, P. M. *Recherches historiques et littéraires sur 'Raoul de Cambrai'* (Paris, 1962).

Mathiassen, F. *The Style of the Early Motet (c. 1200–1250)* (Copenhagen, 1966).

Matoré, G. *Le vocabulaire et la société médiévale* (Paris, 1985).

Mauclère, J. (ed.), *Doon de Mayence* (Paris, 1937).

McGuire, B. P. 'Friends and tales in the cloister: Oral sources and Caesarius of Heisterbach's *Dialogus miraculorum*', *Analecta Cisterciensia*, 36 (1980), pp. 167–247.

—— 'The Cistercians and the rise of the exemplum in early thirteenth century France: a reevaluation of Paris BN MS lat.15912', *Classica et Mediaevalia*, 34 (1983), pp. 211–267.

—— 'Written sources and Cistercian inspiration in Caesarius of Heisterbach', *Analecta Cisterciensia*, 35 (1979), pp. 227–282.

McKinnon, J. *Music in Early Christian Literature* (Cambridge, 1987).

—— *The Church Fathers and Musical Instruments* (Diss., Columbia, 1965).

—— 'The meaning of the patristic polemic against musical instruments', *Current Musicology*, 1 (1965), pp. 69–82.

Medcalf, S. 'Literature and Drama', in Ford, B. (ed.), *The Cambridge Guide to the Arts in Britain 2: The Middle Ages* (Cambridge, 1988), pp. 101–4.

Mehl, D. *The Middle English Romances of the Thirteenth and Fourteenth Centuries* (London, 1968).

Menzel, F. and Stengel, E. (eds.), *Jean Bodels Saxenlied*, 2 vols (Marburg, 1906 and 1909).

Meredith-Jones, C. (ed.), *Historia Karoli Magni et Rotholandi ou Chronique de Pseudo-Turpin* (Paris, 1936; R 1972).

Meunier, F. (ed.), *La Chanson de Godin* (Louvain, 1958).

Meyer, P. 'La chanson de *Doon de Nanteuil*: fragments inédits', *Romania*, 13 (1884), pp. 1–26.

—— (ed.), *L'Histoire de Guillaume le Maréchal*, 2 vols (Paris, 1891–1901).

—— and Longon, A. (eds.), *Raoul de Cambrai* (Paris, 1882).

Michaud-Quentin, P. 'A propos des premières *Summae confessorum*. Théologie et droit canonique', *Recherches de théologie ancienne et médiévale*, 26 (1959), pp. 264–306.

Michelant, H. (ed.), *Der Roman von Escanor* (Stuttgart, 1886).

—— (ed.), *Guillaume de Palerne*, Société des Anciens Textes Français (Paris, 1876).

Miller, S. H. and Sweeting, W. D. *De gestis Herwardi Saxonis*, published as a supplement to *Fenland Notes and Queries*, 3 (1895–7).

Misrahi, J. and Knudson, C. A. (eds.), *Jehan de Saintré* (Geneva, 1965).

Mittellateinisches Wörterbuch (Munich, 1967–).

Molenaer, S. P. (ed.), *Li livres du gouvernement des rois* (New York, 1899).

Molinier, A. *Obituaires de la province de Sens*, 1 (Paris, 1902).

Mollat, M. *The Poor in the Middle Ages* (Yale, 1986).

Mommsen, T. (ed.), *Cassiodori Senatoris Variae*, Monumenta Germaniae Historica, Auctorum Antiquissimorum Tomus XII (Berlin, 1894).

Montaiglon, A. de, and Raynaud, G. (eds.), *Recueil général et complet des fabliaux des XIII° et XIV° siècles*, 6 vols (Paris, 1872–90).

Moore, R. I. *The Formation of a Persecuting Society* (Basil Blackwell, 1987).

Morgan, R. Jr. 'Old French *jogleor* and kindred terms. Studies in medieval Romance lexicology', *Romance Philology*, 7 (1953–4), pp. 279–325.

Morris, C. *The Discovery of the Individual 1050–1200* (London, 1972).

Morton, C. and Muntz, H. (eds.), *The Carmen de Hastingae Proelio* (Oxford, 1972).

Muir, L. R. *Literature and Society in Medieval France: The Mirror and the Image 1100–1500* (London, 1985).

Mullally, R. 'Cançon de Carole', *Acta Musicologica*, 58 (1986), pp. 224–231.

Murray, A. 'Confession as a historical source in the thirteenth century', in Davies, R. H. C. and Wallace-Hadrill, J. M. (eds.), *The Writing of History in the Middle Ages* (Oxford, 1981), pp. 275–322.

— — *Reason and Society in the Middle Ages* (Oxford, 1978).

Nicholas de Braia, *Gesta Ludovici VIII Francorum Regis*, Recueil des historiens des gaules et de la France, 17 (Paris, 1878).

Nicholas de Gorran, *Sermones [Fundamentum aureum]*, (Antwerp, 1620).

Nichols, J. W. *The Matter of Courtesy: A study of Medieval Courtesy Books and the Gawain Poet* (D. S. Brewer, 1985).

Nichols, S. G. Jr. 'The interaction of life and literature in the *Peregrinationes ad loca sancta* and the *chansons de geste*', *Speculum*, 44 (1969), pp. 51–77.

Noiriel, G. 'La chevalerie dans la geste des Lorrains', *Annales de l'Est*, 5th series, 3 (1976), pp. 167–96.

Ogilvy, J. D. A. *'Mimi, Scurrae, Histriones*: entertainers in the early Middle Ages', *Speculum*, 38 (1963), pp. 603–19.

Orbis Latinus, 3 vols (Braunschweig, 1972).

Orme, N. *From Childhood to Chivalry* (London, 1984).

Paden, W. Jr. 'The role of the joglar in troubadour lyric poetry', in Noble, P. S. and Paterson, L. M. (eds.), *Chrétien de Troyes and the Troubadours: Essays in memory of the late Leslie Topsfield* (St Catharine's College, Cambridge, 1984).

Page, C. H. *'Angelus ad virginem*: a new work by Philippe the Chancellor?', *Early Music*, II (1983), pp. 69–70.

— — *Anglo-Saxon Hearpan* (Diss., University of York, 1981).

— — 'German musicians and their instruments: a fourteenth century account by Konrad of Megenberg', *Early Music*, 10 (1982), pp. 192–200.

— — 'Instruments and instrumental music to 1300', in *The New Oxford History of Music* 2, (revised edition), forthcoming.

— — 'Jerome of Moravia on the *rubeba* and *viella*', *Galpin Society Journal*, 32 (1979), pp. 77–95.

— — 'Machaut's "pupil" Deschamps on the performance of music', *Early Music*, 5 (1977), pp. 484–91.

— — 'Music and chivalric fiction in France 1150–1300', *Proceedings of the Royal Musical Association*, III (1984–5), pp. 1–27.

— — 'Secular Music', in Ford, B. (ed.), *The Cambridge Guide to the Arts in Britain*, 2, *The Middle Ages* (Cambridge, 1988), pp. 235–250.

— — 'The performance of Ars Antiqua motets', *Early Music*, 16 (1988), pp. 147–64.

—— 'The performance of songs in late medieval France: a new source', *Early Music*, 10 (1982), pp. 441–50.

—— *Voices and Instruments of the Middle Ages: Instrumental Practice and Songs in France 1100–1300* (London, 1987).

Painter, S. *William Marshall* (Baltimore, 1933).

Palisca, C. (ed.), *Hucbald, Guido and John on Music* (Yale, 1978).

Paterson, L. 'Knights and the concept of knighthood in the twelfth century Occitan epic', in Jackson, W. H. (ed.), *Knighthood in Medieval Literature* (D. S. Brewer, 1981), pp. 23–38.

Pauphilet, A. 'Sur la *Chanson de Roland*', *Romania*, 59 (1933), pp. 161–198.

Payen, J. C. (ed.), *Les Tristan en vers* (Paris, 1974).

Pearsall, D. *Old English and Middle English Poetry* (London, 1977).

Peters, E. *Torture* (Oxford, 1985).

Petrus de Palude, *In quartum Sententiarum* (n.p. 1493).

Pez, B. (ed.), *Thesaurus anecdotorum novissimus*, 6 vols (Augustae Vindelicorum et Graecii, 1721–9).

Pfeffer, W. *The Change of Philomel: The Nightingale in Medieval Literature* (New York, 1985).

Pierre de Palude. See Petrus de Palude.

Pike, J. B. *Frivolities of Courtiers and Footprints of Philosophers* (Minneapolis, 1938).

Pitra, J. B. *Analecta novissima: Spicilegii Solesmensis, altera continuatio*, 2 (Typis Tusculanis, 1889). Includes the *Sermones vulgares* of Jacques de Vitry.

Pizzorusso, V. B. 'La supplica di Guiraut Riquier e la riposta di Alfonso X di Castiglia', *Studi Mediolatini e Volgari*, 14 (1966), pp. 9–135.

Place, E. B. (ed.) *L'Histoire de Gille de Chyn by Gautier de Tournai* (Evanston and Chicago, 1941).

Planche, A. 'Omniprésence, police et auto-censure des pauvres', in Buschinger, D. (ed.), *Littérature et société au moyen age* (Paris, 1978).

Poe, E. W. 'The meaning of *saber* in Raimon Vidal's *Abril issia*', in Keller, H.-E. (ed.), *Studia Occitanica: In memoriam Paul Remy*, 2 vols (Kalamazoo, 1986), II, pp. 169–78.

Poly, J-P., and Bournazel, E. *La mutation féodale X^e–XIIe siècles* (Paris, 1980).

Pope, M. (ed.), *The Romance of Horn by Thomas*, 2 vols (Oxford, 1955 and 1964).

Post, G. 'Masters' salaries and student-fees in medieval universities', *Speculum*, 7 (1932), pp. 181–98.

—— 'The naturalness of society and the state', reprinted in *Studies in Medieval Legal Thought* (Princeton, 1964).

——*et al.*, 'The medieval heritage of a humanistic ideal: *Scientia donum dei est, unde vendi non potest*', *Traditio*, 11 (1955), pp. 195–234.

Prou, M. (ed.), *Raoul Glaber: Les cinq livres de ses Histoires (900–1044)* (Paris, 1886).

Pseudo-Bonaventura, *De institutione novitiorum*, in *S. R. E. Cardinalis S. Bonaventurae . . . opera omnia* (Paris, 1864–71), vol. 12.

Quo[d]libeta . . . Ricardi de Mediavilla (Brixiae, 1591).

Radding, C. M. 'Evolution of medieval mentalities: a cognitive-structural approach', *The American Historical Review*, 83 (1978), pp. 577–597.

—— 'Superstition to science: Nature, Fortune and the passing of the medieval ordeal', *The American Historical Review*, 84 (1979), pp. 945–69.

Rainerus of Pisa, *Pantheologia* (Nuremberg, 1474).

Räkel, H-H. S. *Die musikalische Erscheinungsform der Trouvère Poesie* (Bern, 1977).

Raupach, M. and Raupach, M. *Französierte Trobadorlyrik* (Tübingen, 1979).

Raynaud de Lage, G. (ed.), *Eracle* (Paris, 1976).

Reaney, G. 'The anonymous treatise *De origine et effectu musicae*: an early fifteenth century commonplace book of music-theory', *Musica Disciplina*, 37 (1983), pp. 101–119.

—— and Gilles, A., (eds.), *Franconis de Colonia Ars Cantus Mensurabilis*, Corpus Scriptorum de Musica 18 (American Institute of Musicology, 1974).

Reckow, F. (ed.), *Der Musiktraktat des Anonymus 4*, 2 vols (Wiesbaden, 1967).

Régnier, C. (ed.), *Les rédactions en vers de la Prise d'Orange* (Paris, 1966).

Reichert, B. M. (ed.), *Fratris Gerardi de Fracheto Vitae Fratrum Praedicatorum* (Rome and Stuttgart, 1897).

Reimer, E. (ed.), *Johannes de Garlandia: De mensurabili musica*, 2 vols (Wiesbaden, 1972).

Reinhard, J. R. (ed.), *Amadas et Ydoine* (Paris, 1926).

Richard of Middleton, *Super IV Libros Sententiarum* (Brixiae, 1591).

Richardson, L. B. 'The *Confrérie des jongleurs et des bourgeois* and the *Puy d'Arras* in twelfth and thirteenth century literature', in Fisher, J. and Gaeng, P. E. (eds.), *Studies in Honor of Mario A. Pei* (Chapel Hill, 1972), pp. 161–171.

Rigby, M. 'The education of Alexander the Great and *Florimont*', *Modern Language Review*, 57 (1962), pp. 392–3.

Rivière, J. C. (ed.), *Pastourelles*, 3 vols (Geneva, 1974–6).

Roesner, E. 'The performance of Parisian organum', *Early Music*, 7 (1979), pp. 174–189.

Rohloff, E. (ed.), *Die Quellenhandschriften zum Musiktraktat des Johannes de Grocheio* (Leipzig, 1972).

Roques, M. (ed.), *Erec et Enide* (Paris, 1952).

—— (ed.), *Le Chevalier au lion (Yvain)* (Paris, 1960).

Rosenberg, S. N. and Tischler, H. (eds.), *Chanter m'estuet: Songs of the Trouvères* (London, 1981).

Rosenwein, B. H. and Little, L. K. 'Social meaning in monastic and mendicant spiritualities', *Past and Present*, 63 (1974), pp. 3–32.

Rossi, M. *Huon de Bordeaux et l'évolution du genre épique au XIII⁰ siècle* (Paris, 1975).

Roze, M. l'Abbé, (ed.), 'Nécrologie de l'église d'Amiens', *Mémoires de la société des antiquaires de Picardie*, 3ᵉ Série, 8 (1885), pp. 265–477.

Rubel, H. 'Chabham's [sic] penitential and its influence in the thirteenth century', *Publications of the Modern Language Association of America*, 40 (1925), pp. 225–239.

Ruelle, P. (ed.), *Huon de Bordeaux* (Brussels and Paris, 1960).

Rychner, J. *La chanson de geste: essai sur l'art épique des jongleurs* (Lille, 1955).

Sahlin, M. *Etude sur la carole médiévale* (Uppsala, 1940).

Salter, E. *Fourteenth Century English Poetry* (Oxford, 1983).

Scheler, A. (ed.), *Dits et contes de Baudouin de Condé et de son fils Jean de Condé*, 3 vols (Brussels, 1866–7).

Schmidt, Ph. *Der Teufels und Daemonenglaube in den Erzählungen des Caesarius von Heisterbach* (Basel, 1926).

Schneyer, J. B. *Repertorium der lateinischen Sermones des Mittelalters*, 9 vols (Münster, 1969–79).

Scott, H. von E. and Bland, C. S. S. (trans.), *The Dialogue on Miracles* (London, 1929).

Seay, A. (trans.), *Johannes de Grocheo [sic] Concerning Music*, 2nd edition (Colorado College Music Press, 1974).

Sermones beati Umberti Burgundi, 2 vols (Venice, 1603).

Siciliano, I. *Les chansons de geste et l'épopée. Mythes, histoires, poèmes* (Turin, 1968).

Simpson, W. S. (ed.), *Registrum statutorum et consuetudinum ecclesiae cathedralis Sancti Pauli Londinensis* (London, 1873).

Sjoberg, G. *The Preindustrial City* (New York and London, 1960; R 1965).

Southern, R. W. *Medieval Humanism* (London, 1970).

—— *Robert Grosseteste: The Growth of an English Mind in Medieval Europe* (Oxford, 1986).

—— *The Making of the Middle Ages* (London, 1953).

Sowa, H. (ed.), *Ein Anonymer Glossierter Mensuraltraktat 1279* (Bärenreiter-Kassel, 1930).

Spufford, P. *Money and its Use in Medieval Europe* (Cambridge University Press, 1988).

Stanley, E. G. (ed.), *The Owl and the Nightingale*, 2nd edition (Manchester University Press, 1972).

Stefenelli, A. *Der synonymenreichtum der altfranzösischen Dichtersprache* (Vienna, 1967).

Steffens, G. 'Der kritische Text der Gedichte von Richart de Semilli', in *Festgabe für Wendelin Foerster* (Halle, 1902), pp. 331–62.

Stegmüller, F. *Repertorium biblicum medii aevi*, II vols (Madrid, 1940–80).

—— *Repertorium commentariorum in Sententias P. Lombardi*, 2 vols (Herbipoli, 1947).

Stengel, E. (ed.), *Li romans de Durmart le Galois* (Tübingen, 1873).

—— (ed.), *Hervis von Metz* (Dresden, 1903).

Stevens, J. *Words and Music in the Middle Ages: Song, Narrative, Dance and Drama, 1060–1350* (Cambridge, 1986).

Strange, J. (ed.), *Caesarii Heisterbacensis monachi ordinis Cisterciensis Dialogus miraculorum* (Cologne, 1851; R 1966).

Stroick, P. A. 'Collectio de scandalis ecclesiae: nova editio', *Archivum Franciscanum Hustoricum*, 24 (1931), pp. 33–62.

Stubbs, W. (ed.), *Memorials of St Dunstan*, Rolls Series (London, 1874).

—— (ed.), *Willelmi Malmesbiriensis monachi De Gestis Regum Anglorum libri quinque*, 2 vols., Rolls Series (London, 1887 and 1889).

Subrenat, J. 'Moines mesquines et saint chevalier: à propos du "Moniage" de Guillaume', *Marche Romane: Mélanges de philologie et de littératures romanes offerts à Jeanne Wathelet-Willem* (Liège, 1978), pp. 643–665.

Terracher, A.-L. (ed.), *La Chevalerie Vivien* (Paris, 1909).

Thomae Cantipratani . . . miraculorum et exemplorum memorabilium sui temporis libri duo, 2 vols (Douai, 1605).

Thorpe, L. (ed.), *Le Roman de Silence* (Cambridge, 1972).

Tischler, H. (ed.), *The Montpellier Codex*, 4 vols (Madison, 1978).

Tobler, A. and Lommatzsch, E. *Altfranzösisches Wörterbuch* (Berlin, 1925; Wiesbaden, 1954–).

Todd, H. A. (ed.), *La Naissance du chevalier au cygne*, published as a supplement to *Publications of the Modern Languages Association of America*, 4 (1888–9).

Tubach, F. C. *Index exemplorum* (Helsinki, 1969).

Ulland, W. *'Jouer d'un instrument' und die altfranzösischen Bezeichnungen des Instrumentenspiels* (Bonn, 1970).

Ulrich, J. (ed.), *Robert von Blois: Sämmtlichle Werke*, 3 vols (Berlin, 1889–95).

Vale, J. *Edward III and Chivalry: Chivalric Society and its Context 1270–1350* (Boydell and Brewer, 1982).

Vale, M. *War and Chivalry* (London, 1981).

Van der Veen, J. 'Les aspects musicaux des chansons de geste', *Neophilologus*, 41 (1957), pp. 82–100.

Van der Werf, H. *The Chansons of the Troubadours and Trouvères* (Utrecht, 1972).
—— *The Extant Troubadour Melodies* (New York, 1984).
Van Dijk, C. 'L'instruction et la culture des frères convers dans les premiers siècles de l'ordre de Citeaux', *Collectanea Ordinis Cisterciensium Reformatorum*, 24 (1962), pp. 243–58.
Vellekoop, K. 'Die Estampie: ihre Besetzung und Funktion', *Basler Jahrbuch für Historische Musikpraxis*, 8 (1984), pp. 51–65.
Vennebusch, J. 'Unbekannte Miracula des Caesarius von Heisterbach', *Annalen des Historischen Vereins für den niederrhein*, 184 (1981), pp. 7–19.
Verger, J. 'Abélard et les milieux sociaux de son temps', in *Abélard et son temps* (Paris, 1981), pp. 107–131.
Vernay, P. (ed.), *Maugis d'Aigremont* (Berne, 1980).
Vie de St Louis par le confesseur de la reine marguerite, Recueil des historiens des gaules et de la France, 20 (Paris, 1840).
Vinaver, E. *The Rise of Romance* (Oxford, 1971).
Waddell, C. 'The early Cistercian experience of liturgy', in Pennington, B. (ed.), *Rule and Life*, Cistercian Studies Series 12 (Shannon, 1971).
—— 'The origin and evolution of the Cistercian antiphonary: reflections on two Cistercian chant reforms', in Pennington, B. (ed.), *The Cistercian Spirit*, Cistercian Studies Series 3 (Shannon, 1970), pp. 190–223.
Waesberghe, J. Smits van, (ed.), *Aribonis De Musica*, Corpus Scriptorum de Musica 2 (American Institute of Musicology, 1955).
—— (ed.), *Johannis Affligemensis De Musica cum Tonario*, Corpus Scriptorum de Musica 1 (American Institute of Musicology, 1950).
—— *Musikerziehung: Lehre und Theorie der Musik im Mittellalter*, Musikgeschichte in Bildern, III: 3 (Leipzig, 1969).
Wagenaar-Nolthenius, H. 'Estampie/Stantipes/Stampita', in *L'Ars Nova Italiana del Trecento: 2nd Congress* (Certaldo, 1969), pp. 399–409.
Wagner, F. 'Studien zu Caesarius von Heisterbach', *Analecta Cisterciana*, 29 (1973), pp. 79–95.
Wailly, N. de, (ed.), *Joinville: Histoire de St Louis* (Paris, 1865).
Wallensköld, A. (ed.), *Florence de Rome*, 2 vols., Société des Anciens Textes Français (Paris, 1907 and 1909).
Ward, B. *Miracles and the Medieval Mind: Theory, Record and Event 1000–1215* (London, 1982).
Ward-Perkins, B. *From Classical Antiquity to the Middle Ages: Urban Public Building in Northern and Central Italy AD 300–850* (Oxford, 1984).
Warichez, J. (ed.), *Les Disputationes de Simon de Tournai* (Louvain, 1932).
Wathelet-Willem, J. *Recherches sur la Chanson de Guillaume*, 2 vols (Liège, 1975).
Webb, C. C. I. (ed.), *Ioannis Saresberiensis Episcopi Carnotensis Policratici*, 2 vols (Oxford, 1909).
Welter, J. T. *La Tabula exemplorum secundum ordinem alphabeti: recueil d'exempla compilé en France à la fin du XIIIᵉ siècle* (Paris, 1926).
—— *Le Speculum laicorum* (Paris, 1914).
—— *L'exemplum dans la littérature religieuse et didactique du moyen âge* (Paris, 1927).
Wenzel, S. *Preachers, Poets and the Early English Lyric* (Princeton, 1986).
Whitehead, F. (ed.), *La Chanson de Roland* (Basil Blackwell, 1970).
Wienbeck, E., Hartnacke, W. and Rasch, P. (eds), *Aliscans* (Halle, 1903).
Wilkins, N. (ed.), *The Lyric Works of Adam de la Hale*, Corpus Mensurabilis Musicae

44 (American Institute of Musicology, 1967).

William of Auvergne, *Opera Omnia* (Venice, 1591).

Williams, H. F. (ed.), *Floriant et Florete* (University of Michigan, 1947).

Wilson, E. R. 'Old Provençal *Vidas* as literary commentary', *Romance Philology*, 33 (1980), pp. 510–518.

Wolf, J. 'Die Musiklehre des Johannes de Grocheio', *Sammelbände der Internationalen Musikgesellschaft*, I (1899–1900), pp. 65–130.

—— 'Die Tänze des Mittelalters', *Archiv für Musikwissenschaft*, I (1918–19), pp. 10–42.

Wright, A. R. *British Calendar Customs: England* (London, 1936).

Wright, C. *Music and Ceremony at Notre Dame of Paris, 500–1500* (Cambridge, 1989).

Wright, L. 'Misconceptions concerning the troubadours, trouvères and minstrels', *Music and Letters*, 48 (1967), pp. 35–9.

—— 'The role of musicians at court in twelfth century Britain', in Macready, S. and Thompson, F. H. (eds.), *Art and Patronage in the English Romanesque* (London, 1986), pp. 97–106.

Yeandle, F. G. (ed.), *Girart de Vienne* (New York, 1930).

Yudkin, J. *The Music Treatise of Anonymous IV: A New Translation*, Musicological Studies and Documents, 41 (American Institute of Musicology, 1985).

Index

Abril issia see Raimon Vidal
Adam de la Hale, 125
Adam of Dryburgh, 158
Adam of 'St Victor', 166, 245 n.47
Adamnan, 181
Adele of Louvain, 108
Aegidius of Zamora OM, 181
Aiol, 213 n.45
Albertus Magnus OP, 38-9, 126, 129-32, 172-3
A l'entrade d'Avrillo, 101-2 (mus. ex. 5)
Alexander Nequam, 139
Alexander of Hales OM (Summa Theologica),
    45, 132, 210 n.22, 212 n.36
Aliscans, 213-14 n. 45
alms, 16, 17
Amadas et Ydoine, 230 n. 60
amateur music-making, 81-109 passim
Ambrogio Lorenzetti, 114
Amiens Cathedral, 136
anima see Latin terms
Annales Flodoardi, 32
Anonymous IV, 151-3, 242 n.56; and the
    magistri, 242 n.50
Anselm of Laon, 142, 242 n.56
Anseis de Carthage, 231 n.65
antiqui, of Anonymous IV, 151-3
anti-semitism, 6, 181-2
Aribo (De musica), 214 n.56
Aristotle: 9, 35, 38, 39, 40, 138, 171, 217 n.77;
    Ethics, 35, 37, 39, 77, 139, 172; Politics, 35,
    36, 77, 172-3; Topics, 139
Arnaut Daniel, 46, 225 n.52
Arnaut de Maroill, 58, 65
Arnulphus de Albumeria, 248 n.35
Ars cantus mensurabilis see Franco of Cologne
Arthurian romance, 63, 83-4, 104, 105
artifex see Latin terms
Athelstan, 94
Athis et Prophilias, 232 n.77, 233 n.97
Auberi le Bourgoing, 32, 177
Aucassin et Nicolette, 231 n.65
Auctor B (Vita sancti Dunstani), 229 n.48
auctoritas see Latin terms
audiences: for chansons de geste, 31, 70, 178; for
    troubadour song, 46-60; for secular motets,
    148-54; behaviour in Provence, 58-9

Ave Dei genitrix, 168
Ave maria, 11
Ave maris stella, 97
Ave praeclara maris stella, 168
Aye d'Avignon, 94, 95
Aymeri de Narbonne, 30, 32, 177

bachelers, 86-92 passim
Barbarismus (Book III of the Ars maior of
    Donatus), 138
Bartholomaeus de Pisa OP (Summa Pisana),
    174, 248 n.36
Beatrice of Savoy, 52
Bernart de Ventadorn, 46, 59
Bernward of Hildesheim, 93
Bertrand de Bar-sur-Aube (Girart de Vienne),
    72-3
Bertran de Born, 46
Besalú, 46, 47, 53
Béziers, 52
biblical passages (titles and numberings of
    AV):
    Gen. 1:26-7, 17
        3:1, 245 n.20
        3:19, 16
    Ex. 10:5-19, 198
        15:20-21, 131
        32:19, 130, 132
    Deut. 32:10, 85, 156, 170, 184
    Judg. 21:19-25, 124
    1 Sam. 16:22, 245 n.22
    2 Sam. 6:5, 201
    2 Kgs. 3:15, 199
    Ps. 13:6, 18
        33:3, 201
        35:26, 201
        68:25-6, 130
        95:2, 203
        132:18, 201
        149:1, 1
    Prov. 31:21, 201
    Eccles. 9:3, 198
        9:7, 115
    Isa. 3:16-17, 111, 130
        5:12, 198
        43:26, 203

Index

narrative songs, 23-4, 176-7; see also *chansons de geste*, Lives of Saints
nationes see Latin terms
necessaria see Latin terms
Nicholas de Bayard OM, 117, 235 n.16, 237 n.61
Nicholas de Braia (*Gesta Ludovici VIII Francorum Regis*), 89, 228 n.36
Nicholas de Caen, 12, 13
Nicholas de Gorran OP, 18, 210 n.9
Nicholas de Lyra OM, 176
Nicholas of Guildford (? *The Owl and the Nightingale*), 208 n.5
Normandy, 171, 246 n.3
nota procellaris, 148
notula see Latin terms

officium see Latin terms
Ogier the Dane, 11, 33, 71, 213 n.45
Oliver, 11, 13, 31, 33, 70, 71, 177, 220 n.10
Opus maius see Roger Bacon
Opus tertium see Roger Bacon
oral and literate composition, 224-5 n.42
Orderic Vitalis (*Ecclesiastical History*), 215 n.68
organiste, 142, 144-5, 239 n.29, 240 n.40, 242 n.56
organizator, 74, 144
organum duplum, dissemination of, 149; *see also* performance practice
Osbern (*Vita sancti Dunstani*), 94
Otinel, 213 n.45
otium see Latin terms
ouvrier, 64, 65, 79, 179
Ovid (*Ars amatoria*), 103, 123, 233 n.97
Owl and the Nightingale: 6, 134, 224 n. 26; themes, 3-4; authorship and date, 208 n.5; symbolism of the nightingale, 208 n.7

Pantheologia see Rainerus of Pisa
Paris: 2-3, 9, 13, 21, 31, 33, 39, 40, 44, 61-80, 78 (fig. 5), 98, 111, 114, 119, 129, 133, 171-2, 179, 204-5, 225 n.60; influence of commercial activity on mentality, 2, 36; its artisans, 2, 36, 79; milieux for minstrelsy, 61-80 *passim*; and concept of the professional musician, 66; minstrel schools at, 217 n.85; Grand Pont, 71, 77, 79; Petit Pont, 31, 177, 178; Cathedral of Notre Dame, 2, 19, 135-7, 142, 144-54 *passim*, 147, 148, 156; St Leufroy, 11, 71; La Madeleine, 11; Ste Chapelle, 9, 12, 44; St Antoine-des-Champs, 12; St Germain-des-Prés, 119, 123, 149; St Gervais, 9, 118; Convent of St Jacques, 18; *rue aus jougleurs*, 61, 66
Paris, University: 74, 126, 180; study of polyphony, 137-43; structure of studies, 138; set books in Arts, 138-9; study of Boethius,

139; questions on music, 139-41; neglect of practical music, 141; music and theology, 141-2; music in works of *magistri* and William of Auvergne, 142; formal study of music, 238-9 n.18; music as subject in university disputations, 239 n.19
Pariset, 61
pastourelle, 101-2, 113, 149, 236 n.45, 241 n.50
Pater noster, 11
patristic authority, 14-16, 35, 198, 210 n.11
pauperes see Latin terms
pauperes clerici, 144
peasants, as minstrels, 18
Peire d'Alvernhe, 49, 59, 221 n.32
Peire Roger, 225 n.52
Peire Vidal, 46
Peirol, 49
penance, 6, 14-29 *passim*, 34, 35, 39-40, 120, 121 (fig. 8), 126, 132-9, 174-6, 189, 193-4, 214 n.51, 237 n.57; changes in theology of, 214 n.52
Pepin, 220 n.10
Perceval, 86
Perceval le Gallois see Gerbert
Perdigon, 49
performance practice, the *carole*: performers, 104-5, 110-33 *passim*, 227 n.19, 227 n.21; performing contexts, 114-25, 228 n.41; choreography, 114-15
performance practice, *chanson de geste*: performers, 30-33, 219-20 n.10; manner of performance, 25-6, 70-73; instrumentation, 213-14 n.45; performing contexts, 31, 178; audience, 31, 70-73, 176-8
performance practice, French monody: performers, 81-109 *passim*; performing contexts, 87-8, 94-7, 99, 102-6; audience, 81-109 *passim*
performance practice, Occitan monody: performers, context and audience, 46-60 *passim*
performance practice, *organum duplum*: performers, 144-53, 180; ornamentation, 147-8
performance practice, motet: performers, 148-9, 152-5; performing contexts, 119, 148-55; audience, 148-55
Perotin, 137, 146, 151, 152, 153, 239 n.30
persecution, of Jews, heretics and lepers 6, 174, 182-5 *passim*
Peter Abelard, 155; (*Ethics*), 28, 214 n.53
Peter of Poitiers (*Summa de confessione*), 28
Peter the Chanter, 242 n.56; (*Summa de sacramentis*), 21-8 *passim*, 181; (*Verbum abbreviatum*), 2-3, 6, 17, 19, 79-80, 136-7
Peter the Lombard (*Sentences*), 34, 37, 129, 132, 138, 173, 217 n.73, 217 n.84

276